COOL COLLEGES

for the Hyper-Intelligent, Self-Directed,

Late Blooming, and Just Plain Different

COOL COLLEGES

for the
HYPER-INTELLIGENT, SELF-DIRECTED, LATE BLOOMING, JUST PLAIN DIFFERENT

Including addresses, phone numbers, and Web sites for every accredited four-year institution in the United States and Canada

Donald Asher

TEN SPEED PRESS
BERKELEY TORONTO

Ten Speed Press • Box 7123 • Berkeley, California 94707 • www.tenspeed.com

Distributed in Australia by Simon & Schuster Australia, in Canada by Ten Speed Press Canada, in New Zealand by Southern Publishers Group, in South Africa by Real Books, in Southeast Asia by Berkeley Books, and in the United Kingdom and Europe by Airlift Book Company.

Cover design by Catherine Jacobes
Book design by Paul Kepple & Timothy Crawford @ Headcase Design

Thank you to the following for granting permission to use their work:

"Secret to Finding Scholarships—There Isn't One" by Jane Bryant Quinn (p. 32–34) copyright © 1999, the Washington Post Writers Group. Reprinted with permission.
Excerpt from *Looking Beyond the Ivy League*, revised edition, by Loren Pope (p. 46) copyright © 1990, 1995 by Loren Pope. Reprinted by permission of Penguin Books and the author.
"Western Colleges Finally Get Their Due" (p. 51–53) copyright © 1999 by Janet L. Holmgren. Reprinted with permission.
Excerpt from *Colleges That Change Lives* by Loren Pope (p. 78) copyright © 1996 by Loren Pope. Reprinted by permission of Penguin Books and the author.
"On College Counseling for the Intellectual Student" (p. 100–107) copyright © by Laura J. Clark. Reprinted with permission.
"The 'Rocket Science' of Empowering Faculty to Teach" (p. 108–110) copyright © by Larry D. Large. Reprinted with permission.
Narrative evaluation (p. 127–128) used by permission of New College of the University of South Florida.
"What is Intelligence?" (p. 133–136) copyright © by Ruby Ausbrooks. Reprinted with permission.
"Why Kids Aren't Happy in Traditional School" (p. 143–146) copyright © by Ruby Ausbrooks. Reprinted with permission.
"The Big Meeting" (p. 161–162) copyright © by Crystal Finkbeiner. Reprinted with permission.
"The Filene Center for Work & Learning" (p. 165–167) copyright © by Dan Golden. Reprinted with permission.
"A Life of Work and Learning" (p. 196–197) copyright © by Dennis Jacobs. Reprinted with permission.
"Why I Finally Chose to Attend an Historically Black College" (p. 220–221) copyright © by Amelia R. Shelby. Reprinted with permission.

Library of Congress Cataloging-in-Publication Data

Asher, Donald.
Cool colleges for the hyper-intelligent, self-directed, late blooming, and just plain different : including addresses, phone numbers, and web sites for every accredited four-year institution in the United States and Canada / by Donald Asher.
p. cm.
    Includes index.
    ISBN 1-58008-150-9
1. College choice—United States. 2. College choice—Canada. 3. Universities and colleges—United States—Directories. 4. Universities and colleges—Canada—Directories.
I. Title.

LB2350.5 .A64 2000
378.73—dc21
00-055949

Printed in Canada
First printing, 2000

1 2 3 4 5 6 7 8 9 10 – 05 04 03 02 01 00

For

Lisa Bertschi

CONTENTS

ACKNOWLEDGMENTS

Nobody writes a book like this by himself or herself. Many, many people helped out in ways great and small. First and foremost I must thank my research assistant, Denise Rhiner, of InfoExpeditions in Portland, Oregon, who worked tirelessly to track down thousands of pesky details. There are still plenty of errors in this book, but they are all mine. Denise never makes a mistake. Thanks also to Julie Bennett, my editor and chief whip snapper, without whose assistance this book would still be just a good idea and a couple of filing cabinets overflowing with notes and materials collected over a ten-year span. I also appreciate Kirsty Melville, publisher, and Phil Wood, "like a god," at Ten Speed Press, for their wisdom to publish this book. Thanks to Jean M. Blomquist of Albuquerque for copyediting a difficult manuscript. Special thanks also to Paul Kepple and Timothy Crawford, interior designers, and Catherine Jacobes, cover designer, for developing a look for this book that I am just delighted with. Also, a few thousand people in higher education helped me to research and compile this book, including college presidents, deans and directors of admission, and public affairs officers. My surveys elicited warm and thoughtful comments from the best and the brightest at institutions all over North America, and I am grateful for their contribution. Special thanks to Kate Goldberg, college planning counselor, French-American International School in San Francisco; Laura J. Clark, college planning counselor, Ethical Culture Fieldston School in the Bronx, New York; Larry Large, president, Oglethorpe University in Atlanta; Janet Lavin Rapelye, dean of admission, Wellesley College; Janet L. Holmgren, president, Mills College; Fred Hargadon, dean of admissions, Princeton University; Marlyn McGrath Lewis, director of undergraduate admissions, Harvard University; and Dr. Dan Golden, director, the Filene Center for Work & Learning, Wheaton College in Norton, Massachusetts. Special thanks to L. M. Boyd, the trivia meister, author of "The Grab Bag" syndicated column, and the original source for a number of the academic trivia items in this volume. Very special thanks to Mr. Steve Old Elk, who rescued me when I needed it most. My greatest appreciation goes out to Dr. Judy Jones, one of my earliest mentors, who set this train in motion. Likewise to my mother, Dr. Ruby Ausbrooks, who was in school, like, forever, and my older brother, Bill, and younger brother, Clyde, who proved to me that anything is possible. I also need to acknowledge Professor Walter Englert, classics, Reed College, who is a credit to the profession of professing; and Tom Francis, director of career services, Swarthmore College, a true friend and a fine wrecker of boats.

WHERE THIS BOOK CAME FROM

I didn't really fit in at high school. The classes moved along at a glacial pace, until I felt that I'd just pull my hair out one strand at a time out of sheer boredom.

The dean of students had a personal vendetta against me. I'd be in a crowd of students and he'd see Don Asher and some nice young people. It was probably some kind of pattern recognition thing. Like that time I wore a Native American getup to Western Day, and got sent to the principal's office for my lack of "spirit," whatever that was. I never did really understand school spirit. I always thought school was about learning, and this spirit stuff was usually some blatant glorification of the very students who weren't learning anything. It seemed like a perverted recognition system to me. I didn't fit expectations. Sometime in high school I began to realize that systems in general were not designed for me.

I was not alone. My friends and I were always doing the "challenge" problems in the math books (and sometimes we'd even remember to turn them in). We talked in puns, collected oxymorons, read ahead in the books, wrote poetry, and drew cartoons in class. We gloried in discovering the historical inaccuracies of our texts, and had long arguments about minutiae, often bringing in outside references our teachers knew nothing about. We didn't always get the top grades. We were "difficult." We were trying so very hard to stay interested in an educational system that clearly was not designed for us.

Then I discovered a program whereby I could go straight into the largest university in the state without graduating from high school! All I needed were three things: the right grades (had 'em), the right SATs (had 'em), and a letter of recommendation from my high school principal. The only thing standing between me and this blessed event was a recommendation from my high school principal. He was a thin, bald man, who left all troubles to the dean of students. I knew the dean well, but I'd never actually spoken to the principal. Would he write me a letter? Would he release me? "I'd be glad to," he said, with a smile I couldn't interpret.

And so I went to college. Heaven at last, I thought. A university! Where they'll treat me like an adult! Where learning is the raison d'être for the entire institution!

The first week of classes the dean of students' secretary called me and said, "The dean wants to see you in his office. Would you be available on Wednesday at two?" What had I done now? I wondered. I thought all deans were alike, and I thought maybe my high school dean had called this university dean and warned him about me.

When I got there I was literally shaking. I had to wait only a few minutes before I was ushered into the dean's office. He motioned for me to take a chair with an authority that could not be denied. Then he spoke. I couldn't have been more shocked when he said, "I've been going over your file and I just want to say how delighted we are that you chose this university. We need a thousand students like you, and it's critical that you adjust well and stay here. If you ever need anything, you let me know. I want you to consider me your personal friend." I was terrified of him, and just nodded a lot and left as quickly as I could.

But I did not adjust well. I was shocked that my fellow students were more interested in dating, sports, and avoiding the real world for four years than they were in learning. Students openly discussed cheating, and professors routinely dismissed class well before the scheduled end. I was so disappointed I dropped out after one semester. So I was technically a high school dropout with one semester of perfect college grades.

My dad was livid. I was going to become a bum, he thought. I was going to fall in with a bad crowd. I was throwing my life away. In fact, I was on a mission, and that mission was to find a place in this world where I would fit in, where I was the norm, where I was welcome, and where I felt at home. After three years of research, I found it, in one of the schools in this book. It is absolutely not true that all colleges are the same, or that "the college experience" is largely similar throughout the country. There are very real differences between institutions, and even some wonderful experiments in higher education in America. I found the perfect place *for me.*

I hope you find your college, too, a perfect place *for you,* a place where you'll be happy, excited, welcomed, appreciated, and productive, a place that will launch you into the rest of your life like a trampoline. You deserve this. From the bottom of my heart, I wish you good luck. I wrote this book for you.

RESEARCH METHODOLOGY, BIASES, AND LIMITATIONS

The most important part of research is passion. My passion for this topic, choosing the right college when you are hyper-intelligent, self-directed, late blooming, or just plain different, carried me across a full decade of inquiry. My first vision of this book was that I'd design a methodology to identify cool, and then list and describe the "most cool" colleges in some ordinal ranking until I got to a reasonable number of schools or pages, whichever came first. I naively blundered into this endeavor expecting it to be easy. It proved very difficult after all, and in the end, this book became a hobby I worked on over a ten-year span.

In the spirit of full disclosure, I am forty-two years old. Occasionally I advise young people on college choice, especially when they are hyper-intelligent, self-directed, late blooming, or just plain different, but that is not my main career. I am a self-employed business writer and public speaker specializing in careers and higher education. I guest-speak at undergraduate and graduate schools from coast to coast, usually about career development and graduate study issues. I am not a college administrator or a faculty member, but as part of my job I visit some sixty campuses each and every year. Part of my motivation for finally completing this book is that I have a daughter and a stepdaughter who are both making college decisions as I write. (As is typical, neither is the least bit interested in the contents of this book—one says she doesn't want to go to college at all, and the other says she's going to school in Europe.)

In 1990, when I first began this project, there were very few college guides and they were all as dull as a televised fundraising marathon. From my own early research, I knew of a few dozen of the more interesting and innovative colleges in the United States. But I also knew that I didn't know much. So I wrote to a few thousand college presidents, deans, and directors of admission, explaining my endeavor and asking for their advice.

They were wonderful! They told me about schools I'd never heard of, suggested criteria, alerted me to trends that were underreported in the national media, decried the intellectual dishonesty of the most popular ranking system, applauded my efforts, and predicted, almost every last one, that my project was doomed from the outset.

The problem, according to them, was that the culture of a college, its very ethos, defies depiction. The environment of a college might be described, but it could never be measured. In short, I'd never be able to design a methodology to identify and quantify whatever it meant to be "cool."

I worried about this, but at the same time I noticed clear patterns in the schools they were recommending for study. The same schools kept showing up over and over in the surveys. So I made a list of the most nominated schools and sent out another wave of letters, asking college presidents, deans, and directors of admission to vote on which institutions should be further investigated.

This was unfair, of course, because I was asking them to vote for schools that were both good *and* innovative, without formally defining either term. Although most people can see the problem with formalizing a definition for "innovative," many would argue that "good" ought to be easy to define. However, it is not, unless you want an easy but not very meaningful definition. The problems lie in quantification and practicality. A good college has what overt, measurable aspects? (See p. 58 for a discussion of inputs and outputs.) For example, what calipers would you put on a professor to see if he or she is really a good professor? Does she prepare students for graduate school? Or to be good citizens? Does he have a talent for reaching the chronic underachiever? Or does he spend all his energies on the brightest students? Does she excel at conveying the intellectual traditions of a discipline? Or does she ignite dynamic, new, creative approaches to classic problems? A truly outstanding professor might have any of these aspects, and even if you focus in on certain ones, always and necessarily at the expense of others, you still face the challenge of quantifying qualitative matters.

Even supposing an elaborate methodology for measuring these issues, I projected that problems of access and cost, to say nothing of multistage validation studies, would doom the endeavor. Cost alone would be prohibitive. Even the most basic inquiry into the quality of an institution would involve a host of factors.

So how, then, do the national ranking systems work? They rely on self-reporting of existing data, i.e., they conduct zero original research at any institution. The data they collect is already quantified, collected by the institution for its own purposes, which in almost all cases was never meant to address qualitative issues at all. In the words of programmers everywhere, "garbage in, garbage out." I wanted to get at what it was like to study and live at a certain school, and I didn't think an institution's financial data were going to be particularly illustrative.

In spite of the transparent inadequacies of my surveys, I always got plenty of votes. So whatever "good" and "innovative" means at the institutional level of colleges and universities, it must fall into that "I know it when I see it" category. At least presidents and deans seemed comfortable making decisions based on common understandings of those words.

There are other problems with the "voting" methodology I used in my early research (often derisively known by social scientists as a "beauty contest survey"). Suppose, as is frequently the case, a very good and very innovative school is poorly known. Other schools, perhaps only slightly good and slightly innovative, will receive many more votes. So I conducted further research on schools that were least known but had promising reports on the innovative scale. For example, someone wrote to me about a school called Thomas Aquinas College, where intellectual inquiry is almost a religion. My correspondent wrote, "The president of the college sometimes has the *entire student body* over to his house to discuss ideas. These meetings can take hours, and have nothing to do with the regular class load." Hmmmm. It doesn't take a genius to realize that a school like that belongs in a book like this, regardless of the number of votes it gets.

Finally, there was another problem, and it was not a small one. Not only is it extremely difficult to figure out what makes up the culture of an ever-evolving institution, one student's experience at that institution will always be uniquely individual in any case. For example, the student in Smith Hall 107 may love the institution for reasons A, B, and C, while the student in Smith Hall 108 hates it for reasons A, X, and Z, and the student in Smith Hall 109 loves it for reasons X, Y, and Z. Not only are schools different from one another, but students are different too. Students like and dislike different things. So my solution was simple: provide information on A, B, C, and X, Y, Z, and let the students decide for themselves.

In fact, that is why I decided to consider a few hundred schools instead of a few dozen—sometimes by discussing a type of school and then listing all the members of that category. My original plan was to profile in detail very few schools, and omit those that did not receive enough votes. This proved silly when I kept finding out about really cool classes and programs at institutions that were otherwise absolutely ordinary. The more students I spoke with the more I realized that almost any college or university is "cool" to somebody. Sometimes the reasons are incomprehensible such as that of one student who told me she picked a particular school "because it had two swimming pools," but nevertheless, each and every student has a rationale.

Ultimately, I decided to include every accredited four-year institution in the United States and Canada.

(By the way, two of the most influential factors in the college choice decision are the attractiveness and persuasiveness of the tour guide. This is not logical since prospective students are not likely to ever see this person again, even if they do decide to attend the institution.)

To complete my research, I visited several hundred colleges and universities. I did not visit every one of the schools I recommend in this book, but I did visit enough to be able to translate promotional rhetoric and gossip into very accurate predictors of what I would find if I did, indeed, visit. Visits, while helpful, were more useful for eliminating colleges from further consideration than for ensuring their inclusion.

Over time I became more sophisticated in my understanding of colleges and universities. From more than thirteen years of inquiry, three years on my own behalf and ten years of working on this book, I have come to trust my own judgment. I discovered that some of the schools that educators favored were long past their prime. Others, hardly visible on the national scene and known only to a small circle of faculty and currently enrolled students, were doing exceptional work. A purely statistical methodology of any kind would not reveal these differences, yet a trained observer can spot them immediately. I became a trained observer.

In the end, the colleges featured in this book were chosen by me. They were originally proposed by college presidents, deans, and directors of admission, but if they made the final cut it was a purely subjective decision by one person.

In ten years of tracking this issue I collected thousands of articles and press releases, and like anyone else, was subject to manipulation by particularly skilled (or unskilled) public affairs officers. That is, I might be swayed by their presentation of information. One bias that I do not claim: As much as possible, I did not reward or penalize a school because of interactions with any one administrator. As enticing as it might have been to remove a school because an administrator was rude (or include a school because an administrator was particularly solicitous), I avoided doing so.

Here are my biases as I know them. First of all, I am not sixteen anymore. I am a Baby Boomer, like it or not, and have a different point of view than young people today. I am idealistic to the point of being corny. My daughters and their friends think I am "quaint," and perhaps you will, too. I think education can liberate a soul, and that social meritocracy and individual success can be attained by means of education. (I have tons of data to support this point of view, but that is not the point. The point is that I have this point of view, rather strongly.) I believe in citizenship and responsibility, and have a "right is right" and "wrong is wrong" attitude. These are beliefs I grew up with and I couldn't shake them if I wanted to. That's a bias. In fact, that's nearly the definition of a bias.

Second, I don't think large universities are good places for young people as undergraduates. Again, I have very good reasons for this bias, and I've tried to present some of them in this text, but it is a bias just the same. Just because in large universities students are more likely to report being lonely and isolated, more likely to drop out, more likely to be taught by a graduate assistant than a professor, more likely to cheat, more likely to be unable to name even one friend from college ten years after graduation, less likely to go to graduate school, more likely to be unable to get needed classes, more likely to work more than ten hours a week, and more likely to go through all four or five years of their education without really being changed by it shouldn't create bias, but in my case it has.

Third, I've studied at two large universities, two small universities, and one college mentioned in this text. I'd like to think I've succeeded in being objective about them (if anything I've been overly critical), but nevertheless, my experience must color my report somehow.

Fourth, upon reconsideration of this text, I discovered that I tend to favor some of the lesser-known institutions. I think this provides a service, since we all know about Harvard, Princeton, Yale, and Stanford. This guide is not meant to be the primary guide in a counselor's office, nor the only guide a student should consider. One of my explicit goals is to provide information not readily available everywhere.

Fifth, I did not research college cost while preparing this book. I find the subject obtuse, labyrinthine, and illogical, but those are not the reasons I decided not to cover it. Any statement a college makes about its own cost is intentionally misleading. When the overwhelming majority of students at any institution receive complex and multilayered financial aid, and when even wealthy families are negotiating discounts, the sticker price is meaningless. I'd like readers of this book to look for a good college fit. Every student should apply to his or her dream college or university, and make the financial decision when you have the financial data, i.e., after you have aid offers. For more on this topic, read a book that specifically addresses the issue of college financing, such as Bruce G. Hammond's *Discounts and Deals at the*

Nation's 360 Best Colleges (Golden Books Publishing Company, 1999).

Sixth, I did not research the issue of admissibility. That is, this is not really a book about how to get into college; it is a book about cool colleges one might want to get into. There are many other books on improving your chances of getting into a highly competitive program. I will tell you this, however: the best way to get into an elite school is to be the son or daughter of wealthy alumni.

One final limitation of this book is that it groups together schools in a way that is, ultimately, arbitrary. For example, it has a chapter called "Schools Where Scholarship Is Honored," and another one titled "The Great Books Programs." The decision to put St. John's College in the chapter on Great Books programs was, for me, an agonizing one. It very strongly belongs in the chapter "Schools Where Scholarship Is Honored." The school is extraordinary in its curriculum (Great Books), but even more extraordinary in its ethos (very scholarly). Tough call. Creating a taxonomy of

IS IMPORTANT INFORMATION MISSING FROM THIS BOOK?

In spite of the fact that I wrote to almost a thousand schools a minimum of four times each, some of them didn't provide me with so much as a viewbook. One wrote back, "We as an institution have made the decision not to participate in surveys such as the one you are conducting." Nice. If you have information that belongs in this book, whether you are an alumnus, an alumna, a currently enrolled student, or a member of faculty or administration, I welcome it for the next edition. As you can see, there are a wide range of topics covered. If you know of a way that your favorite school stands out from the crowd, I'd be delighted to hear about it:

Donald Asher · Cool Colleges Project · c/o Ten Speed Press · P.O. Box 7123
Berkeley, CA 94707 · Fax: 415-441-0389 · donasher@ix.netcom.com

You should be careful about believing everything you read in college guides, even this one. Writers can be mistaken or, even worse, intentionally misled either by overzealous school officials or by bad data. For example, at a top liberal arts college students got together twice to intentionally mislead national magazines, both times filling out surveys as if they were taking drugs and binge drinking every single day. This was a big joke to them, but the school suffers from this lingering reputation. The irony is that it would be impossible for students to succeed academically at this school if they even remotely participated in these parties fabricated as a prank. (For a different take on this, see the Tulane University story, p. 369.)

Finally, I know of a nationally ranked business school that hands out "suggested responses" for filling out quality surveys, and reminds students that the cash value of their graduate business education depends on the school's continued high rating in national rankings. Wow. Think about that.

schools, at least for the purposes of organizing this book, was not a pleasant task. Many outstanding and unique schools are lumped into groups. How do you create a taxonomy of unique items anyway? They defy organization.

Then, there was something that I came to call "The problem of Earlham." Earlham is a fantastic college in Richmond, Indiana. I have visited this school, and I know that it is a truly wonderful institution. The students are enthused and engaged. The faculty is smart and caring. The school as a whole has a coherent philosophy of education and service. It has an attractive campus and a solid physical plant. And yet it was hard to find the right spot for it in this book. Do I describe it by itself as the twenty-third example of a liberal arts college? You, dear reader, would go glassy-eyed with that approach, and yet it seemed quite unfair to simply list it as an iteration of a category.

Q. Why are some listings in this book in reverse alphabetical order?

A. I was touring a rather undistinguished institution in the middle of nowhere, whose name begins with an A. I was struck by the number of international students and the number of students from distant states. When I asked the dean why the school had such draw, she said, "We think it's our name. Students start making a list, and we're at the top of it." Since I thought this was a singularly poor reason to choose a college, I resolved to mix up the organization of my listings. I'd do them in random order, but people do want to look quickly and see if one they know of by name is on any given list. Thus, some are in alphabetical order, and some are in reverse alphabetical order.

Q. Why is there no standardized methodology in this book?

A. Finding the right college should be a process of discovery. One profile or even one item of information should be the trigger for you to investigate further and find your dream school. If the descriptions of schools in this book were all alike, even the most avid and serious student's eyes would glaze over shortly. I wrote thousands of letters to research this book, read thousands of letters and e-mails, read hundreds of viewbooks, visited several hundred schools, interviewed thousands of currently enrolled students, and researched comparative data until I was seeing spreadsheets and tables in my sleep. Then I thought about what stood out from the background noise. Whether one college has five thousand more books in its library than another is irrelevant. Physical books are themselves increasingly irrelevant. The culture or feel of a campus cannot be reduced to a ranking or a unilinear measure of any kind. The vitality and creativity of a student body is not visible in mean incoming SAT scores. Whether a professor will help *you* learn cannot be revealed by the number and prestige of his or her almae matres. I invite you to see through the chaos of this book to see that there *is* a methodology, and to see what that methodology suggests to you. Where will you be happy? Where will you learn the most? What is important to you? How can you find out more?

So as you read this book, please be aware of its limitations. Its organization is imperfect, and a little like organizing a car lot by putting all the blue cars and trucks in one corner, and all the red cars and trucks in another. If you're interested in four-wheel drives, you're going to have look all over the lot.

HOW TO READ THIS BOOK

There are three ways to read this book:

Method Number One: I call this the smorgasbord approach—just open it up anywhere and read any amount you want. Fool around with it; don't work at it. To look for interesting items, try the index and the table of contents. If you're not applying to college right away, the best thing you can do with this book is put it in your bathroom and glance through it when the opportunity presents itself. If your parents have their own bathroom, get them their own copy.

Method Number Two: If you are applying to school soon and want to make sure you don't make an egregious, life-ruining mistake by missing the chance to apply to a college you'd really love but have never heard of, then use the table of contents to methodically investigate schools in the chapters that most interest you. Read about all the schools in those chapters that match your personality and approach to education.

Method Number Three: Look up the schools you're interested in, and pay particular attention to the schools listed in the "Cross Apps" feature. This section will lead you from schools you already know a little about to similar schools that you don't know much about, but may like better. This is like surfing the Web—and all you need is one school you're interested in to get started.

SOME FINAL, *VERY* IMPORTANT DISCLAIMERS

This book purports to provide information on every accredited institution in the United States and Canada. You need to know that we have made every effort to identify every accredited institution at the time this book went to press, but it is entirely possible that an institution may have become accredited after this book went to press, or we may have missed an accredited institution through error on our part or on the part of the accrediting authorities, or there may be an accrediting authority that is unknown to us but carries weight for a certain type of institution. Also, we may have listed an institution as accredited when it is not, through error on our part or on the part of accrediting authorities. We made the decision not to mention those institutions that are on warning from their accrediting authorities, as it is very unusual for an institution to be delisted, and many infractions are minor and/or of an administrative sort.

We would be remiss if we did not state forcefully that the institutions listed herein are of vastly differing missions and quality. Just because an institution is described in this book does not mean that it will provide the quality and type of education that you seek. Sometimes students will focus on some aspects of a college that are very attractive, and fail to notice other aspects of that same college that make it a poor match.

Finally, although it is true that there is often only one college in the world that is a perfect match for a student, particularly an unusual student, it is not good strategy to apply to only one college, no matter how strongly you feel about a school you may discover in these pages. We recommend that you make your college choices in close collaboration with your parents, teachers, college counselors, and other advisors, and that you apply to several colleges.

Chapter One

TWO PREP COLLEGES

SIMON'S ROCK COLLEGE OF BARD

early entry program • **no high school diploma required** • *quality college education beginning at age 16, 17, or even 15, if you have what it takes* • **350 students: 60% women, 40% men** • *beautiful environs* • **a unique chance to get on with it**

Simon's Rock is one of the few schools in the nation to seek out students who have *not* finished a high school curriculum. It offers an early start at college for those students who are ready for college before most colleges are ready for them. Strictly speaking, Simon's Rock is not just a prep college, as many students do complete all four years there. Deep Springs is a two-year school like no other. When you think about two-year programs, you're probably not thinking about Simon's Rock and Deep Springs. These two schools are listed first in this book just to give you an idea of some of the different approaches to higher education that are out there once you think beyond the nearest large state university. This section also begins the discussion of the college choice process, which infuses all the sections of this book. The questions under consideration in this chapter will be: Should you go to a large or a small institution? What about scholarship scams? Are there really totally free schools out there?

SIMON'S ROCK COLLEGE OF BARD

Some people are too bright for high school. Is this you? Do you find the level of academic endeavor at your high school slightly beneath sea level?

Are you drowning intellectually while you wait, wait, wait for the day when you can escape and join a real college, where you can be with other people who care

**An old pond
A frog leaping in
The sound of water**

—Matsuo Basho

about more than the senior prom and *Oh, what are you going to wear? Ohmygawd! You can't be serious! That's like, so out of it!*

Well, you are not alone. All over North America smart young people are bored out of their minds by high schools that de-emphasize academics and emphasize sports and a warped view of adolescent social life.

Here's the really important question: Are you ready for college now? There are four main parts to this question, really:

- Do you have the intellectual capacity to perform at the college level today? Are you ready to write college papers and do college-level scientific work and tackle college-level mathematics? This is a question of intellect.
- Are you academically prepared? That is, do you know enough to benefit from college now? This is a question of accumulated knowledge.
- Are you mature enough to perform on your own? Are you able to get out of bed in the morning, manage your own time, and meet your commitments?
- Have you gotten all your high school has to offer you? Not perhaps all your high school has to offer, but all your high school has to offer *you*?

If you can answer an unequivocal yes to each of these four questions, you should consider the early entry program at Simon's Rock College of Bard in Great Barrington, Massachusetts.

Simon's Rock admits students of demonstrated promise straight out of high school. Except for this one fact, it is in most other senses just an innovative New England liberal arts college. It has a carefully designed curriculum emphasizing mastery of critical thinking skills, followed by increasing specialization and the design and execution of a major research project before graduation with a bachelor's degree. You can start a classic liberal arts education here, then transfer after two years to another school—or stay and complete your bachelor's degree.

> **❝It's a really great school for kids who are too bright to do well in high school.❞**
>
> *—An independent college counselor*

I recently went to my high school reunion. Everybody who was really cool in high school was now selling vacuum cleaners door to door while everybody who had been down with the out crowd was a scientist or a college professor or a dot-com millionaire. It was almost a biblical reversal of fortune. Weird.

At the end of the sophomore year, students complete what the school calls the Lower College program, and are awarded an associate of arts degree. At this point, two-thirds of Simon's Rock students opt to complete their studies at another college or university. This was the way the college was originally designed to work, as a sort of early entry prep college for young scholars who were bound for other schools after completing Lower College. Simon's Rock students find admission to such colleges and universities as these:

American University, Washington, DC

American University in Paris, France

Bard College, Annandale-on-Hudson, New York

Barnard College, New York, New York

Bates College, Lewiston, Maine

Berklee College of Music, Boston, Massachusetts

Boston University, Boston, Massachusetts

Brandeis University, Waltham, Massachusetts

Brown University, Providence, Rhode Island

Bryn Mawr College, Bryn Mawr, Pennsylvania

Carleton College, Northfield, Minnesota

Carnegie Mellon University, Pittsburgh, Pennsylvania

Case Western Reserve University, Cleveland, Ohio

Claremont McKenna College, Claremont, California

Clark University, Worcester, Massachusetts

Colgate University, Hamilton, New York

Colorado College, Colorado Springs, Colorado

Columbia University, New York, New York

Cornell University, Ithaca, New York

Dartmouth College, Hanover, New Hampshire

Drew University, Madison, New Jersey

Duke University, Durham, North Carolina

Emory University, Atlanta, Georgia

Eugene Lang College of the New School for Social Research, New York, New York

Evergreen State College, Olympia, Washington

Fisk University, Nashville, Tennesee

George Washington University, Washington, DC

Goucher College, Baltimore, Maryland

Hampshire College, Amherst, Massachusetts

Harvard University, Cambridge, Massachusetts

Hood College, Frederick, Maryland

Howard University, Washington, DC

Hunter College, New York, New York

Johns Hopkins University, Baltimore, Maryland

Knox College, Galesburg, Illinois

Lehigh University, Bethlehem, Pennsylvania

Lewis & Clark University, Portland, Oregon

Macalester College, St. Paul, Minnesota

Massachusetts Institute of Technology (MIT), Cambridge, Massachusetts

Michigan Technological University, Houghton, Michigan

Mills College, Oakland, California

Morehouse College, Atlanta, Georgia

Mount Holyoke College, South Hadley, Massachusetts

New York University, New York, New York

Oberlin College, Oberlin, Ohio

Parsons School of Design, New York, New York

Pitzer College, Claremont, California

Pomona College, Claremont, California

Reed College, Portland, Oregon

Rensselaer Polytechnic Institute, Troy, New York

Rice University, Houston, Texas

Royal Holloway College of the University of London, England

Rutgers University, New Brunswick, New Jersey

San Francisco Art Institute, San Francisco, California

Sarah Lawrence College, Bronxville, New York

Savannah College of Art and Design, Savannah, Georgia

School of Oriental and African Studies of the University of London, England

Skidmore College, Saratoga Springs, New York

Smith College, Northampton, Massachusetts

Stanford University, Stanford, California

State University of New York, Albany, New York

State University of New York, Binghampton, New York

State University of New York, Buffalo, New York

State University of New York, Purchase, New York

State University of New York, Stony Brook, New York

Stevens Institute of Technology, Hoboken, New Jersey

Swarthmore College, Swarthmore, Pennsylvania

Syracuse University, Syracuse, New York

Trinity College, Dublin, Ireland

Tufts University, Medford, Massachusetts

University of Arizona, Tucson, Arizona

University of California, Davis, California

University of California, Irvine, California

University of California, Los Angeles, California

University of California, Santa Cruz, California

SIMON'S ROCK AND BARD

Is Simon's Rock part of Bard, or what? You'd think this would be a simple question to have answered, but it is not. According to the public affairs office of Simon's Rock College of Bard, "Simon's Rock is an independent college with its own board of directors, but it has the same president as Bard, Leon Botstein. Bard is the parent college, but Bard does not 'own' Simon's Rock." Whatever that means. You figure it out. Leon Botstein is one of the most interesting people in higher education today. See the sidebar on his new book, which makes a case for the abolition of high school as we know it.

University of California, San Diego, California

University of Chicago, Chicago, Illinois

University of Colorado, Boulder, Colorado

University of Illinois, Urbana-Champaign, Illinois

University of Maryland, College Park, Maryland

University of Massachusetts, Amherst, Massachusetts

University of Michigan, Ann Arbor, Michigan

University of Minnesota, Twin Cities, Minneapolis, Minnesota

University of North Carolina, Chapel Hill, North Carolina

University of Pennsylvania, Philadelphia, Pennsylvania

University of Rochester, Rochester, New York

University of Utah, Salt Lake City, Utah

University of Washington, Seattle, Washington

Vanderbilt University, Nashville, Tennesee

Vassar College, Poughkeepsie, New York

> **We pick up a fair number of home-schooled students. They tend to do well here.**
>
> —*Simon's Rock administrator*

CoOl BoOk AlErT!

Jefferson's Children: Education and the Promise of American Culture by Leon Botstein (Doubleday, 1997)

Eighteenth-century optimism has been lost in a national morass of pessimism, Botstein contends. Weighing an assemblage of evidence, he charges that we no longer believe we can educate our children to create a better world. Leon Botstein was the youngest person to assume such a post when he became president of Bard College. Now the longest-serving college president *and* director of the American Symphony Orchestra, he makes a bold indictment of present practices in public education. "The American high school is obsolete," he declares, characterizing schools as "breeding grounds for violence, for drug and alcohol abuse, vulgarity, and a totally thoughtless, rampant expression of sexuality," and where the "best are influenced by the weakest." Yet, Botstein portrays public education as doing a better job than political rhetoric would have us believe, despite the deleterious effects of bureaucratic regulations, defensive teachers' unions, and parents more concerned with school prayer than with education. He offers concrete ideas, some of them certain to raise hackles, for creating renewed institutions of learning.

Also check out Stanley Aronowitz's *The Knowledge Factory: Dismantling the Corporate University and Creating True Higher Learning* (Beacon Press, 2000), in which the author calls modern universities "glorified employment agencies." If you want even more fun books along this line, read Martin Anderson's *Imposters in the Temple* (Hoover Institution Press, 1996), Charles Sykes's *ProfScam: Professors and the Demise of Higher Education* (St. Martin's Press, 1990), and Richard Huber's *How Professors Play the Cat Guarding the Cream* (George Mason University Press, 1993).

Washington University in St. Louis, St. Louis, Missouri

Wellesley College, Wellesley, Massachusetts

Wesleyan University, Middletown, Connecticut

Williams College, Williamstown, Massachusetts

Yale University, New Haven, Connecticut

One-third of students decide to complete the bachelor's degree at Simon's Rock by completing the Upper School. The college emphasizes interdisciplinary study and independent study, with strengths in some areas, such as environmental studies and most of the liberal arts, and weaknesses in others. If a student is interested in an area the college feels it cannot support, the student is encouraged to transfer to complete her or his undergraduate program at a more appropriate institution. Students can cross-register with nearby Bard College, and many do. A central part of the Upper School degree program is a year-long independent study leading to the writing of an undergraduate thesis. Expectations are high, and success in this degree program is excellent preparation for graduate study.

Recent thesis projects include:

An Investigation of the Possible Synergistic Mutagenic Effect Created In Vitro by Potassium Chromate and Meta-Stable Barium

My Room: An Exploration of Non-Traditional Performance Art

Whipworms and Water Filters: An Investigation of Intestinal Parasites in Children Living in a Temporary Home in Tegucigalpa, Honduras

Harlem Rising: The Contributions of African-American Music to American Culture during the Harlem Renaissance

Art or Artifact? Historicizing Ancient Egyptian Archaeology

Once Upon a Thesis: An Original Fairy Tale and Dance Narrative

Mud and Myrabolam: An Exploration of Pattern, Fabric, and the Woodblock Printing Traditions of Jaipur, India

The Legacy of French Colonization in Côte d'Ivoire

DOWNSIDE: Many parents are shocked to have their children interested in an early entry program. The student may feel that the program is perfect and a salvation, but the parents may be financially and emotionally unprepared for the student

❝ At first I was relieved. There were a lot of strange people like me. It was the first time I'd ever really felt at home. After a while I realized I wasn't strange at all. ❞

—Simon's Rock alumna

to leave home for college. Can your family afford a school like Simon's Rock? The majority of students at Simon's Rock are on financial aid, and the college grants twenty full-ride merit scholarships every year in national open competition. For more information, contact the college. In short: It may be a lobbying job to convince your parents that you should take an early- entry option. On the other hand, your parents may jump at the chance to see you happy and challenged in school.

Also, it is important to understand that Simon's Rock is a college, not some kind of boarding school on steroids. Students thrive here who are able to manage their

" Everyone is born a genius. "

—R. Buckminster Fuller

A FEW THOUGHTS ON THE LARGE VS. SMALL DECISION

If you play a sport in high school and you'd like to continue to play it in college, consider a smaller college. There probably won't be a scholarship for it, but there will be field time and the camaraderie and the competition and the excitement that you've come to love about your sport. At a large university, you're either a national-level contender, or you don't play.

If you want to write for the newspaper at a small college, all you have to do is find the editor and propose an article. Boom, you're a reporter, maybe even a columnist. At a large university, you'd probably have to be a journalism major, and even then a lot of the newspaper jobs are actually full-time, paid positions.

If you want to be a DJ for the campus radio station, at a small college all you have to do is find the station manager and ask to come on board. You'll start with the worst time slot, but it'll be your show. You can play rockabilly, gospel, and have poetry readings, all on the same show probably, if that's what you want. At a large university, you'd have to follow the playlist.

At a smaller institution, you can more easily become captain or founder or czar of something, compared to major universities where student senate campaigns have a media budget. You can be the lead in a play without being a theater major. You can go on biology field trips without being a biology major. You can play cello in a quartet without taking a single music class. You can *try lots of things out* without specializing yet.

If you want to get to know your professors, and have them know you, it's sure a lot easier if there are ten or twenty students in a class, than if there are one hundred or two hundred.

Suppose you want friends. Maybe you think that on a campus with fifteen thousand students you'd have ten times as many people to know as on a campus of fifteen hundred students. This is like the saltwater sailor's lament, "Water, water everywhere, and not a drop to drink." The larger the campus, the less interaction outside of class. At a large school, you won't know the one thousand people in the student union at any given moment. At a small school, you're likely to know *all* of the few dozen students in the student union at any given time. Also, at large schools, the overwhelming majority of students live off campus. They go home after class, and lots of them go home between classes. You'll see them, alright, walking past you to find their cars.

The most important factor in creating a school's on-campus atmosphere is on-campus living. It is absolutely essential to creating a bond between students and between students and the institution. Very few universities succeed in providing this—Yale, Princeton, and Rice are the only that come to mind—but practically *all* the smaller colleges do.

15 LARGEST COLLEGES/UNIVERSITIES

University of Texas at Austin - 48,906
Austin, Texas

Ohio State University, main campus - 48,514
Columbus, Ohio

University of Minnesota, Twin Cities - 46,973
Minneapolis, Minnesota

Arizona State University, main campus - 43,732
Tempe, Arizona

Texas A&M University, College Station - 43,389
College Station, Texas

Michigan State University - 43,189
East Lansing, Michigan

University of Florida, Gainesville - 42,336
Gainesville, Florida

Pennsylvania State University, University Park - 41,114
University Park, Pennsylvania

University of Wisconsin, Madison - 39,565
Madison, Wisconsin

Purdue University, main campus - 38,757
West Lafayette, Indiana

University of Illinois at Urbana-Champaign - 38,307
Urbana-Champaign, Illinois

University of Michigan at Ann Arbor - 37,197
Ann Arbor, Michigan

New York University - 36,719
New York, New York

University of California, Los Angeles - 35,795
Los Angeles, California

Indiana University, Bloomington - 35,600
Bloomington, Indiana

(Source: Department of Education, National Center for Education Statistics)

15 SMALLER COLLEGES/UNIVERSITIES

Black Forest Hall - 1
Harbor Springs, Michigan

Yeshiva Toras Chaim Talmudic Seminary - 20
Denver, Colorado

Monterey Institute of International Studies - 20
(Primarily grad; talented undergrads study in grad classes)
Monterey, California

Magnolia Bible College - 47
Kosciusko, Mississippi

Alaska Bible College - 51
Glennallen, Alaska

Vennard College - 61
University Park, Iowa

The Thomas More College of Liberal Arts - 62
Merrimack, New Hampshire

Southeastern Baptist College - 64
Birmingham, Alabama

Cleveland Institute of Music - 64
Cleveland, Ohio

Pacific States University - 66
Los Angeles, California

Hebrew Union College - 66
Los Angeles, California

Cincinnati College of Mortuary Science - 70
Cincinnati, Ohio

American Indian College of the Assemblies of God - 71
Phoenix, Arizona

West Suburban College of Nursing - 75
Oak Park, Illinois

Kentucky Mountain Bible College - 76
Vancleve, Kentucky

(Source: Department of Education, National Center for Education Statistics)

time well, who welcome intellectual challenge, and who are mature and independent. Many young people, fifteen to eighteen years old, overestimate their maturity and self-motivation. Does your mother wake you up? Drive you to school? Nag you about the due dates on assignments? Wash your clothes? Your mother's probably not going to be around, so how would you really do without this type of support?

Here's what one administrator told me: "The student who thrives here is very self-directed, has an inner set of values, and is somewhat sure of himself or herself." Let's face it, this is not the typical sixteen-year-old, no matter how smart he or she is.

CROSS APPS: If you're interested in early entry programs, you should know that before the American high school was invented it was the norm for students to enter college at fifteen or sixteen years of age. For years, Simon's Rock was a lone voice in this wilderness, championing the early-entry option. Now, more programs are coming on line. Some states, such as my home state, allow early entry under special circumstances, but it's not always that great an advantage to be just thrown into the regular university system. Check out the early-entry program for women at Mary Baldwin College in Staunton, Virginia, the summer program at Johns Hopkins University's Center for Talented Youth, The University of North Texas-Denton's Texas Academy of Mathematics and Science, and the University of Washington-Seattle's Students in Transition School. These are outstanding programs designed for this type of student. See also the National Research Center on the Gifted and Talented at

IN TODAY'S LESSON, CLASS, WE EXPLORE THE INCREASING ISOLATION OF THE INDIVIDUAL IN SOCIETY.

> **The greatest shortcoming, I believe, of most attempts at liberal education today, with their individualized, unfocused, scattered curricula, and ill-defined purpose, is their failure to enhance the students' understanding of their status as free citizens of a free society and the responsibilities it entails.**
>
> —Donald Kagan, professor at Yale and author of Reconstructing History, in an essay in the Chronicle of Higher Education (1 October 1999).

www.gifted.uconn.edu and the National Association for Gifted Children at 202-785-4268 or www.nagc.org.

If you're interested in the idea of doing an undergraduate research project and/or thesis, be sure to read the section on Reed College, beginning on p. 62, and New College of the University of South Florida, beginning on p. 122.

Simon's Rock is particularly strong in environmental studies. If this is of interest to you, see also Evergreen State College in Olympia, Washington; University of California, Santa Cruz; Prescott College in Prescott, Arizona; Green Mountain College in Poultney, Vermont; and College of the Atlantic in Bar Harbor, Maine, among many others.

If you're interested in a school that can see you're smart in spite of some iffy grades, also check out St. John's College in Annapolis, Maryland, and Santa Fe, New Mexico, and to some extent, Reed College in Portland, Oregon. All of these schools will look beyond your overall GPA, but don't overinterpret this as a license to quit worrying about your GPA. They will be looking for certain grade patterns that might be misleading in aggregate. For example, they may look for many very high grades offset by a few very low grades, with no grades in the middle (a smart nonconformist), or all As in some years and mediocre grades in other years (a smart student who gives up). No school is going to agree with you that your collection of Bs and Cs really should be counted as As, no matter what your rationale. Remember, all schools are looking for concrete reasons to admit you, real evidence you can perform, rather than mere claims of such ability. You can't be all potential and no actualization. By seventeen years of age, you should have done something that can serve as evidence of your abilities.

If you're interested in Simon's Rock's small size, see Marlboro College, p. 147; New College of the University of South Florida, p. 122; College of the Atlantic in Bar Harbor, Maine, p. 140; or Deep Springs, next page, which is truly small with only twenty-six students, all male. Deep Springs is also a two-year prep program leading to entry to the most elite colleges and universities in the nation. (See the next section for a complete description of Deep Springs.)

Simon's Rock College of Bard
84 Alford Road
Great Barrington, MA 01230
413-528-0771
www.simons-rock.edu

DEEP SPRINGS COLLEGE

26 students · *all male* · **on a working ranch** · *students run everything* · **unbelievably strong two-year program** · *prep here, then finish at almost any top college or university* · **campus is 80 square miles** · *oh, and it's free*

Many colleges and universities claim to be "unique" or "distinctive," but Deep Springs is a college like no other. This tiny men's college is built upon three pillars: scholarship, self-governance, and labor. The founder, a visionary named L. L. Nunn, started the college in 1917 as an educational experiment, an "idealistic vision of what an education should be." With a student body limited to twenty-six young men, the college is a bastion of brilliant eccentricity in the "rising tide of mediocrity" that is higher education in this country today.

Deep Springs's isolation is quite intentional. Located between Death Valley and Yosemite National Park, the college is precisely in the middle of nowhere. It is a place so remote that the mail gets delivered to a post office in another state. The campus is in fact an eighty-square-mile cattle ranch and organic alfalfa farm. L. L. Nunn thought that cities were a distraction to the academic studies of young men, and morally corrupting, so he sought a place where such distractions would be at a minimum.

The ranch itself is quite a distraction, however, as the students run it—fish, tarp, and spindle. They provide the labor, from sowing to reaping, and are charged to wring

> **Hey, we've got the Internet. We're global.**
>
> —*Student*

The school has a perennial debate about whether to go coed. In fact, the school has a perennial debate about everything, but this is one of the more serious issues that keeps coming up.

> # " One of the most selective and innovative colleges in the world. "
>
> —*New York Times*

a profit out of the "living endowment" of the ranch. The labor is one cornerstone to the educational experience that is Deep Springs. Students need to keep up with their chores while studying one of the most demanding curricula available anywhere (more on that in a moment). The ranch work is not for the overly squeamish, as it includes the grunt work of neutering steers and slaughtering stock, as well as entering production figures on a computerized spreadsheet. Nevertheless, the student body usually includes some vegetarians, who somehow find a way to do their part.

Students run Deep Springs. Like labor, self-governance is a cornerstone of the college. The students are completely responsible for the conduct of their own numbers as well as for the governance of the college and the ranch. I interviewed a first-year student who was a member of the board of trustees, a sworn fiduciary of the college, a member of the curriculum committee, a member of a faculty search committee, and a member of the committee planning the next year's academic calendar. (Remember, this is a student, who presumably finds time to study as well.) Nunn

GET THE NAME RIGHT!

When you're looking for a college or university that you know only a little about, be careful to get the name right! Several people have told me that upon hearing for the first time that "Penn" was an Ivy League school, they thought of Pennsylvania State University, especially if they heard this in casual conversation. Pennsylvania State University-University Park is in State College, Pennsylvania, and "Penn" is the University of Pennsylvania in Philadelphia. Very different.

Also, many state universities sound alike. There are twelve institutions calling themselves "Rutgers." Check it out. And Washington University in St. Louis changed its name from Washington University to "Washington University in St. Louis" in 1976 to keep this strong national university from being confused with the eighteen other schools in the country with "Washington" as part of their name.

There's a Saint Francis College in Loretto, Pennsylvania, and another one in Fort Wayne, Indiana, as well as a St. Francis College in Brooklyn Heights, New York. Then there's St. John's College in Annapolis, Maryland, and her sister campus in Santa Fe, New Mexico, and a totally different institution by the exact same name in Winnipeg, Manitoba, and the St. John's University in Jamaica, New York, and the Saint John's University in Collegeville, Minnesota, a St. John's Seminary College in Camarillo, California, and another one in Brighton, Massachusetts, not to be confused with St. John Vianney College Seminary, in Miami, Florida, to say nothing of the St. John Fisher College in Rochester, New York.

There's a great little liberal arts college called Wheaton in Norton, Massachusetts, and a great little liberal arts college called Wheaton in Wheaton, Illinois. One is a Christian college, and one is famous for its career development program (see p. 165). I suppose it matters whether you want most to advance in this life or the next, but it would pay to get it right either way.

wanted his college to build citizenship and leadership, and viewed the college as an incubator for mastering those skills.

Finally, Deep Springs academics are second to none. The school sets the highest standards for students and faculty. Classes are small, ranging from one student to maybe twenty. (Obviously the largest possible class, under any circumstances, is twenty-six.) The workload is heavy, and there is certainly no way to fake it or coast in an environment where everybody knows everything about everybody's business. The school accepts approximately one applicant out of twenty, making it, arguably, the most exclusive and competitive college in the nation.

The curriculum changes annually, depending on the interest of the students and the available faculty. "We do not have a Great Books program," says one student. "We pretty much follow the Western canon, but it is not a Great Books program per se. We try to keep a balance of social sciences, humanities, French literary theory. Right now, for example, we have a class in Marcel Proust's *In Remembrance of Things Past*, a class on nationalism in the twentieth century from an anthropological perspective, and classes on postmodernism and literary theory, James Baldwin, geology, sustainable agriculture, natural moral philosophy (taught by a professor from Oxford who is coming here just to teach that class), ancient Greek language, patristic theology, ecology, and history of higher education, taught by our college president, Jack Newell." The classes move along at a blazing speed, with a year made up of six seven-week terms. The only required course is public speaking, which every student takes every term.

There is no tenure at Deep Springs, and the faculty rotate in from places like Stanford and Swarthmore for periods from one to five years. Even the presidency tends to rotate. Half the student body changes every year. A running joke on campus is that the longest-lasting residents on campus are the dogs. The real winner is a cat, rumored to be twenty years old, older than many of the students.

Who goes to Deep Springs? Very smart, very motivated male students who want to have a very different college experience. Those who are admitted need no outdoor experience at all, but they must want to participate in the working agrarian community that is Deep Springs. Last year's incoming class included one sixteen-year-

> **Nunn was a self-made man in the storybook way, a poor man who worked hard and became a multi-millionaire industrialist. He observed in the late 1800s that the country was being run by an old boys' club, and decided that those who would become members of that club needed some moral training. The original student body were the sons of wealthy industrialists, sent here to keep them from becoming spoiled.**
>
> —*Deep Springs student*

Deep Springs is bigger than the City and County of San Francisco, yet it exists to serve just twenty-six students. Institutional continuity is an issue. But somehow the school has stayed remarkably consistent over the last eighty years.

old, one student who worked for three years before even applying to college, and a couple of transfers, so out of an incoming class of thirteen, roughly one-third were not traditional eighteen-year-old high school graduates. However, the average combined SAT is "about 1500" according to the dean of academic affairs, making this an elite student body indeed.

Deep Springs is free. Tuition, room, and board are absolutely free. A student's only expenses are books, travel, and a laptop if he wants one.

L. L. Nunn wanted to create a place with democratic self-governance to develop respect for democracy and justice, manual labor to develop character, and strong academics to sharpen the mind and reasoning capabilities. If this appeals to you, apply.

DOWNSIDE: This is an intense college choice. Any man who could get in here could probably go anywhere else, so this is obviously a place students choose, rather than just accept. The admissions process is grueling, including a visit where you will have to try to be yourself while interacting with your future peers, who are in fact your admissions committee, too. If you go to Deep Springs, you'll never have a simple answer to the question, "Where'd you go to college?" If you've been coasting through high school to make straight As, that won't work here. And finally, they are dead serious about the work aspect. Students work like ranch hands at Deep Springs College—because they are.

MORE UPSIDE: Students who complete the two-year degree program at Deep Springs are generally able to write their own tickets to any top college. In the world.

CROSS APPS: Deep Springs does not have any meaningful cross apps. It is simply not like any other school.

Deep Springs College
Off California Highway 168
Deep Springs, California
c/o HC72 Box 45001
Dyer, NV 89010
760-872-2000
www.deepsprings.edu

ON CREDIT

You no doubt have a credit card. You may have several. There is no finer thing you could do for your long-term welfare than to destroy those cards immediately. College is always financially difficult. No matter how much you've saved or how much your family supports you, you will not have enough money. Worse than that, you may be shoulder to shoulder in school with others who *do* have seemingly unlimited access to cash. The temptations will be constant. A consumer item here, a car repair there, a "celebratory" dinner for some triumph, a dollar here and a fiver there, and just like in Congress, pretty soon you're talking about real money. Get a debit card if you like the convenience or, even better, get a credit card with your name on it that really belongs to a parent. Then, if you have an emergency, you've got a card, but you're not likely to abuse the privilege, as your parents will get that bill every month and notice how many "emergencies" you were having.

First, don't dream for even one moment that your parents will bail you out if you run up your cards. They're going to be spending a fortune on your college education, and your credit line with them is very likely to dry up before you graduate. Your parents' financial advisors are busy telling them *not* to pay off your credit cards, so you can "learn from" your mistakes.

Second, you will have real trouble after you graduate trying to rent an apartment and buy a car if your credit is wrecked. You may land a great job and be in a really embarrassing bind because you don't have adult access to credit. No apartment, no car, no business clothes, and you'll look like a jerk.

Third, you will have trouble getting financial aid for graduate school if you accumulate credit card debt. Student debt, even tons of it, is factored in to graduate school financial aid, but consumer debt never is, even if you only bought books with those credit cards.

Fourth, credit card companies make the most money from the least creditworthy customers, and that means you. You'll face high interest rates and punitive late fees, and that's just if you have a reputable card provider. The unscrupulous ones have

---

Deep Springs may have the best food in higher education. Their chef was trained at Chez Panisse, and they grow their own organic vegetables, slaughter their own beef and pork, and make their own cheeses. Not exactly cafeteria food.

---

devised more ways than you can imagine to squeeze money out of people who get in over their heads. Why enrich them?

These credit card companies should be banned from campus. If a drug dealer came and set up tables and gave away free T-shirts, the whole academic community would be up in arms. But credit card companies do it every day, offering free sign-ups and fancy enticements reminiscent of the drug dealer's clichéd come-on, "Here, try one of *mine.* No charge the first couple of times." They're extending thousands of dollars of credit to people *most of whom don't even have a job.*

They know that no matter how high the interest rate and how many fees they pile onto your account, sooner or later you're going to need new credit bad enough to clean up your old account. And that's how they get paid. Oh, and by the way, even after you pay them off, you still have bad credit on your record. That means more years of higher interest rates.

Your goal: Don't get involved with them at all. Get a debit card, or get a card in your name on your parent's account. If you do get your own account, pay it off every month and *always* pay off 100 percent of your credit card debt before the first day of school every year. If you fail, burn the card and live without it. Don't let it get any worse.

Warning signs of credit problems

Using credit cards to get cash advances.

Using credit cards to pay rent.

Using credit cards to buy groceries.

Using credit cards to pay off other credit cards.

Getting dinged with late fees.

Failing to pay off your outstanding balance every month.

Making only the minimum payment every month.

Borrowing money from others to make credit card payments.

Bumming money from your parents to pay off credit card bills.

Running out of money before you run out of month.

Lying about your debt.

If you run up $2,000 and then stop, you could make the minimum payment every single month for the rest of your life and, if you were never late once, *every year you would owe more than the last.* Wow, is that dumb.

Don't even get started.

For more on this, get the Real Credit Cost Reminder Kit from Access Group, Inc., www.accessgroup.org, 800-282-1550.

AN UNUSUAL APPLICATION ESSAY

3.A. Essay.

IN ORDER FOR THE ADMISSIONS STAFF OF OUR COLLEGE TO GET TO KNOW YOU, THE APPLICANT, BETTER, WE ASK THAT YOU ANSWER THE FOLLOWING QUESTION: ARE THERE ANY SIGNIFICANT EXPERIENCES YOU HAVE HAD, OR ACCOMPLISHMENTS YOU HAVE REALIZED, THAT HAVE HELPED DEFINE YOU AS A PERSON?

I am a dynamic figure, often seen scaling walls and crushing ice. I have been known to remodel train stations on my lunch breaks, making them more efficient in the area of heat retention. I translate ethnic slurs for Cuban refugees, I write award-winning operas, I manage time efficiently.

Occasionally, I tread water for three days in a row.

I woo women with my sensuous and godlike trombone playing, I can pilot bicycles up severe inclines with unflagging speed, and I cook Thirty-Minute Brownies in twenty minutes. I am an expert in stucco, a veteran in love, and an outlaw in Peru.

Using only a hoe and a large glass of water, I once single-handedly defended a small village in the Amazon Basin from a horde of ferocious army ants.

I play bluegrass cello, I was scouted by the Mets, I am the subject of numerous documentaries. When I'm bored, I build large suspension bridges in my yard. I enjoy urban hang gliding. On Wednesdays, after school, I repair electrical appliances free of charge.

I am an abstract artist, a concrete analyst, and a ruthless bookie. Critics worldwide swoon over my original line of corduroy evening wear. I don't perspire. I am a private citizen, yet I receive fan mail. I have been caller number nine and have won the weekend passes. Last summer I toured New Jersey with a traveling centrifugal-force demonstration. I bat .400.

My deft floral arrangements have earned me fame in international botany circles. Children trust me.

I can hurl tennis rackets at small moving objects with deadly accuracy. I once read Paradise Lost, Moby Dick, and David Copperfield in one day and still had time to refurbish an entire dining room that evening. I know the exact location of every food item in the supermarket. I have performed several covert operations for the CIA. I sleep once a week; when I do sleep, I sleep in a chair. While on vacation in Canada, I successfully negotiated with a group of terrorists who had seized a small bakery. The laws of physics do not apply to me.

I balance, I weave, I dodge, I frolic, and my bills are all paid. On weekends, to let off steam, I participate in full-contact origami. Years ago I discovered the meaning of life but forgot to write it down. I have made extraordinary four-course meals using only a mouli and a toaster oven.

I breed prize-winning clams. I have won bullfights in San Juan, cliff-diving competitions in Sri Lanka, and spelling bees at the Kremlin.

I have played Hamlet, I have performed open-heart surgery, and I have spoken with Elvis.

But I have not yet gone to college.

NOTE: This essay appeared all over the Internet in the nineties, and undoubtedly belongs to an actual student, who is also undoubtedly a politician by now. Do not copy or even imitate this essay. Believe me, the original was the best that ever will be. However, do be encouraged by this student's bravery and creativity, and see that you can be brave and creative in your essay as well.

SECRET TO FINDING SCHOLARSHIPS— THERE ISN'T ONE

by Jane Bryant Quinn

I dialed a toll-free number and heard a cheerful, recorded voice.

"Hi! And thanks for calling the College Funding Seminar Hotline," it chirped. "Discover the little-known, inside secrets to getting the most money possible to pay for your child's education. . . . Receive all the details at our next, upcoming free seminar that's saving other parents just like you thousands of dollars."

Oh, dear. The old "secret scholarship" game, updated for the seminar age. The postcard promoting this seminar promised the "Shocking Truth!" about scholarships and "amazing facts . . . never before revealed!"

Why, one wonders, would colleges want to keep scholarships secret? Why would the facts be revealed only to a seminar company that bulk-mails postcards with no return address? Why would you think these amazing facts would be revealed for free?

Maybe something's fishy here.

I left a message on the hotline, saying who I was and asking someone to call. No one did. So I can't tell you more about this particular seminar.

But I can tell you this: There are *no* secrets—amazing or otherwise—to unearthing student financial aid. You'll find all you need to know below.

The Federal Trade Commission sees an upswing in seminars offering scholarship information and advice. You'll get a piece of junk mail at home saying that your student is "scheduled for an interview" on college costs or "has been identified" as eligible for aid.

But the so-called interview "isn't so much educational as it is a sales pitch," says attorney Gregory Ashe of the FTC's Bureau of Consumer Protection.

At the meeting, a salesperson may imply that thousands of hidden scholarships lie within your grasp. To find out where, however, you'll have to pay.

Alternately, you might be told that you can win more federal aid dollars by rearranging your assets to appear more needy. Most of these asset-protection methods involve costs, such as taking loans or buying annuities. And there's no guarantee that you'll get a larger student grant.

Yet other seminars offer to help you with college and aid applications. But you still have to gather all the information for the application, which is the hardest part of the paperwork.

If paperwork is your problem, your high school guidance office often will help you, at no cost. So will www.finaid.org (a Web site that has lots of other good information, besides).

Among the sales tactics to be wary of, according to the FTC: claims that you can't get this information anywhere else (false!); pressure to sign up for the paid service now, now, now; testimonials from people who say they got big scholarships (they might be paid shills); money-back guarantees hedged with lots of conditions.

Pitches to worried parents are commonplace during the precollege years. Telemarketers get your student's name from lists of people who buy yearbooks, order class rings, and show up in student directories. You get a mass-mailed postcard urging you to call a toll-free number.

The FTC recently shut down eight companies that, for a fee, "guaranteed" they could find you $1,000 or more in private student aid. They charged $10 to $400 up front and delivered a lot of useless information.

After the FTC actions, scholarship companies quit "guaranteeing" money, Ashe says, and switched to "identifying" $1,000 to $5,000 scholarships for which you supposedly qualify. But the information you get might be inappropriate or out of date.

No legal action has been brought yet against any seminar operations, which cost in the $750 range. But the FTC's Project ScholarScam is still functioning, so one can assume that the field remains under observation.

Here's the real "Shocking Truth" about finding college aid: It's easy to locate for free. You high school guidance office (or www.ed.gov) has the government forms and timetables. The colleges do the rest after you apply.

"Between 90 percent and 95 percent of all student aid, including federal aid, is packaged for you by the college you attend," says Bruce Hammond, a college counselor at Sandia Preparatory School in Albuquerque, New Mexico, and author of *Discounts and Deals at the Nation's 360 Best Colleges.*

Most of the remaining aid comes from corporations, in the form of employee benefits.

Those "secret" private scholarships account for no more than 2 percent of all college aid money, Hammond says. You can locate them yourself, through www.finaid.org.

But guess what? If you find a $500 private scholarship, many colleges deduct $500 from your aid package, leaving you no better off. You'd pay a seminar for that?

Near the end of my freshman year I got a letter informing me that I had won an academic scholarship based on "demonstrated and sustained merit and recommendation of the faculty." It was for $1,000. I was proud about earning this scholarship. I even began to think about how I could use this $1,000 to pay my account at the bookstore. In fact, I went to the bookstore and charged a couple hundred dollars in books in anticipation of receiving an actual check for $1,000. Two days after that I got a letter from my financial aid officer, informing me that he was reducing my overall financial aid award by $1,000 due to my recent good fortune. Ouch. Thanks for nothing. The scholarship "money" went from one ledger to another without ever leaving the business office. And I worked all summer to pay off my bookstore account.

A LIST OF TOTALLY FREE COLLEGES AND UNIVERSITIES

What does free mean? It certainly doesn't mean that a school will have no cost for students and their parents. Free means tuition-free, but it does not mean that you won't have expenses for living, books, and travel to and from home. California, for years, had the ruse that its colleges and universities were "free," but they charged thousands of dollars in "fees" until it was the same thing as tuition. It is important to realize that many expensive private colleges and universities are cheaper than many seemingly inexpensive public universities, because their financial aid awards are comprehensive, that is, they take your total college expenses into account (tuition, room, board, books, fees, travel). Most public university awards amount to a waiver of all or part of the tuition, leaving a student to patch together monies to cover the other parts of college costs. Unfortunately, the only way to tell how much a college will cost you is to apply, and be accepted. There is a book purporting to provide X-ray vision into the process, however: Bruce G. Hammond's *Discounts and Deals at the Nation's 360 Best Colleges* (Golden Books Publishing Company, 1999). The following schools are tuition free. Each provides an outstanding education. And with some planning and some hard work, it is possible to enter some of these schools without any more than a summer's savings, and graduate debt free in four years.

TUITION-FREE INSTITUTIONS

Alice Lloyd College

(No tuition for individuals from select mountain counties in Kentucky, Ohio, Tennessee, Virginia, and West Virginia—only small fees and room and board; students outside these counties pay $4,000 per year.)
100 Purpose Road
Pippa Passes, KY 41844
606-368-2101
www.alicelloyd.edu

Berea College

101 Chestnut Street
Berea, KY 40403
800-326-5948 or 606-986-9341
www.berea.edu

College of the Ozarks

Opportunity Avenue
Point Lookout, MO 65726
800-222-0525 or 417-334-6411
www.cofo.edu

**The Cooper Union for the Advance-
ment of Science & Art**

(Has "mandatory student fee" of $500
per year.)

30 Cooper Square

New York, NY 10003

212-254-6300

www.cooper.edu

The Curtis Institute of Music

1726 Locust Street

Philadelphia, PA 19103

215-893-5262

www.curtis.edu

Deep Springs

Off California Highway 168

Deep Springs, California

c/o HC72 Box 45001

Dyer, NV 89010

760-872-2000

www.deepsprings.edu

United States Air Force Academy*

2304 Cadet Drive

Colorado Springs, CO 80840

719-333-1110

www.usafa.af.mil

United States Coast Guard Academy*

31 Mohegan Avenue

New London, CT 06320

860-444-8444

www.cga.edu

**United States Merchant
Marine Academy**

300 Steamboat Road

Kings Point, NY 11024

800-732-6267 or 516-773-5000

www.usmma.edu

United States Military Academy*

(The whole city is the academy
and military base.)

Stony Lonesome Road

West Point, NY 10996

914-938-4200

www.usma.edu

United States Naval Academy*

121 Blake Road

Annapolis, MD 21402

410-293-1000

www.nadn.navy.mil

Webb Institute

(A school of naval architecture and
engineering)

Crescent Beach Road

Glen Cove, NY 11542

516-671-2213

www.webb-institute.edu

*Post-baccalaureate active-duty service commitment
of five to six years. See the section on "The Military
Academies," p. 188.

(Source: Web searches and a partial list provided
by U.S. News & World Report at the following
location: www.usnews.com/usnews/edu/dollars/
howtopay/dsfree.htm)

THE IVY LEAGUE AND MORE

What is the Ivy League? What are your chances of getting into an Ivy League school? What would improve your chances? There used to be no greater cachet in American higher education than to attend an Ivy League college or university. Unfortunately, there are some significant challenges involved in applying to these schools due to the overwhelming competition from other outstanding students applying from all over the world. What do you think of a school that rejects the majority of students who apply with a perfect SAT score (800 Math, 800 Verbal)? What do you think of a university that rejects more than 20,000 students *every year*? In spite of these increasingly oppressive statistics, parents still push for an Ivy League or other big name school. Obviously, it is time for students to educate themselves and their parents on what "highly competitive" means in higher education today. A great education is available at hundreds of schools, but only a handful of schools attract this level of attention. Where did the name "Ivy League" come from, anyway?

THE IVY LEAGUE

The Ivy League was originally a football conference between eight venerable Northeastern schools close enough together to play intercollegiate games: Harvard (formed in 1636), Yale (1701), Pennsylvania (1740), Princeton (1746), Columbia (1754), Brown (1764), Dartmouth (1769), and Cornell (1853). Over time, the name came to refer to the schools themselves, rather than to the football conference. There is a tremendous mystique to the Ivy League schools. They are now, in effect, a collective brand identity.

The name allows them to continue to attract very good students and very wealthy benefactors. For example, Harvard's endowment of more than $14 billion makes it one of the larger fiduciary entities in the world. (Bill Gates, a Harvard dropout, has more, but Bill Gates has more money than God.) The schools are really quite different from one another. Cornell is best known for its engineering and technical programs, and certainly has one of the most regal and beautiful campuses in

In the most recent year, Harvard rejected 89 percent of applicants. The applicant pool included:

3,000 class valedictorians

11,000 students in the top 10% of their graduating class

2,100 students with a perfect 800 on Math Level II

400 students with a perfect SAT score (double 800s)

the world. Columbia is in New York City, and is inseparable from that fact. The University of Pennsylvania, almost always known as Penn, is also an urban school, set in Philadelphia. Dartmouth used to be known as a bastion for politically conservative students, although it has been busy distancing itself from that reputation. Yale is known as the most liberal and socially conscious; students belong to colleges within the university, giving it a small feel for a large school. On the cool scale, Brown is the coolest Ivy League school. It doesn't have any distribution requirements whatsoever (which means there aren't any required classes), some classes can be taken credit/no credit, and the students are more laid-back and open than at the other Ivy League schools. Princeton and Yale are arguably the most willfully intellectual, as in intentionally and self-consciously intellectual. Of course, these are gross generalities. One thing I've learned about these schools is that the department you're in makes all the difference in the world. You may go to Harvard or Dartmouth or Yale, but whether you are happy or not will depend on your relationship with the faculty in your department.

A lot of people consider Stanford (1885) to be the ninth Ivy League school, but that's not what it says in the dictionary. Incidentally, Stanford was started by Jane and Leland Stanford, with a railroad fortune. Stanford's original fortune came from selling mining supplies to forty-niners suffering from gold fever. Leland Stanford became one-quarter of the Big Four, who built the Central Pacific Railroad from Cal-

Completing a minimum of two years of foreign language study as an undergraduate is required for admission to most graduate programs, and learning a market language is beneficial in any career. (Market languages are Chinese, Japanese, Spanish, Arabic, French, Indonesian, and any language used as a lingua franca by a region of the world.) Learning a foreign language is difficult in three classroom hours a week. If you really want to learn a foreign language, take a language or literature course every semester, spend a lot of hours in the language lab, join a conversation group, live in the language dorm, spend a semester or year abroad among native speakers, and spend your summers and breaks the same way. (Just for trivia: They still speak Latin in the Vatican.) Some of the best programs try to recreate an immersion environment. For example, Beloit College in Beloit, Wisconsin, has a summer languages institute providing intensive, nine-week, residential immersion programs in Arabic, Chinese, Japanese, Russian, Portuguese, and other languages. Check it out. Also, if you're really into languages, you've got to look at the Monterey Institute of International Studies, Monterey, California. It is the preeminent foreign language-focused institution in the United States. Its strengths are education in spoken foreign language, interpreting, translating, diplomacy, international trade, international business, commercial diplomacy, and international environmental policy.

ifornia over the Sierras to Promontory Point, Utah. At one time, the Big Four owned the entire town of Reno, among their other vast holdings. Leland dedicated his quarter of the fortune to found Stanford University. There is an unsubstantiable story that Leland and Jane originally tried to give a gift to Harvard University in the name of their son, Leland, Jr., who had died tragically. Neither institution has any interest in this story being true, and both call it an urban legend. Stanford was started on the site of Stanford's Palo Alto stock farm, and is still affectionately called "The Farm." (Incidentally, Harvard Yard was originally a cattle lot, too.) If you want to really tease a Stanford student, remind him or her that the institution's official name is Leland Stanford Junior University.

The Ivy League schools have far more applicants than they need. One of the problems with higher education enrollment management today is that students are becoming a national commodity without becoming savvy to national levels of competition. That is, students are looking past their local and regional schools and concentrating on national schools, but they and their parents are downright naive about the admissions process. The result of this is that students vastly overestimate their admissibility to these elite schools. The ugly truth is that very bright and capable students are rejected by these schools every day. Students with a 4.0 GPA are routinely rejected. Students with a 4.0 GPA and two sports and six hobbies and three community service activities are *routinely* rejected. Basically, everyone in North America is applying to the same ten or fifteen schools, creating a classic market imbalance of supply and demand. It is not really the school's fault that they are forced to reject the overwhelming majority of applicants.

High school counselors call these schools "lottery schools." If a student gets in to one of these institutions, it's partially a matter of chance. You can improve those chances, however, by being born to an alumna mother or an alumnus father, which would make you a legacy (that's the term). According to the *Wall Street Journal*, that will increase your chances by approximately 15 percent. You might start your appli-

"Bizarro" copyright © Dan Piraro. Reprinted with permission of Universal Press Syndicate. All Rights Reserved.

Princeton's commencements are still delivered in Latin, and students are instructed in a set of signals when to laugh or applaud or gasp or express other crowd emotions, so that their parents and guests are convinced they understand Latin. This innocent ruse has been going on for at least a hundred years. Presumably, before then, Princeton graduates did not need signals to know when to laugh in Latin.

cation essay with this line: "My uncle, for whom your library is named. . . ." That might work. You also can play sports that are favored by these schools, such as lacrosse or crew. (Interesting that these are the same sports favored by elite private high schools in the Northeast. So much for valuing diversity.)

Students and their parents need to know these data. Students with a connection, or a particularly strong attraction, to a specific Ivy League school should of course apply to that school. Truly outstanding students should of course apply to some of these schools. But students without a nearly perfect record should think twice before racking up a stack of rejections from these hypercompetitive institutions. A better idea all around is to go out there and learn how many good schools there are that you've never heard of, places that would be delighted to admit you, fund you, care for you, and send you out into the world with a first-rate education.

These are certainly all good schools, but that doesn't mean that you'll thrive at one of them. Well, that said, here is the Ivy League:

Brown University
45 Prospect Street
Providence, RI 02912
401-863-1000
www.brown.edu

Columbia University
2960 Broadway
New York, NY 10027-6902
212-854-1754
www.columbia.edu

> " Of all the young men who come to me with letters of introduction from friends in the East, the most helpless are college young men. "
>
> —Leland Stanford, founder of Stanford University

THE MOST COMPETITIVE SCHOOLS IN AMERICA

How hard is it to get in? Here are the most competitive schools in North America:

Harvard rejects 89%	Brown rejects 85%	Dartmouth rejects 80%
Caltech rejects 88%	Stanford rejects 85%	Georgetown rejects 79%
Columbia rejects 87%	Yale rejects 84%	Swarthmore rejects 79%
Princeton rejects 87%	Amherst rejects 81%	Williams rejects 77%
Deep Springs rejects 86%*	MIT rejects 81%	University of California Berkeley rejects 74%

Keep in mind that the average acceptance rate, nationwide, is three out of four, and many institutions have what amounts to an open door policy. So these schools are, indeed, difficult to enter.

*Deep Springs is so small that this figure varies tremendously. In some years it is 95%.

Cornell University

410 Thurston Avenue

Ithaca, NY 14850-2488

607-255-2000

www.cornell.edu

Dartmouth College

East Wheelock Street

Hanover, NH 03755

603-646-1110

www.dartmouth.edu

Harvard University

(Technically Harvard College is the

undergraduate college; Harvard Univer-

sity refers to the entire institution,

including all its graduate schools and

affiliated institutes.)

Massachusetts Hall

Cambridge, MA 02138

617-495-1000

www.harvard.edu

Princeton University

Princeton, NJ 08544

609-258-3000

www.princeton.edu

The University of Pennsylvania

(almost always known as Penn)

34th and Spruce Streets

Philadelphia, PA 19104

215-898-5000

www.upenn.edu

Yale University

New Haven, CT 06520

203-432-9300

www.yale.edu

The Ivy League has wonderful professors, right? Well, yes, but maybe as an undergraduate you won't see much of them. "Undergraduates at Yale University are twice as likely to be taught by a graduate student or an adjunct instructor as by a tenured professor," says *The Chronicle of Higher Education* (9 April 1999). Yale is

In the last year for which complete data are available, Harvard University rejected 80 percent of the valedictorians who applied and the majority of the students with a *perfect* SAT score (double 800s). The best activities for applicants: those that are only really popular in the Northeast prep schools, such as lacrosse and crew. Bowling? Forget it. Also, it's easier to stand out if you excel in something a little unusual. "We're always looking for oboes," says Janet Lavin Rapelye, dean of admission at Wellesley. For more on this, see "Beating the Ivy League Odds," in the *Wall Street Journal* (16 April 1999).

hardly unusual in this practice. And undergraduate classes are often huge, with several hundred students sitting in large lecture halls.

THE YALE SYNDROME

Sometimes ambitious students pushed by ambitious parents will view admission to one of these schools as a major life goal, rather than education for its own sake or success in later life. The student may spend years preparing to be a good applicant to college, weighing every activity and endeavor by how it might look to an admissions officer. The parents may exacerbate this effect by speaking frequently about how much it would mean to them for the student to be admitted, and how much it would fulfill somebody's, usually not the student's, lifetime dream. The whole process is made much worse if some family member attended the school in question, or tried and failed to attend. Of course, the importance is magnified when the boy from up the street gets into Stanford, or the daughter of an office rival gets into Yale.

This creates an odd psychological horizon for a young person. Instead of fantasizing about future careers and professional and personal relationships with others, the student has a short chronological horizon: the event of college admission. Students may spend so much emotional and developmental energy preparing to apply that they may not develop a plan for actually being at a college or university. Further, if their decision-making process-

Well, we go to school to explore our creative talents, to gain self-understanding, to acquire useful knowledge and to get into a college of your father's choice
—Princeton.

Q. What is the biggest warning sign of parental overinvolvement?

A. Pronoun confusion. If your parents say "we" got into MIT or "we" had an interview at Knox or "we" are wait-listed at Stanford, you've got a problem. How do you get help for overinvolvement? (1) If your parents are a problem, don't allow them to sit in on interviews with admissions counselors. (2) Arm yourself with information, so you can reassure them that you know what you're doing. (3) Ask your guidance counselor to ask them to back off. (4) Move in with your Uncle Bob until you turn eighteen. This is your life, and yes, they're probably going to pay for some of it, but you can't let anybody else make this decision for you. If you are happy in the place of your choice, you will thrive in college and succeed in life. If you are unhappy in the place of your parents' choice, you will lose joy in life, start to cut corners, become boringly predictable, and slide into a slimy pit of loathsome mediocrity. It's your life. What's it gonna be?

es have been colored by measuring every decision against its impact on admissibility, they can fail to successfully function in school after admission.

This is called the Yale Syndrome. Students afflicted with the situation described above need counseling to rediscover what it is that they themselves actually might care about. They feel lost, unmotivated, confused; they may report that life has become meaningless; many drop out.

The same thing happens when some people apply to medical school and law school. They may have made the decision to apply *years* prior and not reconsidered that decision. They drive and strive until they are admitted, and then feel guilty and conflicted and miserable to discover that they don't actually like medicine or law.

These are usually family-system problems. That is, it's not the students themselves who are driving this train. Think over your reasons for wanting to go to college, and find a college that can meet those needs. Think for yourself, because you are the one who is going to live this.

For students, parents, and counselors, here are a couple of great books touching on this topic: *Hand Me Down Dreams: How Families Influence our Career Paths and How We Can Reclaim Them* (Harmony Books, 1999) by Mary H. Jacobson, and *The Ambitious Generation: America's Teenagers, Motivated but Directionless* (Yale University Press, 1999) by Barbara Schneider and David Stevenson.

If you think you may be building a big case of the Yale Syndrome, show this passage to your school counselor and ask for help. This is serious. This is not a joke.

THE SEVEN SISTERS

All of the eight Ivy League schools were originally men's colleges. The Seven Sisters were a collection of women's colleges, some closely affiliated with certain men's col-

---

At the University of California, Berkeley (aka Cal or Berkeley), the average GPA of the most recent incoming class was 4.16. That's right, *above* a 4.0. Advanced placement classes are weighted, allowing GPAs above 4.0. By the way, Berkeley rejects thousands of students every year who have a GPA of 4.0 or better. Imagine that. Thousands. Are you starting to understand the national market now? To keep Berkeley from howling, I should tell you that they admit many students with less-than-perfect GPAs because those students are interesting, passionate, involved in their communities, and good essay writers. But rejecting *thousands* of 4.0s? Wow. In all, Berkeley rejected 22,854 students in the most recent application year.

leges, and others always and wholly independent. It's not accurate to speak of Seven Sisters anymore, as Radcliffe has really merged with Harvard and Vassar has gone coed, but here they are, the original Seven Sisters, with notes on their status today:

Barnard College
(still a women's college;
cross-registration with Columbia)
3009 Broadway
New York, NY 10027
212-854-5262
www.barnard.edu

Mount Holyoke College
(still a women's college, prides itself
on its strengths in math and science)
50 College Street
South Hadley, MA 01075
413-538-2000
www.mtholyoke.edu

Bryn Mawr College
(still a women's college; cross-registration with Swarthmore, Haverford, and
others in a Philadelphia-area consortium)
101 North Merion Avenue
Bryn Mawr, PA 19010
800-BMC-1885 or 610-526-5000
www.brynmawr.edu

**Radcliffe Institute for
Advanced Studies**
(the current iteration of what was once
Harvard's "Sister")
10 Garden Street
Cambridge, MA 02138
617-495-8601
www.radcliffe.edu

It is very interesting to get hundreds of letters from college presidents. When I was writing to them asking them for nominations for this book, I included a running list of schools other presidents had recommended. My correspondents often criticized the choices of other college presidents, and advocated for their own choices, quite eloquently. Nevertheless, I noticed that the institutional knowledge of college presidents, and academicians in general, is geographically determined. They recommended schools closer to them, and criticized schools farther from them, as if they were infecting their neighbors with quality. Ernest L. Boyer, in his book, *College: The Undergraduate Experience in America* (Carnegie Foundation for the Advancement of Teaching, 1997), found that high school counselors were generally quite unknowing of institutions more than five hundred miles distant. I believe, really, that knowledge of academic institutions is regional, while the market for students has quietly become nationalized. So students are entering the national marketplace with advice, from parents, teachers, counselors, and even family friends in higher education, that is quite localized. This has allowed national rankings, whatever their limitations may be, to thrive. They are filling this vacuum of knowledge. Of course, rankings cannot determine which students will be happy at which schools. Ultimately, that task falls to the students themselves.

CoOl BoOk AlErT!

Looking Beyond the Ivy League: Finding the College That's Right for You (Penguin USA, 1996) by Loren Pope, Director of the College Placement Bureau and former education editor for the *New York Times*

In this pull-no-punches, take-no-prisoners book, Loren Pope attacks the myths of college choice. Here are a couple of typical passages:

"The university's oft-cited claim that having many fine research scholars affects the quality of undergraduate teaching is a false position that has misled the public too long. If the great scholar teaches undergraduates at all—and most teach few or none—he is likely to be only an animated book or a television performer in a big lecture hall."

"Every year brings more proof that a college's effect on one's life has little to do with its prestige, and that the university, with its worship of research and its cheating of undergraduates, should be sued—or at the very least chastised—for false and misleading advertising."

How's that for taking a stand? In the land of hyperpolite understatement that is academic journalism, Loren Pope is a breath of fresh air. This book is a must-read for students, parents, and educators. Here are his myths.

Myth One: An Ivy League college will absolutely guarantee the rich, full, and successful life.

Myth Two: If you can't make an Ivy, a "prestige college" is next best, because the name on your diploma will determine whether you do something worthwhile in life.

Myth Three: Eastern institutions are the best and most desirable.

Myth Four: The big university offers a broader, richer undergraduate experience.

Myth Five: A college you've heard about is better than one you haven't.

Myth Six: What your friends say about a college is a good indicator.

Myth Seven: The college catalog can help you decide if this is the school for you.

Myth Eight: You should make your college selection early in your senior year, before Christmas if at all possible.

Myth Nine: Your college should be bigger than your high school.

Myth Ten: Going more than 200 miles away from home will cost more and may result in isolation.

Myth Eleven: If you're in the top 10 percent of your class with SATs of 1300 or better, you belong in an Ivy or prestige college.

Myth Twelve: Ivy League schools are looking for students who don't have excellent grades.

Myth Thirteen: SAT scores are the most important thing; good ones will get you in and poor ones will keep you out.

Myth Fourteen: A coaching course will improve your SAT scores.

Myth Fifteen: A bad recommendation from a teacher or counselor will ruin your chances.

Myth Sixteen: Your choice of major will decide your career path, so the quality of the department should govern your choice of college.

Myth Seventeen: A high school diploma is needed to get into college.

Myth Eighteen: Going to a private prep school will enhance your chances of getting into a good college.

Myth Nineteen: Millions of dollars in unused scholarships are going begging every year.

Myth Twenty: A good college is hard to get into.

For a full explication of each point, you'll have to read his book.

Smith College

(still a women's college, has an
engineering department)
Elm Street
Northampton, MA 01063
413-584-2700
www.smith.edu

Wellesley College

(still a women's college,
but men are in some classes
through an exchange program)
106 Central Street
Wellesley, MA 02481
781-283-1000
www.wellesley.edu

Vassar College

(now fully coed)
124 Raymond Avenue
Poughkeepsie, NY 12604
914-437-7000
www.vassar.edu

Oh, and just for the record, women comprise the majority of under-graduates, and the majority of graduate students.

WHY WE STILL HAVE MEN'S, WOMEN'S, AND MINORITY-FOCUSED COLLEGES

All the Ivy League schools were originally men's colleges, and all of them have been coed for years. When men's colleges go coed, they can, for a period of time, be an awful place for women. The only men's college to go coed gracefully in recent years was Rose-Hulman Institute, a top engineering school in Terre Haute, Indiana. Rose-Hulman made an institutional commitment to *inviting* women to Rose-Hulman; it searched the nation for bright, well-prepared women who were interested in science, engineering,

SKULL AND BONES AT YALE

In addition to its residential colleges, which give Yale the intimate feel of a much smaller institution, Yale has a long history of student-run, student-managed secret societies. The rituals and practices of these societies are supposed to remain a tightly guarded secret. Duh! That's why they call them "secret societies." For some of them even membership itself is supposed to be kept secret, and members are supposed to deny that they are members. At least one former president blabbed to all the world that he was a member of Skull and Bones. Skull and Bones may have held a meeting in their clubhouse, a windowless building known as The Tomb, to discuss what censure would be applied to George Bush the Elder, our 41st president (or 40th, depending on whether you count Grover Cleveland twice). Their decision is, of course, unknown.

and math. It worked hard to bring large numbers of women to the campus all at once, rather than dribbling away at it over a period of years. It also explained to the students why the institution was going coed, and prepared the young men who were then enrolled in how to act like gentlemen, and what was expected of them.

The administration of Rose-Hulman Institute, now smoothly coed for years, ought to be applauded from the Atlantic to the Pacific for the good job they did in this transition.

Contrast this with The Citadel of Charleston, South Carolina, which was dragged kicking and screaming into compliance with a series of court orders. The Citadel

The highest paid employee on almost any major university's payroll is the head football coach.

allowed hazing and harassment of its first female cadet, Ms. Shannon Faulkner, to the point that she decided to withdraw.

Why are there still men's colleges and women's colleges? For several very good but also very divergent reasons. Although the students and admissions staff at these institutions can tell their own stories best, here are some things I know:

There are still women's colleges because men still hog the majority of attention in most classrooms. Read *How Schools Shortchange Girls* by the American Association of University Women (Econo-Clad Books, 1999), or just look around you. It is an established fact that men speak out more in class than women. It is an established fact that faculty (male or female) spend more time on and give more approval to the opinions expressed in class by men. It is an established fact that our greater society, beyond the boundaries of the ivory tower, is also male dominated. Women often feel that they are guests in the land of the men, strangers in a strange land that does not belong to them and that they did not design. This is easily established by a walk

Rice University in Houston also has residential colleges patterned after the Oxford and Cambridge model, with faculty and students living together. With top-caliber students, strong science and engineering programs, and a cost close to half of the typical Ivy League college, it delivers real bang for the investment. Bruce G. Hammond, author of *Discounts and Deals at the Nation's 360 Best Colleges* (Golden Books Publishing Company, 1999), calls Rice "the nation's preeminent bargain among elite private universities."

across campus at any women's college. Mills College, in Oakland, California, is a perfect example. The statues on the lawn are of women. The art on the walls is of and by women. The quotes posted on professors' and students' doors are primarily by women. There are women everywhere, studying, reading, talking, walking, exercising. In every class, all the students are women. If you are a woman, this is a new experience, and it can be a life-changing experience. Ever since Betty Friedan wrote *The Feminine Mystique* in 1963, it has been a tenet of gender theory that the nondominant gender does not even know the cost of living in nondominant status. In my opinion, every female in the world would benefit from living for a year in non-nondominant status. Every female in the world would benefit from going to a girls-only high school or a women's college for at least a year. *It can change your life forever.*

The exact same argument can be made for attending a college that serves a large proportion of your race. If you have spent your life living in a dominant white culture (or any other dominant culture), it can be a truly liberating experience to spend time in college where your race or your culture is dominant. See the essay by Amelia R. Shelby of Howard University, "Why I *Finally* Chose to Attend an Historically Black College," on p. 220.

Further, there are many people, young men and young women, who would like to put off the whole question of sexuality for a few more years. They choose to spend their college years concentrating on their studies, and worry about sexuality at a later time. They choose a single-gender school because they find it less distracting. A tremendous amount of energy is spent on dating and partying at coed institutions, and not all students want to spend their time in this way.

Also, there are many religions and cultures in the world where men and women are commonly separated for education and worship. When people from these religions and cultures send their children to college, they prefer to send them to single-gender institutions. Many extremely powerful and wealthy families from other countries have sent generations of their offspring to the same U.S.-based, single-gender schools.

Applying to a large university? Be sure to use your full legal name, and put your social security number on everything. You *are* your social security number. According to the *Chronicle of Higher Education* (2 April 1999), Truman Bradley of Boulder, Colorado, received a letter from Arizona State University that started out like this: "Congratulations on 345-62-2439's admission to Arizona State University!" Bradley decided to go elsewhere.

Furthermore, there are people who just prefer the company of their own gender, and that is reason enough for them. For most of history and in most of the world, this has been a common sentiment, requiring no further explanation.

And finally, some of these schools have massive endowments, and can provide full-ride scholarships for students who might otherwise not be able to afford to pursue a quality education.

So for these important reasons, we still have, and still *ought to have,* single-gender schools and schools that focus on serving specific minorities.

For more on this, check out these lists later in the book:

THREE SCHOOLS THAT ARE KICKING BUTT

Beloit College, Beloit, Wisconsin

Many of the prestigious old-line schools are on autopilot. Their reputations are based on glory from decades past. But Beloit College in Beloit, Wisconsin, is an "up and coming" college. The students at Beloit are happy and confident, the faculty are energized, the physical plant is in great shape, it's in a picture-postcard little town, and . . . I think you get the picture. I think it is the students, themselves, who stand out the most. They are the opposite of moody and depressed. Maybe it's that healthy Wisconsin air.

Whitman College, Walla Walla, Washington

Whitman is one of those gems that should be overrun with students from all over the country, but is not well known outside of its region. I asked an auditorium of sixty of their students, "How do you like this college?" Not one, *not one,* had a complaint about it. They all said: "It's great." "This place really supports you." "The professors here are excellent." And so on. I dare you to fill an auditorium at any school and get these kinds of endorsements. This was in the week before midterms, when most students are naturally grumpy. (Just for the record, the students were gathered to hear a guest speaker, and they were definitely not prepped by the admissions or public affairs offices.)

Washington University in St. Louis, St. Louis, Missouri

According to its students, Wash U. is the perfect size for a university. With about 5,000 undergraduates and a cloistered feel to the campus, students get the university experience without being lost in a faceless crowd. Students are showered with attention, the academics are excellent, and the administration is responsive. Students have been known to launch their own classes, which is very unusual for a university. Wash U. offers no athletic scholarships, so "if you were a starter in high school you'll probably get to play here, too." St. Louis, always a gateway city (that's what the arch is all about), is cross-fertilized, a little bit Southern, Northern, Western, and Midwestern. The campus is extremely well cared for, almost to country club standards.

WESTERN COLLEGES FINALLY GET THEIR DUE

by Janet L. Holmgren, president, Mills College

Higher education is hot again in the national press, as millions of American high school students—and older students, too—go through the challenging ritual of deciding to which colleges they will apply.

Two California independent/private higher educational institutions were recently ranked No. 1 by *U.S. News & World Report* and *Time/The Princeton Review*. Ranked as the top national university in *U.S. News*'s "America's Best Colleges," The California Institute of Technology (Caltech) was recognized in part for spending more per student ($192,000) than any other college or university in the nation.

The University of Southern California (USC) was named *Time/Princeton Review*'s college of the year in "The Best College for You," having transformed itself from a widely known party school to a committed partner helping to revitalize Los Angeles.

As president of Mills College (one of California's oldest institutions of higher education) and chair of the executive committee of the Association of Independent California Colleges and Universities, I am delighted to see long overdue recognition lavished on Western universities. While occasionally acknowledging Stanford and Berkeley, the national media often seem to have difficulty seeing beyond the Northeast corridor when covering higher education. However, it is a sign of our times that *Time/The Princeton Review* and *U.S. News* focused on the extremes of what a college education represents. While I believe national magazine rankings should play a minor role in the decision-making process, they can provide useful lessons about how institutions distinguish themselves.

CoOl BoOk AlErT!

The Public Ivys: A Guide to America's Best Public Undergraduate Colleges and Universities by Richard Moll (Viking Penguin, 1985)

Caltech values science and technology and recruits the nation's top students in these fields. These areas of study are expensive as well as valuable to society, and the students who go to Caltech are very well supported.

However, as in many research universities, the faculty is overwhelmingly white and male, and Caltech lags in the recruitment of women and people of color to the student body. USC was chosen college of the year because across the curriculum and throughout the university's hierarchy, USC has "discovered ways to inspire the quality of education everywhere," according to the editors of *The Princeton Review*.

The popularity of these rankings teaches us that the public is hungry for evaluations that will guide them about the merits of a variety of institutions. An undergraduate education can be an expensive proposition and researching the right college is crucial. Yet, with more than 2,000 baccalaureate-granting colleges and universities in the United States, and nearly 200 in California alone, how does one make sense of their strengths and weaknesses? And how does one find out what an institution values?

A Mills parent recently approached me at a reception and said that when she and her daughter visited many liberal arts colleges, they heard similar messages: the college would educate her daughter well, spend a lot of money on her, and support her to become a successful alumna. What they heard at Mills made the difference in

"Shoe" copyright © Tribune Media Services, Inc. All Rights Reserved. Reprinted with permission.

When Florida State University didn't like how they came out in a ranking by the *Princeton Review*, they gave the company the "Golden Gargoyle" award for The Most Bogus Survey in Higher Education. Said university president Sandy D'Alemberte, "There was a lot of competition for this award, so I think the *Princeton Review* should be proud." Reed College refuses to participate in *U.S. News & World Report*'s annual ranking surveys, saying that their methodology is "without merit."

their decision. We told them that we educate women to make the world a better place. And, in addition to offering a first-rate, liberal arts education, we do everything we can to develop a student's leadership abilities, to engage her in meaningful community service, and to help her learn how to make responsible choices for using her education into the future.

Other colleges and universities articulate educational values similar to Mills', and it is important to consider written materials as well as personal encounters with the institutions, students, faculty, staff, and alumni to determine whether the institution "walks the talk." The faculty and students at any institution are drawn to it because of its values—its history and traditions, and its current orientation—as well as its academic strengths, physical facilities, and financial resources. So, before you make your final choice, find out what the college or university values and compare it to your own values and aspirations.

Reprinted by permission of the author.

THE PUBLIC IVYS

Miami University of Ohio
University of California at Berkeley
University of California at Davis
University of California at Irvine
University of California at Los Angeles
University of California at San Diego
University of California at Santa Barbara
University of California at Santa Cruz
University of Michigan at Ann Arbor
University of North Carolina at Chapel Hill
University of Texas at Austin
University of Vermont at Burlington

University of Virginia at Charlottesville
William and Mary College of Virginia

Worthy Runners-Up:
Georgia Institute of Technology at Atlanta
New College of The University of South Florida
Pennsylvania State University at University Park
State University of New York at Binghamton
University of Colorado at Boulder
University of Illinois at Urbana-Champaign
University of Pittsburgh
University of Washington at Seattle
University of Wisconsin at Madison

It is important to realize that most of these are very large and highly competitive institutions, perhaps much more appropriate for graduate education and adult commuters than for the benefit of traditional-age undergraduates. The exception would be New College of the University of South Florida, see p. 122.

Q&A WITH A DEAN OF ADMISSION: WHAT *HIGHLY COMPETITIVE* REALLY MEANS

with Janet Lavin Rapelye, Dean of Admission, Wellesley College

Wellesley College is a highly selective women's college in Wellesley, Massachusetts.

Q. What's it like to be a dean of admission?

Virtually everyone I know who is a dean of admission went into this work because he or she was committed to higher education, and to students in particular. At the height of the selection season, our jobs are all encompassing. The volume of material is relentless. We essentially give up our personal lives. We give up evenings. We give up weekends. Having said that, the reason it's exciting and the reason we do it is because behind every application is a student. Every piece of paper we get has a story behind it. It's incredibly humbling to read these applications, to read about these students' lives, whether they are traditional-age students or more experienced students applying as transfers. It is extremely hard work, and a huge responsibility.

Q. Students want to know, How do you make the decision?

Well, I can't answer for other schools. At Wellesley we make the decision by

---

SCHOOLS WITH MASSIVE ENDOWMENTS

Private Institutions

Rockefeller University ($6,748,889)

Woods Hole Oceanographic Institution ($1,708,889)

Princeton University ($875,321)

Grinnell College ($760,484)

Harvard University ($727,522)

Bryn Athyn College of the New Church ($721,910)

Webb Institute ($718,872)

Agnes Scott College ($692,914)

Rice University ($684,313)

Curtis Institute of Music ($674,036)

Public Institutions

VMI Foundation (Virginia Military Institute, $166,663)

Oregon Health Sciences Foundation ($126,036)

University of Texas System ($70,842)

University of Virginia ($65,842)

University of California at San Francisco Foundation ($55,640)

University of Michigan ($51,916)

University of Delaware ($50,404)

Endowment Association of the College of William and Mary ($50,038)

Texas A & M University System ($49,469)

Georgia Tech Foundation ($45,020)

(Figures show endowment per student. Source: Chronicle of Higher Education, 27 August 1999)

committee. Our committee is made up of admissions professionals, faculty, administrators, and even some students. The faculty are elected to the committee by the Wellesley faculty, and the student members are chosen by the Wellesley students, and I think we are unusual in that. Ultimately, decisions are made by majority vote of this committee. There are no decrees. I can be outvoted by others, and have been, and the committee decision stands. We are choosing the next class of students, and it is truly a community process.

The decision about every student is made individually. We have no quotas, no set formula. Every single decision is made individually. Every file is read by three different readers, and then goes to committee for discussion and a vote. Sometimes a recruiter will champion a candidate. She may say, "I met this student on the road, and she impressed me as being incredibly mature, poised, and well spoken." She may try to sway the other members of the committee. Sometimes she can. Sometimes she can't, but we do value the ability to speak well and to write well. Can these arguments overcome a mediocre transcript? No. Will they override weak letters of recommendation? No. But we take everything into consideration.

Incidentally, if students or parents want to know how a college or university makes its admission decisions, I'd recommend they ask. Most schools will tell them.

Q. How much do grades and scores count? And how much do activities count?

I think admissions offices can always quantify their classes at the end of the process, how many admitted, average GPA, range of SAT, and so on, but this process is much more an art than a science. While we do have the transcript in front of us, which is the most important part, we ask: Has she taken the most challenging load? Has she done well in the more challenging classes? Has she taken advantage of everything her high school has to offer?

Then we're trying to measure the intangibles—the motivation, the creativity, the potential. We're looking for talents the student will bring to our campus. And we're looking for diversity in the broadest sense of the term, diversity of thought, diversity of backgrounds, diversity of talents. And that's why we rely on the committee

Swarthmore College and Occidental College do an outstanding job of attracting, retaining, educating, and graduating minority students in a small liberal arts college setting. Check them out.

process. Because certain things appeal to different readers. The essay is very important. In the essay we're looking for how well a student writes. But essays can be more or less appealing depending on the reader, and then again, that's where the committee process comes in.

Students are not just academics. They're not just numbers. Whether a person plays field hockey or the oboe matters to us. Art and music and theater and dance are all part of our curriculum. They're part of what we do. So they're not just "extra"-curricular for us.

So we look at the academic piece, and the talents, and the overall background, and then we look even further, for the intangibles. For example, leadership. Leadership is an intangible that is generally best articulated by someone else, besides the student in question. When you're talking about selective admissions, you have to talk about potential *and* performance. It can't be all potential. A student who has very high scores and low grades is probably not going to fare well in a selective admissions process. When a student says, "I have the potential for leadership," but they haven't really done it, they need to realize that there are a lot of other students out there who have done leadership, who have already demonstrated it.

Q. How competitive is it to get into a top school?

Most of the highly selective schools publish the range of students that they admit. We do. It's important for parents to look at the range, and look objectively at their own daughter. Most of the guides have this information, and most viewbooks are frank about the competition, and we're not kidding.

The problem is that most parents think that their child will be the exception in this process. They look to see if we admitted anybody at all with a statistical profile similar to their daughter's, and if so, they think that surely we'll see that we should admit her, too.

Selective admissions means that we don't have enough spaces for all the qualified candidates. That's exactly what it means. We have to turn down many qualified students each year. That's what makes our jobs so hard for us. We're not going to

One administrator at a highly selective institution (not Wellesley) told me, "We don't need any more applicants. It will just cost us money to reject them." That's a pretty amazing statement. "Okay. I won't send you any," I promised.

expand the size of the college, so we have to make decisions. These decisions are very hard to make, sometimes.

It's very important for parents to be realistic about what their son or daughter looks like on paper. Like it or not, students will be judged by what they look like on paper, their transcripts, recommendations, grades, scores, essay, extracurricular activities, and how they put the application together. Applications that are done at the last minute look like applications that were put together at the last minute.

SHOULD YOU GO TO THE BEST COLLEGE YOU CAN GET INTO?

How many times have you heard this: "You should go to the best college you can get into"? This is a really common belief held more by well-meaning parents than by most educators. If you somehow manage to get into a program vastly above your preparation and skill levels, you could be very poorly served by picking "the best" school you can get into. You may be frustrated and overwhelmed, or lose your confidence as a scholar. In general, it is better to pick a school where you will be challenged, where you will need to work very hard but not relentlessly, where you can earn grades you can take satisfaction in. The exact same student could be an admired scholar at one school or a reviled laggard at another. And grad schools are definitely going to be more interested in strong grades from a weaker school than weak grades from a stronger school. Upon thinking deeper, you will realize the whole question has a built-in fallacy. There is no such thing as a unilinear ranking of colleges. Therefore, there is no meaningful arbiter of good, better, best *across all departments* and *for every student*. Colleges and universities cannot be reduced to rankings like so many baseball teams. Departments will vary. Specific instructors will have more to do with your experience than any abstract notion of the overall quality of an institution. And what about the differences between students? You may fit in socially at one college and feel completely out of place at another. Your academic interests may be much better served by one college or another, but all of these factors are unlikely to have anything to do with any college's ranking on a "good, better, best" scale. Imagine this: Rank all the sports teams on the North American continent from "best" to "worst." Mix in NHL teams with MLB teams with NFL teams with NBA teams with women's Olympic soccer with two towns competing in a regional Mexican rodeo. Now tell me: Does that make any sense? Why not? They're all sports teams. This is exactly like the process of ranking undergraduate institutions in unilinear ordinal rankings. Finally, real-time quality lags reputation. You may pick a school because of some published ranking, and find that it has passed its prime. The academic officers and the professors that made the place special are no longer in charge. The administration no longer has a commitment to excellence. The current students are more bland and homogenous and predictable than the ones who helped build the reputation for excellence in the first place. I can name half a dozen highly ranked schools that haven't, together, generated a new idea in years. My tip: Start thinking for yourself. Start looking for a team you want to play on, where you can be a starter every day and at least occasionally a star.

INPUTS AND OUTPUTS

Most measurements of college quality are actually input measurements. For example, they measure the quality of students entering the college, not the quality of students exiting the college. Here are some inputs and outputs:

INPUTS	OUTPUTS
High School GPA	GRE Scores
SAT/ACT Scores	Satisfaction Surveys
Endowment	Student Debt at Graduation
Faculty Salaries	Career Placement
Spending per Student	Average Salary Offer
Freshmen in Top 10% Ranking	% Admitted to Graduate School
Faculty with Terminal Degree	% Who Get Ph.D.'s
Full-Time Faculty	Citation Analysis
Faculty-Student Ratio	% Who Tithe to Their Alma Mater
Parental Lifetime Income	Student Lifetime Income

Think of a college as a black box device, with high school seniors entering on one side and college graduates exiting on the other. It is clear that the "best" college would have the greatest difference between inputs and outputs, and the "worst" college would have the least difference between inputs and outputs. No national survey has taken this approach, but it would sure be interesting to see which colleges would win this ranking query.

As another example of input vs. output, an administrator at Wells College in Aurora, New York, told me, "We take a lot of A students here, but our greatest strength is taking a student who was maybe a B student in high school and turning her on to education, and making an A student out of her in college." In my opinion, that's an excellent college.

Some other measures are slightly less clearly an input or an output. For example, retention. Some would argue that retention is an output, for it is a result of the educational process itself. Thus, high retention leading to a high graduation rate could be seen as an indicator of quality. This is how it is treated by *U.S. News & World Report*. But Steve Koblik, president of Reed College, told me he thinks otherwise. "Retention is not an indicator of academic rigor. Quite the opposite. If your program is truly challenging, some people are going to have a hard time with it. The idea that retention is a sign of academic rigor is—on the face of it—absurd." He does have a point.

When evaluating a college, remember that it is the output you'll have to live with. What kind of graduate school and career experiences do graduates have? That is the question. Because once you graduate, you're an output.

So a refuse decision does not mean that a student could not have succeeded at our school. But it does mean that I have to write her a letter denying her admission, a letter that feels very inadequate to me. I have to say that we simply do not have enough places at Wellesley College, and I'm sorry but we had other candidates who just had to come first.

It's very hard for that group just below the top group to understand why they weren't included. In fact, we believe they'll be terrific college students. Let me be clear. Selective admissions is not a decision about how worthy a child is. This is not a report card for parents on their parenting, nor is it a judgment call on a student's intrinsic value as a person or even as a candidate. As hard as it is to accept, it is a decision about what an individual student looks like on paper compared to the rest of the applicant pool of a particular college in a given year. It's as simple as that, and as complicated as that.

Q. Any final words of advice for applicants and their parents?

Well, two things. One is a pet peeve. We're seeing an increase in the anxiety level of families about whether application materials have arrived in our office. Let me tell you, if you mailed your application, or any piece of it, within the prior five

MEASURING THE VALUE OF AN IVY LEAGUE DEGREE

There is a famous and oft-cited study conducted in the sixties by Patricia Salter West while she was at Columbia University, that attempted to set a cash value for the Ivy League education. The study factored out socioeconomic status of incoming students, but failed to factor out academic preparation, intelligence, and drive (i.e., very important inputs), thus establishing nothing. Scores of studies since have suffered from the same methodological weakness. One would almost begin to believe that researchers had a systematic bias, i.e., a desire to find a high value for an Ivy League education. A more useful study is one done recently by Alan B. Krueger (Princeton) and Stacy Berg Dale (Andrew W. Mellon Foundation), sponsored by the National Bureau of Economic Research. Their findings: For the middle class student, going to a college with average SAT scores of 1000 will result in higher income later than going to a college with average SAT scores of 1200. Read that last sentence several times. Some factors to consider are these: Of two students who are otherwise equal, the one attending a slightly less selective institution will have a higher class rank, will stand out more to faculty, will probably earn higher grades, and will be more confident of his or her own abilities.

This study, like all the studies in this genre, is controversial and has its critics. For a discussion of many of the research projects on this topic, see "Measuring the Value of an Ivy Degree," in the *Chronicle of Higher Education*, 14 January 2000.

days, it's entirely possible that it's in our office, but it's physically impossible for us to tell you whether it's here or not. You have to trust the process. Just be sure to keep copies of everything.

As a related point, it's very important that they fill out the forms to tell us how they would like us to contact them and to mail to them. If they prefer to use a middle name or even a nickname, we'll honor that, but they've got to let us know and they've got to be consistent. And in an ideal world, their teachers and counselors would also use that exact same name.

Finally, I have this to say: Virtually every student that we see coming through the process has wonderful qualities and talents and skills. They have the ability to push the intellectual limits of a college campus, and there's a right college out there for them. There's a place out there looking for them. Their goal should be to find that right campus.

Oh, and one final, final thing: If you're a bright young woman reading about this, we'd like you to consider Wellesley as possibly that right campus for you.

EASTERN OREGON UNIVERSITY

Eastern Oregon University is located in the middle of nowhere near the corners of Washington, Idaho, and Oregon. It is nestled in a quaint little town of La Grande, Oregon. They do not charge out-of-state tuition for students from Washington and Idaho. Why is this college in this book? Because it offers a much better education than most of the large universities near you. Almost all the students are undergrad, so the focus is on them. There is no big and distracting social scene revolving around big-time football and Greek Row. The pace is relaxed, but the students are engaged. Nobody has to go to college in La Grande, so the students I met were, in general, quite interested in getting the most out of their educational opportunity. In fact, that's the point: They viewed it as an opportunity. "People come here to go to school. There's not much else to do," said an administrator. "A lot of them play athletics, or they hunt and fish, or they hike and ski. It's a great place for those things, but many, if not most, just concentrate on school."

Eastern Oregon University • 1410 "L" Avenue • La Grande, Oregon 97850 • 541-962-3511 • www.eou.edu • admissions@eou.edu

Chapter Three

SCHOOLS WHERE SCHOLARSHIP IS HONORED

What is the purpose of the college experience? Is it to prepare a student for a successful career? Or a meaningful life? There used to be a consensus in higher education in America that education was supposed to build citizens. That consensus is outdated, however, and nothing has stepped up to replace it. There is no longer agreement among institutions of higher education about the main purpose of those four or five or six years after high school. Worse yet, there is often great dissent within a single institution about its own purpose. The schools in this chapter, however, have not lost their sense of identity and purpose. They believe that a student is not just a vessel to be filled like so many gallons in the tank. They believe an education should change the vessel as well as fill it.

Also in this chapter, a college president weighs in on the role of faculty, and we will continue our discussion of college choice with attention to college ranking systems and how college counselors provide guidance to the hyper-intelligent, the self-directed, the late blooming, and yes, even the just plain different.

REED COLLEGE

a community of scholars • all design and conduct a major research project, and write a thesis, before they can graduate • *junior qualifying exam to advance to senior status* • one of the only small liberal arts schools that is also outstanding in the sciences • *used to be called The Reed Institute* • has its own nuclear reactor • *science seniors get their own labs* • everybody takes the same humanities core • *no Greek system* • no football team • *honor code* • ski cabin • *no published grades (weird!)*

If there were a way to quantify cool, Reed College would rank at the very top. (Actually, it does. See the ranking on p. 374.) The shortest way to describe this school is to say that it is an extremely liberal student body wedded to an extremely conservative curriculum. That's liberal in the old sense of free, and conservative in the old sense of guarding a known good.

The college takes the radical approach that it is admitting adults, who will conduct themselves accordingly. So it does not spend a lot of institutional energy on controlling the social and personal lives of its students. The students manage student life. On the other hand, the curriculum is sacrosanct. It has hardly changed since the college was founded. Students have almost no input to the curriculum. The faculty are the guardians of the canon, and interestingly enough, Reed students are content to let them be so. The faculty are not in the habit of tinkering with the curriculum, which is a classic liberal arts and Great Books program. At Reed, if it was good enough for the Greeks, it's good enough for students today. Every decade or so something is added, such as Chinese Humanities, but other than that nothing much changes.

In this day and age of treacly concern for "the whole student," Reed is not afraid to stand up and say it is interested only in the student's mind. This school exists for the life of the mind. Reed is the epitome of an ivory tower. It is a place where students and faculty have discussions for days over whether words can ever completely convey a personal reality, and whether calculus was invented or found. It is a place where ideas matter. A lot. For their own sake.

All students participate in a humanities core, whether they are majoring in chemistry or philosophy. With an emphasis on small group seminar discussions and reading original texts, the humanities core provides a common bond for students. But the thing to "get" about Reed is that there is an academic culture here that goes well beyond the classes. You could take all the classes that are offered at Reed at many other schools, but you wouldn't capture what happens at Reed. The very atmosphere at Reed is filled with discourse. If Reed students learn nothing else, they learn to present and defend their ideas.

An interesting thing about Reed is that it is a liberal arts college that is outstanding in the sciences. Harvey Mudd is also like this, but in reverse: It is a science school that is strong in the liberal arts. Usually science and engineering schools only give lip service to liberal education, but Reed and Harvey Mudd provide the type of education that serves as a real foundation to a scholarly life. Reed has its own nuclear reactor, which will give you an idea of the level of science done here.

The students manage their own affairs through an honor code and a peer judicial board. The honor code is simple. *"The members of the Reed College community believe that they should take upon themselves a responsibility for maintaining standards of conduct that ensure an atmosphere of honesty and mutual trust in their academic and social lives. Such standards of conduct rest upon a principle of honor rather than a constitutional system of right and law. This principle entails the unquestioned integrity of the individual in all areas of his or her intellectual activity, and a*

> **The most important skill to acquire now is learning how to learn.**
>
> —*John Naisbitt, futurist*

CoOl WoRd LiSt!

coprolite • limivorous • emporiatrics • exobiology • newel • hierodule • mortmain • sural • vidette • wen • uroboros nimbus • menhir • acedia • confubuscate • hokey-pokey • scaffolder • sibilate • shvontz • oysvurf • boid • hippopotomonstrosesquipedalian • loganamnosis • kakistocracy

shared responsibility for enabling the college as a whole to achieve its highest aims as a community of scholarship and learning." This code is taken very seriously, and there are many ramifications to that fact. For example, there are no test proctors at Reed. Faculty assume that no student would ever cheat, so a common faculty practice is to pass out a test and then leave the classroom.

WHY REED DECLINES TO PARTICIPATE IN NATIONAL RANKINGS

Reed has refused for years to participate in national ranking surveys, taking the position that they are not meaningful. Even the schools that rank at the top of these lists find them controversial. The first year Swarthmore was ranked number one, there were protests on that campus about the questionable nature of the honor. Was Swarthmore honored by this association with *U.S. News & World Report*, or was *U.S. News* honored by its association with Swarthmore?

Reed's stance is self-serving, but not entirely disingenuous. Reed used to show up in any list of the top liberal arts colleges in the country before *U.S. News & World Report* started its rankings in 1983. As long as it showed up on the tops of the lists, Reed never complained. What changed? Reed, or the lists? Prior to *U.S. News,* most lists were surveys of academic reputation. A magazine or other interested party would survey college presidents or deans of admission or departmental chairs on what liberal arts colleges were of highest quality. Even *U.S. News* started its controversial rankings using this methodology. Reed's reputation among college presidents, especially, is exalted. Reed is a known original source for outstanding faculty,

In a survey on academic integrity at nine large public institutions, three quarters of respondents admitted to one or more instances of "serious" cheating on tests or examinations. (Research authors: Linda K. Trevino, Pennsylvania State; Kenneth D. Butterfield, Washington State; Don McCabe, Rutgers-Newark.) Those who cheated cited "pressure to succeed." Obviously, all three-fourths of these students are at the wrong institutions for the wrong reasons. When you are at the right college for you, your goal will be to learn and discover and compete against your own standards and expectations. Cheating probably exists on every campus, but it is rare indeed at some of the schools in this book. Who would cheat at St. John's, or Reed, or Thomas Aquinas, or Hampshire, or Prescott? The concept is almost absurd.

(*Source:* Chronicle of Higher Education, *15 October 1999*)

intelligent scholars who really care about teaching at the college level, and researchers who bring creativity and passion to their work. *U.S. News* surveys, however, focus on other, more quantifiable data, such as size of the endowment, the percentage of alumni who contribute to the college, and so on. These data are then weighted, and combined into a single, unilinear ranking of best-to-worst schools.

This is not a trivial exercise, but it is of limited validity. If you happen to personally care about the exact same criteria to the exact same weight as the editors of *U.S. News & World Report,* then the rankings will be valid for you. If you care about different things, or care more and less about the same things, *U.S. News* rankings are simply not valid for you. Think about it. Finally, you need to know that from time to time they tinker with the criteria. They claim this is in response to input from college administrators, but if that were true, they'd stop calculating unilinear ordinal rankings altogether in favor of compiling and reporting categorical data, and letting students and parents decide what mattered the most to them. I believe the real reason they remain dedicated to the ordinal rankings is so that schools will move up and down in the rankings and generate controversy and publicity.

At a convention for the National Association for College Admission Counseling, I heard a senior *U.S. News & World Report* editor actually admit, "I realize our methodology excludes some important factors. I realize that it excludes what goes on in the classroom." *What's strong about Reed College is what goes on in the classroom.*

> **❝❝ I taught at Reed for six years and found it a wonderful, quirky, and absolutely intense academic experience. The ethos of the college—to study hard and master fields—permeated not simply the classroom but every activity on campus. ❞❞**
>
> *—A Reed professor*

SIZE DOES MATTER

One of my post-undergraduate almae matres is one of the highest ranking public universities in the world. Although I was impressed with the quality of the professoriate, I was very disappointed in the student body. They were, statistically, brilliant. But you would never know that from sitting in class with them. They very diligently wrote down whatever the professor said. They seldom spoke. They never ran even five minutes of class discussion. Mind you, this was at the graduate level. When one professor was too busy being famous to grade his own mid-term, I decided to leave and pursue studies elsewhere.

One of my brothers went to one of the larger Ivy League universities. His freshman calculus class had hundreds of people in it. He watched the professor on a projection screen from an assigned seat near the back of an auditorium. It was a really good thing that he already knew calculus.

> **Basically the faculty here try to guide you but stay out of the way. In fact, if you ask me, the whole place is set up that way. The student has total access to the academic endeavor. I have keys to the chemistry building, and I work all night whenever I want to. A lot of us do.**
>
> —*Reed student*

If you're really interested in comparative data on colleges, go to more complex data and think for yourself. Check out *Educational Rankings Annual* (The Gale Group, 1999), where Reed shows up on these lists:

U.S. colleges and universities

- offering the best overall academic experience for undergraduates
- where students study the most
- with excellent instructors
- with the most accessible instructors
- which produced the most papers cited and citations for papers published
- de-emphasizing varsity sports

Private, four-year undergraduate colleges and universities

- producing the most Ph.D.'s in all fields of study
- producing the most Ph.D.'s in life sciences, chemistry, computer sciences, economics, English, history, mathematics, physics, astronomy, political science and international relations, psychology, anthropology, and sociology
- top baccalaureate colleges for bachelors degrees awarded to science and engineering Ph.D.'s
- innovative and/or unorthodox colleges

And more. In fact, whatever college or university you are interested in, I recommend you check it out in *Educational Rankings Annual*. It's a great resource and fun to surf through, or you can just cut to the index and find out as much as you can about a specific institution.

Also, if you're into educational statistics leading to ordinal rankings, read Jeremy Fox's home page at www.stanford.edu/~jerfox/laissez_faire_1999_2000.txt,

PHILOSOPHICAL DIFFERENCES

At many major universities, public and private, renowned and mediocre, undergraduate classes are taught by teaching assistants, that is, graduate students who may have been undergraduates themselves a few months ago. There are notable exceptions, such as Caltech, but not many. Reed has no graduate assistants.

where, as a public service, he publishes "A New Ranking of American Colleges on Laissez-Faire Principles." Jeremy Fox is a Ph.D. student at Stanford who got interested in educational data, and he has a sense of humor to boot.

Reed is a prep college, which means that the curriculum is designed to prepare students to succeed in graduate school. All seniors design and conduct a major original research project, write a thesis, and defend their entire undergraduate education in front of an orals board. Reed even has a comprehensive written exam at the end of the junior year just to qualify to *become* a senior. After passing these hurdles, most Reed students report that graduate school is easy.

In order to de-emphasize grades, Reed has one of the weirdest grading systems in higher education: students get regular A to F grades, but they are not reported to the students. Students have to make a specific type of appointment with a dean or

> **The lecture method of instruction: A process by which the notes of the professor are transformed into the notes of the student without passing through the minds of either.**
>
> *—Anonymous*

To: Friends & Colleagues

Re: Rankings

I really wish we could get past the idea that academic programs can be rated—as if all students interested in a particular field were identical. I'm teaching at a small school not often heard of nationally; are we *the best* at anything? Maybe not, compared nationally; but we're way ahead of some of the most prestigious schools in being able to help some of the students who seek us out (and who would have no chance to go to a prestigious school). And certainly size and resources have much to do with the ratings. My department simply can't offer all the courses that a major university department does, nor can we afford the large library acquisitions that state funding and huge endowments can. I nonetheless think that it is a superlative department, able to prepare students better than the two major (and ranked) state universities I attended as a graduate student.

Why not focus on making the best possible match between students with their particular circumstances, and schools most able to benefit them?

Maybe that would be *the best* for everybody.

Regards,

Phil Hey

English and Writing

Briar Cliff College

Sioux City IA 51104-2100

712-279-5477

hey@briar_cliff.edu

a faculty advisor to learn their grades, and many go all four years without doing so. This is not wise, however, as Reed also has one of the toughest grading systems in the country, along with Harvey Mudd and Swarthmore. It is extremely difficult to make an A at Reed, and only four students have graduated with a 4.0 in the last sixteen years. One faculty member explained the rationale for this system this way: "We want students to focus on faculty comments, not the letter grade. We want them to focus on the learning itself, not the measurement of it."

In keeping with its overall philosophy, Reed has no football team and no Greek system. Students manage a few intercollegiate teams, the most popular being men's and women's rugby, but the administration does not sponsor them. Most students live on or very near the campus, and the most common social activity is going to the Paradox Café for coffee and then more coffee. The library is open from 8 A.M. to 2:30 A.M., and most students spend far more time at the library than anyplace else on campus. Seniors get their own desks in the library, and seniors in the sciences get access to their own lab space. The Reed Student Union is open twenty-four hours a day, and is the only building in the country that is 100 percent under student control by explicit writ in the constitution of the college.

Reed is its own little self-contained island in an affluent suburb of Portland. Surrounded by tree-lined streets with elegant homes, it's across the street from one of Portland's famous botanical gardens, and next to a golf course. The campus itself is a wildlife refuge, but tame ducks looked like the main "wild" life. Portland is one of the nicest small cities in the United States, with a good public transportation system. (A car is not needed at Reed.) Although Portland is in the Pacific Northwest, the annual rainfall is only 37 inches. That's less than New York City (44") and Pittsburgh (38"), and way less than Miami (56") and New Orleans (65").

Reed has a ski cabin on Mt. Hood, where, at least in theory, you can ski twelve

REED SCHOLARS WIN HONORS

National Science Foundation (73)	Fulbright (43)	Goldwater (11)	Danforth (2)
Watson (55)	Rhodes (30)	Marshall (2)	Carnegie (2)
	Mellon (18)	American Association of University Women (2)	Churchill (1)

months of the year. Any currently enrolled student can stay there at any time, for free. The Pacific Ocean is a couple of hours away, with Cannon Beach, Haystack Rock, and an elaborate system of tide pools being the top attractions.

DOWNSIDE: Reed was once called the "Parris Island of prep schools," after Parris Island, South Carolina, the famed boot camp for the United States Marine Corps. Although Reed glories in its reputation as a tough place, it can seem at times almost butch. The college has beefed up student support services in recent years, but still, some students are going to prefer a kinder, gentler place to spend four years. Students who thrive at Reed are often a little more mature, a little better able to take care of themselves, and dedicated to their studies. Students who fail at Reed often fail because they can't handle the social freedom or they lack the self-discipline to keep performing when external motivators are withdrawn. For example,

> 99 **You could take from me everything I've learned at Reed, and I could get it back on my own. What they really teach you here is how to learn.** 99
>
> *—Reed student*

EVERY REED SENIOR WRITES A THESIS

Here are a few examples, out of a few thousand:

Platonic Soul Theory in the Middle Dialogues: The Phaedo, The Republic, The Phaedrus

Deamidation of Glutamine and Asparagine Residues: An Approach to the Study of Protein Folding

Acetylcholine in the Barnacle Central Nervous System, Or, The Light That Never Did Shine

Olympia: The Plural Ideal, Modern Greek Spacetime & The Art of Mass Consumption

Acousto-optics and Real-Time Fourier Spectrum Analysis of Radio-Frequency Spectra

Jews Burn Too: The Development of Hell in Judaic Theology from the Exile through the Herodian Period

Cannibalism and Anticannibal Behavior in Bombina Orientalis: The Oriental Fire Bellied Toad

Time Out of Mind: Conciousness and the Bourgeoise

An Additive Synthesis of Jungian and Eliadian Archetypal Theory

Dueling Galaxies

Electron Relaxation in a Quantum Dot by Defect-Assisted Tunneling

The Dynamics of Flylines and Other Classical Strings

Energy Czars and Hot Boxes: Appropriate Energy Matching Using Second-Law Efficiency and Solar Dynamics

Death from Above: The Global Smiting of the Amphibian

Aplusia Californica: It's Not Just for Breakfast Anymore

Borders & Boundaries: Cowboys, Cactus & Cuervo in El Paso, Texas

Regeneration of Rear Derailleur Efficacy Following Chronic Exposure to Substantial Litterfall in Pacific Northwest Forests & Xenopus Laevis Splenocytes

faculty don't assign busy work to see if students are keeping up with the class assignments. Many classes are graded on two papers or two exams per semester, and that allows a student to get *way* behind before anyone else will notice.

One student told me that she felt the faculty fawned over those students who were going on to graduate school, especially the ones who planned to become college professors themselves. [Just to be fair, this is a common complaint at all institutions of higher learning.] She told me, "If you weren't one of their darlings, you just didn't get the same attention. A lot of Reedies are just after a good education, and then they plan to go to work, or they may not even know what they want to do after graduation. It would be nice if the school acknowledged that better."

Reed has an egalitarian flavor, with a complete range of socioeconomic backgrounds, but the college has no minority-focused scholarships. (On the other hand, if you do get into Reed you'll know it wasn't because of your race.)

Finally, Reed is so intense that students sometimes don't plan for the day after graduation. They are so focused on finishing their theses and passing their oral exams that they wait until June to even think about what to do after Reed. This is a minority of students, of course, but a noticeable phenomenon nonetheless. This doesn't seem to keep them from succeeding later, however.

CoOl WeB SiTe!

Check out the latest and past winners of the annual Bulwer-Lytton Fiction Contest for bad writing, named after Edward George Earl Bulwer-Lytton, who once began a novel, "It was a dark and stormy night . . ." Here's a recent winning entry for worst first sentence of an imaginary novel:

Through the gathering gloom of a late-October afternoon, along the greasy, cracked paving-stones slick from the sputum of the sky, Stanley Ruddlethorp wearily trudged up the hill from the cemetery where his wife, sister, brother, and three children were all buried, and forced open the door of his decaying house, blissfully unaware of the catastrophe that was soon to devastate his life.

Perhaps your entire freshman dorm would like to enter this year's contest. Check it out at www.bulwer-lytton.com.

While we're on this topic, a popular dorm activity at many colleges is to try to get a letter in Dear Abby, Ann Landers, or Miss Manners. Students invent all types of maladies, dilemmas, and pickles, and see if Abby, Ann, or Judith will step forward with the solution. Handwritten letters work best. I believe the reigning champions for this are Yale students, but I am not sure who's keeping score. Oh, and one more tip: You can't all have the same postmark.

MORE UPSIDE: Understanding that many of the most brilliant students are poorly served by the secondary education system in this country, Reed will sometimes take a chance on a student with great potential whom other schools would pass over. If you have evidence that you're brilliant, or even just unusually driven to succeed, Reed is probably going to be interested in you. Reed is the best school in the country that will consider a student with an imperfect background. The other top schools just won't, although many say they will.

You know Reed is doing things right when you talk to Reed alumni. They are almost cultlike in their devotion to this school. I met an alumnus who named his son after the college, and while reading student theses in the library, I came across this dedication, "To Reed College, with love." That's just not going to happen at most institutions. To Reed College, with love.

See for yourself.

Also, all the top schools that I have visited have different cultures; you might even call them atmospheres. Some of the schools full of the best and the brightest students have a leaden atmosphere, humorless, maybe even almost oppressive. But Reed has an undercurrent of irreverence and lightheartedness that offsets the seriousness of the academic workload. When I visited, there was a television buried face up in the middle of the lawn, showing Oprah reruns to the sky. Near it was a labyrinth laid out by hundreds of toothbrushes no doubt stolen from the dorms. Reed has an almost British acceptance of eccentricity. There's a Reed professor whose patents have done well, who has a Rolls-Royce with a uniformed driver wait for him outside his classes. Somewhere else this might be odd. Not at Reed.

Finally, because of all the communicating, orally and in writing, that Reed students have to do, they become highly effective and productive scholars later. Reed students win Fulbright, Rhodes, Mellon, and Watson and other prestigious academic honors and fellowships in numbers all out of proportion to the size of the college.

> **I would not trade the thesis experience for anything. Being involved in a project of such length and scope has prepared me for future writing and work in ways I could have never imagined. It has taught me that I can do high quality, consistent work for a year on one question and learn about a subject to a depth that I didn't even realize existed, let alone existed within my grasp. Being a senior writing a thesis with every other senior creates a bond. And one day when I was feeling particularly discouraged, I went into the thesis tower and read the Beat poets' theses from the '50s. Being connected with them made me feel connected to the academy and, quite frankly, to the past and the world in a way I didn't think I could ever feel. The experience has been priceless.**

—*Reed senior*

Reed comprises one-third of a book by Burton R. Clark, *The Distinctive College* (Transaction Publishers, 1992), in which Clark explicates what makes Reed an unusual and distinctive institution. The other two schools covered in the book are Antioch and Swarthmore.

Reed actually does offer underwater basket weaving as an activity during winter break.

CROSS APPS: If you're interested in the scholarly community aspect of Reed College, check out the University of Chicago, St. John's College, Swarthmore College, and to a greater and lesser degree, any of the better liberal arts colleges. See p. 81 for a partial list. Also, check out The University of the South (aka Sewanee), which is very different but oddly similar, and not well known.

If you're interested in the Great Books aspect of Reed College, see also Shimer College, St. John's, Thomas Aquinas, The Thomas More College of Liberal Arts, and the University of Chicago.

If you're interested in the senior thesis, see also Princeton University, New College of the University of South Florida, and Davidson. I want to stress that this is an incomplete list, and that many other schools also allow, and some may require, a capstone project. Pay attention to the details, however. Some schools' "capstone project" is little more than a scrapbook of "stuff I learned while I was in college," while other schools' senior research project results in a thesis that could be published as an academic book. By the way, at some of the schools I visited, the undergraduate theses were vastly superior to many of the graduate theses I've read in my day.

If you're interested in Reed's honor code, you should know that approximately twenty of the older liberal arts schools still have them. At some schools the honor code is still taken seriously, while at others it's a vestige of more quaint times. At Reed, it remains the law of student conduct. As an interesting trivia item, many of these honor codes were first compromised when Ronald Reagan decided that each school receiving federal funding should have "an alcohol and drug abuse policy." That codified policy compromised the intellectual tradition of having a moral code embodied in the students themselves, and at many schools was an invitation to trash the honor code system in favor of rules and regulations provided by the administration.

INTERESTED IN A CAREER IN HIGHER EDUCATION?

Whether you are interested in being a college professor or an administrator, start reading the *Chronicle of Higher Education* while you're an undergraduate. You can read it for free at any college library. It's hilarious—full of intrigue, sexual shenanigans, embezzlements, bold power plays, cheating, and lots of government conspiracies. In fact, it reads like a police blotter for the ivory tower set. Of course it also has scientific breakthroughs and such, but it is the soap opera aspect of it that I find fascinating. And you thought these people were stuffy and staid . . .

Reed College

3203 S.E. Woodstock Blvd.

Portland, OR 97202

503-771-1112

www.reed.edu

A SHORT HISTORY OF EDUCATIONAL REFORM

The second to the last big education reform movement came about because the Russians launched Sputnik, the Earth's first human-made satellite, in 1957. A few years later President John F. Kennedy and his advisors, a lot of Eastern-school academics commonly known as the "Brain Trust," belatedly decided this constituted a national emergency. They poured money and rhetoric into education like it mattered. This wave pretty much died out after we walked on the moon twelve years later and the Russians could only watch. Not long after that NASA laid off thousands of engineers and scientists.

The last big education reform movement, which is still reverberating, was sparked by "A Nation at Risk," a special report of the National Commission on Excellence in Education. It contained the famous comment that U.S. education was facing "a rising tide of mediocrity" and bemoaned that "secondary school curricula have been homogenized, diluted, and diffused to the point that they no longer have a central purpose. In effect, we have a cafeteria-style curriculum in which the appetizers and desserts can easily be mistaken for the main courses." The report also pointed out that 25 percent of high school student credits were in health and physical education or remedial classes. The same trend was afoot at universities, covered in a later study funded by the Carnegie Foundation for the Advancement of Teaching and

> **And, as a final comment, I think 'priceless' is the best word to describe the quality of my Reed education. Priceless in the same way that an Egyptian artifact is priceless: you can put a monetary value on it, but the monetary value has nothing to do with the true value. Reed has changed my life for the better in ways I didn't know my life could be changed when I arrived here. It has put me in touch with an intellectual and ideological rigor without which I would not be the human being I am now. It has given me the insight and training which I think I need to be a healthy, happy, and productive human being. I will be eternally grateful and incapable of expressing how valuable the experience truly was.**
> *—Reed alumna*

THE MOST INTERESTING THING EVER SAID
TO ME BY A COLLEGE PRESIDENT

President of Reed College, Steve Koblik, told me that the key to a good college is a strong faculty to check the power of the presidency. He suggested that the faculty's role as protector of the curriculum and the academic culture of an institution is absolutely critical for institutional continuity and integrity. He may be the only college president in history to suggest that what the world needs is a stronger faculty.

reported in Ernest L. Boyer's *College: The Undergraduate Experience in America* (Carnegie Foundation for the Advancement of Teaching, 1997), a book frequently cited in this text. At the same time, Americans were told to fear the Japanese, that the Japanese were overtaking us in mathematics and the basic sciences, and something "needed to be done."

This spawned the call in state legislatures from coast to coast for a return to "basics" and "standards," which they believed, being legislators and lawyers, they were best suited to define. Academics, who spent their lives studying how students learn and what they might benefit from learning, were ignored. This trend is still in full swing, with calls for a national high school exam and more and harder teacher testing.

During this same time, say, the last twenty years, there has been a totally separate and countervailing trend to reinvestigate the notion of a canon. In short, the proponents of this trend wanted an answer to this question: Ought we to study the thoughts and writings of only dead, white, European males?

Some major universities with academic reputations of the first order, busy diluting, homogenizing, and diffusing their curriculum "to the point that they no longer have a central purpose," caved in totally to this trend and threw the baby out with the bath water. "All thought is equal," they capitulated, "and whatever students want to study is fine with us, so long as they pay the tuition." Without naming names, let us

---

SO YOU THINK COLLEGE PRESIDENTS HAVE IT EASY?

Recently, college presidents have had to resign for plagiarizing a speech, for having a long-term affair with a family member's wife, for "misappropriating" $1.5 million, and for sexually harassing subordinates and downloading "sexual content" on college computers. And a trustee resigned in protest when a college president refused to resign after "misleading statements" were found on the resumé he used to get his appointment. Hmmmm. Looks like college presidents are "just folks" after all.

While we're on this topic, it is common practice for advising professors to list themselves as the primary author on work that is overwhelmingly, and sometimes entirely, done by graduate students. One professor at a "research university" was so in the habit of this that it is unclear when he last did any research of his own. One of the papers he so appropriated turned out to have been plagiarized by the student in the first place. What a dilemma! Beg off that he stole the work in the first place? Or fall on his sword as a plagiarist? Thief? Plagiarist? Tough call. He and his department just decided that he should retire early. Maybe there is a God.

say these were some of the very best institutions. Some of these same institutions have also been suffering massive grade inflation, as the average grade went from a C+ to an A-, presumably without the student work improving so dramatically. Student reviews of faculty were also popularized in higher education during this time, and the locus of power in many institutions shifted from the faculty toward the students.

We have to ask ourselves, Is this entirely good?

Certainly, some of it *is* good. But there is a reason that we still concern ourselves with the Greco-Roman-European tradition, and there is a reason that that tradition survived and accrued for some twenty-five centuries to come to us virtually intact. You can learn many things at a smorgasbord school, but will it be, ultimately, a coherent education? The schools without a pandering faculty resisted abandoning the canon in favor of improving it. They saw that the students had a point in wanting to add female and minority voices and points of view to the canon, and wanting to learn more about other, separate-but-just-as-important traditions, such as the five thousand years of Chinese history. But they did not decide that any collection of courses stacked up to an education.

Check out www.collegiatechoice.com for a selection of college tour videotapes made by independent college counselors, as in, not affiliated with the school covered in the videotape. They vary in quality, but the interest factor and the honesty are astounding.

CoOl BoOk AlErT!

The Fiske Guide to Colleges by Edward B. Fiske (Times Books, 1999)

There are dozens of college guides, many of which are very good at getting the basic statistics out about a college. There are none that I would censure. However, there is a special place in my heart for the *Fiske Guide*. Edward B. Fiske has spent almost two decades publishing his guide, which goes beyond the statistics to give you an idea of the flavor of a place. He respects the student who might be interested in something a little different, and does the best job of describing the schools that are not cookie-cutter copies of the norm. Also, and this matters, he actually *likes* colleges. He writes about them as if they might be great places to go and learn, and in this, he is right. Check it out. Want to know the best way to check out a guide? See if the schools are organized nationally or by state. If by state, the guide was not written for the student interested in a nationally significant institution.

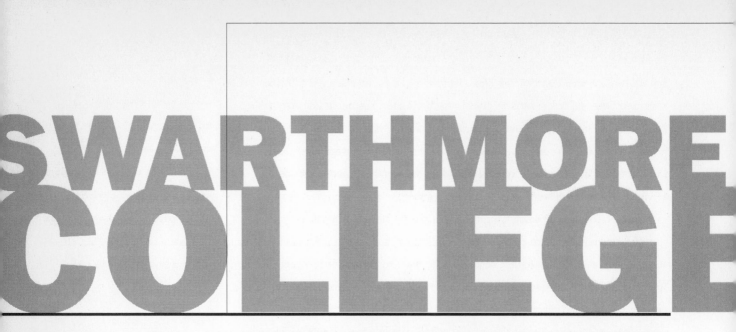

SWARTHMORE COLLEGE

Swarthmore is the quintessential liberal arts college. It is both academically excellent and just the right amount of insular, creating a scholarly community virtually free of distractions. It is located on a campus of green lawns and tree-studded rolling hills in a suburb of Philadelphia. In fact, the entire campus is a nationally registered arboretum. It snows in the winter. You can take a train from the edge of campus to downtown Philadelphia, and with one transfer you can be in New York City. When you see the college experience in old movies, this is what they were trying to re-create. Except at Swarthmore, it's not a movie; it's the real thing.

Swarthmore has long had a preference for valedictorians, and has at times claimed the highest percentage of valedictorians of any institution in the United States. Although not every student is a valedictorian by any stretch of the imagination, their presence permeates the campus as a whole. Valedictorians set very high standards for themselves, and tend to be good citizens as well as good students. The student body at Swarthmore is respected by the faculty, and there is an understanding here that students will conduct themselves with professionalism and decorum.

In fact, student housing is mixed in with faculty offices and classrooms. Nowhere else would the administration be crazy enough to put students and their stereos so close to classrooms and professors' offices, but at Swarthmore this has not created many problems. The school is committed to the practice. The value of mingling faculty, student life, and teaching spaces is seen as more than worth an occasional disrup-

> **❝ This is a fantastic place to be an undergraduate. We're the focus of the whole school. I can go into a professor's office and discuss the course. I can use all the lab equipment. A lot of students work with professors on original research. We're the only game in town. ❞**
>
> *—Swarthmore student*

tion. "Class" as a discrete activity that happens within four walls and fifty minutes is a misnomer at Swarthmore, where learning spills over into all hours and all places.

Swarthmore is very intentionally a culturally diverse community. The school goes to great lengths to recruit minority and international students with outstanding academic preparation. Originally started by Quakers, Swarthmore continues to have a service tradition. The students and the institution itself are more involved in local and regional affairs than would be the case at many liberal arts colleges.

The students work hard, some would say very hard, but mostly they compete with their own expectations. Like Reed and Harvey Mudd, Swarthmore has very tough grading. A popular campus T-shirt reads, "Anywhere else it would have been an 'A.'" Making Bs is often shocking to students who were valedictorians at their high schools, but the grading system lets everyone know there is always room for improvement.

Swarthmore is organized like a mini-university, with black studies, engineering,

GRADE INFLATION

Swarthmore is one of three colleges with virtually no grade inflation. (Harvey Mudd and Reed are the other two.) Students who have never made a B learn how at Swarthmore. At any of these schools, a B is an indication of extreme effort *and* talent, and an A still means "outstanding." An A is, in fact, extraordinary in the literal meaning of the term.

Grade inflation originated in response to certain U.S. military draft policies of the Vietnam War era. For a time, young men could get a draft deferral by being full-time college students. Faculty members became reluctant to give young men failing grades, as they could be sentencing those young men to tours of duty in Vietnam. So students who should have flunked out received a C, and students who were legitimately earning a C now "deserved" a B, and students earning a B got an A. The "Gentleman's C," originally a weak effort that nonetheless complied with all course requirements, became a solid B. Eventually, a C became something it had not been before then: shameful. Grade inflation has been exacerbated in recent years by student aid policies with minimum GPA requirements ("Prof. Wilson, if you give me a B I'll lose my scholarship!") and the continuing devolution of higher education into a pander bear for students as consumers (grade harshly and watch your student reviews drop like a rock). So today students who come to class and comply with the minimum course requirements strongly believe that they "deserve" an A.

In 1976, 19 percent of all college students had a GPA of A- or better; by 1993, 26 percent did. Although I haven't found any studies since the 1993 one, anecdotal reports are that the problem is continuing to worsen. It starts in high school, where students with a pulse expect to make an A. This is one reason that admissions deans are spending more time on activities, evidence of focus and strength of character, and SATs and ACTs. There are so many young men and women with nearly perfect GPAs that it is just not that useful to use the GPA as an admissions decision-making tool.

CoOl BoOk AlErT!

Colleges That Change Lives by Loren Pope, Director of the College Placement Bureau and former education editor for the *New York Times* (Penguin USA, 2000)

Loren Pope is no fan of large research universities, which he proves "cheat undergraduates" using an array of statistical, rhetorical, and anecdotal presentations. Graduates of small colleges are overrepresented in the faculty of major research universities. The faculty of major research universities are more, not less, likely to send their own children to small colleges. An analysis of *Who's Who,* Nobel, and other national and international honor listings shows that graduates of small colleges are overrepresented, statistically. A small college can turn an indifferent high school student into a lifelong scholar. And on and on. Pope identifies and describes forty colleges that "change lives." This is a fantastic book for any student, teacher, or counselor. Here are Pope's forty schools, in reverse alphabetical order:

Whitman College, Walla Walla, Washington

Wheaton College, Wheaton, Illinois

Western Maryland College, Westminster, Maryland

Wabash College, Crawfordsville, Indiana

Ursinus College, Collegeville, Pennsylvania

Southwestern University, Georgetown, Texas

St. Olaf College, Northfield, Minnesota

St. John's College, Annapolis, Maryland, and
    Santa Fe, New Mexico

St. Andrews Presbyterian College, Laurinburg,
    North Carolina

Rhodes College, Memphis, Tennessee

Reed College, Portland, Oregon

Ohio Wesleyan University, Delaware, Ohio

Millsaps College, Jackson, Mississippi

Marlboro College, Marlboro, Vermont

Lynchburg College, Lynchburg, Virginia

Lawrence University, Appleton, Wisconsin

Knox College, Galesburg, Illinois

Kalamazoo College, Kalamazoo, Michigan

Juniata College, Huntingdon, Pennsylvania

Hope College, Holland, Michigan

Hiram College, Hiram, Ohio

Hendrix College, Conway, Arkansas

Hampshire College, Amherst, Massachusetts

Guilford College, Greensboro, North Carolina

Goucher College, Towson, Maryland

The Evergreen State College, Olympia, Washington

Emory and Henry College, Emory, Virginia

Eckerd College, St. Petersburg, Florida

Earlham College, Richmond, Indiana

Denison University, Granville, Ohio

Cornell College, Mount Vernon, Iowa

College of Wooster, Wooster, Ohio

Clark University, Worcester, Massachusetts

Centre College, Danville, Kentucky

Birmingham-Southern College, Birmingham, Alabama

Beloit College, Beloit, Wisconsin

Austin College, Sherman, Texas

Antioch College, Yellow Springs, Ohio

Allegheny College, Meadville, Pennsylvania

Agnes Scott College, Decatur, Georgia

Also see Cool Book Alert! on p. 46 for Pope's *Looking Beyond the Ivy League.*

computer science, and other emphases that are not common at liberal arts colleges. It also has one of the most vigorous career planning and placement offices available at any college, with 265 companies recruiting Swarthmore students every year. (In case you don't realize it, this is *very* unusual at a liberal arts college.) Basically, Swarthmore packs a major punch in a little package.

The college offers an honors option that is similar to Reed's senior thesis project, leading to oral examinations. A Swarthmore degree, with or without the honors option, is a valuable ticket to life. Swarthmore graduates are all over the world, but they are particularly well represented in the Northeast. Once you are a member of this family, you are well connected.

Most of the socializing at Swarthmore seems to focus on small group gatherings, many of them impromptu. The college puts Adirondack chairs on the lawn in front of Parrish Hall, and students can be found reading in them even in inclement winter. (They call it "Parrish Beach.") The Greek and varsity athletic systems are typical, but definitely take a back seat to academics.

DOWNSIDE: It is quite difficult to get into Swarthmore. They reject four out of five applicants. I found Swarthmore administrators to be very friendly and approachable, in spite of this. Some schools that I won't name have absolutely arrogant administrators, but Swarthmore seems to be staffed by conscientious administrators who seem genuinely delighted to get to work with this student body.

> **All my classes are taught by full professors. They earned their doctorates at the best graduate programs. When I get ready to go to graduate school, they can open a lot of doors for me. That's just not true as an undergraduate at a large university.**
>
> —*Swarthmore student*

" Swarthmore? Intense. In a word, intense. "
—*Swarthmore student*

Swarthmore can be a draining experience. Students who are happy at Swarthmore like to study; they enjoy the work itself. Students who are unhappy at Swarthmore tend to be unhappy because of the workload and the unrelentingly high expectations. On the other hand, many of the students at Swarthmore exacerbate the workload by committing to a list of activities that would wear out a pair of identical twins pretending to be one person. The admissions materials coming out of Swarthmore today downplay the workload, but it is very real.

MORE UPSIDE: Swarthmore is frequently ranked at or near the top for liberal arts colleges in the United States by U.S. News and World Report, which means you don't have to explain your decision to go there to your parents or your friends. Swarthmore is in a very secure position, with good management and good funding, and is unlikely to fall very far from its lofty perch any time in the immediate future. It has deep pockets, which allow it to make competitive or superior financial aid offers. If you can get into Swarthmore, you'll probably survive it financially.

Finally, Swarthmore graduates seem universally grateful for the experience. I've interviewed a number of them, and they seem to have some *je ne sais* what, a kind of confidence that comes from substantial and real personal accomplishment. At the risk of being corny, they glow from within.

CROSS APPS: Swarthmore is not unlike many elite liberal arts schools; it just happens to do a very, very good job of being a liberal arts college. If you are attracted to Swarthmore, also consider the schools in the following section, or any good liberal arts school in the nation.

Swarthmore College
500 College Avenue
Swarthmore, PA 19081
610-328-8000
www.swarthmore.edu

CoOl ScHoLaRsHiP!

You've heard of the Rhodes and perhaps the Watson and the Fulbright and the Javits, but have you heard of the Wofford Presidential International Scholarship? Wofford College of Spartanburg, South Carolina, offers a fully supported year of international travel in the developing world to "the singular student best fitted to benefit humankind." Students submit travel and service plans in an open competition to win this scholarship. Wofford also publishes the first novels of select creative writing students under the Benjamin Wofford Prize. How's that for a college that honors and supports its own students? Check them out.

THE CONSORTIUM OF LIBERAL ARTS COLLEGES (CLAC)

The Consortium of Liberal Arts Colleges (CLAC) evolved from a series of meetings of college presidents at Oberlin College in the 1980s. The original concern was for the future of the liberal arts college as an educational institution with a clear vision of what it wanted to provide to undergraduate students. It has since evolved to focus on academic and administrative computing and related technologies, ways to create economies of scale by consortium, and so on. Basically, it serves as a forum for the exchange of ideas among its members. These are all excellent schools.

The present membership includes the following colleges and universities, in reverse alphabetical order:

Williams College, Williamstown, Massachusetts

Whittier College, Whittier, California

Wheaton College, Wheaton, Illinois

Wesleyan University, Middletown, Connecticut

Wellesley College, Wellesley, Masschusetts

Washington and Lee University, Lexington, Virginia

Washington College, Chestertown, Maryland

Wabash College, Crawfordsville, Indiana

Vassar College, Poughkeepsie, New York

Union College, Schenectady, New York

Trinity University, San Antonio, Texas

Trinity College, Hartford, Connecticut

Swarthmore College, Swarthmore, Pennsylvania

St. Olaf College, Northfield, Minnesota

Smith College, Northampton, Massachusetts

Skidmore College, Saratoga Springs, New York

Sewanee-The University of the South, Sewanee, Tennessee

Reed College, Portland, Oregon

Pomona College, Claremont, California

Ohio Wesleyan University, Delaware, Ohio

Occidental College, Los Angeles, California

Oberlin College, Oberlin, Ohio

Mount Holyoke College, South Hadley, Massachusetts

Mills College, Oakland, California

Middlebury College, Middlebury, Vermont

Manhattan College, Riverdale, New York

Macalester College, Saint Paul, Minnesota

Lawrence University, Appleton, Wisconsin

Lafayette College, Easton, Pennsylvania

Kenyon College, Gambier, Ohio

Kalamazoo College, Kalamazoo, Michigan

Hope College, Holland, Michigan

Haverford College, Haverford, Pennsylvania

Harvey Mudd College, Claremont, California

Hamilton College, Clinton, New York

Grinnell College, Grinnell, Iowa

Gettysburg College, Gettysburg, Pennsylvania

Franklin and Marshall College, Lancaster, Pennsylvania

Earlham College, Richmond, Indiana

Dickinson College, Carlisle, Pennsylvania

CoOl BoOk AlErT!

College: The Undergraduate Experience in America by Ernest L. Boyer

(Carnegie Foundation for the Advancement of Teaching, 1997)

Ernest L. Boyer conducted a national review of undergraduate education as part of a grant from the Carnegie Foundation for the Advancement of Teaching. The result was *College: The Undergraduate Experience in America.* The book investigates the undergraduate educational process, what is done well and what is done poorly, and goes beyond a purely descriptive approach to attempt to be prescriptive. It is a bold book. It makes an argument for an integrated core of knowledge followed by a thoughtful accumulation of expertise in a major field of study; it rejects the smorgasbord approach to curricular offerings. It reveals the trials and tribulations of being a professor, or a student, at different types of institutions. Anyone involved in higher education, either as a student or a member of faculty or staff, should check it out. This will probably be the last book of its type, as higher education sinks into relativism, curricula become "student oriented," and grade inflation is the law of the land. For the latest research findings, go to SUNY Stony Brook's home page, www.sunysb.edu, and click on "Boyer Commission Report."

DePauw University, Greencastle, Indiana

Denison University, Granville, Ohio

Davidson College, Davidson, North Carolina

Connecticut College, New London, Connecticut

Colorado College, Colorado Springs, Colorado

The College of Wooster, Wooster, Ohio

College of the Holy Cross, Worcester, Massachusetts

Colgate University, Hamilton, New York

Colby College, Waterville, Maine

Carleton College, Northfield, Minnesota

Bucknell University, Lewisburg, Pennsylvania

Bryn Mawr College, Bryn Mawr, Pennsylvania

Bowdoin College, Brunswick, Maine

Beloit College, Beloit, Wisconsin

Bates College, Lewiston, Maine

Amherst College, Amherst, Massachusetts

Alma College, Alma, Michigan

Albion College, Albion, Michigan

Check out the CLAC Web site at www.liberalarts.org. Also, be sure to remember that there are at least two hundred other excellent liberal arts colleges that just don't happen to belong to this association.

THE HIGHEST PAID PROFESSORS IN AMERICA
(AVERAGE SALARY OF FULL PROFESSOR)

Rockefeller University $125,400

Harvard University $122,100

Stanford University $117,000

Princeton University $114,900

California Institute of Technology $114,600

Yale University $113,100

University of Chicago $112,000

University of Colorado Health Sciences Center $111,500

New York University $110,000

Columbia University $109,200

(*Source:* The Chronicle of Higher Education, *23 April 1999*)

THE UNIVERSITY OF CHICAGO

one of the world's great universities • with a quirky student body who would rather study than . . . well, anything ranked dead last for social life, and proud of it • *more Nobels than a Swedish phone book (70, to be exact)* • 3,900 undergraduates • *8,550 graduate students*

The University of Chicago is like a Roman city, rising from the shores of Lake Michigan just south of downtown Chicago. It *feels* like a great university, with massive English gothic architecture framing expansive green lawns. Totally lopsided in favor of graduate studies, it nevertheless offers its undergraduates a chance to go to university with like-minded overly studious young scholars. Serious intellectualism is in here, and the type of career-minded lollygaggers you find at some of the Ivy League campuses is totally absent. Welcome to a study hall that never ends.

The University of Chicago is famous among the academic crowd for three things. First, it ranked dead last in a survey of social life at colleges and universities. Instead of bemoaning this fact, the students printed up T-shirts with this number on them, "300," a cryptic reference to being found 300th, dead last, in this ranking. ("No social life" generally means more or less sober students sitting around and discussing books and ideas.)

> **Chicago students continue to revel in the stereotype that they are library-shackled intellectuals.**
>
> —*Chronicle of Higher Education (18 June 1999)*

Professors at Chicago are not called "Dr." or "Professor," as this is thought to detract from the community-of-scholars concept. Also, for the same reason, freshmen are called "first-year students."

Second, Dr. Hanna Grey, a former University of Chicago president, told her students that they needed to get out more, go to the bars in Chicago, and get more of a social life going. This caused quite a stir. While other colleges and universities are fretting over excessive alcohol use by their students, Dr. Grey thought that what her students needed most was a good night out on the town. At least once a month or, if that was too distracting, once per semester. Recently, the students held a mock "Fun In" after the administration again focused on their lack of a social life.

Third, the University of Chicago asks the weirdest questions on its application essay. A recent example: "Given the probability that the federal tax code, nondairy creamer, Dennis Rodman and the art of mime all came from outer space, name something else that has extraterrestrial origins and defend your hypothesis." Another one invited the candidate to pitch a TV pilot involving Van Gogh's ear, a proton accelerator, and Muddy Waters guitar. Students are warned: "Remember that this is Chicago so it is better to err on the side of intellectual pretension than on the side of pure silliness." One thing is certain: The University of Chicago does not want your form essay.

Although usually mentioned in the company of Princeton and Yale, Chicago goes its own way. It is a very intentionally scholarly place, interested in truth and thought for its own sake, tolerant of all manner of quirkiness as long as it is accompanied by a razor-sharp mind. It once refused to give an honorary doctorate to Queen Elizabeth "because she hadn't made significant contributions to a field of study."

So, what do you learn at the University of Chicago? There is a core curriculum somewhat like Reed's and having a great deal in common with St. John's. It focuses on a Great Books sequence and mastery of a second language. After that, you can branch out in many directions at one of the great research universities in the world. Chicago claims, with no false humility, that "in the wake of the national hue and cry over the failings of higher education the College does not seek a 'return' to higher standards because it never left them."

DOWNSIDE: Chicago has no traditional collegiate social life. This is either a draw or a repulsion, but it would be a mistake to be neutral about it. Like Swarthmore,

> A little learning is a dang'rous thing;
> Drink deep, or taste not the Pierian spring:
> There shallow draughts intoxicate the brain,
> And drinking largely sobers us again.
>
> —*Alexander Pope*

Chicago has a Smart Museum. This is an inside joke, really, but you'll have to visit to get it.

Chicago is one of the few schools that is roughly gender balanced. It has approximately half men and half women. Women outnumber men in most schools except engineering specialty schools and some business programs. Where are all the men? Not in college, is what the sociologists say.

Chicago can certainly be relentless. Also, Chicago has just completed a period of turmoil, in which the core curriculum was cut by one-seventh amid great protest, eventually resulting in the ousting of the prior president of the university. Perhaps that will be old news by the time you arrive. Finally, Chicago really is a Class I research university (see the Carnegie Foundation system for classifying colleges and universities, this page). It has teaching assistants, bigger classes, and a more impersonal atmosphere. It's like its own town, with several newspapers and more than one culture. It's the only university strongly recommended in this book (if you don't count the *much* smaller Caltech or the overnamed University of the South). It's here for two reasons: one, it makes minimal use of teaching assistants, and two, the quality and particular nature of the program are too strong to overlook.

MORE UPSIDE: This is a quality education, certainly one of the very best available in the country for an internally driven and self-consciously intellectual person.

University of Chicago
5801 South Ellis Avenue
Chicago, IL 60637
773-702-1234
www.uchicago.edu

THE CARNEGIE FOUNDATION FOR THE ADVANCEMENT OF TEACHING CLASSIFICATION SYSTEM

There are two major classification systems for colleges and universities in the United States: the National College Athletic Association's Divisions I, II, and III, with subcategories that have to do with intercollegiate athletic competition, and the Carnegie Foundation for the Advancement of Teaching Classification System, which has to do with the missions of the institutions themselves. Academics everywhere refer to the Carnegie system, but rarely is it explicated. Here it is. Now when an academic intones to you, "This is a Class I research university," you'll know to respond, "What you mean is that educating bright young undergraduates is not really the central mission of this institution."

Research Universities I

1. Full range of baccalaureate programs

2. Committed to graduate education through the doctorate

3. Give high priority to research

4. Award 50 or more doctoral degrees each year

5. Receive $40 million or more in federal support per annum

Research Universities II

1. Full range of baccalaureate programs

2. Committed to graduate education through the doctorate

3. Give high priority to research

4. Award 50 or more doctoral degrees each year

5. Receive $15.5 million to $40 million in federal support

Doctoral Universities I

1. Full range of baccalaureate programs

2. Committed to graduate education through the doctorate

3. Award at least 40 doctoral degrees annually in five or more disciplines

Doctoral Universities II

1. Full range of baccalaureate programs

2. Committed to graduate education through the doctorate

3. Award at least 10 doctoral degrees in three or more disciplines, or at least 20 doctoral degrees in one or more disciplines

> **❝ I wanted to go to a place where it wouldn't be weird to spend Saturday night in the library, and indeed, all my friends would be there too. ❞**
>
> *—University of Chicago student*

A NOTE ABOUT URBAN DANGER

The University of Chicago keeps showing up in national articles as a "dangerous" school. This is based on crime statistics from a nearby neighborhood that has almost nothing to do with the campus itself. Chicago students are as safe as any urban institution's students as long as they don't hang around on street corners in that particular neighborhood. Columbia and the University of Pennsylvania are also in challenging urban environments, yet they have somehow avoided the undue attention that the University of Chicago has had to endure. Visit the campus and you'll see that it's really a matter of zip code boundaries, not safety.

Master's (Comprehensive) Universities and Colleges I

1. Full range of baccalaureate programs

2. Committed to graduate education through the master's degree

3. Award 40 or more master's degrees annually in three or more disciplines

Master's (Comprehensive) Universities and Colleges II

1. Full range of baccalaureate programs

2. Committed to graduate education through the master's degree

3. Award 20 or more master's degrees annually in one or more disciplines

Baccalaureate (Liberal Arts) Colleges I

1. Offer a baccalaureate degree

2. Focus on undergraduate education

3. Award at least 40 percent of their degrees in the liberal arts

4. Restrictive in admissions

Baccalaureate Colleges II

1. Offer a baccalaureate degree

2. Focus on undergraduate education

3. Award less than 40 percent of their degrees in the liberal arts

4. Less restrictive in admissions

Associate of Arts Colleges

1. Offer only the associate of arts degree

Specialized Institutions

Offer degrees ranging from the bachelor's to the doctorate with at least 50 percent awarded in a single discipline, including:

1. Schools of engineering and technology

2. Medical schools and medical centers

3. Other health profession schools

4. Schools of business and management

5. Schools of art, music, and design

6. Schools of law

7. Teachers' colleges

8. Graduate-only institutes and centers

9. Maritime academies

10. Military institutes

11. Tribal colleges and universities

12. Theological seminaries and Bible colleges

13. Institutions that do not fit any other classification category

It is important to note that these are not rankings, and should in no way be considered or construed as rankings. This was never the intent of the Carnegie Foundation for the Advancement of Teaching. This is a system for categorizing institutions by their missions, i.e., that which they strive to be best at. One problem is that an institution might very well meet some of the criteria in one category, and some in another, as the criteria are divergent but not mutually exclusive. For these and other reasons, the Carnegie categories are under revision at the moment, with changes expected to be released in two phases, in 2000 and 2005.

(Source: The Carnegie Foundation for the Advancement of Teaching, www.carnegiefoundation.org)

C o O l   B o O k   A l E r T !

The Innovative Campus: Nurturing the Distinctive Learning Environment by Joy Rosenzweig Kliewer (Oryx Press, 1998)

The Innovative Campus investigates many of the same institutions listed in this guide, but unlike the book in your hands, it has a defensible academic methodology. For example, Ms. Kliewer defines "innovative college," which you have to admire. She also does an admirable job of providing a context for the genesis of many of the innovative colleges, describing the history of their launch, the motivations of the founders, and the twists and turns of their evolution, and even their prognosis for future success. This is a great book for the innovating educator, the serious college counselor, and the more serious high school student, and for the parent who wants to know more about the innovative college her son or daughter wants to attend. She gives full-chapter profiles to these colleges:

Pitzer College, Claremont, California

New College of the University of South Florida, Sarasota

Hampshire College, Amherst, Massachusetts

The University of Wisconsin-Green Bay

University of California, Santa Cruz

The Evergreen State College, Olympia, Washington

Definitely worth a read.

THE UNIVERSITY OF THE SOUTH (SEWANEE)

a world unto itself • a liberal arts university on a mountaintop • *an old-fashioned gentility* • a 10,000-acre campus • *a small university? or a large college?*

The University of the South is one of those institutions that defies categorization. It is partially like a university, with sororities and fraternities and football, and partially like a small and quirky liberal arts college, with an academic tradition based on the British model. It's not particularly unusual in some respects, but it is very unusual in others.

With that said, here's what's important to know about Sewanee:

First of all, Sewanee was the Indian name for the mountain the school is situated on. The 10,000-acre campus is called "The Domain." It's off the beaten path, and no one comes here by accident. The campus is Gothic-ed to the max, but they do have a hewn log cabin, too.

The honor code here is sacrosanct. When students go through orientation, they ceremoniously sign the honor code in a massive ledger, containing the signatures of all the students who have so sworn before them. Students also sign their work, from tests to papers, with the simple word, "Pledged." That means they've done the work

The University of Virginia, founded by Thomas Jefferson, does not have freshmen. They have first-year, second-year, third-year, and fourth-year students. Jefferson thought that since learning should be a lifelong endeavor, no student should ever claim the status of "senior."

in compliance with the academic honor code. This has the gravitas of the sharia. When I was on tour I noticed a faculty member's office door was open. The light was off, she was gone, and the door stood open. I asked the guide about it and he said, "Someone might want to leave her a note."

Academic performance here is revered, and scholars have special status. At so many universities, special privileges are showered on athletes. Football players leave early, skip class, arrange to take exams at home and with help. Here, scholarship is

" Even brilliant students find it difficult to make the As they're used to. "

the focus. This is evidenced by the fact that students who maintain honors status and are indoctrinated into the Order of the Gownsmen *wear academic robes on campus.* This is a symbol of their accomplishment, and they are to be honored and respected by others as exemplifying what the institution is all about.

Many men wear a coat and tie to class, and many of the women wear dresses.

Professors hold some classes in their homes. Everybody eats dinner with professors often.

Sewanee's outcomes are impressive:

23 Rhodes scholars

26 Watson fellows

70 percent pursue graduate study

HAMPDEN-SYDNEY COLLEGE

At all-male Hampden-Sydney College, until recently young men could still be found wearing dinner jackets for evening conversation in the dorms. Although dress is somewhat more relaxed now, it remains one of the last semi-aristocratic institutions in the United States.

Hampden-Sydney College · College Road · Hampden-Sydney, VA 23943 · 804-223-6000 · www.hsc.edu

95 percent of graduates applying to law school are accepted

89 percent of graduates applying to medical, dental and veterinary school are accepted.

Students take comprehensive examinations in their majors, called comps, which they must pass to graduate, no matter what their GPA or other accomplishments are.

Sewanee. Told you it defied classification.

The University of the South (Sewanee)

735 University Avenue

Sewanee, TN 37383

800-522-2234 or 931-598-1238

Free video: 800-255-0384

www.sewanee.edu

CoOl BoOk AlErT!

The Templeton Guide: Colleges That Encourage Character Development edited by the John Templeton Foundation
(Templeton Foundation Press, 1999)

The John Templeton Foundation was established in 1987 with the purpose of supporting higher educational programs and institutions that encourage character development by inspiring "students to lead ethical and civil-minded lives." Mr. Templeton felt that previous to the college years, the student is shaped by his or her parents and school experiences, but once in college that development can either continue or stagnate depending on what type of support and guidance is provided in the higher educational environment. Our society tends to focus on the younger years as those being important for shaping the personality and character, when in reality it is also the college years that are "critical to forming a strong and steady character."

The Templeton Guide is a collection of approximately 550 programs and institutions found by The Templeton Foundation to encourage character development through volunteering, community service projects, substance abuse prevention programs, superb guidance and mentoring throughout the college years, a curriculum dealing with ethical and character issues, and programs supportive of spiritual development. The book is a good resource for students looking for an educational experience that goes beyond just the books. Full of detailed program descriptions, the guide will give the reader a very good idea of which institutions will provide the right environment for the type of growth they are interested in.

THE ROBERT E. COOK HONORS COLLEGE

a school within a school • **emphasis on critical thinking** • *residential retreat, a world apart, right on campus* • **like the rich uncle you never had** • *an intellectual family of peers* • **every possible advantage, at your fingertips**

Suppose you were to take truly bright kids who grew up in modest or perhaps challenging circumstances, and ship them off to a rich uncle's mansion. Further suppose that this uncle were wealthy, wise, and caring, and took it upon himself to be sure that his young charges would learn about philosophy and history and language and art and music and culture and the ways of the world. Wouldn't that be an educator's fantasy? Wouldn't that be the best way to actualize the potential of these bright young people?

The Robert E. Cook Honors College is exactly that rich uncle, and it takes exactly such kids, bright as all heck but not necessarily worldly, and gives them every advantage that education can bestow on those thirsty for the benefit. Conveniently located in the middle of nowhere in western Pennsylvania, The Robert E. Cook Honors College is part of the Indiana University of Pennsylvania (IUP) in Indiana, Pennsylvania. It is the brainchild of Robert Cook, "the rich uncle" and an alumnus of IUP, and Janet Goebel, "the governess" and IUP faculty member who is now director of the Honors College.

The thing to realize about the Cook Honors College is that it is designed, right down to the magazines on the tables and the wallpaper on the walls, to foster a life of intellectualism and culture. Many colleges have "honors classes" or an "honors program." Don't mistake an "honors program" for the Cook Honors College. First of all, this is a residential immersion program. All freshmen and most sophomores live in the dorm, which is a world apart from the rest of IUP and its remote surroundings.

Paintings cover every wall, well-stocked bookshelves line every common room, sculptures and antiques and tapestries are just everywhere, and most amazing of all is it's all available for you to touch, pick up, admire, inspect, or rearrange for a different silhouette. The classrooms, the dorm, the great hall, and the administrative offices are all mixed together in the same building. The college has two kitchens,

You can't be anonymous here.

and the students often make meals here family style (as well as partake of the university's dining hall across the street). There are many study salons, where students can study and gather to talk.

While I was on tour, I noted that on a single coffee table were *The Congressional Record No. 114-Part II*, *The New York Times Review of Books*, *The Economist*, *Opportunities for the Academic Year Abroad*, *The Tunnel* by William H. Gass, and *Infinite Jest* by David Foster Wallace. At the reception desk was a three-foot tall stack of the

THE REAL TRUTH ABOUT THE COOK HONORS COLLEGE

Q. What should a prospective student know about your program?

A. That this is an extremely nurturing place, where people will find out who you really are and help you to become the best person you can be. We try to spoil our students. We work at it. We demand a lot from them, but then we're going to take care of them in return. We took some students to Vienna last year, and through personal connections we were able to have some of our musicians play on one of Beethoven's pianos. Imagine that. These are the kind of life experiences that we strive to provide. This goes way beyond the curriculum or the reading list. And what we're *not* looking for are cynics or nihilists. We're looking for kids who are hungry, who will see what we're trying to offer here, and go for it. This is not a school with a parking lot full of BMWs, where the students run off to the Caribbean for spring break, and where your roommate is spending more to board her horses than your parents make. This is, however, a place where you can be a scholar in a community of scholars, where the people you go to class with are the ones you hang out with, where the professors have high expectations, where we listen to your input on how this place is run. If this sounds right to you, then we'd love to hear from you.

Q. Who would be unhappy here?

A. Someone who doesn't want to work. Someone who likes things really clean cut. Someone who brings a full set of opinions with them, but doesn't want to put them on the table. A whiner.

current day's *New York Times,* one for each and every student in the college. Two students were in the great hall playing chess next to a Roman bust, while another walked by with a tray of cookies he'd just made in the kitchen. All three were barefoot, since this was also their dorm.

In the women's rest room I counted thirty-four different paintings, all images of women. (The men's room wasn't nearly as interesting, with some moody art shots of staircases.) There is a lightheartedness to the decor and the program, as well, which makes it seem inviting and fun and unintimidating. For example, one classroom is decorated with sixty-three paintings all related to the Arthurian legends. It's absolutely lyrical. In another classroom, a little knight in armor guards the door. One gets the impression that all this is not to be taken too seriously.

So, maybe by now you're saying to yourself, "Enough with the interior decorating, already. What's the curriculum like?"

The Cook Honors College has an innovative core curriculum. The core courses bring an integrated, cross-disciplinary approach to "Great Questions." The program is designed to hone critical thinking skills while providing a survey of the important writings in several disciplines. And, in a rather old-fashioned way, the curriculum means to impart a moral education, one of the goals of the college experience for hundreds of years before the "training school" and "smorgasbord" trends took root. (It is not at all designed to tell you your moral obligations, but is designed to get you to discover and develop your own thinking on such matters.)

The core courses are in the process of being expanded and revised right now with heavy student input. At the time this book went to press, here were the core units:

Unit A: "What do we know? What do we believe? What, therefore, should I do?"

Unit B: "What is good. What is evil? What, therefore, should I do?"

Unit C: "What is art? What, therefore, should I do?"

> **The application to the university was like a page. The application to the Honors College was like a book. Totally different. You definitely couldn't just photocopy an essay from some other application.**
>
> —*Cook Honors College student*

The most interesting thing the director said to me at the Robert E. Cook Honors College of IUP: "Anyone could do this. Dorms are remodeled every year at any university. Professors would be teaching classes anyway." "What about the decor?," I asked. "Surely it cost a fortune." "No way," she said. "We did all this on the cheap. All the paintings are prints, everything else is a reproduction, and the students hung the wallpaper." I guess you just have to know which reproductions to get, which professors to select, and which innovative curriculum to develop. Somehow I think there's a little more to it than just hijacking a dorm.

Unit D: "What is history? What, therefore, should I do?"

Unit E: "How do we understand the sacred?"

Unit F: "Must the need for social order conflict with personal liberty?"

Each semester, students write a major paper that is peer-reviewed through four revisions. This fosters close interaction, critical thinking, communication skills, mastery of the English language, and cooperation rather than competition among the students. This is, without a doubt, the beginning of one of the most cutting-edge curricula in North America. It is possible that the school will expand the core sequence to eight, one for every semester of a four-year undergraduate program, but that is not certain.

One good thing about the Cook program is that it is attached to a university. You can be in the honors program and pursue any major the university offers, from business to art to anthropology. One bad thing about the Cook program is that it is attached to a university. Once you get used to being an involved and engaged stu-

---

TRUMAN STATE UNIVERSITY

How important is visionary leadership in an academic setting? In 1970, when Charles J. McClain became president of Northeast Missouri State University, it was just another state university in Missouri. In fact, they joked about it being so obscure it wasn't just a directional university—generally not a sign of a distinguished institution—it was a *bi*directional university! But President McClain had the vision and the power and the persuasiveness and the stamina to create something special. So he installed what he called "outcome objectives," actual measurements of pedagogical performance, which he captured and analyzed by department. In plain English, he decided to "measure if learning was really going on here." Then he sold it to the faculty, which was the first miracle. Then he decided there was no honor in being all things to all people, and got NEMSU's mission changed to "the liberal arts school in the Missouri state system." That was the second miracle. Then he went up and down the state telling anyone who would listen that NEMSU was the best place for the brightest and most inquisitive young people. He preached something like this: "Those other state schools are just fine for the engineers and whatnot, but the best and the brightest belong at NEMSU." (I feel the need to point out that there was no statistical evidence for this position whatsoever.) And by the power of his persuasion, the people of that entire region of the country began to believe that NEMSU was the best school for the brightest and most well prepared. "We don't need to send our children to distant and expensive schools! Dr. McClain and his dedicated teaching faculty are doing a great job right here in our own backyard," people began to say. So, Northeast Missouri State University became, in fact, what President McClain had envisioned: the place for the best and the brightest. In 1995 it was renamed Truman State University, and as a frequent visitor I can vouch that the students and the faculty there are doing some impressive work. Jack Magruder is president now, and he is continuing to build on the legacy of Charles J. McClain, a person with a vision and the leadership ability to actualize it.

dent, it can be rather discouraging to sit in lecture classes where the professor is not accustomed to being challenged, and where the other students only want to know what's going to be on the test.

DOWNSIDE: Although the HC students are always bonded to their core class brethren, some majors dominate student schedules in the upperclass years, which draws students away from the community at the Honors College building. Also, since the dorm is a virtual mansion right in the middle of a university campus, security is tight. If residents can pick up everything in the building, so could thieves. And, once again, it is important to remember that students cannot take all their classes at the Honors College, so it is important to be sure that you like the rest of the community, including the curriculum, the professors, the students, and the infrastructure.

MORE UPSIDE: This was the most genuine, unpretentious place I visited. The students were friendly, the staff was gracious, the building was beautiful, the whole thing was like a television show from the fifties. This is not a perfect program or a perfect school, but it is certainly one that is trying to be. And that's worth a lot, all by itself.

Also, check out the essay, "The Big Meeting," on p. 161, by a Cook student.

WARNING: Over two hundred universities claim to have honors colleges or honors programs, but most of them are not like this at all. They are not residential. They do not have an innovative, coherent, sequenced curriculum. They do not have a cultural component. They may or may not have caring staff interested in you as a

---

WHAT GRAD SCHOOL ADMISSIONS OFFICERS LOVE TO SEE ON YOUR APPLICATION

- Research or teaching assistant to professor (paid or unpaid)
- Departmental or subject tutor (college or high school levels)
- Writing center tutor/counselor/coach (especially if you really learned how to do it)
- A *completed* independent study class (incompleted counts less than zero)
- Residence hall advisor/peer counselor (shows maturity, plus you passed screening and training)
- Any extended research project (especially if you write a thesis or capstone paper, and doubly especially if you do a good job)

NOTE: For more on planning now to get into grad school later, read the sections on strategies to gain admission to highly competitive graduate programs in my book, *Graduate Admissions Essays: How to Write Your Way into the Graduate Program of Your Choice* (Ten Speed Press, 2000).

whole person. They may not have handpicked professors. They won't help you pick a semester overseas that you can afford. So what do they have? Slightly more demanding workload and a chance to study in a class with other students more like yourself than the average. In short, they are nothing more nor less than the higher education equivalent of "tracking," placing the smarter kids together. That's not nothing, but it's not like the Cook program at all.

That being said, you can visit the National Collegiate Honors Council at www.runet.edu/~nchc, and click on "Member Institutions," to explore other options. There *are* some good programs out there, working hard to offer elite educational opportunities at bargain prices. While you're at the NCHC Web site, check out the "Characteristics of a Fully-Developed Honors Program," which is interesting in its banality, if nothing else. The single most important factor to look for in a program would be the residential component. Without that, you're really just headed for another anonymous university experience.

The Robert E. Cook Honors College at Indiana University of Pennsylvania
290 Pratt Street
Indiana, PA 15705
724-357-4971
800-487-9122
www.iup.edu/honors/

A COLLEGE OFFICER WRITES ABOUT DISTINCTIVENESS AT A COLLEGE

You are correct that it is extremely difficult to "pin down" the concept of distinctiveness in a college. That is precisely why the mass-market college guides resort to common quantifiable formulae in order to rank colleges. There are some colleges which seem always to leap to mind whenever terms such as "special" or "distinctive" are bandied about, but it is difficult to explain exactly why this is the case. Many of these colleges appear on the list you have supplied.

The problem you have bought with this project is that even faculty and staff who have extensive experience at these institutions sometimes have difficulty explaining what it is that makes their institutions distinctive. I will describe common characteristics which I believe these institutions should share:

A DOMINANT ETHOS: There is an old "professor's tale" in higher education about a distinguished German visitor to an American university. After the visitor was taken on a tour of all the buildings, the laboratories, the classrooms, and after he spoke to many of the students and faculty, the visitor said, "You have shown me all your facilities, and you have allowed me to speak with many of your students and faculty. And I have enjoyed wandering on your lovely grounds. But where is the spirit of your university?"

When you arrive at a campus with a dominant ethos, you can sense it. It permeates every aspect of campus life and goes beyond the physical features of the campus. It can be described as a defining culture, and the very self-descriptive language of the college carries the ethos in its semiotic content. You can see it in the way the students, faculty, and staff speak of the institution, and even when they are complaining about the institution, they somehow do not doubt this ethos but rather the way the ethos is being used or abused. It is a self-defining niche in the grand scheme of higher education. It is the lack of this ethos which is palpable at many of the "diploma mills" which dot our landscape.

A SENSE OF HISTORICAL CONTEXT: A distinctive institution must have a sense of its own place in the history of our culture and in higher education. This does *not* mean that an institution must be old in order to be distinctive. This sense of historical place is precisely what some of the newer colleges on your list are attempting to capture when they design a curriculum focused on the great works or when a predominantly black college designs programs to refocus on its African-American heritage. Without a sense of historical place a college has an incomplete identity.

A REFLECTIVE PHYSICAL PLANT: By this I mean that the physical plant of a college should reflect its ethos and historical place. I was recently at [a large university in the Southwest] and was struck by an interesting paradox along these lines. My tour guide proudly showed me two structures. One was a magnificent fine arts center designed by [a famous architect]. The building itself was remarkable, and yet when I pressed the guide on how the building fit into the heritage of the school, he was unable to make any meaningful connection. Then, only two minutes later, I was shown the new library which was built mostly underground. As part of the guide's automatic spiel, I was told how the architecture emulated a desert arroyo and how the landscaping and materials were reflective of the desert Southwest heritage. This is what I mean by a reflective physical plant. When asked to think of great examples of this, we readily think of the Cloisters at Mr. Jefferson's University of

Virginia or the eating clubs at Princeton. I, of course, immediately think of the neo-Gothic architecture of my own institution.

AN APPROPRIATE CURRICULUM: The college curriculum must reflect the ethos and historical place of the institution. In other words, the curriculum must "fit" the institution. What would St. John's at Annapolis be without its Great Books curriculum or West Point without its vocationally oriented technological curriculum and its cocurricular military programs, or Antioch without its humanistic/revisionist curriculum? The day Princeton or Harvard injects remedial education into their curricula is the day they cease to be Princeton or Harvard.

These comments are not comprehensive but do include criteria I feel are necessary for a college to be considered distinctive. The proof is in the living, not in the telling.

ON COLLEGE COUNSELING FOR THE INTELLECTUAL STUDENT

by Laura J. Clark

College Counseling Office

Ethical Culture Fieldston School

Bronx, New York

This is the text of a talk delivered at an annual convention of the National Association for College Admission Counseling (NACAC). It was intended for those inside the profession who work with high school students on a daily basis and are passionately concerned with placing them in suitable institutions of higher learning, but it also may be of great interest to parents and students who are interested in how these particular students are matched to (we hope) the right institutions.

Often intellectually advanced students are not recognized as a challenge by counseling professionals in the college placement process, either because they are self-sufficient and not well known or because they will get in wherever they apply. This is a mistake, since for these students an appropriate match, both academically and socially, is extremely important.

The first step is identifying the young intellectual, the student for whom the life of the mind is of paramount importance. Though grades and scores indicate some ability, sometimes the most "intellectual" students do not have a perfect numerical record. Frequently high school academics bore them and they can feel disconnected from their peers so they don't "show" in traditional measures. Often they have been traumatized by high school social life and their best talents may well emerge in what they do on their own, outside the curriculum. They may not be student leaders or star performers in other areas. This can be a problem as well for counselors, parents, and sometimes the students themselves, who may not feel intellectually gifted. I have tried to adopt an approach with all students that will foster trust and help me to identify the student for whom the life of the mind is of paramount importance.

To this end, in a first meeting with the family I ask students who their friends are, what they do for fun, and what they don't like about high school. (The parents are always *very* interested in this—I am sure to ask the students again later, without the parents, so they can tell me what they left out the first time.) I also ask to see artwork if they have made any, and an academic paper they are proud of. Sometimes art, theater, and music programs become a safe haven for intellectuals, since the students interested in these pursuits are often more socially tolerant of students who may not fit in.

Parental input also helps to form a clearer picture of the student. I ask them to write a letter specifically describing how their child learns best. In some cases, however, this letter tells me more about the parents. The therapist who talks about the "five salient personality traits" and the mother who writes in thirty-five different ways "I love my son" on flowered stationery give me insight into the student's support network at home, and thus into the student.

I also ask the teachers of the junior class for a list of their most interesting students and for information on how these students learn best to discover which students think originally in the classroom and on paper. The college match for these highly motivated students is crucial. Most importantly, high selectivity at the college level does not necessarily indicate an appropriate match for a bright student. It may indicate a reasonably bright student body, but selectivity does not predict social comfort, an intellectual atmosphere, an appropriate curriculum or professor availability.

I remember one student who was always trying to create independent study projects, with any teacher who would support him, on everything from Asian frogs to jazz in the thirties. No surprise that he loved his time at Hampshire College. I had another extremely bright student who was so shy that during one college interview he rolled his T-shirt up until it was collected under his arms and then used it to mop his brow. He found academic heaven in the large lecture halls of a big state university's math department, where no one called on him, ever, and he was free to think without fear of interruption.

It is important to be able to predict this sort of thing. Questions to ask both teachers and students might be:

- Is the teacher's personality the thing that excites the student so that small classes are imperative?
- Does she need a core curriculum to structure her study?
- Is this a student who can tolerate a fraternity/sorority system, or are other social options a better idea?

Through this process the student begins to know him or herself and the parents begin to see who their child is. If these discussions are exhaustive it helps a great deal later on when trying to get past some of the stereotypes about "intellectual" environments that rankings and the media in general produce.

The problems which emerge as students research college choices are obvious to all of us. Students are inundated with newspaper articles, brochures and documents, most of which don't speak to them and some of which actually mislead them. Many commercially published general guidebooks encourage misleading stereotypical judgements about campus life. Some colleges have "no social life," are "party schools," or "encourage hallucinogens." Try convincing even the hippest parent that one of your favorite small colleges for brilliant students is a great place for her child after that comes out in print!

Rankings are clearly influential and often lead even very bright students to conclusions that have far more to do with prestige than academic aspects related to their own learning styles. A breath of fresh air came for me last week when one of my best students asked me what could have changed enough in one year for a college to move from #42 to #12 in the *U.S. News and World Report* rankings.

Most printed information seems to encourage students to stereotype colleges based on small "bites" that have no texture. It is the counselor's job to cut through this and help the student find the truth. Counselors also must be careful, by the way, not to stereotype the students in the same way: "He's a real (fill in the college name) type." Our brightest students need to do a special type of research and we, as educators, have to make sure that they do it. All colleges are not right for all students and we are not doing our jobs if we become merely distributors of leaflets, keepers of records, and spin-doctors.

I keep a list of former students willing to host on Friday and Saturday nights; my most intellectual students need to look at social life to find out what there is to do and talk about when much of the college population is drinking beer. I have another list of students at college who will take visiting students to class with them and talk to prospectives on the telephone. Students should visit courses in the disciplines that interest them. I remember one science student who visited small humanities classes recommended by admissions at one university and loved them enough to enroll. When he began to attend his freshman science and math courses, he was shocked to find they were 200- to 400-student lecture classes.

I also have accumulated the names of a number of professors who like to talk to prospective students. I'll never forget when I was still in admissions taking one of my favorite physics recruits interested in astronomy down to meet the expert in string theory at Princeton. I watched them "talk" to each other in numbers on blackboards for forty-five minutes. The student's comment when we left: "That was great." I had had no idea what was going on at the time.

It is also important to make sure the Nobel laureates and Pulitzer novelists so attractive to voracious readers and researchers really teach undergraduates. The young intellectual may also want graduate courses as a junior or senior, independent research with professors, and special programs that link courses like the Structured Liberal Education program at Stanford, the Honors College at Michigan, and Saint John's entire curriculum. Some students need special major programs, like one unusual environmental expert who wanted a major in waste management. It is also worth considering that a student like this may have "focused" her interests in high school to feel socially secure, to give herself an area of expertise that no one can assail. We need to be sure she realizes what else is out there, too.

My students taught me something about bashing stereotypes and breaking the media code—it is difficult! Last year one of my students methodically visited only colleges with "poor social life" ratings in the college guides. His list grew to include seven of them when he found "no social life" tended to mean sitting around talking about books and listening to music. Public relations efforts can mystify rather than clarify as students try to cut through to the truth. In a fervor to lure more attractive applicants, colleges represent themselves as both more selective than they are, and as having all things for all students.

That student and his girlfriend also worried, when an article came out in the *New York Times* about University of Chicago being in short, "a fun place after all," that maybe it was not in fact as intellectual as it seemed, or that the administration was trying to change its focus on academic life in some way. Another student asked me if the huge number of brochures that arrived from [a major university] meant that the college was having trouble filling its freshman class, or was not so strong academically as it once had been.

The word "pressure" in guidebooks, usually seen as a negative, can mean "stimulation" for students with certain learning styles. One of my students asked for a place where kids "cared enough to compete."

As an aside, admissions work is an exhausting job, demanding passionate dedication, long hours of isolation on the road and reading files for relatively low pay; no wonder admissions offices have trouble keeping experienced and knowledgeable personnel for any length of time. In-depth knowledge of an institution—both the college and the high school—takes time; if they go to high schools, most admissions officers visit four to six a day, for forty or fifty minutes each. This sort of presentation encourages the sound bite. Because time constrains both class periods and their own schedules, it is near impossible for them to address individual questions in depth, give a deep and individualized picture of their institution, or get to know the students in their audience.

There is also the danger of the students equating the personality of the admissions representative with the personality of the college, misleading at best. Last year the Haverford College representative to our school was so charismatic that every student who attended his presentation wanted to apply because they liked him. Probably not the most sensible reason to choose a college, though Haverford is a fine institution. Some admissions personnel use these trips to get to know the school instead, and educate me so I can pass on the information to the appropriate students. This seems to work well. Of course, many high schools are not on the "visiting trail" for one reason or another, and colleges are beginning to doubt the efficacy of this use of personnel, since Web pages and brochures can do much of what these whirlwind tours can.

Some colleges seem to have mastered the way to approach the young intellectual. These colleges know themselves and are not afraid not to be all things to all people. In a survey I handed out to my "intellectual" students attending college, they chose, among others, Colgate, Harvard, Hampshire, Macalester, University of California at Santa Cruz, Bard, Kenyon, University of Chicago, Johns Hopkins, Oberlin, Union, McGill, and the University of Wisconsin at Madison as some of the colleges who "were most honest" in their public relations. Altogether these represent an eclectic list. Students told me that these places had put them in touch with professors to talk to and sent them to a wide variety of classes. They had been honest about the social life and intellectual rigor in their mailings, and sent them selected brochures about special programs that showed they had looked carefully at the students' applications.

In several cases, the students had spoken to or e-mailed admissions personnel and received real and thought-provoking answers to their questions rather than what they felt was standard public relations. One admission officer admitted to a student during a recruiting function that his college probably did not have the best academic program for that student. The student was grateful and considered attending that college simply because the admission officer was so honest.

There is nothing more liberating than when a really bright student can find her element. One student I worried desperately about in high school because he had no friends, though he was fiercely interested and interesting, e-mailed me last week. "I'm popular here," he said. "I can't believe it. People here like me. No one thought it was weird when my roommate and I spent all night making an alarm clock out of the contents of the hallway trash can!"

A few words about presenting students to a college. I tell my students that admissions officers are not the IRS or the House Judiciary Committee. I tell them the application should be fun and interesting to fill out, that they should feel they risked something, and that it could make them laugh. I tell them to list *all* the ways they spend their time, including reading books, going to films, etc., and say how long they spend doing each activity. Many of my most intellectual students don't have lots of organized activities. It isn't necessary to have them, but they need to say what they *do* do with their time.

I also tell them if there is something the application doesn't ask for that they want to say, put it in. I spend time with our teachers talking about being clear on paper about our brightest kids, I try to do it myself, and I try to let admissions know in one way or another, who the special ones are. Many teachers, particularly in math and science, think that grades tell the whole story, and spend their letters telling what a nice person the student is, or, how the student seems "nerdy" and cut off from his/her peers. I remember a discussion I had with a science teacher who told me how one of her students had drawn a completely original conclusion from an experiment. She later showed me her college letter, which detailed only the student's extracurricular activities.

I try to review the student's entire file, if I can, to see if it gives a complete picture. If it does not, I may ask for an extra letter of reference, enclose an English paper I have seen, or ask the student to document something else.

Content of student essays is so important for these particular students, far more, I think, than grammatical accuracy. One of the best essays I ever read I saw when I was at Princeton in admissions—a one-sentence stream of consciousness piece on race relations in Los Angeles. I could tell from the rest of the application that the student was traditionally articulate, but it was this risky piece that packed the intellectual punch.

There are also a few brilliant students I have worked with who have represented a "hunch" for the admissions dean who accepted them. These successes have been the result of searingly honest phone conversations with people who have been kind enough to trust me about kids who didn't show their stuff in traditional ways. This is not the norm, but many of these kids are the ones I was most excited about and for whom the rewards of an intellectual environment were immense. It may seem obvious, but developing relationships with admissions colleagues around these issues teaches us what is available and can, occasionally, really help us place our students intelligently. It has also helped me immensely in these conversations to be a classroom teacher. I often have seen these kids in action and it keeps me thinking about what college professors need.

There is often a huge gap between what counselors and admissions professionals know and even the best-educated world assumes. For a little while my teaching and my admissions career overlapped at the same institution. I remember vividly a faculty meeting where a professor was ranting on about his two favorite students, two he assumed had high verbal scores on the SAT, since they were so articulate and such good writers. I went back and looked at our files and found that the two students in question had low 600 verbals and that one of the "passive" learners he was complaining about had an 800. He was, of course, blaming admissions for their lack of consistent rigor and was astounded when I set the record straight. Not surprisingly, the two he loved had been admitted primarily based on their grades, essays, and the strength of teacher support. One had had a fabulous creative writing portfolio.

One of my worries is that in a world where rankings determine numbers of applicants and perceived quality, increasing emphasis on testing and grade point averages close doors at some of the places most challenging to young intellectuals. By quantifying and oversimplifying the process of research and of academic evaluation, the media forces colleges to collude with it in order to "sell spaces." Colleges may find themselves compelled to bypass students admissions officers know to be intellectually interesting and dynamic to admit more conventional students who spent time on test preparation, and hounded their teachers for grades.

These students help the rankings and please trustees and college presidents who don't have to teach them. Granted, often the really intellectual student has managed to master the conventional approach as well without really thinking about it, but I find more and more that my most interesting students rebel against the time, money, and energy it takes to prep for SATs and maintain the perfect record. They would rather be reading philosophy, grinding the perfect telescope lens, or taking the intellectual risk that may not get them the A.

The way to get past these problems is to find more accurate and creative means, first, to teach the students about their academic options, then to evaluate those students. Clearly this means a more individualized approach, which in turn means more personnel and more money in an age where great faith has been placed on the computer statistics and mass mailings to deal with an ever-expanding population.

Most high schools don't have the luxury of one counselor for each 50 to 70 students, and most admissions staffs have huge turnover, making the close relationships between counselors and colleges difficult. There are lots of us on both sides struggling to make a difference in this area, but to serve our most intellectual students we need to retrench and redirect some funds to come up with new tactics. In the meantime, students need to take more responsibility for their own destinies, researching more deeply, challenging the process with harder, more thought-provoking questions and applications that represent who they really are, rather than some prepackaged idea of what the colleges want. They need to use both their intuition and common sense to see past rankings, prestige, and empty publicity to analyze what kind of education they will actually receive at the college of their choice. In turn, the colleges need to work to see through to the real student in whatever creative ways are available, rather than relying on statistics and standardized measures.

THE "ROCKET SCIENCE" OF EMPOWERING FACULTY TO TEACH

by Larry D. Large, Ph.D., President, Oglethorpe University, Atlanta, Georgia

Whether a learning institution consists of five instructors with a set curriculum delivered over the Internet to students at remote locations, a thousand instructor/researchers delivering lectures to classes of several hundred students in a lecture hall, or a faculty of fifty to a hundred professors meeting with groups of five to twenty students in an idyllic setting of stone and ivy—whatever the size, the location, and the delivery of instruction might be, the heart and soul of any learning institution is its faculty.

The set of beliefs about learning that are commonly held by the majority of the faculty determine the shape and structure of the curriculum. Those same beliefs influence the hiring of new faculty members, thus perpetuating the commonly accepted model. And beyond the general influence of the majority views of the group, the interests of the individual faculty members influence the particular course offerings at any given time.

Yet while this shaping of the curriculum is a major role of the faculty, the most critical factor in defining a learning institution is the faculty's ability to interact with students. The nature of this interaction in large measure determines the quality of the learning experience.

In the model of learning on the Internet, the student becomes a consumer in every sense of the word, not only because the student is a paying customer, but also because "to consume" is the only possible action open for that student. Such learning is virtually a one-way process. In the large lecture hall setting, the learning process is little different from the Internet mode. The students do share the same physical space, but the professor is a remote figure at a lectern, delivering a message in a stream of one-way communication.

In the best of academic settings, learning takes place in small groups, each consisting of a highly skilled, academically outstanding professor meeting face to face with well-prepared, eager students. In this setting, faculty approach their teaching and learning responsibilities actively, providing information, knowledge, scholarly techniques, and, now and then, even wisdom. Such faculty teach with a level of confidence and of psychological security that facilitates students' learning from one another, and on occasion, such faculty even learn from their students. What a powerful moment occurs for students when a faculty member acknowledges having learned something from a student! The combination of these dynamics—strong and well-prepared students and a well-prepared and secure faculty who are committed to good teaching—is what defines interactive learning. In this ultimate form of learning the student is neither passive nor anonymous, but an active and valued contributor to the learning process. While many types of institutions may try to create such a learning environment, the uniquely American educational institution, the small liberal arts college, is the prototype.

And yet, though this educational setting may in some ways be a time and a place apart, it cannot exist except as a valued part of the world at large. To be specific, this ultimate learning model requires the following three things. First, both students and faculty have to be able to commit sufficient time to learning together. While a few facts can be quickly learned and stored in memory, the process of expanding the ability and capacity to think critically about ideas both old and new—reading, discussing, and assimilating new information and others' ideas into one's own way of thinking and deciding which of those views one wishes to discard and which to make his own—takes an investment of time as well as energy. New ideas must be tried on trusted friends and colleagues, tested for validity in a nurturing environment, and accepted or discarded as a part of the growth process. The process takes time.

In addition to this investment of time on the part of both students and faculty, the institution has to make an investment in resources to support the learning community. Learners need physical space for class meetings, office space for study and research, informal spaces for discussion and thinking, library resources to support further reading and research, technological resources to facilitate communication and additional research, spaces to sleep, eat, and study—and the list could continue. The point is that providing a physical environment where real, interactive learning can happen is an essential component that cannot be shortchanged or bypassed. This environment must provide adequate spaces, yet remain comfortably small enough to be nurturing, not overwhelming.

Finally, because of the necessary investment of time and resources, the institution, the faculty and the students all must have the support of the larger community. This personal, interactive learning model is expensive. Students cannot bear the entire burden of the cost, nor can they make the necessary investment of time if they are constantly worried about how to pay the bills. Students have to have enough resources to buy their own time. The community at large must support them with money and also with a commitment to the value of their education. If the society does not place enough importance on providing a real learning environment to support it financially, not only can the student not afford the financial burden, but students and their families will not be willing to invest their time either. The entire social order—including families, government, business, and philanthropic organizations—must recognize that providing faculty and students with the time, the space and the resources they need benefits not only those students and their families, but their communities and the whole of human society for years to come. Students who have experienced a faculty who make them valued colearners will be the thinkers, the doers, the leaders, the citizens who have the intellectual skills required not just to deal with day to day living and working, but to think creatively and act decisively to solve the problems and realize the possibilities of a world we cannot yet imagine.

Thus, the role of faculty today, tomorrow, and always is to empower the learner to realize to the fullest extent his or her own abilities to learn, to think, to act, and to commit all his or her talents to making a unique contribution to the human endeavor.

MIT'S CHARM SCHOOL

During winter session, MIT has a charm school for its famously eggheaded scientists and engineers, covering such subjects as "Walking," "Table Manners," and the all-important "Buttering Up Big Shots." The busiest lobbies on campus are set up like a carnival. Bright yellow banners reading, "Please," "Thank You," and "You're Welcome," are hung from the rafters, while red and white streamers and bows mark off the "Ballroom Dance" instruction area. The Beaver (MIT's mascot), wearing top hat and tails over his costume and carrying a cane, mingles with the crowd throughout the day.

Students entering Charm School choose the booths they wish to attend. A yellow coupon is given to each student who participates in a Charm School "class." If students attend at least six classes, they receive a Charm School Bachelor's Degree. If they attend eight, they receive a Master's and if they attend twelve, they receive a Charm School Ph.D. Charm School is fun, with the Fashion Police giving out neon orange "fashion violations" for such improprieties as being a "walking jewelry store," or "using both straps on a backpack."

Charm School has its own commencement ceremony, and recent guests of honor have included Judith Martin (better known as "Miss Manners"), and Dan Zevin, reporter for *Rolling Stone* and author of the book *Entry-Level Life: A Complete Guide to Masquerading as a Member of the Real World* (Bantam, 1994). The event is accompanied by the music of The Chorallaries, playing Pomp and Circumstance on kazoo.

The event is intended to be humorous, but it has a serious side, too. Every future techie millionaire needs to know "How to Be the Perfect Host," and "How to Deliver News Someone Really Doesn't Want to Hear."

Chapter Four

THE GREAT BOOKS PROGRAMS

Once upon a time all colleges had "Great Books" programs. In other words, scholars everywhere believed that great thought from the past was useful for understanding the present. In the latter half of the last century this fell out of favor, as students clamored for vocational training and more pluralistic points of view. The Great Books programs are dedicated to the theory that great thought, thought that has survived the centuries, is quite relevant to life today. Many of these programs have revised their curricula to allow pluralistic points of view by finding them in the past, not by turning to whatever was written in the paper last week. These programs provide a classical education that will illuminate any life, even a very modern one.

ST. JOHN'S COLLEGE

"the freedom of no choice" • **the curriculum is exactly the same for everybody** • *professors teach across the curriculum* • **profs are called "tutors"** • *professors demonstrate continued learning themselves* • **the most intelligent and the most contrary** • *a Great Books program where intellectualism is the norm—all day, every day* • **one in the East, one in the West**

St. John's College is the Rock of Gibraltar in higher education. It is an institution that ignores every trend, as if it existed on a separate plane altogether. Perhaps it is its own universe, even. St. John's harkens back to the origins of higher education in this country, when faculty set the curriculum and directed students to get to it. St. John's has a pure Great Books program, all the way through. This is not some core curriculum that students get through before they go on to specialize, this is *the entire curriculum.* Students read original works starting with Homer. They learn Greek and Latin and French. They re-create the great experiments from the history of science. They produce Shakespearean plays without updating the language. They study the great problems of math through the minds of the mathematicians who were there.

Not only is the curriculum an anachronism, the students and the faculty and the very atmosphere of the place are as well. For example, the students dress almost neatly, and they are very civil to one another. Broadsides in the student newspaper read like a transcription of a Senate debate, wherein anything might be said but only in the most overly polite manner. Students are taught the art of civility, conversation, and rational discourse in class, and carry this over to their everyday interactions. The main activity here, night and day, is conversation. All students used to learn to waltz, and although that tradition has faded in recent years, it tells a lot about the community's expectations of its members.

St. John's College has no busy work and no pop quizzes. St. John's students are simply expected to do their work for the intrinsic interest of learning from it. There are oral exams, and many papers to write, but few tests. A student here will never see a multiple choice test or learn what a Scantron is. There is no such thing as cheating at St. John's, for the only person to cheat would be oneself.

The faculty are expected to teach across the curriculum, which means that whatever their expertise was when they were hired, they have to learn everything in the curriculum eventually. Faculty study groups are common, both to advance mastery of the curriculum, and to pursue outside interests. This is truly an intellectual community, with the camaraderie of shared experience virtually universal.

In addition to all of the above, each student designs and conducts an independent research project leading to a thesis and public oral defense. The examination also serves as a comp, and St. John's students can be asked a question from any part of their four-year education.

St. John's is famous among academics and virtually unknown elsewhere. In academic circles, a St. John's graduate is a known quantity, and a degree from here is well respected at the best graduate schools. On the other hand, your parents' nosy neighbor may be clueless about what you're up to.

> **An education at St. John's provides students the opportunity first to learn to think well, second, to learn to learn, and third, to learn to apply what they learn to any situation.**
>
> *—St. John's admissions publication*

> # The true University of these days is a collection of books.
>
> *—Thomas Carlyle*

Although St. John's is the third oldest college in the nation (after Harvard and William and Mary), the lockstep Great Books curriculum only dates back to 1937. It was the trough of the Depression, and the college was one step away from closing its doors. Several benefactors convinced the college to reject a watered-down curriculum in favor of becoming a very distinctive academic community. Thus this great institution was reborn as a survival measure. It is secure today, and has been for decades. Although different, it is not really, anymore, experimental.

THE READING LIST FOR FRESHMAN YEAR (PARTIAL)

Aeschylus	Cannizzaro	Herodotus	Nicomachus	Sophocles
Archimedes	Euclid	Homer	Plato	Thucydides
Aristophanes	Euripides	Lavoisier	Plutarch	Virchow
Aristotle	Fahrenheit	Lucretius	Proust	

THE READING LIST FOR SOPHOMORE YEAR (PARTIAL)

Apollonius	Beethoven	Epictetus	Pascal	Shakespeare
Aquinas	Chaucer	Haydn	Plotinus	St. Anselm
Aristotle	Copernicus	Luther	Plutarch	Stravinsky
Augustine	Dante	Machiavelli	Ptolemy	Tacitus
Bach	Descartes	Montaigne	Rabelais	Viète
Bacon	Donne	Mozart	Schubert	Virgil

THE READING LIST FOR JUNIOR YEAR (PARTIAL)

Adam Smith	Eliot	Kepler	Molière	Spinoza
Austen	Galileo	La Fontaine	Mozart	Swift
Bernoulli	Hobbes	La Rochefoucauld	Newton	
Cervantes	Hume	Leibniz	Pascal	
Dedekind	Huygens	Locke	Racine	
Descartes	Kant	Milton	Rousseau	

THE READING LIST FOR SENIOR YEAR (PARTIAL)

Ampère	Einstein	Jay, Hamilton, and	Millikan	Valéry
Baudelaire	Faraday	Madison	Nietzsche	Wagner
Bohr	Faulkner	Kierkegaard	O'Connor	William James
Booker T. Washington	Freud	Lincoln	Rimbaud	Yeats
Conrad	Hardy	Lobachevsky	T. S. Eliot	
Darwin	Hegel	Marx	Tocqueville	
Dostoevsky	Heidegger	Melville	Tolstoy	
DuBois	Heisenberg	Mendel	Twain	

You also need to know that St. John's is not after perfect students, but the most interested students. It will take a chance on students with As and Cs, if they have the curiosity and the eagerness that are hallmarks of a St. John's student. And unlike so many of the colleges we've discussed so far in this book, the workload is not quite so oppressive here. I am sure that some students and faculty at St. John's will vigorously protest this statement, but it is my impression that there is more time for discussion, more time to reflect, than at so many of the schools that we've covered so far. Since the assignments are the same for everybody, there's always someone nearby to discuss whether beauty has utility and whether society has purpose. This is the perfect place for the student who is interested in ideas for their own sake, and for whom the title intellectual is the opposite of scary.

St. John's has two campuses with exactly the same curriculum: one in Annapolis, Maryland, and one in Santa Fe, New Mexico. Technically, they are separate institutions, but they function seamlessly as one. Students and faculty interchange between the East and the West, gaining the flavor of both places. However, you should know that the great croquet game with the United States Naval Academy is only available in Annapolis.

CROSS APPS: If you are interested in the Great Books concept, check out Shimer and, especially but not only if you are Catholic, Thomas Aquinas College in pastoral Ojai, California, (see p. 204) and The Thomas More College of Liberal Arts in Merrimack, New Hampshire. The University of Chicago and Reed College offer core curricula based on the Great Books concept. If you want to read the books yourself (without the benefit of honing the meaning through lively discourse), *Encyclopaedia Britannica* has compiled a list in *Great Books of the Western World* edited by Mortimer J. Adler (Encyclopedia Brittanica, 1990).

DOWNSIDE: The students at St. John's gain mastery of an intellectual tradition that goes back several thousand years, but they may not know the latest in teenage street fashion or other aspects of contemporary culture. However, the

---

DOES ST. JOHN'S EVER CHANGE?

St. John's curriculum does in fact evolve, just not very fast. It changes on the time scale of a glacier, or perhaps the evolution of a species.

---

students I spoke with didn't care. Basically, the students who are drawn to this curriculum seem not to find any fault with it.

St. John's College
60 College Avenue
Annapolis, MD 21404
410-263-2371
www.sjca.edu

St. John's College
1160 Camino Cruz Blanca
Santa Fe, NM 87501
505-984-6000
www.sjcsf.edu

THE THOMAS MORE COLLEGE OF LIBERAL ARTS

This is one of the smallest colleges in the country, with only seventy students, thirty-five men and thirty-five women. Located in Merrimack, New Hampshire, this school provides a rigorous curriculum in the humanities. It is affiliated with the Catholic faith, but claims to be "dedicated to providing a Catholic education for students of all faiths." All students learn Greek and Latin so they can read texts in their original language. All students study in Rome at the college's Roman campus. All students take the same sequence of core courses at the same time, before branching off into majors in the upper classes. All students belong to one of the most intense academic communities in the country. To learn more, read the description of the college in *Choosing the Right College* by William J. Bennett (Eerdman's, 1998), or call Dr. Kristen S. Kelly, director of admissions, at 603-880-8308, who will have a long talk with you if you want to know what the school has to offer. Web site: www.thomasmore college.edu. The buzz: "This feels like a much bigger school than it is, because there's

Also check out the College of Saint Thomas More in Ft. Worth, Texas, www.cstm.edu.

always someone to discuss your readings with and there's no difference, really, between being in class or not in class. This whole place is a class."

The Thomas More College of Liberal Arts

Six Manchester Street

Merrimack, NH 03054

603-880-8308

www.thomasmorecollege.edu

SHIMER COLLEGE

Shimer College is one of the least-known jewels in higher education today. Working strictly and only from original classical texts, Shimer makes scholars out of all who are willing to be so molded. With a virtual open admission policy, Shimer proves that the curriculum and the faculty make the college, not outstanding entering freshmen. Shimer usually admits around 90 percent of those who apply, but all of those who are admitted will become scholars. The school's admissions documents say, "Once a student has encountered original sources—works often thought to be too difficult for the undergraduate—that student knows that no material is too complex, no subject too arcane to be approached and mastered." Located in Waukegan, Illinois, Shimer has loose affiliations and much philosophical alignment with the University of Chicago. Shimer classes are limited to twelve students or fewer, working directly with a curriculum designed to give students a strong background in the humanities, social sciences, and natural sciences. With a diploma from Shimer, students know they have an education. There would be no doubt about it.

Shimer College

438 North Sheridan Road

Waukegan IL 60079

847-623-8400

www.shimer.edu

RECENT PILOT GREAT BOOKS PROGRAMS

There is a revival of interest in the Great Books canon, as evidenced by new programs at the following institutions:

Wilbur Wright College of the City Colleges of Chicago

University of Wisconsin, Milwaukee, Wisconsin

University of Montevallo, Montevallo, Alabama

Middle Tennessee State University, Murfreesboro, Tennessee

Louisiana State University, Shreveport, Louisiana

Gardner-Webb University, Boiling Springs, North Carolina

Delta State University, Cleveland, Mississippi

Clemson University, Clemson, South Carolina

California Polytechnic State University (Cal Poly),
   San Luis Obispo, California

Bethel College, St. Paul, Minnesota

Austin Peay State University, Clarksville, Tennessee

(*Source:* Chronicle of Higher Education, *19 November 1999*)

Just for the record, a DWEM is a dead, white, European male.

Chapter Five

INNOVATIVE CURRICULA AND SCHEDULES

This chapter covers some of the most innovative and interesting schools in higher education today. Some offer you a chance to design the bulk of your educational process. Many do not have traditional grades. Others offer a chance to combine work and learning into an integrative whole. If you're interested in professors who are more coaches than instructors, then one of these schools may be for you. If you're interested in idealistic campuses that view the global environment as part of their educational purview, then perhaps one is perfect for you. Also, as part of our continuing discussion of the college choice process, there are essays that consider "What is intelligence?" and explore the main reasons some students do not thrive in the traditional educational environment. And you'll also find a discussion about the fairness of the SAT, and some schools that do not require test scores at all.

NEW COLLEGE OF THE UNIVERSITY OF SOUTH FLORIDA

you get to design your education • **small classes** • *a committed teaching faculty* • **the Learning Contract—you negoti-**
ate your efforts in advance • *a private school education at a public school price* • **only for the self-motivated and self-**
directed • *no hand holding here, but all the help you need* • **no grades, but you'll hear what your profs really think**
what's this got to do with a circus magnate? • **596 students: 323 women and 273 men**

New College was founded in 1960 by a small group of educators and civic leaders to address the dissatisfaction they felt with the Northeastern educational establishment, which they felt was promulgating "a collegiate culture that tolerated amateur academics while promoting professional sports."

They founded the college upon four principles, which still guide the college's every action today:

1. A student should be responsible for his or her own education.
2. The best education demands a joint search for learning by exciting teachers and able students.
3. Students' progress should be based on demonstrated competence and real mastery, rather than on the accumulation of grades and credits.
4. Students should have from the outset opportunities to explore in-depth areas of interest to them.

A distinctive feature of the New College program is the Learning Contract. Learning Contracts are agreements developed and negotiated individually between a stu-

> **Most colleges, whatever their roots, have become consumer-driven, offering something for everyone. It becomes difficult to distinguish between them. New College, in contrast, embodies very strong, definitive educational intent.**
>
> *—Administrator*

dent and a faculty member. The student decides which main and ancillary readings to pursue, how many papers to write, and what field or lab work to conduct. At this college, the faculty member's guidance usually consists of paring down the student's ambitions into a coherent project that can be completed sometime during the student's lifetime.

> **People don't come here by accident. The first essay question is "Why New College?"**

CoOl WeB SiTe!

Do you shake in your shoes about having to take all those "tests" that may determine your "eligibility" to get into college? You'll find that in the past several years there has been an ongoing discussion in the educational community about the usefulness of such tests, like the SAT, as a measurement of one's academic abilities. Whether you value the worthiness of these tests or think they are a disgrace of our system, you might want to check out the National Center for Fair and Open Testing (FairTest). They now have a Web site, www.fairtest.org, with news, resources and publications, advocacy support, and fact sheets addressing these issues.

There are currently a fair number of schools that either no longer require the SAT for admission or have limited these requirements to certain cases. Here are a few that do not insist on the SAT, according to FairTest.

Academy of Art College, San Francisco, California

Antioch College, Yellow Springs, Ohio

Bard College, Annandale-on-Hudson, New York

Bates College, Lewiston, Maine

Bowdoin College, Brunswick, Maine

City College of City University of New York (CUNY), Manhattan, New York

College of the Atlantic, Bar Harbor, Maine

Dickinson College, Carlisle, Pennsylvania

Goddard College, Plainfield, Vermont

Golden Gate University, San Francisco, California

Hampshire College, Amherst, Massachusetts

Julliard School, New York, New York

Lewis & Clark College, Portland, Oregon

Muhlenberg College, Allentown, Pennsylvania

New England College, Henniker, New Hampshire

Prescott College, Prescott, Arizona

San Francisco State University, San Francisco, California

Shimer College, Waukegan, Illinois

St. John's College, Annapolis, Maryland

St. John's College, Santa Fe, New Mexico

Wheaton College, Norton, Massachusetts

If you'd like to take a look at the whole list (including schools that still require the scores but have reduced their role in the admissions decision), check out: www.fairtest.org/optinit.htm. Perhaps you won't have to go through a night of no sleep and three hours of sweating after all. But before you blow off the SAT completely, be sure to check with the admissions offices of those colleges you are applying to. Policies change annually, and you don't want to realize too late that you've overlooked a required piece of your application.

The school is strong in the sciences as well as all areas of the humanities, and just completed the addition of a major science building. As you would expect, students have access twenty-four hours a day, everyday.

Students here participate in regular seminar classes, but a big part of the New College education is designed and conducted by the student independent of the

IS THE SAT REALLY FAIR?

Check out these data.

AVERAGE SAT SCORES AS A FACTOR OF FAMILY INCOME:

Income	SAT verbal	SAT math	combined
More than $100,000	559	571	1,130
$80,000–$99,999	539	543	1,082
$70,000–$79,999	527	531	1,058
$60,000–$69,999	520	523	1,043
$50,000–$59,999	514	514	1,030
$40,000–$49,999	505	506	1,011
$30,000–$39,999	493	493	986
$20,000–$29,999	476	478	954
$10,000–$19,999	449	458	907
Less than $9,999	427	444	871

AVERAGE SAT SCORES AS A FACTOR OF RACE:

Race	SAT verbal	SAT math	combined
Asian, Asian-American	498	560	1,058
White	527	528	1,055
American Indian	484	481	965
Hispanic, Latino	463	464	927
Black	434	422	856

(Source: Educational Testing Service)

classroom workflow. Every student completes three significant independent study projects (one of the undergraduate experiences that graduate schools favor the most). All students plan and conduct a yearlong research project leading to writing a thesis. They defend their theses in public oral baccalaureate examinations, at which no question is barred. (*The* undergraduate experience that graduate schools favor most.) The school offers twenty-one majors, which it calls disciplines, but the truth is you can design any major you want if you can find a faculty member to collaborate with you. The theses that I read here were some of the best I've ever seen by undergraduates. Many represented serious, original scholarship by undergraduates. Here are but a few titles:

Rigidity Theorems Involving Principal Curvature

Theory of Justice in Ancient Law Codes

The Significant Pleasures of Roland Barthes: From Structuralism to Post-Structuralism through Political Myths

The Eyes of Fishes: Ganglion Cell Densities in the Retina of the Teleost-Holocentrus Rufus

Comparison of Forest Floor and Canopy Humus in a Costa Rican Cloud Forest: Seasonal Fluctuations in Soil Moisture and Effects on Nitrogen Cycling

Sea Level Rise in Southwest Florida: An Economic Benefit-Cost Analysis of Policy Alternatives

Children's Eyewitness Testimony: The Effects of Narrative Style on Adult Perceptions of Credibility

No visit to the college would be complete without taking significant time to look at some of these theses in the library.

> **Faculty serve as facilitators and mentors rather than as purveyors of information.**
>
> —New College student

How important is climate to you? Top students spend a lot of time in libraries and labs, and air conditioning and heating are pretty similar at all latitudes and elevations. You might really enjoy going to school where the weather is more than a casual conversation topic. For example, Michigan Tech in Houghton, Michigan, has its own ski run, the steepest in the Midwest, Mont Ripley Ski Hill. Students build giant snow and ice sculptures for Winter Carnival, and they last the rest of the winter. They also have sled dog races, with a twist: Teams of students pull dogs in sleds on a race course. Whether this is fascinating or horrifying to you, just remember, in the library it's 68 to 72 degrees Fahrenheit all over North America.

The college also offers competitive grants. Students without the financial means to pursue exotic interests can compete for grant money to fund their research.

New College is well known among academics, though little known outside of academic circles. If New College students do a credible job on their classes and their theses, admission to graduate school should be a snap. Alumni have attended over sixty graduate programs from coast to coast, including virtually all of the A-list schools.

The campus itself is a special added benefit. It is right on the shore of Sarasota Bay, on the grounds of the estate of Charles Ringling, the business manager brother of the Ringling Brothers, Barnum and Baily Circus. It has taken over several marble mansions that were built by monies from The Greatest Show on Earth. Next door is the John and Mabel Ringling Art Museum, an impressive collection. New College is affiliated with the University of South Florida, but there is little interaction between the schools that would matter to a student. The University of South Florida and New College merged in 1975 to keep the college from financial disaster. It is one of the only working relationships in the United States between an independent-minded and innovative academic program and a public institution. The University provides stability to New College, and New College provides bragging rights to the Florida state university system. It seems to be working.

New College has no grades, instead using a narrative evaluation that faculty give to each and every student they teach or advise. (For more schools that de-emphasize grades, see p. 137.)

On the facing page a sample narrative evaluation. The collection of these becomes, in fact, the student's transcript. When graduate schools receive these records, they have to take the time to actually look at the candidates. They cannot reduce them to a number and plug it into a formula. The real advantage, however, is to the students, who get feedback on what their strengths are and how they can improve as a scholar. Wouldn't you rather get one of these than an A? An A is a single letter, entered on some spreadsheet in a registrar's computer program by the stroke of a single key. Perhaps neither the professor—nor the registrar—nor even the student-thinks one minute about that grade. This, on the other hand, is a communication of real value and integrity.

Student: Nancy Adams

Project advisor: Dave L. Lawson

Title of the class: Three Works by Friedrich Dürrenmatt in the
German Original

For this project Nancy read in the original German the following
works by Friedrich Dürrenmatt: the dramas *Der Besuch der alten
Dame* and *Die Physiker*, and the novel *Der Richter und sein Henker*.
She also consulted relevant secondary sources and critical material
contained in the Continuum translation of Dürrenmatt's works. As a
final project Nancy submitted two medium-length essays in German,
and one essay in English.

Nancy's first essay on *Die Physiker* showed a good appreciation of
the play's comic and serious aspects. She focused on Dürrenmatt's use
of thematic contrasts and the work's reflection of his dramaturgical
principles. Her second essay on *Der Besuch der alten Dame* utilized
Jean-Paul Sartre's *Huis clos* as a point of departure for an exploration
of Dürrenmatt's representation of the character Ill's acknowledgment
of his guilt and self-induced torment. Nancy correctly noted where
Dürrenmatt and Sartre differ. Both these essays showed a good command of German stylistics for a student with Nancy's background of
three semesters. She had clearly worked hard to locate good equiva-
lents for abstract English expressions, and she avoided fundamental
slips. To be sure, Nancy did not always locate the correct terms, and
several errors in hypotactic structure and related mistakes did occur.
But this is to be expected at this stage.

Nancy's English essay, "Objects of Concern: Dürrenmatt's Focus on
Justice and Chance," linked *Der Besuch der alten Dame* with *Der
Richter und sein Henker*. Her analysis of the role of chance in both
works was quite effective, particularly with regard to the novel,
where coincidence is a key concept. Nancy also brought up salient features of Dürrenmatt's treatment of justice. Here she noted the important Christian implications of Ill's suffering in *Der Besuch der alten
Dame*, and she also traced the transformation in the town's position

on Ill's "crime." On this point I would have liked to have seen more analysis of the process which the townspeople undergo as they abandon Ill and then "justify" his "execution" in the name of the very "Western values" they had invoked when they initially rejected Claire's offer of money in exchange for Ill's life. In her analysis of justice in *Der Richter und sein Henker*, Nancy recognized the ambiguity of Bärlach's moral position with respect to Gastmann and the legal form of justice the latter had successfully evaded. Her writing was clear and careful, and her argument was supported with relevant textual references.

Nancy's work for this project was very good. She learned a lot about Dürrenmatt and enhanced her active and passive command of German in the process.

DOWNSIDE: New College is quite small, and you have to make your opportunities. If you're looking for a sequence of classes you can pick out of a catalog, you're not going to like New College. Many of the students spend significant amounts of time working alone on projects unique to their own interests, which actually cuts down on the academic community aspect of the school, despite its small size. Since faculty members spend so much time in one-on-one academic "coaching,"

CoOl BoOk AlErT!

This Way Out: A Guide to Alternatives to Traditional College Education in the United States, Europe, and the Third World by John Coyne and Tom Hebert (Dutton, 1972)

This is a fascinating book, not only for the hundreds of colleges and programs that it describes but also as a period piece. It is one of a rash of irreverent, counterculture college guides that came out in the late '60s, early '70s. It's long out of print, but a cult favorite among college admissions deans and ex-hippie college counselors. I stole my copy from Audrey Smith at Hampshire College, swearing I would mail it back as soon as I read it. That was eight years ago. If you can find a copy, it's worth a trip to the copier machine. Sample: "Visually there is little difference between the freaks and the hippies, though at Goddard we noticed hostility between them. The freaks talked disparagingly about the hippies tinkling bells over brown rice, and dumped on the commune living. The freak is a private person who has taken from the hippie's counter-culture his dress, style of life, flexibility and is using the college to gain skills." Wow.

some of the seminar classes are actually surprisingly large for the size of the school. Finally, applicants must really ask themselves, "Am I self-motivated enough to run my own study programs?" The school warns: "We have found that students who attend college largely because all of their friends are doing so, or because no other alternatives seem open to them, lack the day-to-day motivation necessary to exploit learning opportunities available at New College." They are not kidding. Some students attracted to the experiential aspects of New College fail to realize that all learning here needs to be tied to a sound theoretical approach involving abstract and reflective thought. Activity without thought will result in failure at New College.

MORE UPSIDE: The faculty and staff that I have met at New College have all been completely engaged and committed. I can name no other place I visited where so much care was afforded the students by the faculty. Everyone here seems to realize that they're involved in a noble endeavor, something special, uncommon, and even precious.

CROSS APPS: New College is pretty unusual, but one place like it is the Johnston Center for Integrative Studies at the University of Redlands in Redlands, California. If you're interested in writing a thesis, check out Reed, Davidson, and Princeton, among many others. You may be interested in Prescott College, which has learning contracts, narrative evaluations, and extensive self-designed study blocks (see p. 138). Prescott is a very different school, however, and a different type of student would be happy there than at New College. Hampshire College and The Evergreen State College use learning contracts as well. These comparisons conceal major differences between New College and all these referenced institutions, however, so investigate the differences as well as the similarities.

New College of the University of South Florida
5700 North Tamiami Trail
Sarasota, Florida 34243-2197
941-359-4269
ncadmissions@sar.usf.edu
www.newcollege.usf.edu

HAMPSHIRE COLLEGE

the freedom to design your own program • **a liberal student body with a global perspective** • *saving the world is okay, even expected* • **being creative is okay, even expected** • *community service requirement* • **no grades per se, but narrative evaluations** • *learning contracts* • **extensive self-designed study blocks** • *it pays to be a self-starter* • **also welcomes nontraditional students who are ready to make a total commitment to their undergraduate education** • *1,160 students: 44% male, 56% female*

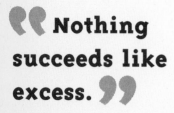

Nothing succeeds like excess.

—Oscar Wilde

Hampshire College doesn't do anything halfway. I asked them to send me some basic information on their program, and I received an eight-inch stack of materials. That's how Hampshire works. If you are someone who has always had more ideas than time to do them, more energy than anyone you know, more creativity than was ever required by the situation, then Hampshire could be for you.

Hampshire is a college of action, for people of action. Its motto is *non satis scire*, which means "To know is not enough." If memorizing and passing tests are your gig, Hampshire is not. If you want to be engaged by integrating your studies with the world around you, Hampshire might be just right.

Hampshire used to be known as "that school in Amherst where you can get a degree in Frisbee." People thought you could go to Hampshire and just do whatever you pleased. But that's old news. The college is maturing, evolving, and improving. Hampshire has distribution requirements (required courses) now, and a coherent approach to learning across the curriculum. Students are required to complete a mix of basic studies (Division I) within the first two years, then pursue a concentration to the level of mastery satisfactory to their advisor (Division II), then complete advanced studies, which is a major self-designed project (Division III). "Each Hampshire student's intellectual or artistic vision culminates in a substantial independent project—an academic or research thesis, a scientific experiment, a film, an art exhibition, an original invention, or a project in theatre, music, or dance."

Students learn to initiate, plan, conduct, and finish projects in each class, as they prepare for greater personal responsibility for their own learning process. By the time students are doing Division III work, they are prepared. Hampshire doesn't have departments; it has schools: Cognitive Science; Humanities, Arts, and Cultural Studies; Interdisciplinary Arts; Natural Science; and Social Science. This reduces "compartmentalizing" of academic exploration, and allows students to approach any issue from multiple angles. There are no grades at Hampshire; students receive narrative evaluations on their performance in the past, with suggestions on preparing for future academic objectives. At Hampshire, the faculty believe that giving students an A may keep them from doing their best work.

Hampshire students benefit from a consortium of Amherst-area schools, all allowing cross-registration for classes and open participation in many (but not all) student activities. The consortium consists of Hampshire, Amherst, Mount Holyoke, Smith, and the University of Massachusetts, allowing local access to 6,500 courses without paying extra. This is a key part of the Hampshire program as students pursue Division II concentrations. Amherst itself is a quintessential New England town, dominated by the colleges, with a coffee-house-and-poetry-reading flavor. Emily Dickinson is from here, and everyone goes by her house on their first visit to Amherst.

DOWNSIDE: Hampshire College is liberal, and if that doesn't appeal to you, you might need to think about that. Being gay is no problem, but cooking up a fat steak in the dorm or throwing away perfectly good recyclables may create a scene. Students are sometimes drawn to Hampshire because they want to escape the structure and control of their current learning environments, but escaping from is not a good enough reason to come to Hampshire. You must be *drawn to* the Hampshire program to find a genuine fit. The program is demanding in ways that are not at first

> ## " Imagination is more important than knowledge. "
>
> —*Albert Einstein*

Hampshire has a student club called Basic Character Flaws. And another called Stage Combat. And another one called Mixed Nuts.

---

obvious. You cannot just go through the motions and turn in a certain volume of work. Your work must improve in quality over your time at Hampshire or you will not be allowed to advance to Division III and complete the program. Students who are unhappy at Hampshire are the ones who don't listen when the school says it expects a lot from its students. Finally, as at New College, students are applying themselves to so many different projects that the academic community tends to diverge in the final year. The best way to beat that is to keep living on campus.

MORE UPSIDE: Hampshire College is growing stronger every year, so it's a good horse to bet on. Almost any Hampshire student can identify with Mark Twain's boast, "I never let schooling get in the way of my education." Hampshire alumni become powerful academic citizens. For example, Hampshire alumni have started no fewer than twenty-six graduate programs at other institutions. Hampshire College will not get in the way of your education.

CROSS APPS: If you're interested in the capstone project, check out Kalamazoo College in Kalamazoo, Michigan, as well as New College, Davidson, and Reed, and Prescott College, which is covered later in this chapter. Prescott is in many ways the most similar college to Hampshire, but they are, you guessed it, very, very different. New College has narrative evaluations, student-planned learning, and no grades, but the atmospheres at these two colleges are very different. Visit the school, and you will know if it appeals to you. If you are interested in the liberal student body and social involvement aspects of Hampshire, consider Earlham in Richmond, Indiana.

Hampshire College
893 West Street
Amherst, MA 01002
413-549-4600
www.hampshire.edu

Hampshire College has a working farm. Students can study sustainable agricultural practices on a micromodel basis. The School-to-Farm program brings K-12 students on campus for education in organic farming, global agricultural issues, and sustainable agricultural practices.

WHAT IS INTELLIGENCE?

by Ruby A. Ausbrooks, Ed.D., master teacher and secondary education consultant

Did you ever wonder why everybody thinks the person with an "A" in math is smart, but no one seems to be much impressed with another person's "A" in music or art? Why not? Doesn't achievement in those fields—music or art—require as much attention, evaluation, synthesis, and work as math demands?

What *is* intelligence? What do we mean by *smart*?

The astronomer Carl Sagan believed a long pass by a quarterback to the end zone is an example of a fantastic combination of fine motor skills and applied physics. While maneuvering through a field of shifting obstacles, a quarterback must adjust his throw for direction, speed, distance, and wind vectors. If people can do this extremely well, sports journalists call them brilliant.

There is more than one way of being smart. On some level we always have understood this. We've used descriptive words that illustrated this understanding, phrases such as "talented musician," "wise investor," "witty humorist," or "gifted chess player." British writers seem to have favored "quick" as a necessary criterion of intelligence.

Is intelligence, then, a concept dependent on its context?

Yes. What if we lived in a less technical culture? What if there were no stock markets for the investor, no laboratories for the scientist, no machines for the engineer? Would a chess player have high status in a society of hunters and gatherers? Valuing and nurturing intelligence depends on context.

And no. Outstanding persons would seek other outlets or create new ones. Mathematicians and astronomers looked to the stars. Naturalists became herbalists and healers. Someone in an ancient community built a toy steam engine.

Pacific island navigators have demonstrated ability to cross a trackless ocean, guided by celestial features, currents, and color of the water. Writers have claimed that Columbus carried a spatial awareness inside his head, locating himself by those same celestial features, currents, direction, and sailing time (although, this seems unlikely if he believed he had reached Asia). Columbus and the islanders possessed skills derived from the same kind of intelligence.

If a superior intelligence means better ability to learn, solve problems, make logical judgments, and direct one's actions, we see immediately the problem with such a definition. Examples are all around. What are they thinking, we wonder, the millionaire athlete who murders his girlfriend, or the respected physicist who knowingly risks global annihilation?

The implication is that a person can be smart and dim-witted at the same time. Jimmy Carter is generally rated as one of the most intelligent presidents the U.S. ever had, but he was ineffective as a chief executive. Ronald Reagan is considered by many historians to be one of the great leaders of the last century, but he was certainly near average in classical intelligence.

The concept of intelligence as something to define and measure wasn't even around before 1900. Alfred Binet created for Parisian administrators a test that attempted to measure ability in children. Americans seized the idea of measuring intelligence, and within a few years a test score and a chronological age became the familiar IQ, intelligence quotient.

Few are in agreement about what IQ tests actually measure, except that it probably isn't intelligence. IQ tests have been misused widely. Officials used fear of diluting our national pool of intelligence, whatever that is, to promote restrictive immigration laws. IQ scores became part of personnel files, affecting promotion in business and industry. Schools separated students into college preparatory and vocational tracks.

More recently, the author of a best-selling book offered IQ scores as proof that some racial and ethnic groups are superior to others. One of those superior groups, Asians, was also one of the groups most feared eighty years earlier because they might dilute the national IQ.

Howard Gardner grappled with some of these same problems when he was developing the theory of multiple intelligences which he presented in the book *Frames of Mind: The Theory of Multiple Intelligences* (Basic Books, 1993). Educators greeted Gardner's book with a nation-wide, "Aha!" It was the kind of response that occurs when someone organizes intuitive knowledge and states it in understandable terms.

Like theories on cell biology that appeared before anyone saw inside a mitochondrion, the theory of multiple intelligences was a working model that could be used to understand the present and to investigate the future.

If there is more than one way of being smart, and common sense tells us there is, how does one isolate an intelligence? Neurobiology offers little help; the brain uses many different sites and millions of neurons to process information from one sensory perception.

Gardner drew on biological and anthropological research to answer the question of what intelligence is. He developed several criteria; among the more specific are the following essential characteristics:

An intelligence can exist in the absence of other abilities. Gardner cited instances where brain injury or birth defects damaged other mental capacities while leaving intact outstanding ability in one area, a savant, for example.

If an intelligence is distinct, there will be persons who demonstrate exemplary performance in that intelligence, such as a musical prodigy or a mathematical theorist.

A set of core information-processing functions can be identified with an intelligence.

An intelligence can be destroyed, even though other abilities remain (a condition opposite of that in the first statement; again, true instances were cited).

Gardner initially described seven distinct intelligences:

1. Logical-Mathematical—involves deductive reasoning, detecting patterns, analytical thinking. Persons who exhibit exemplary ability likely will be mathematical theorists or scientists.

2. Linguistic—mastery of language and nuances in the use of words, uses language to interpret and process information. This is the intelligence domain of novelists and poets.

3. Spatial—the ability to create and manipulate images and shapes and to orient objects in space. This is the special intelligence of architects, artists, and some explorers.

4. Musical—involves recognition and understanding of pitches, tones, and rhythms; a dominant musical intelligence interprets the world in these terms, exemplified in great musicians and composers.

5. Bodily-Kinesthetic—mastery of fine motor skills and utilizing physical skills to maximize mental abilities. Outstanding examples are superior athletes and dancers.

6. and 7. Personal—combines two separate intelligences, understanding ourselves (Intrapersonal) and how we relate to others (Interpersonal). Philosophers and essayists, Henry Thoreau, for example, have exceptional ability in intrapersonal intelligence. Charismatic religious leaders, teachers, and politicians may be gifted in interpersonal intelligence.

Gardner expected more distinct intelligences to be identified.

He himself soon added more distinctions. Gardner's eighth intelligence is the naturalist. This is intelligence which notes differences and similarities in plants and animals and the environment, and which appears to recognize interconnections in the natural world. Charles Darwin demonstrated outstanding ability, although it is said that as a young man his mental ability wasn't particularly memorable. Other achievers in this intelligence are the persons admired in colloquial terms as the man or woman with a "green thumb."

Other psychologists, notably, Peter Salovey, a Yale psychologist, Reuven BarOn, an Israeli researcher, and Daniel Goleman, author of *Emotional Intelligence* (Bantam Books, 1997), incorporated part of Gardner's theory of multiple intelligences and placed greater emphasis on emotional development.

Goleman expanded Gardner's idea of a personal intelligence into a sweeping concept—the command of ourselves and how we relate with others make up the set of skills that determines whether or not we succeed in workplace, home, or personal satisfaction.

No intelligence functions alone in a healthy person, and accordingly, Goleman links emotional intelligence closely with kinesthetic intelligence and sensory processing, music, and artistic awareness. In Goleman's view, emotional development is the key to making sound judgements and to nurturing the development of all mental abilities.

It appears now, looking at implications for schools and education, that we have completed a circle—returning to the importance of school climate, attention to emotional development, and a goodness of fit for the student who lives outside the middle of the Bell curve.

SCHOOLS THAT DE-EMPHASIZE GRADES

New College of the University of South Florida has no grades at all. In place of grades, students receive very personal narrative evaluations (see sample on p. 127). The small size of the college, combined with the close interaction with faculty, allows this system to flourish. Faculty and students alike love it. The Johnston Center for Integrative Studies at University of Redlands has a similar system. Prescott College also works very similarly, with a narrative evaluation system. Brown University, certainly one of the best small universities in the world, has grades but students can opt to take a significant number of classes on a credit/no credit basis. Brown students strive to excel in those classes for the sake of learning, not for a grade. (Interestingly, Brown also has no distribution requirements. They trust their students to select a mix of classes appropriate for their aspirations. Amherst and Grinnell also have no distribution requirements.) Reed College has regular grades, recorded in the registrar's office, but not distributed to students. Reed students need to make an appointment with a faculty advisor or the dean of students to discover their grades. Most don't. How do Reed students get feedback? Faculty members write narrative remarks on papers and labs that are then returned to the students. Sarah Lawrence has a similar system. Sarah Lawrence and Reed have the same philosophy as Brown, i.e., students should pursue learning for its own sake and not worry about earning a grade. The University of California, Santa Cruz, had no grades at all until 1997, using instead a narrative evaluation system. Since then, students have had a class-by-class option to choose a grade over evaluations. The majority of students do not choose this option. A vocal minority of the UCSC faculty successfully pushed for grades, arguing that the school has grown too large (11,000 students) to continue what was basically an experiment in the first place, and they should not be required to write so many evaluations for students they "hardly know." Perhaps they revealed more than they intended, but they also took a distinctive and innovative campus and basically screamed, "Hey, there's nothing special here." Many students are furious, but my prediction is that this is one change that sticks.

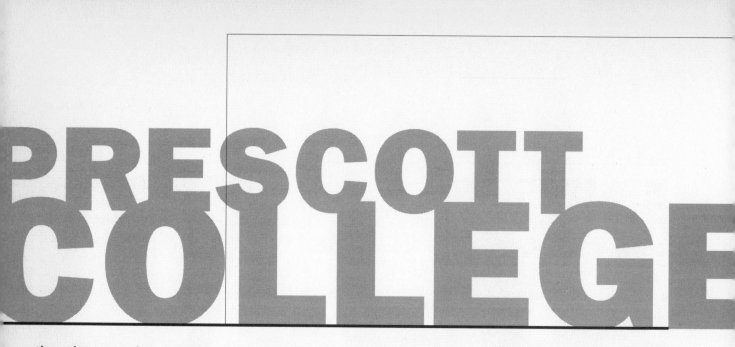

PRESCOTT COLLEGE

the coolest way to learn: outside • **heart, hands, head** • *experiential eco-school* • **the environment, the Great Southwest, and the liberal arts** • *every day is Earth Day* • **where students really matter** • *block system* • **things go way too fast to get bored** • *510 students* • **very small class size** • *50% male, 50% female* • **students come from all over the nation only 6% are from the Southwest**

Prescott College is an "experiential education" school, which means that students learn by doing, going, seeing, hearing, tasting, experimenting, working, thinking, reflecting, and touching as much as they learn from reading and being lectured at. High quality research and scholarship happens at Prescott, but it happens in a very different way than at most other schools.

Although there is a regular core of classes, the point of Prescott is to master self-directed learning. Students design the direction and the methodology of their overall degree program, in close collaboration with their advisors. They enter into contracts of learning, as at New College, and must prove mastery of subject matter to advance. Tests are relatively rare, and multiple choice tests almost unheard of, but papers and direct oral examinations are common. Students receive narrative evaluations of their performance, and letter grades are only entered on the transcript if a student specifically requests it.

The locals pronounce "Prescott" with the same cadence as "biscuit," not with a two-beat "Press Scott," as most outsiders say.

The school uses a novel "block and quarter" trimester. A block is an intensive, four-week long course dedicated to only one subject, and a quarter is an eleven-week period when students can take several classes simultaneously. During block periods, students are expected to be 100 percent available and dedicated to the class. Many classes move off campus, going on-site throughout the Southwest and even in Mexico. With this calendar every class moves along at warp speed, and students are expected to keep up with the academic side of their assignments as they travel, camp, relocate, mesh with local communities, conduct field studies, and otherwise pursue the "experiential" side of their educations.

Prescott is a good place to be an eco-vegetarian. Many students are veggie, and the environment is the point of this college. Prescott College was an early adherent of the outdoor education and adventure education movements, that is, they believe that being in, surviving, exploring, and paying very close attention to the outdoors is educational and character forming in and of itself. All new students spend three weeks in the Wilderness Orientation Program, a program intended to be an acclimation to the ecology of their new home as much as to the institution that they have joined.

> **All genuine learning is active, not passive. It involves the use of the mind, not just the memory. It is a process of discovery in which the student is the main agent, not the teacher.**
>
> —*Mortimer J. Adler in The Paideia Proposal: An Educational Manifesto (Macmillan, 1982)*

The Southwest Is Our Classroom.

Many incoming students are transfers from other institutions, where they may have become disillusioned by an educational process that favored learning meaningless and isolated facts over understanding a world of interlinked systems. Prescott definitely favors the meta-level in everything: the meta-cognitive approach to education, and the meta-view of subject matter. If you come here, you'll never view a fact in isolation again, even when seemingly confronted by one.

The faculty-student interaction at Prescott is different from classroom-based programs. Faculty and students travel and study and research and write and work more closely together than at any other institution in this book. Students are involved in

A Prescott professor of environmental studies has spent twenty years leading safaris in Africa, and Prescott students frequently accompany him on these educational and research-oriented treks.

every aspect of running the college, and their opinions matter. This is an academic community unlike others, perhaps less bookish than others but with more emphasis on community.

How academic is it? As academic as you want to make it. Prescott grads have advanced to graduate study at Cornell, Stanford, Tulane University Law School, Tufts University School of Medicine, Union College, University of Oregon, University of Arizona, Loyola University, and Antioch College, among many others. They have also gone on to thrive in roles as educators, ecologists, conservationists, field biologists, botanists, public policy consultants, museum docents, social workers, authors, storytellers, outdoor guides, kayak instructors, emergency medical technicians, financial consultants, recording engineers, journalists, poets, psychologists, and activists, to name just a few examples.

Throughout the student's Prescott career, he or she builds a learning journal, or portfolio, and students cap their time at Prescott by designing and conducting a major project as a senior. These projects also become the high point in their portfolios. The learning journal is intended to help students tie all their learning experiences together as they occur, to make coherence out of their program as it actually develops. Most courses also require their own portfolio, which is then subsumed into the student's larger collection. The content and nature of portfolios vary widely, according to the college, but may contain course portfolios, personal journals, statements of learning goals and objectives, essays, exams, photographs, maps, drawings, letters, and awards.

COLLEGE OF THE ATLANTIC

College of the Atlantic is a small eco-school at Bar Harbor, on an island close in to the coast of Maine. It offers only one degree: bachelor of arts in human ecology. Small like Marlboro, it uses student-designed curricula like Hampshire, practices participatory democracy like Marlboro, and emphasizes experiential learning like Prescott. And yet is unlike any of them. If you are interested in ecology and want to go to school with other students and a faculty that is dedicated to the same issue, check out College of the Atlantic.

College of the Atlantic • 105 Eden Street • Bar Harbor, Maine 04609
800-528-0025 or 207-228-5015 • inquiry@ecology.coa.edu • www.coa.edu

Here are some sample senior and independent study projects by Prescott College students:

Sacred Earth, Sacred Self: Implementing a National Ecopsychology Conference

Verde Basalt: A Climber's Guide

Socio-Political Survey of Ecuador

Wolf Conservation

Girls' Wilderness Therapy

Nature Conservation in Japan

Native Alaskan Cultural Studies

Siberian Exploratory River Expedition

Storytelling

Health Care in Central America

Interdisciplinary Synthesis: Connecting Photography and Science

Economics of Sustainability

Straw Bale House Design and Construction

Orchard Planning, Design, and Implementation

Embodying the Dream World

Avalanche Forecasting and Snow Dispersal

Prescott College is also home to a NASA-funded Sustainability and Global Change Program, an attempt to use educational outreach to link local community practices to global environmental impacts. The program focuses on such topics as, for example, local causes of global warming and sea-level rise. NASA hopes the program will help disseminate information about the Earth as an interlocked ecosystem.

THE PRESCOTT COLLEGE MISSION

The mission of Prescott College is to educate students of diverse ages and backgrounds to understand, thrive in, and enhance our world community and the environment. We regard learning as a continuing process and strive to provide an education that will enable students to live productive lives of self-fulfillment and service to others. Students are encouraged to think critically and act ethically with sensitivity to both the human community and the biosphere. Our philosophy stresses experiential learning and self-direction within an interdisciplinary curriculum.

Prescott is one of the top five sources of baccalaureate degrees for Native Americans. Prescott students frequently travel to Arizona reservations to gain understanding of Native American spiritual and ecological traditions, and while "on the res" they are expected to assist with farm and herd chores just like everyone else. The college also hosts the Center for Indian Bilingual Teacher Education, an innovative program to develop community teachers with local ties and traditional cultural knowledge to earn the Arizona teaching credential. All Prescott students are eligible to pursue an Arizona teaching credential, either concurrent with their undergraduate studies or after their baccalaureate degree is complete.

The students who are happiest at Prescott are those who revere the out-of-doors but never forget they are at college. Those who don't make it are those who forget that the papers have to be written and the projects finished. This is not a four-year vacation, as students soon find out. The fast pace of Prescott's calendar makes it easy for students to get behind, and those who catch the last bus out of town, so to speak, are usually carrying a load of incompletes.

DOWNSIDE: Prescott College is not wealthy, and cannot afford to sponsor many full-ride scholarship students. There is financial aid, but not as much as is needed. Prescott lacks infrastructure; although it has plans to build it; if you've got to have great big Tudor halls to feel that you're at college, Prescott may not be for you. Also, at the time this book went to press, Prescott College was searching for a new president. With young, small, innovative institutions, a president can have a disproportionate impact on the college, for better or for worse. A new leader may make Prescott better than ever, but I'd inquire about it all the same.

MORE UPSIDE: How many colleges advertise for a president with "a deep personal commitment to the environment"? This is not your everyday college. It's definitely not for everybody, but it may be perfect for you.

MAHATMA GANDHI'S SEVEN SINS

Wealth without work

Pleasure without conscience

Knowledge without character

Commerce without morality

Science without humanity

Worship without sacrifice

Politics without principle

CROSS APPS: If you're interested in other schools where you can design your own curriculum and pursue opportunities for independent study, see Hampshire, Marlboro, and New College.

If you're interested in the small size of Prescott, see Marlboro, New College, and College of the Atlantic, among others. Also see the list of "Smaller Colleges and Universities," p. 22.

If you're interested in Prescott as an eco-school, also check out College of the Atlantic, Green Mountain College, Berry, Unity, and Evergreen.

If you are attracted to building a portfolio of your college experiences, check out Kalamazoo College in Kalamazoo, Michigan, and Wheaton College in Norton, Massachusetts.

Prescott College

220 Grove Avenue

Prescott, AZ 86301

520-778-2090

www.prescott.edu

WHY KIDS AREN'T HAPPY IN TRADITIONAL SCHOOL

by Ruby A. Ausbrooks, Ed.D., master teacher and secondary education consultant

Why does one person sail through schooling while a sister or brother suffers through the grade structure as if each year were a jail sentence?

Why do so many smart people flounder through public school like fish caught in a net? Or accumulate a record of detentions and instant recognition by the principal responsible for discipline?

Even those who discover or create a niche for themselves often hate school. One young woman, now a college junior and who was almost a stereotypical cheerleader and member of the *in* crowd, says her high school years were wasted. She got through it by concentrating on the social life and taking a course load that got her out in three years.

Recent research on individual differences and how we learn allows us to speculate on part of the answers.

> **Gie me ae spark o' Nature's fire, That's a' the learning I desire.**
>
> —*Robert Burns*

Some people have different learning clocks. A student may be ready to read, say, at eight years instead of six—so she spends three years feeling stupid—or she's ready to tackle algebra at ten, but she has to sit through years of stupefying boredom.

Some students have a dominant sense for learning, just as important for dealing with daily life as being right- or left-handed, that doesn't fit the popular mold. We no longer force left-handed people to write with their right hands, but we think nothing of forcing auditory learners, who learn by listening, or kinesthetic persons, who learn by doing, to sit silently for hours with books their only source of instruction.

If we're doing some things wrong, we've been doing them wrong a long, long time. Egyptian papyri bear the copying work of school children: letter forming exercises, lists of nations, phrases of moral instruction. In the archives of Duke University there is a bit of papyrus with margin notes that mention Argos, Troy, and Helen.

An educator friend, whose experience includes both upstate New York and Nevada, points out schools have used many of the same methods for centuries because these methods work. There have been always, he says, students who don't like or fit the system; that's the way people are.

A former high school principal and superintendent of schools in Illinois, Bill Hayes, had this comment, "Schools are very narrow minded and short tempered in dealing with someone who disagrees with the way they have their system set up."

Sometimes, the people who don't like the way things are effect changes when they get their chances. Sometimes, they give up.

For a number of years, I was a teacher, director, and curriculum coordinator in a cooperative high school that served five separate school districts. The students who came to our school were creative, talented, and bright. Some of them were angry. Most had one thing in common—they didn't fit the stereotypes.

Our school had a number of young men and women who suffered from a lack of goodness of fit. When I remember some of them, their individualities stand out like sapphires sparkling in a fuzzy web.

Angela wanted to be an auto mechanic after she graduated, and she was already working through an apprenticeship despite a ton of pressure from her family and friends who insisted that girls didn't repair cars.

Our school had an unusually large number of musicians, so large that for my own satisfaction I did the numbers. According to the statistical software I used, the probability was less than .0005 that, strictly by chance, one school would have so many young men whose tests indicated music as the primary interest in their lives.

People who are born musicians hear music and rhythms in everything around them, the sound of air brakes on a truck, the beat of tires hitting pavement grooves, voices blending in a crowded hallway. These students might thrive in a school where there is as much emphasis on music as there is on sports in the traditional secondary schools. History can be learned through studying and listening to the changes in musical tastes over decades as well as through memorizing data. Playing in a band is the usual compromise.

Stephanie appeared, at first, to fit the stereotype our culture constructs for young women. She was thin to the point that I wanted to grab her and start spoon-feeding her chicken soup. Her long blond hair shined and waved around a thin face that was expertly made up. Her clothes bore the approved labels.

One of the most fascinating things about Stephanie was that through the influence of a former boyfriend she had developed a hobby. She raised goats for showing in competition. Trophies and award ribbons adorned her room at home. This was what consumed her interests and time.

Steve was a talented mechanic who was left in the charge of two older brothers while his parents, both truck drivers, made long-distance runs from ocean to ocean. The brothers, serious burly men who would tolerate no problems from their younger sibling, were the guardians who came to parent conferences. They looked overpowering, tall, scowling, and obviously able to lift tall buildings. I hesitated to say anything that might be used against Steve once the family returned home.

Steve, however, was a real pain in the neck. He hated schools, teachers, "busy work" assignments, persons in authority, a lot of his fellow classmates ("these dumb jerks"), and who knows what else. Steve invented a device that simplified unloading large trucks. A trucking company purchased Steve's invention for a good sum, which Steve used to set himself up in business after he got out of school, and today he is a successful businessman. I doubt that he ever learned to tolerate busy work.

Except for a few magnet or theme schools sprinkled sparingly like exotic spice, traditional high schools are designed to fit no one, although many students do fit well enough that they prosper.

Goodness of fit is a real-world phenomenon that really does matter. There exists somewhere a public high school for performing arts, a school of science and mathematics, a school for creative writers and artists, a school of applied sciences. Somewhere. As yet, none except that for applied sciences is in my neighborhood.

Adults choose, if they can, to work and live among people of similar lifestyles and interests. It makes nights more interesting, mornings more worth getting up for. Artists like access to galleries, musicians to concerts and opportunities to make music with other musicians. Golfers prefer neighborhoods with golf courses. Hikers look for open countryside. Athletes want handy gyms, handball and basketball courts.

Selecting a college is the first opportunity most of us have to find a goodness of fit. College is the single most important leap, outside choosing a life partner, in creating the kind of life we really want. Somewhere is the college that fits our learning styles, personalities, and interests, where there never again need be more square pegs pounded into round holes.

MARLBORO COLLEGE

self-directed study • **on an isolated mountaintop** • *a real community, in the sense of a Swiss village* • **direct democracy** *a strong writing curriculum* • **the opportunity to do a major research project, but you have to be self-directed and self-motivated** • *special invitation to home-schooled students*

Marlboro College is a very small academic community perched on a mountaintop. The entire community—faculty, staff, and students—totals only 370 people. The whole place gets snowed in every winter, sometimes several times. This institution offers an extraordinary college experience.

The first two years of the program are writing intensive. The student works closely with faculty to explore the curriculum with an emphasis on bringing the student's writing up to a high standard. The college offers an impressive array of classes for so small an institution, from organic chemistry to early Soviet cinema to Irish history to "Zap! Hands-on Electricity & Magnetism." Check out the course list at www.marlboro.edu/academics/courselist2000spring.html.

By the end of the freshman year, students must pass the writing requirement, and those who do not are asked to withdraw. From that point on, all writing is expected to meet publishable-level standards. At the beginning of the junior year,

Q. What do you like most about Marlboro?
A. It's really small.

Q. What do you like least about Marlboro?
A. It's really small.

students embark on a two-year endeavor to garner and demonstrate mastery of a subject matter, usually using a multidisciplinary approach. In collaboration with faculty advisors, students develop reading lists and study plans that they will, predominantly, pursue on their own. The library is the center of this campus, and reading is the central activity. The library is open twenty-four hours, and students check out their own books, on the honor system.

The faculty and the students become colleagues and peers during the process, with rapport similar to that at the best graduate programs. The faculty at Marlboro cannot rely on yellowed lecture notes, but are charged to keep up with student interests that are ever changing. As one said to me, "No two students have done anything the same."

Students complete the research project by writing a thesis, and must defend their thesis before an orals board of two professors plus an outside examiner. The outside examiner sets the grade. Marlboro is extremely well thought of in academic circles, and has no trouble getting experts from all over New England to come up on their mountain. Rarely, the student and both faculty members will travel to the outside evaluator's turf.

Marlboro tends to appeal to more mature students, who know what they want. It draws a lot of transfers, in some years as much as one-third of the incoming class. Nontraditional and home-schooled students are welcome. If you visit, be sure to read some of the theses by past students.

The governance aspect of Marlboro is very exciting, reminiscent of Deep Springs. Students are involved in every aspect of college operations, but Marlboro goes beyond that. The college is run like a Swiss village democracy, since the entire community regularly assembles to discuss and decide on community issues en masse. Students hold a majority on Community Court, which "has the power to fine any community member and suspend or expel students who violate community rules or violate state or federal law."

DOWNSIDE: Being at Marlboro is like being at home, smack in the center of a 400-acre lawn. If you went to a high school with two thousand students, as more and more students do, this could be an attractive adventure. However, there is nowhere to hide in a school this small. If you don't do your work, your professor will know, and so will everyone else. Most eighteen-year-old students who have been coasting through high school would find it difficult to succeed at Marlboro, unless they are uncommonly mature and self-motivated. It helps to hit the ground running here, and if you don't keep moving along you won't finish on schedule.

MORE UPSIDE: You'll have friends for the rest of your life, as close as siblings. You'll be more than ready for graduate school. You'll know how to write much better than I. The cornerstone of the program is one-on-one faculty attention, and you can't beat that anywhere. My favorite admissions booklet: "After Marlboro: One Hundred Marlboro Graduates and Where They Are Today." Finally, the Internet has been a real boon to places like Marlboro. If you want to learn something, you can do it just as easily on a mountaintop in Vermont as in Manhattan. Probably easier, because there're a lot fewer distractions.

Marlboro College
South Road
Marlboro, Vermont 05344
800-343-0049 or 802-257-4333
www.marlboro.edu

> We do not offer institutional research projects, major collegiate sports, extensive social endeavors, or any of the other activities which are 'sold' in various ways at universities or large colleges. We offer learning.
>
> —*Administrator*

A lot of schools claim that they are small and intimate. At Marlboro you will know *everybody* in the community.

THE BLOCK PLAN SCHOOLS

concentrate on one class, full-time • **moves really fast** • *students are available to go on-site, all of them, anywhere, even out of the country* • **it's focused and intense**

COLORADO COLLEGE

Colorado College has an unusual schedule. Students study one course at a time, full time. Classes last three and a half weeks, then students get four days off, and then the next block begins. "The class bells never ring at Colorado College." Students concentrate on one class with no interruptions and no distractions from other classes. This has unique advantages over most schedules. It allows professors to take their classes out of town, or schedule events at night, or overnight. They can coordinate with the schedules of cultural events, even in distant cities. At Colorado College in Colorado Springs, Colorado, students may take a two-week trip to the Grand Canyon to do hands-on research, something that simply isn't possible with a traditional semester or quarter system. Says a professor, "We tend to draw students who are obsessive about their studies, and they like the block plan." One problem: You absolutely must keep up with your work, *every day,* or you'll be in serious trouble fast.

Colorado College

14 East Cache la Poudre Street

Colorado Springs, CO 80903

719-389-6000

www.coloradocollege.edu

CORNELL COLLEGE

Cornell College in Mount Vernon, Iowa, also has the block plan, which it calls "One-Course-At-A-Time," a phrase that it went to the trouble to protect with a trademark.

Cornell College

600 First Street, West

Mount Vernon, IA 52314

800-747-1112 or 319-895-4000

www.cornell-iowa.edu

❝ Education is the sleeping pill that makes dreams happen. ❞

—Peggy Hill, King of the Hill

TUSCULUM COLLEGE

Tusculum College in Greeneville, Tennessee, is also using this innovative schedule.

Tusculum College

60 Shiloh Road

Greeneville, TN 37743

423-636-7300

www.tusculum.edu

Also note that Prescott College (p. 138) uses a modified block plan schedule.
If you are "a little bit obsessive" the block plan schedule could be of interest to you.

THE CO-OP SCHOOLS

go to school, go to work, go to school • **real world integrated with the ivory tower** • *the most employable graduates in the world* • **very diverse choices in programs**

UNIVERSITY OF CINCINNATI

Co-op education was pioneered by the University of Cincinnati, launched in 1906 by Herman Schneider, dean of the University of Cincinnati college of engineering. Dean Schneider thought it would be useful for students to alternate between classroom learning and learning on the job. His idea was an instant success, and thus was "co-op" born.

The University of Cincinnati today has the largest co-op program of any post-secondary school in the United States, with four thousand students participating in a variety of fields from engineering to business to French. Co-op is "a key component of the institution's overall mission."

University of Cincinnati
2624 Clifton Avenue
Cincinnati, OH 45221
513-556-2201
www.uc.edu

The #1 indicator of the first full-time job you'll hold after college is the last full-time job you held before you graduated.

ANTIOCH COLLEGE

Perhaps co-op's best known adherent is Antioch College in Yellow Springs, Ohio. This is a small liberal arts college with a big reputation. The thing to understand about the co-op program at Antioch is that it is about education, not vocation. "Our educational philosophy is driven not by the three Rs, but by the three Cs: classroom, co-op, and community."

This is a school for activists and would-be activists. The college's home page unabashedly asks, "Do you want to change the world?" If the answer is yes, then maybe Antioch is for you.

Antioch students alternate between classroom and co-op sessions, stretching the college term to five years. Students are independent and self-reliant by the time they graduate, because they've moved five or ten times and gotten the equivalent of five jobs. Co-op experiences are valued for numerous and in some ways divergent reasons: They offer a student a chance to make a difference in this world, to serve a community, or to work on a social problem. They provide the student with an opportunity to test out career options (and many find that it is just as important to find out what you don't like as it is to find out what you do like). Many earn money dur-

Purdue University has a Rube Goldberg contest. Rube Goldberg was a cartoonist who drew pictures of elaborate machines that performed mundane tasks, like opening a window or making toast. Teams of engineering students from all over the country work all night for weeks in preparation for the event held on-site at Purdue University in West Lafayette, Indiana. Each machine must have at least twenty steps, operate mechanically, and take no further guidance from its maker after the "on" switch is triggered. Some of the machines operate for many minutes before completing a run. If you and your pals are interested in competing, contact the engineering department at Purdue, and start planning now.

ing co-op sessions that can be used to offset the cost of their educations. And finally, as a student nears graduation, the co-op can be used to create a smooth launch into the career world.

Antioch College
795 Livermore Street
Yellow Springs, OH 45387
937-767-7331
www.antioch-college.edu

NORTHEASTERN UNIVERSITY

Northeastern University is also a proponent of co-op education, but they have evolved a unique approach that they call "practice-oriented" education. By integrating professional education and the liberal arts and sciences with cooperative education, Northeastern hopes to maximize the impact of all three disciplines. Whether you study business or art, Northeastern wants you to experience the real world as part of your education.

Northeastern University
360 Huntington Avenue
Boston, MA 02115
617-373-2000
www.neu.edu

KETTERING UNIVERSITY

Kettering University is another exemplar of the co-op model of education, also with a five-year rotational program. Kettering was an engineering institute sponsored by General Motors that evolved into a national university specializing in engineering, applied sciences, mathematics, and business management. Kettering graduates

As an odd piece of trivia, Kettering has tunnels connecting almost every building on campus. A student never has to step outside during the cold winter months. As a variation on this theme, Wartburg College in Waverly, Iowa, put in skyways between many of its buildings, providing the same utility with the added benefit of a good view.

more mechanical engineers than any school in the United States. Its students enjoy a 99 percent placement rate, that is, 99 percent of Kettering students have a job or are admitted to graduate school *before* they graduate from college. Kettering is the only university in the United States with two first days of school, as it staggers its classes to match up with the co-op rotations.

Kettering is an engineer's dream school. It's much more applied than Harvey Mudd or Rose-Hulman; it is loaded with labs and equipment, and students have lots of access. The school is "very aggressively recruiting women and minorities" and has a high minority retention rate as well, so it must be treating them right after it recruits them. Check it out.

Kettering University
1700 West Third Avenue
Flint, MI 48504
810-762-9500
www.kettering.edu

While we're on this topic, engineering students at LeTourneau University in Longview, Texas, are charged to walk on water. To pass Introduction to Engineering, they have to design and mount a water-walking device, and successfully traverse the campus pond. Dry.

Chapter Six

ENTREPRENEURIAL STUDIES

Is a liberal arts education compatible with a strong interest in business? The short answer is yes, but there is more than one good answer to this question. Babson College is a unique liberal arts college dedicated to business in general, and entrepreneurial studies in particular. At Babson, students learn how Shakespeare might spice up a business meeting, among many other things. One thing that is clear from the direction of the economy: Only those who can learn quickly and continuously will survive. With this in mind, we've also covered the approach that many liberal arts colleges take to career development, in a series of "best practices" items collected from schools around the country, and we've included an essay from a student who describes using her liberal arts education to advantage. In a section we refer to as "career planning in two pages," we cover how to major in anything you want, from art to architecture, zoology to zymurgy, and succeed in your career.

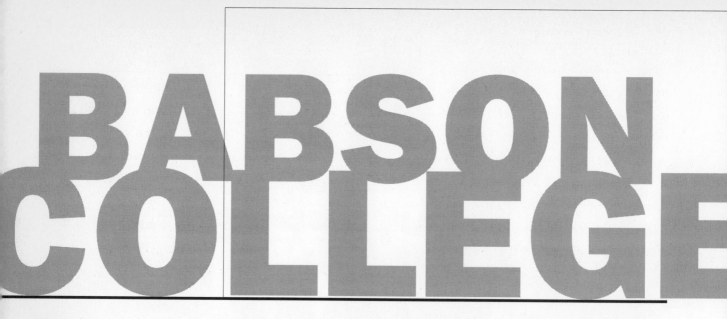

BABSON COLLEGE

the world's best small college of and for business • **a leader in entrepreneurial studies** • *hands on* • **innovative competency model for curriculum** • *students run businesses while still students* • **business plan competition** • *a solid liberal arts core as well* • **a leader in every way** • *1,701 students from all over the world* • **64% men, 36% women**

> **Students are challenged in a curriculum that helps them become innovative problem solvers and future leaders in the world of business.**
>
> —*Babson admissions publication*

Babson College is a phenomenally successful small school founded in 1919 by Roger Ward Babson, an inventor, entrepreneur, and policy advisor to six U.S. presidents.

This school does not try to be all things to all people, but it does, with great self-confidence, say that it will prepare you for success in business and success in life. By combining business and liberal arts curriculum with a vigorous program of internships and "real life" learning activities, it promises to instill expertise in the student in five general skill areas, which it calls "critical competencies":

- Rhetoric and communication
- Numeracy and analysis
- Ethics and social responsibility
- International and multicultural perspectives
- Leadership, teamwork, and creativity

There are more *Wall Street Journals* delivered to Babson every day than there are students enrolled.

All students participate in the Foundation Management Experience, including "launching, managing, and liquidating an actual for-profit venture." The profits from the business are plowed into a community service endeavor, which is an integral part of the assignment. In the upper classes, student internships and entrepreneurial endeavors are closely integrated with the on-campus curriculum.

The school sponsors a business plan competition, and the prize is a cash award to be used toward launching the proposed venture. Babson is extremely well connected with business leaders throughout the country, and Babson grads have the benefit of that network for the rest of their lives.

Located in Wellesley, Massachusetts, it draws students from across the United States and Canada, and forty other countries. Babson reflects the business world of the future: global, multilingual, multicultural, entrepreneurial, and maybe even in-your-face. Eighty-five percent of Babson students live on campus, allowing students the type of close interaction and collaboration that a business incubator or a dot-com would offer.

Babson students recently had internships with these employers, among many others:

Arthur Andersen LLP	Fidelity Investments
BankBoston Securities	GE Medical Systems
Bear Stearns	KPMG Peat Marwick LLP
Calvin Klein	Lycos, Inc.
Chase Manhattan Bank	Smith Barney
Deloitte & Touche LLP	Walt Disney World
Dun & Bradstreet	Plus some dot-coms and pre-IPO-you-
EMC Corp.	never-heard-of-its
ESPN	

Babson ranked #1 in a recent survey of academics' choices for best graduate entrepreneurship programs, ahead of Wharton (Penn), Harvard, Stanford, Anderson (UCLA), USC, and Sloan (MIT).

At Illinois Wesleyan University in Bloomington, students taking an investment management class control IWU's Student-Managed Portfolio, now standing at more than $660,000. By investing real money, students studying business and economics can test out investment theories in a forum where the results matter. Profits are used for scholarships.

Students who are happy at Babson are entrepreneurial self-starters who can work well with others. Students who don't make it fall into two flavors: adenoid-grabbing-testosterone-driven-my-way-or-the-highway me-firsters, and those students who don't want to learn about anything *but* business. This is in many ways a liberal arts college, with a theatre and sports teams and a coffee shop where students discuss movies and art and literature, as well as business.

Most popular T-shirt on campus: Babson Means Business.

DOWNSIDE: If you major in business as an undergraduate, you may find an MBA later to be overkill. You'll already know a lot of what they'll throw at you in a graduate business program, so think that over before deciding to concentrate on business as an undergraduate. Also, in spite of its entrepreneurial bent, Babson is a little too cozy with big, old-line East Coast companies. Finally, if you change your mind about business and decide you want to pursue a career in peace and social justice, or studio art, or whatever, you are probably going to have to transfer.

MORE UPSIDE: In spite of the above, if you love business, and you're interested in a business-focused but still rounded undergraduate education, you can't beat Babson.

CROSS APPS: The most common alternative to Babson would be to major in business at a university with a good business school. However, most business schools focus on graduate students and none that I know of offers any business-only residential cluster, which makes the experience of being a business undergraduate entirely different from Babson. Two colleges sometimes mentioned with Babson are Bentley College in Waltham, Massachusetts, and Bryant College in Smithfield, Rhode Island, for business.

Graduates of Rockhurst University in Kansas City are remarkably accomplished. One in ten of them holds the title of CEO or president. Reed College in Portland, Oregon, also boasts an unusually high percentage of officers and entrepreneurs among its alumni, "nearly 10 percent have been or currently are founders, CEOs, or presidents of private companies," says Reed's public affairs office. These figures are eclipsed, however, by the independent-minded graduates of Hampshire College in Amherst, Massachusetts, one-fifth of whom have started their own businesses.

Babson College

231 Forest Street

Babson Park, MA 02157

800-488-3696 or 617-235-1200

www.babson.edu

THE BIG MEETING

by Crystal Finkbeiner, The Robert E. Cook Honors College

It was the first week of my internship. I realized the company went out on a limb to give me this position working side by side with one of the sportswear buyers. Somehow I even convinced them to pay me. I quickly became conscious that I was expected to do everything the assistant buyer did. After the first day, I was put in charge of some of the daily activities. If a sales report needed to be generated, I did it. If a purchase order needed to be created and faxed, I did it. Things were going smoothly as I adjusted into my new routine.

My buyer felt that I needed to experience all aspects of what goes on to keep the business up and running. This is why he invited me to sit in during a meeting to decide the collection for spring slacks. In order to maintain a consistent look throughout the stores, there needed to be an agreement between sportswear and formalwear. The meeting consisted of the buyer I was working with, the vice president, planner, and assistant buyer for the sportswear division along with the buyer, vice president, planner, and assistant buyer for the formalwear division. The two most important people in attendance were the general merchandise manager and the CEO of the company. Before any decision could be made, it had to go through these two gentlemen first.

During the first two hours of the meeting, I felt we were going in circles. There were not any decisions made so far on which pants to purchase for the spring. The group went off on so many tangents that I thought for sure no decisions were going to be made during this meeting. By the look on everyone else's faces, I concluded this was their feeling too.

This is when one simple question changed the whole outlook of the meeting. Out of frustration, the CEO turned to me—I had been silent up until this point—and asked if I bought men's pants. I was taken back by this question and muttered a simple no. I knew I could have just sat there until he moved on, but I decided to seize the opportu-

> **Never confuse brains with a bull market.**
> —*Saying on Wall Street*

Listen to Babson Radio at www.radio.babson.edu.

nity. I quickly mentioned that I had worked for one of the stores as a cashier for the past two years and witnessed many men buying pants. That did it, I caught his attention. I went on to explain the demographics of our customers. I explained how the accurate picture of what happens during the day cannot be determined solely on numbers, especially sale dollars. Honestly, I do not know much about men's pants. I do, however, know how to look at the bigger picture of a situation and use everything to form support for my ideas. During Honors Core, I learned that I could not just use something little to support my thoughts, unless it agreed with all the other information supplied. For example, the message of a whole book, with all of its reasoning and conclusions, is a much better source of support than one statistic from the book that may be deceptive.

Honors Core taught me that people will not only listen to me, but they will learn from me. I had nothing to lose when I was talking during that meeting. My internship was going to be over in four weeks and I didn't think I'd get fired for saying something wrong.

The conclusion of the meeting was better than I had hoped. Not only was the spring collection of pants decided upon, but I impressed everyone in attendance. Everyone shook my hand and personally thanked me, yes me, the new intern, for being an instrumental part of what they said was the most productive meeting ever. The realization that I can apply my critical thinking skills I acquired in college to the real world gives me confidence for when I enter the full-time work force.

ON CHOOSING A MAJOR AND LAUNCHING A LIFE

Today, on average, it takes more than five years to graduate from college. Families may be dismayed that their offspring take more than four years, but that is, in fact, the norm. Lighter loads taken by students who have to work while they are in school contribute to the problem, as does "difficulty in obtaining classes needed to graduate." If you change your major frequently, it will definitely add to your time in school. Take as many survey courses as you can as a freshman and sophomore. This increases your chances of choosing a major you'll actually like enough to keep through your upperclass years.

Remember, you can major in anything you want if you'll master these skills:

INTERPERSONAL SKILLS: If you will learn to work effectively with others on teams, it will help launch your career. If you can persuade others orally and in writing, you'll be ahead of your peers. If you learn in college to manage, supervise, and delegate effectively to others, your future career path will be accelerated.

How do you master interpersonal skills? By taking an interest in extracurricular activities, by learning how to work with others on team projects in class, and by taking seminar classes where you have to present your ideas before others. If you're on a team, try to be selected as the one who presents the team's work to the whole class. Even if you're shy, you need this practice. In fact, the more shy you are, the more you need it.

TECHNOLOGY SKILLS: If you will learn as much as you can about standard business applications, you can major in anything you want. Standard business applications are rather secretarial, really, but here they are:

Word processing

Spreadsheet

Database

Project management

Contact management

Visual presentation

HTML and Web-page design

Even if you major in business you may not gain much exposure to these applications, but they are as common as dirt in the real world. An internship is the best place to learn more about these programs, or just install them all on your college computer and teach yourself.

GENERAL BUSINESS CONCEPTS: How can data support decision making? Where does profit come from? How do workers create value? These concepts are relevant whether one wants to create peace and social justice or simply amass a personal fortune. (If you advance in the peace and social justice world, you will eventually face budgets that can be spent well or poorly, advancing or hindering your cause. Think about it.)

The best way to gain expertise in this area really is to take a sequence of two courses: microeconomics, and intro accounting or accounting for managers. You can pick this up on the job, if you want, but theoretical understanding makes it faster.

> " Success is not the key to happiness. Happiness is the key to success. If you love what you are doing, you will be successful. "
>
> —Dr. Albert Schweitzer

Muhlenberg College in Allentown, Pennsylvania, offers entrepreneurial studies, and has a unique "Entrepreneur in Residence" to support the program. Finally, Rensselaer in Troy, New York, has its Incubator Program, which turned a student idea into a $60,000,000 company.

What's a Dead-Cat Bounce? A dead-cat bounce is when the stock market rebounds for a bit after hitting bottom, then settles back down to stay down.

INDUSTRY-SPECIFIC KNOWLEDGE: This is generally picked up by having internships in a specific industry. This is not a classroom assignment at all. You need to know what jobs exist in any given industry. What are the entry-level jobs? What skills are needed to get those jobs? What jargon is needed to identify yourself as an insider? How does one advance after gaining one of the entry-level positions? What ensures continued success?

It helps if you discover your values, so that you can pick a career direction that aligns with those values. For example, if you have to help others or be creative in order to be happy, any career that lacks an element of helping others or exercising creativity would be a poor choice. Also, try to learn your own abilities and limitations, and how to be honest and forthcoming. But that's about it.

So, if you'll take care of these career-readiness skills, you can major in whatever you want. Major in art or philosophy or business or calligraphy or hieroglyphics, it doesn't matter. It's generally best to major in what you love, because then you'll be an enthusiastic student. Your enthusiasm will carry you over the hurdles you will face. You'll be more creative in overcoming obstacles. You'll study more and harder without viewing it as a grind. You'll be happier. People will be drawn to you. You'll find the weather is consistently better.

There it is. Career planning on three pages, but the advice is sound.

Economics is considered the "business" major at most liberal arts colleges that don't have a school of business, which is, in fact, most of them. Most liberal arts schools are very weak in business, and most business schools are very weak in liberal arts. Babson is a business school that delivers liberal arts. As another take on this whole issue, Wheaton College in Norton, Massachusetts, is a liberal arts college that delivers on career planning and preparation, whatever your major, through a combination of curriculum, service learning, internships, reflection, and intensive one-on-one career counseling from *before* the first day of classes. Check this out; it's considered by many to be the best career center model in the nation.

There have been complaints at Harvey Mudd, MIT, and several other institutions about student ideas being appropriated and patented either by professors, venture sponsors, or by the schools themselves. Think carefully about whether meager funding today warrants giving all future benefit of your idea away. Challenge, especially, those clauses that require you to turn over patents, etc., for a few thousand dollars. Some "honors" are better turned down in advance.

THE FILENE CENTER FOR WORK & LEARNING

by Dr. Dan Golden, director, Wheaton College, Norton, Massachusetts

In the early 1980s, Hannah Goldberg arrived on the Wheaton campus as its new provost and academic vice president. Exploring ways to link the educational experience of Wheaton students to the world of work, she developed the central concepts for transforming the Office of Career Planning into the Center for Work & Learning.

At the heart of the change was the incorporation of the new Center into the administrative structure of the provost, signaling that, at Wheaton College, an integrated approach to life-planning was inseparable from other classic academic services such as the library, academic computing, and the curriculum itself. This organizational positioning of the new Center was at the time (and still is) fairly unusual in higher education reporting structures, with fewer than ten percent of similar offices housed on the academic side of college or university campuses.

I took over the Center for Work & Learning in 1986 as the founding director. To deliver on our mission of helping Wheaton's liberal arts students connect their academic education with the world of work, we began by building on our strong innovative history in career planning. In the past, Wheaton's mentor program had garnered national recognition for its junior-year alliances of students and alumni professionals, and since the late 1970s our students had been field-testing their career interests with an internship program during winter break periods.

In 1988 the Center took an expanded and more prominent nomenclature as it was renamed the Filene Center for Work & Learning, to honor distinguished alumna Catherine Filene Shouse (Class of 1918) on the occasion of her 75th reunion.

In its early years, the Filene Center for Work & Learning spent much of its energy identifying and developing strategies to help students extract meaning from their work experiences. Aided by grants from private foundations such as the Charles A. Dana Foundation and the Consortium for the Advancement of Private Higher Education, the Filene Center was able to send its message of work and learning to students and faculty through a variety of innovative programs, a sample of which I describe below.

- Wheaton Serves!
  Every year hundreds of Wheaton students donate thousands of hours to local and global community service programs.

- The "Life Aims" Project

    This program creates opportunities for students to reflect on their personal and professional goals by writing a fictional letter to an old friend on the occasion of a future high school reunion. In discussion with faculty, staff, and peer advisors, first-year students are encouraged to discuss their aspirations and anxieties about their future. The goals of life aims are to help new students develop an aspirational vocabulary—a way of thinking and talking about themselves and their hopes—and to reflect on the role their college experience will play in the future. This program was so successful that in 1990 a version of the life aims essay became the core element of Wheaton's admission process.

- Orientation Service Day

    The experiential capstone of their first four days on campus, Orientation Service Day pairs new students with public and community service organizations for a day of volunteer work in communities surrounding the campus. Every year since its inception in 1990, hundreds of students have worked at service sites focusing on a wide array of social, political, and environmental issues.

The Filene Center helps students understand the conditions that underlie their choice to attend college. It teaches students to take control of their learning by understanding both their learning styles and their primary accountability in the learning process, and it encourages students to perceive their education as a whole, seamless interweaving of courses and experiences that continue far beyond graduation.

Do we have a "secret" to what we do? We are flattered by the favorable attention our programs receive from other institutions, and remind our visitors that the central components of our successes are:

- a vision of academic and trustee leadership that believes in graduating "whole" learners in a fragmented world
- a commitment of sufficient resources to ensure our programming, stipend programs for students, and labor-intensive advising structure can deliver on its promises
- an integration of field-based learning across the curriculum that deepens student exposure and commitment to learning outside the classroom

- daily attention on our part to ensure that the messages of the Filene Center
  serve the larger cause of Wheaton's core mission

To this end, the Filene Center has worked even more explicitly on strategies to meld the reflective approach of work and learning into other Wheaton core competencies and values. We expanded our reflective learning instructions to help students examine the relationships between work and learning and other institutionally-related issues encountered in their jobs, internships, or public service settings.

What makes us different is that we're a relentlessly liberal arts college without overt preprofessional curricula. The Filene Center is the answer to students and families who want our kind of education, but who also want to be prepared to make their way in the world. The Filene Center captures students and "professionalizes" them through the integration of experiential opportunities—like community service, jobs, and internships—in both their college courses and their career exploration. To do so demands a lot of staff and funding, two items that are in short supply, not to mention the support of the founding vision.

We are heavily supported partly because we're an academic service that provides our faculty with valuable resources in the way of field placements and underwriting of their work, partly because we provide free lifetime career service for alumni, and partly because we are at the center of the admissions marketing campaign—not only do we attract students, we have also proven to be influential in retaining students.

The "second transcript" our students get as a result of their involvement with the work and learning program is incidental to the role we play, but it's fronted as the credential that separates a Wheaton grad from the rest of the pack. Of course not every student embraces and benefits from the second transcript, but having the documentation system does aid them in picking majors, clarifying career direction, and proving to employers and graduate schools that they are thoughtful practitioners. Matters of technology, diversity, ethics, and integrity are played out on site. All of these are core Wheaton values, and as students see the interconnections, their synthesis of vision and those values—of the practical and the philosophical—will combine to produce the learners and workers of the future.

BEST CAREER PRACTICES FROM OTHER COLLEGES & UNIVERSITIES

Oglethorpe University's Shadowing Program, aka "Sophomore Choices"

At Oglethorpe, students participate in four weeks of occasional preparation including an assessment instrument and instruction on how to act and what to expect. They are then sent out on assigned shadowing experiences, usually three or four different one-day experiences per student. The students provide the Oglethorpe career center with a wish list of interests, and the center develops the shadowing sites. The program takes advantage of fall and spring breaks to send students out on all-day treks that won't cause them to miss class. The only real requirement of the students is punctuality and professional dress.

A key part of the program is the evening debriefings, when students meet back at a dorm, eat free pizza, and share with other students what they discovered for the day. A faculty member will often join this group to discuss transferable skills, and how the liberal arts and sciences curriculum meshes with job skill-sets.

This program evolved from institutional research that identified "unfocused" students as an attrition demographic, especially on the cusp of the sophomore-junior year. Sophomore Choices was originally intended to be a semester-long career management for-credit course, but the director launched the program rather than wait for faculty approval.

Students love Sophomore Choices, and program attendees often make enthusiastic presentations to prospectives and their parents.

Nevertheless, this is, so far as I know, the best shadowing program in the nation, in large part because the director has made such a personal commitment to making it work. Students cannot rave enough about how much they get out of it.

Oglethorpe University
4484 Peachtree Road, NE
Atlanta, GA 30319
404-261-1441
www.oglethorpe.edu

Kansas State University Academic & Career Information Center's Peer Counselors

KSU uses undergraduate peer counselors to run every aspect of the career exploration process, as well as the center itself. (Please note that the ACIC is a support program to the career services center, and is housed separately.) Peer counselors are trained in the peer model, starting with process (e.g., how to ask nonthreatening, nonjudgmental questions) and continuing with content (e.g., how to administer computer- and paper-based assessment instruments). The students spend a good deal of their time in outreach and marketing. The development opportunity for the peer counselors themselves is explicitly a benefit of the program, enhancing their leadership and presentation skills and improving self-confidence. Students even get to teach a one-hour for-credit course, "Major Decisions."

The hiring process for peer counselors is complicated. The director says, "We don't just look for extroverts. We also look for quieter people, who may process information a little bit differently. We like to reflect the student body. We start advertising in January, and send nomination forms to advisors and student services administrators. Then, we use a group orientation session, stressing the paraprofessional aspect, that this is not just another student job. Then we hand out applications. Using a blind screening technique (names removed), we'll screen down from thirty-eight to twenty-three applicants. All of those twenty-three will go through interviews. We give them an "All about Me" form to fill out and bring into the meetings. Everybody goes through three meetings. We use the forms to generate nonintimidating talk in the first interview. Then, in meetings two and three, they face increasingly pointed questions. "Who have you admired and why?" plus some behavioral interviewing. Same questions of each applicant, in the same order. We strive to have qualitative and quantitative info in each weeding session. After meeting with the inter-

---

Would you still study just as hard if you were filthy rich? Many professors show up every day to teach who are exactly that. One professor at MIT is worth $2 billion, and shows up every day. Another at Cal Berkeley is worth $800 million. One-third of Stanford's computer science department are millionaires. A professor at Reed used to have a chauffeured Rolls wait for him outside class, yet he showed up every day. One would hope that you would, too.

(*Source:* Chronicle of Higher Education, *2 March 2000*)

viewing committees, there will be sixteen candidates left. All sixteen will go through a structured thirty-minute interview with a hiring panel. We start with general questions, behavioral based, situational based, same questions, same order, for example, "Registration is here, you have two papers due, and your personal life is in turmoil. You come to work with a full day ahead of you. How do you deal with it?" Or, "You have a friend who's interested in a demanding career choice, but just failed biology, what do you do? What do you tell her?" Then, that clincher, "Why should we hire you over the other fifteen people we're meeting with today?" We extend an offer to eight of the sixteen who complete this round. Then, all eight accept. We train twenty hours in the spring, and in the fall they come in a day early for eight hours, plus one hour a week for staff meetings and in-service development.

Kansas State University

Seventeenth and Anderson Streets

Manhattan, KS 66506

785-532-6011

www.ksu.edu

Beloit College

Beloit College also uses peer counselors, which it sharply distinguishes from student clerical staff. They receive one-week in-service training (forty hours), plus a team-building retreat. Training covers role playing, explicit instruction on confidentiality and ethics, leadership development, all basic office skills, publicity design, and career content. The assistant director says one of the hidden benefits to the peer counselor model is increased student utilization of career center services.

In one of the only large, long-term studies of career outcomes for liberal arts graduates, AT&T's Bell System Management found that liberal arts graduates were more likely to be promoted into management than hires with business or technical majors. The study found that 43% of them advanced to senior management, compared to 32% of business graduates and 23% of engineering graduates. The researcher, Robert E. Beck, wrote, "The humanities/social sciences majors showed especially strong interpersonal skills and were similar to business majors in administrative skills and motivation for advancement."

(*Source:* Liberal Education and Careers Today *by Howard Figler [Garrett Park Press, 1989]*)

Beloit College

700 College Street

Beloit, WI 53511

608-363-2000

www.beloit.edu

Principia College's Career Summit

Principia College hosts a paradigm Career Summit for some lucky departments. For example, the Biology/Environmental Science Seminar involves professors, students, alumni, and practicing professionals. They meet to discuss career options for people in fields related to this cluster of majors. This serves as a career development seminar and mini-reunion for department alumni as well. This collaboration between the faculty and the career services function seems to be the exact model that would ensure success.

Principia College

One Maybeck Place

Elsah, IL 62028

800-277-4648 or 618-374-2131

www.prin.edu

COOLEST "JOBS" ON CAMPUS

Guest speakers committee: meet the phat and famous

Student activities committee: hire bands, poets, jugglers

Campus radio or CC TV god: on-air talent, or be a technician, producer, manager

Campus newspaper reporter or columnist: it may as well be you

Admissions tour guide: gain the most important business skill

Student government: rule today, rule tomorrow

NOTE: At the beginning of every school year there is usually an "activities" fair, where all the clubs and organizations seek new recruits. The larger organizations may hold their own open houses. Hot tip: Seek out the president, chief, czar, or director of any organization you're interested in *before* the open house or fair, so you can learn about the coolest assignments and pitch yourself for them ahead of the crowds.

Junior Decision Programs: Santa Clara University and Washington University in St. Louis

Junior Decision Programs are career and graduate school planning days that, in both cases, started out as weeklong programs that were later shortened to one or two days. Regular classes are suspended during the event. Speakers are brought in to cover career planning, resumés, self-directed career launch, graduate school application essays, credit and financial management, and so on. Washington University in St. Louis charges students to participate and takes a no-nonsense approach. Santa Clara does not, and throws in business theater and corporate games-type experiences to keep attention. By the way, the official name of Washington U. is "Washington University in St. Louis," to keep it from being confused with more than a dozen other schools with a similar name.

Santa Clara University

500 El Camino Real

Santa Clara, CA 95053

408-554-4764

www.scu.edu

THE FIVE HIGHEST AND FIVE LOWEST PAYING MAJORS

THE FIVE HIGHEST PAYING MAJORS ARE:

Chemical Engineering

Aerospace Engineering

Computer Engineering

Physics

Electrical Engineering

THE FIVE LOWEST PAYING MAJORS ARE:

Special Education

Elementary Education

Home Economics

Music

Drama

(Source: The College Majors Handbook *[JIST, 1999])*

This does not mean, however, that you should start studying chemistry if you have no talent for it. It does mean, however, that if you would be equally happy as a chemical engineer or an elementary school teacher, you might remember that chemists earn, on average, 95 percent more than elementary school teachers. Every year.

Washington University in St. Louis

One Brookings Drive

St. Louis, MO 63130

314-935-5000

www.wustl.edu

St. John Fisher College's Fisher Commitment

Fisher enrolls freshmen into a covenant called the Fisher Commitment. Should the student participate in a series of required career center activities, and fail to find a job in his or her field of choice within six months of graduation, Fisher will pay the student $417 per month ($5,000 maximum benefit) and provide intensive out-placement-style intervention. This received some press when it was announced several years ago.

The requirements of the program are ordinary: maintain 3.0 GPA, attend career workshops, seek and find an internship. In the spring, the director runs Fisher Goes to Work, taking students to nearby Boston for walk-through-style visits with professional alumni and at other businesses.

St. John Fisher College

3690 East Avenue

Rochester, NY 14618

716-385-8000

www.sjfc.edu

Studies of millionaires are pretty interesting. It turns out that the most important skill for someone to have, if interested in accumulating wealth, is not the ability to earn a lot but the ability to save a lot. If you're interested in accumulating wealth, read *The Millionaire Next Door* by Thomas Stanley and William Danko (Simon & Schuster, 1999) or *The Millionaire Mind* also by Thomas Stanley (Andrews McMeel, 2000).

Juniata College in Huntington, Pennsylvania, has a business plan competition and a venture fund sponsored by faculty, as do MIT in Cambridge, Massachusetts, and most of the well-established business schools.

This is a sort of boot camp for liberal arts majors, an "intense crash course in business." The school brings in alumnae from all over the world to teach the course, all experts in such topics as accounting, finance, marketing, information technology, advertising, human resources, or manufacturing. Juniors and seniors have first crack at seats, limited to fifty per class, offered in the winter session. The fee is "several hundred dollars," but the experience is invaluable.

Wellesley College
106 Central Street
Wellesley, MA 02481
781-283-1000
www.wellesley.edu

Career counselors will tell you that success in life is fundamentally based on finding work that you enjoy. If you enjoy your work, you will succeed. If you don't, you won't. So make your choice of a major based on what you really enjoy, but do watch out for accumulating those skills mentioned on pages 162 through 164, mostly gained outside the classroom, during your college career. For more on this, see Patrick Comb's *Major in Success* (Ten Speed Press, 2000), profiled in the Cool Book Alert! on p. 399.

Chapter Seven

THE ENGINEERING SCHOOLS

While we're in this chapter, we'll consider where millionaires come from and take a look at some of the greatest schools of engineering in the world. Interested in science? Want to study at a school with the best opportunity to prepare you for a Ph.D., or set off your meteoric rise in a career in industry? Then you need to consider more than just who has the most Nobel Prize-winning scholars. You may read about a school's atom smasher or other "Big Science" project, but those are mostly reserved for grad students, even post-docs. As a prospective student you need to find out about access. The thing that engineers want more than anything is unfettered access to labs. In the schools in this section, undergraduate engineers and scientists have plenty of access to labs and equipment, in some cases twenty-four-hour access to their own labs and equipment. Be sure not to miss the fine engineering schools in the next chapter as well, "Flying, Sailing, and Militarizing." Oh, and what the heck is a jackalope? And why is it so hard to photograph?

There are numerous specialty engineering schools in the United States. Here are the ones I know the most about, followed by a list of the rest.

HARVEY MUDD COLLEGE

science and engineering plus liberal arts • **a team-based, real-world curriculum that is also steeped in theory** • *access to four other colleges that you'll be too busy to take advantage of* • **famously tough grading system** • *designed for versatile thinkers*

Harvey Mudd is one of those schools that everyone in higher education knows about and few not in higher education know about. It is an engineering college with a strong liberal arts component. Harvey Mudd puts out engineers who can think, write, and present their ideas before a group. They learn to work well in teams, not always part of the curriculum at other engineering schools. In the past their incoming class routinely had the highest average SATs in the nation, as they needed both analytical talent and verbal talent, thus hitting on both cylinders for the SAT. Last year they had nine freshmen with perfect 800 SATs, on both math *and* verbal. They don't have any grade inflation at all and, along with Swarthmore and Reed, a B is a good grade and an A really is what it used to be: "Outstanding."

Harvey Mudd is a prep college, and most "Mudders" go on to graduate school, if not right away at least within a few years. HMC is number one in graduating students who go on to complete their engineering and science Ph.D.'s, according to *Chemical and Engineering News* (3 August 1998). Harvey Mudd is the kind of place where the faculty and the students built their own supercomputer, from scratch, because they thought they needed one. They have their own cable TV show on technology developments.

Harvey Mudd is part of the Claremont Colleges, a five-college consortium with literally adjoining campuses. Although cross-registration is touted as a benefit of this arrangement, the Harvey Mudd curriculum is so intense and time consuming that a student pretty much needs to come in the door running and never slow down. Here are the consortium members:

Harvey Mudd College (strong in science and engineering)

Scripps (women's college; strong in humanities and arts)

Pomona (strong in liberal arts and humanities)

Claremont McKenna (strong in liberal arts and business and government)

Pitzer (strong in social and political sciences)

If you want to tease Harvey Mudd students, ask them about Harvey Mudd's nightlife. Not the college's. The founder's.

Harvey Mudd students have a sense of humor. They spend their time stealing Caltech's cannon.

Harvey Mudd College

301 East 12th Street

Claremont, CA 91711

909-621-8120

www.hmc.edu

They are ill discoverers that think there is no land, when they can see nothing but sea.

—Francis Bacon

The doctor who knows only disease is at a disadvantage alongside the doctor who knows at least as much about people as he does about pathological organisms. The lawyer who argues in court from a narrow legal base is no match for the lawyer who can connect legal precedents to historical experience and who employs wide-ranging intellectual resources. The business executive whose competence in general management is bolstered by an artistic ability to deal with people is of prime value to his company. For the technologist, the engineering of consent can be just as important as the engineering of moving parts.

—Norman Cousins (in "How to Make People Smaller Than They Are," Saturday Review, *December, 1978)*

CALIFORNIA INSTITUTE OF TECHNOLOGY (CALTECH)

one of the best technical institutes in the world • **more grad students than undergrads** • *no teaching assistants, just real professors* • **do real science, don't just read about it** • *focus on advanced skills at the undergraduate level*

Caltech is nerd central, and proud of it. The lucky undergraduates at Caltech do *not* get taught by graduate assistants; all classes are taught by full professors, who are, good news, among the best in the world. Undergraduates are coddled here. Caltech is currently ranked number one for spending per student by *U.S. News & World Report.* With only nine hundred undergraduates and about one thousand graduate students, Caltech is, like Harvey Mudd, a very small but globally important science and engineering school.

You can check Caltech's Web site for its latest list of inventions and awards and scientific breakthroughs, but what you really need to know about is "Ditch Day."

Major universities usually claim that they produce the greatest number of Ph.D.'s, but this is a blatantly misleading statistic. If you have forty thousand students, you're going to produce some Ph.D.'s by accident, if nothing else. Smaller colleges are actually much greater producers of Ph.D.'s relative to their size. Among all undergraduate institutions of any size whatsoever, Caltech, Harvey Mudd, and Reed rank as the top three *per capita* producers of Ph.D.'s. Considering only undergraduate colleges, Oberlin ranks number one for total numbers, but after the above schools on a per capita basis. Over the years, Oberlin has been a prodigious producer of future Ph.D.'s. If you're interested in more statistics like these, read the academic journals in a specific discipline, check out the National Center for Education Statistics at http://nces.ed.gov, and check out *Educational Rankings Annual* (Gale Press, 1999). Don't be fooled by press releases from mega-universities.

Ditch Day is a day in the spring when all seniors at Caltech ditch classes and leave campus for fun and revelry. Since this is pretty much the only time the students go out for fun and revelry, the faculty tolerate this. The underclassmen, however, do not. If seniors are caught on campus on Ditch Day, they are summarily duct-taped to the nearest tree.

The actual date of Ditch Day is changed every year, and is a secret. To protect their rooms while they are away on Ditch Day, Caltech seniors use "stacks." Stacks are like locks, except that they may be physical locks, or they may be conceptual locks. They come in several flavors:

Brute Force Stack: This is when a senior will, for instance, pour a concrete slab in front of the door to her room. Underclassmen have been known to rent jack-hammers to remove Brute Force Stacks. This is not an exaggeration. (Obviously, seniors not using a Brute Force Stack are safe on the honor of the underclassmen not to use brute force to enter their rooms.)

Treasure Hunt Stack: The senior may, for example, leave a clue on his door. That clue leads to other clues. In a recent year, the final clue was a lap dance from an exotic dancer, after which the underclassman was presented with the key to the senior's room, by the dancer. Other Treasure Hunt Stacks have involved taking airplanes to distant places and looking behind pictures in certain bars in other cities, for example. Remember, all of this has to be done in one day.

Puzzle Stack: A senior may leave very difficult physics problems on her door. The underclassmen must solve the problems before entering. In a recent year, a Nobel laureate was unable to solve a student's problems, and his door remained unopened.

Finesse Stack: A senior may leave a series of Herculean tasks for the underclassmen to perform in order to advance to the magic "open sesame."

So what does an underclassman get for entering a senior's room? Usually booze, food, or candy, sometimes money. If the underclassmen feel that the prize was chintzy in proportion to the effort expended, they may trash the senior's room, or they may set their own stacks, which the senior is honor-bound to resolve before returning home. One perennially popular stunt: dismantling the senior's car and reassembling it in her room.

Caltech students begin planning their senior stacks from the moment they receive their acceptance letters, while still in high school.

California Institute of Technology (CalTech)

1200 East California Boulevard

Pasadena, CA 91125

626-395-6811

www.caltech.edu

ReAlLy CoOl ScIeNcE!

You don't have to go to a world-famous institution like Caltech or MIT to get to do really cool science. As mentioned elsewhere, the science departments at regular liberal arts colleges can be exciting, hands-on places. For example, Reed College is also known as the Reed Institute. Senior science majors get their own labs to do independent research, something that would never happen at major research universities where students almost always contribute to professors' research. Santa Clara University in the Silicon Valley seeks a mix of people in its engineering programs, and has increased enrollment of women by 25 percent. "Like in any other field, a diverse population means more creativity," said Terry Shoup, dean of Santa Clara's school of engineering. "So if we want to produce the best engineers, we've got to have more women." Six of their students recently designed three satellites with off-the-shelf parts and put them into orbit (*San Francisco Chronicle*, 17 January 2000). Here's the team: Maureen Breiling, aka Mars, project manager, VLF receiver; Dina Hadi, attitude control, antenna deployment; Corina Y. Hu, sensor subsystem, systems engineer; Theresa Kuhlman, materials, thermal and radiation analysis; Duncan Laurie, computer sciences and flight code; Amy Slaughterbeck, power subsystem; Adelia Valdez, communication systems.

ROSE-HULMAN INSTITUTE OF TECHNOLOGY

outstanding science and engineering education • **faculty dedicated to teaching, not just their own research** • *studying night and day here is just fine* • **rural campus allowing total focus** • *unfettered undergraduate access to labs and equipment*

Rose-Hulman is an outstanding engineering school. At the time this book went to press, it was ranked number one in the nation by *U.S. News & World Report*. However, you need to know that the president of the college made it an institutional goal to rise in the *U.S. News* rankings. In other words, the school was trying to rank highly, and it succeeded.

Rose-Hulman and Harvey Mudd are mainly different in that Rose-Hulman is in Terre Haute, Indiana, and Harvey Mudd is in suburban L.A. Rose-Hulman appears more conservative and more laid back, but the students actually work very hard here. As mentioned on p. 47, Rose-Hulman is to be commended for having one of the smoothest transitions to coed status.

Rose-Hulman Institute of Technology

5500 Wabash Avenue

Terre Haute, IN 47803

800-248-7448 or 812-877-1511

www.rose-hulman.edu

After these three institutions of astounding quality, there are many very good engineering schools.

COLORADO SCHOOL OF MINES

The Colorado School of Mines favors a laboratory and hands-on approach to engineering training, and students are quite studious there. One told me, "People study on Saturday night. No one will think you're weird if you like to study here." That says a lot. Colorado School of Mines is *right next* to the Rockies. They literally come up to the edge of campus. They also have one of the only known pictures of the elusive jackalope. Ask to see it if you visit.

Colorado School of Mines

1500 Illinois Street

Golden, CO 80401

800-446-9488 or 303-273-3000

www.mines.edu

THE COOPER UNION FOR THE ADVANCEMENT OF SCIENCE & ART

Cooper Union is a school of art, architecture, and engineering, and it is truly outstanding at all three. This is why it defies easy categorization. Oh, and by the way, it's free. As Cooper Union says about itself, it is "the only full-scholarship School of Architecture, Art, and Engineering in the country."

Needless to say, it is extremely competitive to get into Cooper Union. It draws students nationally and internationally, because of its quality and the fact that it is tuition-free.

When rankings came to Sweden recently, educators were understandably upset. Sigbrit Franke, head of the Swedish National Agency for Higher Education, was quoted in the U.S.-based *Chronicle of Higher Education* saying that ranking Swedish colleges and universities was like comparing a hockey team to the Swedish Radio Symphony Orchestra. "What's best for you," she said, "may not be best for another student." *Asiaweek* has for a few years ranked universities throughout Asia, but the school that was consistently ranked number one, the University of Tokyo, decided to refuse to participate. Hasumi Shigehiko, president of the University of Tokyo, said that the decision will stand "so long as I am president." Thus globalism rocks along, with bad ideas just as likely to be exported as good. *U.S. News & World Report* is now ranking hospitals. If they conduct the studies the same way they rank U.S. colleges, the hospitals that admit the healthiest patients and have the largest financial reserves will be found "best."

There are things you need to understand about the school, however. It is really three schools in one. You must know your field in advance. You do not go to Cooper to experiment around with art and architecture and engineering. Like many engineering and architecture programs, you have to begin working on your degree requirements right from the freshman year. You cannot falter or you will be unable to finish in time. The architecture program is heavily theoretical, and is often mentioned as one of the best in the world. Located in Manhattan, you will also have to cover your living expenses, which can be tremendous.

Cooper uses a problem-solving orientation in its curriculum. "We try to look at problems as they really exist, rather than at a problem divorced from the environment," says the dean of admissions. "We address real problems in our society as they are manifest today." Assignments in the past have included how to design an ergonomic and energy-efficient taxicab, and what to do with the recycled glass piling up nationwide. This is an intense school. Students take six and seven courses per semester, and students are in a lab or a studio constantly if they are not in class.

The dean warns, "We won't hold your hand here."

The Cooper Union for the Advancement of Science & Art

30 Cooper Square

New York, NY 10003

212-254-6300

www.cooper.edu

> **In my younger days, when I was pained by the half-educated, loose and inaccurate ways women had, I used to say how much women need exact science. But since I have known some workers in science, I have now said how much science needs women.**
>
> *—Maria Mitchell, first woman member of the American Academy of Arts and Sciences Hall of Fame (in Great Quotes from Great Women)*

Homo sapiens has been a separate species for approximately 400,000 years, but civilization, every aspect of it, is brand new. We've had villages for only 11,000 years; before that, there was no human organization larger than a band. We've had writing for about 5,000 years, and it took all of that to make it global. Imagine what *homo sapiens* can do in, say, 500,000 years of civilization—500,000 more years of science and discovery.

On the other hand, we may wipe ourselves out long before then. For the last fifty years the biggest global fear was nuclear annihilation. Now the biggest risk comes from bioengineering. Nature took 3 *billion* years to develop this planet's DNA stockpile, and scientists are now combining it in new and unpredictable ways on a daily basis. The history of plagues and the introduction of nonnative species into new ecosystems is full of catastrophic disasters sparked by just this type of activity. Whether you become a scientist or a social theorist, remember this.

MORE ENGINEERING SPECIALTY SCHOOLS

Wentworth Institute of Technology, Boston, Massachusetts

Webb Institute, Glen Cove, New York (see p. 188)

State University of New York College of Technology, Farmingdale, New York

Southern Polytechnic State University, Marietta, Georgia

South Dakota School of Mines and Technology, Rapid City, South Dakota

Oregon Institute of Technology, Klamath Falls, Oregon

New Mexico Institute of Mining and Technology, Socorro, New Mexico

Milwaukee School of Engineering, Milwaukee, Wisconsin

Kettering University, Flint, Michigan (see p. 154)

Capitol College, Laurel, Maryland

SOME OTHER SCHOOLS OF ENGINEERING TO CONSIDER

Smith College, Northampton, Massachusetts

Rochester Institute of Technology, Rochester, New York

Rice University, Houston, Texas

Rensselaer Polytechnic Institute, Troy, New York

The Military Academies (see next chapter)

The Maritime Academies (see next chapter)

Georgia Institute of Technology, Atlanta, Georgia

The Aeronautics Schools (see next chapter)

MOST MILLIONAIRES COME FROM THE MIDDLE OF THE PACK

Who wants to be a millionaire? Conventional wisdom says it's the students who get straight As, blow the roof off the SAT, and go to Ivy League colleges. Or maybe it's the children born into wealthy families with brilliant connections. Neither is typical, says Thomas J. Stanley, who surveyed 1,300 millionaires for his book, *The Millionaire Mind* (Andrews McMeel, 2000). The average millionaire made Bs and Cs in college, Stanley says. Their average SAT score was 1190—not good enough to get into many top-notch schools. In fact, most millionaires were told they were not intellectually gifted, not smart enough to succeed. Attending a top-rated college ranked twenty-third as a cause for wealth accumulation, and doing well in college ranked even worse, at thirtieth.

-Associated Press (in the San Francisco Chronicle, 8 February 2000)

WARNING: Choosing an engineering college, or even an engineering major, frequently involves a commitment to your major from the freshman year. These schools are not designed so much for exploring your interests, but mastering an interest that you have already selected. Changing your major can result in an inability to graduate on schedule. Just something to think about.

> **Fact: Introverts, on average, have higher grades than extroverts.**

Chapter Eight

FLYING, SAILING, AND MILITARIZING

You can be a woman and you can be a man, but you cannot go the United States Military Academy at West Point if you are married.

If you've ever fantasized about being the captain of an oil tanker, or the pilot of a 747, or, for that matter, the space shuttle, then the right school for you might be in this chapter. The military academies are one option, but they're not the only access point to these types of careers anymore. Check out the schools of aeronautics, the Webb Institute of Naval Architecture, and the academies for the merchant marine. Several of these schools are free, and consider this: For the military academies, the job placement rates are always 100 percent. These options are not for everybody, but for the student attracted to one of them, they can be an opportunity for a unique college experience.

THE MILITARY ACADEMIES

If you are patriotic, in good physical condition, self-disciplined, and have kept your drug experimentation to the legal kind, you should consider one of the military academies. And especially if you have a tradition of military service in your family, you should consider one of the military academies. Perhaps you should think of it this way: Do you think you *ever* want to join the military? If the answer is yes, consider going to academy; if the answer is no, skip to the next section.

The academies want you to focus on the fact that theirs is perhaps the best free education in the world. But that is not the most important part of applying to academy. This is: If you are accepted, and if you go, you are joining the military and choosing to have the first part of your career, at least, in the military. Don't forget that, no matter how much the full ride means to you and your family.

DOWNSIDE: These programs are demanding. They're physically tough, mentally challenging, and there's no such thing as taking a year off. They require complete loyalty and all of your attention. If you wash out, it's probably better that you

WEBB INSTITUTE OF NAVAL ARCHITECTURE

Also, check out the Webb Institute of Naval Architecture in Glen Cove, New York. It is tuition free, but only accepts a handful of students each year. Note: Webb is not a military academy.

Webb Institute of Naval Architecture · Crescent Beach Road
Glen Cove, NY 11542 · 516-671-2213 · www.webb-institute.edu

had never gone. They are occasionally racked by scandal (drugs, sex, cheating), which can tarnish your reputation even if you're not involved. These degrees are not transferrable between branches. If you decide you don't like the army, the navy is not going to give one whit's care if you are a West Pointer.

MORE UPSIDE: If you go to academy, you will not only enter the affiliated branch of the United States military as an officer, but you will forever be one of the elites in that branch. Whatever your eventual career goals, from politics to engineering to achieving a high rank, this is an illustrious beginning.

Some of these programs have elaborate application procedures, so check out the school's Web site as early as possible so you can set everything in motion.

United States Air Force Academy

2304 Cadet Drive

Colorado Springs, CO 80840

719-333-1110

www.usafa.af.mil

United States Coast Guard Academy

31 Mohegan Avenue

New London, CT 06320

860-444-8444

www.cga.edu

United States Military Academy

(usually just called West Point)

Stony Lonesome Road

West Point, NY 10996

914-938-4200

www.usma.edu

United States Naval Academy

121 Blake Road

Annapolis, MD 21402

410-293-1000

www.nadn.navy.mil

> **❝I seem to have been only like a boy playing on the seashore, and diverting myself in now and then finding a smoother pebble or a prettier shell than ordinary, whilst the great ocean of truth lay all undiscovered before me.❞**
>
> —*Sir Isaac Newton*

When football players wear Super Bowl rings they are partaking of the fine tradition of wearing academic class rings, which started at West Point and spread to every college and high school in the country. It's not entirely clear what this has to do with professional football players, but it's probably a good idea not to argue with any of them.

AVIATION AND AERONAUTICS

Since the First World War the military has kept the commercial aviation industry in pilots. As soon as a war would end, there would be plenty of surplus pilots, and well before that batch was ready to retire, there'd be another. In peacetime the military still turned out loads of freshly trained pilots. Traditionally, 80 percent of commercial pilots were originally trained in the military. But there hasn't been a big enough war lately to keep up with pilot demand, and commercial air traffic has been on a steady increase for decades. So, for the next fifteen years, becoming an entry-level commercial pilot should be a good career choice.

To be licensed in the United States means four years of engineering training and flight school leading to a bachelor's degree and a pilot's license. There are 120 colleges or universities with aviation schools, of varying quality. The best ones combine a strong engineering curriculum with flight training, and the worst ones basically graduate anyone sober who has passed their licensing exams and flight time. If it appeals to you, it can be a good career, involving lifelong learning, cool uniforms, and lots and lots of travel. Most beginners start as copilots for regional airlines. Pay is low to begin with, but can be seriously into six figures for a full captain on international routes. The schools have vastly different infrastructures, so ask pointed questions about flight simulators and other equipment available to students, and be sure to get "available to students" defined precisely. There are too many schools to list, but if this appeals to you, here are a few schools to start your search. Oh, and one final thing: this is one route to becoming an astronaut.

College of Aeronautics
La Guardia Airport
Flushing, NY 11371
718-429-6600
www.aero.edu

Embry-Riddle Aeronautical University
3200 Willow Creek Road
Prescott, AZ 86301
800-888-3728 or 520-708-3728
www.pr.erau.edu

Embry-Riddle Aeronautical University
600 South Clyde Morris Boulevard
Daytona Beach, FL 32114
904-226-6000
www.embryriddle.edu

Western Michigan University
1201 Oliver Street
Kalamazoo, MI 49008
616-387-3530
www.wmich.edu

John D. Odegard School of Aerospace

Sciences at the University of

North Dakota

University Avenue

Grand Forks, ND 58202

800-258-1524 or 701-777-2011

www.und.edu

THE MERCHANT MARINE

If you don't want to join the military, perhaps you'd be interested in the merchant marine. The nation's maritime academies graduate able-bodied seamen and women, engineers, mates, and pilots for U.S. flagships carrying all types of cargo around the globe. The curriculum focuses on engineering and the sciences related to maritime issues (for example, you can study oceanography or meteorology). Just so you know, a typical oil tanker captain's schedule is six months on, six months off, so this is not the same as airline pilots who flit here and there and are back for dinner at least once a week. Also, these jobs can be cyclical, depending at least in part on global trade, but also on U.S. policy related to that trade. In the past, some of the maritime academies had placement rates as high as 100 percent, which is vastly higher than *any* other type of college or university, but that may not be the case by the time you get to the end of your program.

If this appeals to you, following are all the maritime and merchant academies in the United States and Canada. You should know that some of these have really cool programs, like all-sail tall ship training programs, and industrial salvage and repair scuba schools, and so on. Check them out. One thing to realize, however, is that the merchant marine can be pressed into service in case of severe need in wartime, and war zone merchant marines are considered veterans. But if that happens, there'd probably be no New York, so what the heck.

MARITIME COLLEGES AND ACADEMIES IN THE U.S. AND CANADA

Note: Not all of these are undergraduate degree-granting institutions.

California Maritime Academy
200 Maritime Academy Drive
Vallejo, CA 94590
800-561-1945 or 707-654-1000
www.csum.edu

Canadian Coast Guard College
1190 Westmount Road
Westmount, NS B1R 2J6
Canada
902-564-3660
www.cgc.ns.ca

Great Lakes Maritime Academy
Northwestern Michigan College
1701 East Front Street
Traverse City, MI 49686
800-748-0566 x1200 or 231-922-1200
www.nmc.edu/~maritime

Maine Maritime Academy
Pleasant Street
Castine, ME 04420
800-227-8465 or 207-326-4311
www.mainemaritime.edu

Marine Institute of Memorial University of Newfoundland
155 Ridge Road
St. Johns, NF A1C 5R3
Canada
800-563-5799 or 709-778-0497
www.mi.mun.ca

Massachusetts Maritime Academy
101 Academy Drive
Buzzards Bay
Cape Cod, MA 02532
800-544-3411 or 508-830-5000
ww2.mma.mass.edu

Seattle Maritime Academy
4455 Shilshole Avenue, NW
Seattle, WA 98107
206-782-2647
www.seattlecentral.org/maritime

State University of New York Maritime College
6 Pennyfield Avenue
Throggs Neck, NY 10465
718-409-7200
www.sunymaritime.edu

Texas A & M Maritime

200 Seawolf Parkway

Galveston, TX 77553

800-850-6376 or 409-740-4854

www.tamug.tamu.edu

U.S. Coast Guard Academy

31 Mohegan Avenue

New London, CT 06320

860-444-8444

www.cga.edu

U.S. Merchant Marine Academy

300 Steamboat Road

Kings Point, NY 11024

800-732-6267 or 516-773-5000

www.usmma.edu

U.S. Naval Academy

121 Blake Road

Annapolis, MD 21402

410-293-1000

www.nadn.navy.mil

Woods Hole Oceanographic Institute

360 Woods Hole Road

Woods Hole, MA 02543

508-457-2000

www.whoi.edu

Chapter Nine

THE WORK COLLEGES

Work colleges differ from co-op colleges in the way they view work itself. Co-op colleges view work as means to an end, as preparation for a career, as a complement to the curriculum, and so on. To perhaps overgeneralize, work colleges view work as a sacrament, as something beyond a means to an end, as something to be pursued, enjoyed, and mastered for its own sake. Work is central to the educational experience at these schools, not a peripheral annoyance or a distraction from studies.

A LIFE OF WORK AND LEARNING

by Dennis Jacobs, project director, Work Colleges Consortium

In the past three years, I have been employed by the nation's seven work colleges. In addition, I have been privileged to conduct research regarding student perspectives on the experience of work. In so doing, I have come to understand the importance of work in the lives of students and the need to enhance and integrate that experience on college campuses. The value of work is largely overlooked in higher education. This is unfortunate as 81 percent of undergraduates work at least part-time during any given year. Undergraduates know, or soon learn, that they must work in order to deal with the financial strain of attending college. The ability to pay influences whether or not they can continue, and affects the quality of their lives while enrolled.

Who we are is shaped largely by our experience of work. Many students have already worked long hours in difficult jobs in order to have the opportunity to go to college. The world of work has made an authentic contribution to what they have learned. Work has shaped their activity and often determined their opportunities.

Work is a vital part of human experience. Educators tend to see work as either contributing to the students' career development or as an unfortunate interference. This devaluing of the students' experience devalues students as well. At the work colleges, educators are reminded that they are in a position to help students understand, evaluate, and integrate this experience. Work is more than career development. People engage in study in order to enhance the quality of their lives. Whether or not work contributes to the advancement of a particular major, it has significance as a context for development of character, understanding, and of critical thinking skills, essential factors in building better communities. The world of work is a relevant part of our students' lives, not only as a contributor to future goals, but also as current experience.

It is within the context of work that graduates test not only their knowledge, but their character. Students understand that there are ethical issues related to the experience of work. Opportunities to examine these issues in an academic setting prepare students for ethical leadership. It is primarily in the contexts of work and family that students integrate academic understanding with out-of-class experience.

Faculty and staff at the nation's work colleges understand the importance of work. They also understand that work can, in fact, interfere with a student's academic endeavors. That is why the work colleges have created programs that balance work experience with quality academic programs. Class schedules and job assignments are designed to reduce conflicts between work and study. All of the work colleges are committed to reducing student debt through work.

The work colleges challenge students to contribute in a real way to college operations and departments. They benefit from being team members rewarded for admirable performance, and from the increased opportunities for representatives of the college to be involved in their development.

Involvement of all resident students in these programs builds an awareness of the needs of the community and an appreciation for the contributions of others. Work is seen as a service to the campus community. Students, thus, gain respect for the dignity of all work as they prepare themselves to lead in this new millennium. Students work in all areas of the colleges, from the mailroom and the kitchen to media service sites, computer centers, and public relations offices. As one work college student put it, "We are this place."

The work colleges create increased opportunity for related discussions and activities through the Work Colleges Consortium. These colleges collaborate to engage in service projects and partnerships, to share ideas about administration of student work programs, to examine academic links, and to promote open exchange regarding the role of work in higher education and in society. The work colleges serve as consultants for other higher education institutions and groups interested in improving student work programs.

Institutional missions and histories shape the work programs differently. Values other than work inform and shape the curriculum, work programs, and campus life. The colleges serve diverse populations and geographic regions. They provide a wide range of academic majors and extracurricular programs. Their educational philosophies are distinctive. Consequently, the work colleges offer a wide variety of experiences. Perhaps one is right for you.

THE WORK COLLEGES

ALICE LLOYD COLLEGE

Pippa Passes, Kentucky

Alice Lloyd offers full-ride tuition packages to students who are expected to go on to become doctors, lawyers, teachers, and other professionals before returning to serve their own hometowns in Appalachia. The college's mission: "At Alice Lloyd, we are preparing leadership for Appalachia." The college was founded by a visionary, Alice Spencer Geddes Lloyd, with quite a personality in her own right.

Alice Lloyd College
100 Purpose Road
Pippa Passes, KY 41844
606-368-2101
www.alicelloyd.edu

BEREA COLLEGE

Berea, Kentucky

Berea College has offered work learning opportunities since its inception in 1855. Currently, they provide full-tuition scholarships for all students who attend, and financial need is a prerequisite for acceptance. The labor grant is part of that scholarship, and all students work on campus. The college serves students from throughout Appalachia, and reserves some 20 percent of its admission slots for outstanding applicants who apply from throughout the world. Academic expectations are high, and Berea grads can be found in industry, education, and government throughout the country.

Berea College
101 Chestnut Street
Berea, KY 40403
800-326-5948 or 606-986-9341
www.berea.edu

All work is relevant. All work is valid. Work is not just career development, not just educational, not just an opportunity to provide service, but it is all of these things.

—Dennis Jacobs, project director, Work Colleges Consortium

BLACKBURN COLLEGE

Carlinville, Illinois

Students hold all management positions in the work program at Blackburn. The college offers a minor in leadership, which links work-program processes and opportunities with academic reflection. Its worker-managed teams mimic state-of-the-art management theory vis-à-vis employee empowerment.

Blackburn College

700 College Avenue

Carlinville, IL 62626

217-854-3231

www.blackburn.edu

COLLEGE OF THE OZARKS

Point Lookout, Missouri

College of the Ozarks also offers full-tuition scholarship to all admitted students. Their work program reaches beyond the campus to farms, the fire department, the Red Cross, and a summer camp for needy children. College of the Ozarks, aka "Hard Work U," allows a student to get a first-rate education without accruing a back-breaking load of debt.

College of the Ozarks

Opportunity Avenue

Point Lookout, MO 65726

800-222-0525 or 417-334-6411

www.cofo.edu

GODDARD COLLEGE

Plainfield, Vermont

Based upon a progressivist philosophy, Goddard strives to help students to reflect upon all life experience as a laboratory for learning. The work program provides a unique context for this reflection. As the school's home page says, "Your education at Goddard focuses your attention on the real world needs of community for beauty, justice, goodness and equity."

> **What I hear, I forget; what I see, I remember; what I do, I understand.**
>
> —*Unknown*

Goddard College

123 Pitkin Place

Plainfield, VT 05667

802-454-8311

www.goddard.edu

STERLING COLLEGE

Craftsbury Common, Vermont

Sterling College's campus features a family farm on which all students do "chores." The Dean of Work prefers the title of Dow, which stresses the spiritual and holistic nature of work involvement.

Sterling College

16 Sterling Drive

Craftsbury Common, VT 05827

800-648-3591 or 802-586-7711

www.sterlingcollege.edu

THE SAGA OF A MOUNTAINTOP SCHOOL

Tiny and innovative, World College West closed down in the summer of 1992 and devolved into a homeless shelter. You wouldn't want this to happen to your alma mater. According to newspaper reports at the time, the homeless particularly enjoyed the gym and weightroom at the former college. The site was later bought by Dr. Y. King Liu, lock, stock, and barrel. He has launched the University of Northern California. This school is not yet accredited, but it "aspires to become a premiere engineering university with substantial programs in the liberal arts and sciences." Curious? Check it out:

University of Northern California • 101 South San Antonio Road

Petaluma, CA 94952 • 707-765-6400 • www.uncm.edu

WARREN WILSON COLLEGE

Asheville, North Carolina

Students contribute 150 hours of volunteer community service as well as work at paying jobs. In addition to the regular curriculum, Warren Wilson periodically offers courses in which students reflect upon the very nature of work.

Warren Wilson College

701 Warren Wilson Road

Asheville, NC 28815

704-298-3325

www.warren-wilson.edu

BERRY COLLEGE

Berry College in Rome, Georgia, also offers all its students on-campus employment, and admits students regardless of need. Approximately 90 percent of Berry students work on campus. Started in 1902 by Martha Berry, Berry College today emphasizes a comprehensive curriculum combined with "high academic standards, Christian values, and practical work experience in a distinctive environment of natural beauty." Berry College claims to have the largest campus in the world, 28,000 acres of fields, forests, lakes, and mountains in northern Georgia, little more than an hour's drive from Atlanta, but a couple of worlds away from urban bustle and strife. The college has its origins in a one-room log cabin school, but today it boasts a central campus patterned after Oxford University's central quadrangle, a gift of car magnate Henry Ford.

Berry College • 2277 Martha Berry Boulevard, NE
Mount Berry, GA 30149 • 706-232-5374 • www.berry.edu

Chapter Ten

MORE COOL IDEAS

Should you consider a religious or church-affiliated school? This is a very satisfying option for many students, but there are some caveats, as we will cover in this chapter. Also, we'll consider some of the options for nontraditional-age students and single parents, who may not want to go to school where everyone is eighteen and single. Schools of art and music are covered, albeit briefly. This chapter also houses a grabbag of unusual college options, such as schools focusing on textiles, computer games, foreign languages, culinary arts, auctioneering, railroading, stand-up comedy, and surfing, among many others. Finally, what about options for those students who want to consider taking a year off before hitting the college books? Programs ranging from Semester at Sea to Americorps are briefly described, as well as a Web site offering thousands of activities a young person can pursue instead of a freshman year.

THOMAS AQUINAS COLLEGE

The best college class I ever attended, undergraduate or graduate, was at Thomas Aquinas College, a school affiliated with the Catholic faith and with a rigorous great books curriculum. All the students had read and thought about the assignment, a difficult passage in philosophy of religion with which I happened to be familiar. All the students participated equally, the men and the women, and intelligently, which was easy to discern due to the nature of the passage. They backed up their comments with evidence and careful, logical arguments. They were politely influenced by one another's thoughts, with the conversation building in a sequence (instead of that compounded non sequitur that happens when students are simply waiting their turn to say what *they* think). The reading itself was the focus of the class, and any tangents that did come up were gently steered back to the central question by the professor. The professor was a master of the material, and had read the original in Latin, which he occasionally used to discern the most exact meaning of the more esoteric sentences. The students spoke for perhaps 90 percent of the time, the professor only occasionally interjecting guidance. No one knew for sure where the conversation was headed. The hour passed as if it were a moment.

This class had begun with a prayer, for which the professor and all the students but one stood. The one student who did not stand was an atheist, who had chosen this school as an excellent place to get an education, and had said as much to the admission committee, both that he was an atheist and that he thought they offered an outstanding education. They admitted him, he came, and his presence was proof positive that this was an institution of higher learning, a place where critical thinking was the goal, not indoctrination. I shall remember this class, where I was but a guest, for the rest of my life.

SHOULD YOU GO TO A RELIGIOUS OR CHURCH-AFFILIATED SCHOOL?

If you are a member of a faith, should you go to a school closely affiliated with that faith? This is certainly an option you should consider. Great reasons to go to a religious school:

- You don't have to explain your religion to nonbelievers.
- You don't have to put up with professors and fellow classmates who insult your beliefs in class (out of class, maybe, but in class probably not).
- Your parents will probably endorse your choice.
- You can explore your faith in an environment where such exploration is the norm, rather than something you feel you need to conceal from others.
- Some religiously affiliated schools have outstanding financial aid.

One warning, however: faith is explored, intellectually, at many religious and religion-affiliated schools. If you cannot articulate, expound upon, support, defend, and otherwise dissect your faith, you may be uncomfortable. It is, after all, a college not a church. Furthermore, you should not think that there is not sexual and substance use exploration at religious schools. This is a naive belief, leading to great disappointment by students who were expecting all the other students at a religious school to be as pious as are they.

I interviewed an atheist who went to a Christian college because it had a great TV studio and students had unlimited access to it. He was admitted and even given an academic scholarship. Nowhere in his application did he discuss his religious beliefs or misrepresent himself, but he did not volunteer this information either. He was delighted with the television studio, and ended up making a student film that won national awards. Nevertheless, he was absolutely miserable for his entire undergraduate career. "I felt like a pariah," he told me. "Once people found out I was an

Schools that claim to promote a religious environment for religious students do not always have that environment. Some students select these schools to please their parents, without personally endorsing the lifestyle they are expected to exemplify. Others choose a college while in a particularly strong period of faith, and later stay on with a religious college after they are no longer as devout. Furthermore, the schools themselves pass through more and less secular and more and less pious periods in their cultural and collective histories.

atheist, they ostracized me or tried to convert me. Nobody could leave it alone. I wasn't allowed to just be me. I was always 'that atheist.' Professors and students alike did this. I have only one friend from my entire four years as an undergraduate, and he lives in another state." Caveat emptor.

I have visited some outstanding religious schools, and for those who have strong religious beliefs, they can be the best college choice. Here are a few options:

If you are Catholic, **Thomas Aquinas** in Ojai, California (see p. 204), and **The Thomas More College of Liberal Arts** in Merrimack, New Hampshire, provide outstanding—and rigorous—academic experiences. Neither is exclusively Catholic, but Thomas Aquinas is overwhelmingly so.

Alverno College in Milwaukee, Wisconsin, provides women of all faiths with an innovative curriculum focusing on mastering a specified set of life skills. Alverno prides itself on serving disadvantaged and nontraditional students, including single mothers. (See p. 208 for more on Alverno.)

The twenty-eight **Jesuit universities** are also an option. The affiliation is not overly strong, and most view themselves as liberal institutions of education; nevertheless, and especially if you've attended Catholic parochial schools, it's an option to consider. For a complete list, see www.ajcunet.edu.

If you are Protestant, **Wheaton College** in Wheaton, Illinois, was repeatedly cited in my surveys as a strong liberal arts college with a purposeful Christian atmosphere.

Perhaps less demanding but equally interested in providing a purposeful Christian atmosphere are two schools I visit often: **George Fox University** in Newberg, Oregon, and **Grove City College** in Grove City, Pennsylvania. George Fox was origianlly a Quaker school, but now welcomes all denominations.

There are, of course, many, many others. If you are a Christian Scientist, the best school in the world for you is **Principia** in Elsah, Illinois. It combines a strong liberal arts education with a practicing Christian Science community. The school has a strong endowment, a beautiful campus up on the bluffs overlooking the Mississippi River, and a truly global perspective from the heart of the Midwest. If you are interested in more on Christian religious colleges, both the decision to attend and specific colleges to consider, see Peterson's *Christian Colleges & Universities* (Peterson's, 1999), and talk to your religious leaders about options for your faith.

SPECIAL PROGRAMS FOR NONTRADITIONAL STUDENTS, SINGLE PARENTS, AND WOMEN

Here's a personal tale for you: When I was in high school, my mother was in college. Starting from scratch, she graduated Phi Beta Kappa in three and a half years, was president of the academic honor society for her discipline, and provided an academic role model for her teenage children. My mother loved learning, and every day she'd come home and tell us everything she'd learned that day. At one time there were five full-time students in my household. Were we deprived because our mother went to school while we were growing up? On the contrary, I think we were well served by this experience. My mother didn't bake cookies, but if you brought home a box of rocks with fossils in them, she was always first to recommend that you dump them on the table and find the magnifying glass that came with the big dictionary.

So, no matter whether you are twenty-one or ninety, if you want to go to school there is a way. And, lest you think you are going to be too old by the time you complete that degree, I always quote my favorite wise woman, Dear Abby, who asks, "And how old will you be in four years if you *don't* complete that degree?"

Many colleges and universities have on-site daycare for students and staff. Your status as head of household *is* taken into consideration in financial aid offers. Single mothers often have preferential placement in campus-owned married and family housing. You may be able to get an assignment as a residence hall advisor, where you can be "dorm mom" and save on your expenses.

Here are two programs that focus on the needs of nontraditional women students.

THE FRANCES PERKINS PROGRAM AT MOUNT HOLYOKE COLLEGE
South Hadley, Massachusetts

This is a program for women twenty-four and older, sometimes *a lot* older, "married, single, divorced, or widowed." Frances Perkins was a Mount Holyoke alumna and secretary of labor under Franklin Delano Roosevelt. She implemented many worker protections that we all take for granted now, such as the minimum wage, child labor restrictions, and unemployment insurance. The Frances Perkins Program at Mount

Robert Lopatin began his medical education at the Albert Einstein College of Medicine in 1995 at the age of fifty-one, and he's a doctor today. So go for it!

There are no programs concentrating on the needs of single fathers, but if you can get a place in the married and family dorms you can take advantage of on-campus daycare and you'll be the most popular bachelor in town.

Holyoke College is an opportunity for the scholarly minded woman to complete her degree at the oldest institution of higher learning for women in the United States. The program purports to smooth the transition for women, including those who have not been in a classroom in years. The program is integrated into the larger campus, thereby being able to offer forty-four different majors.

Frances Perkins Program at Mount Holyoke College
50 College Street
South Hadley, MA 01075-1435
413-538-2000
www.mtholyoke.edu

ALVERNO COLLEGE

There is no place like Alverno College, a Catholic women's college with a unique curriculum and mission. Alverno is a teaching college, with intense, small classes, and an emphasis on team work and in-class presentations. "There's nowhere to hide at Alverno. It's not cool not to do your work here." The curriculum is designed to establish mastery over self and subject matter. There are over sixty majors and concentrations, but no one graduates who cannot demonstrate mastery of Alverno's "Eight Abilities":

Communication	Social Interaction
Analysis	Global Perspectives
Problem Solving	Effective Citizenship
Valuing in Decision Making	Aesthetic Responsiveness

Students of traditional age are welcome at Alverno, but many of the students are returnees who work, or are parents, or both. Most live off campus and commute, 85 percent receive financial aid, almost 70 percent are first generation, and almost 40 percent are minority. You don't have to be a top student to get into Alverno, but you will be one by the time you get out.

Alverno College

3400 South 43rd Street

Milwaukee, WI 53234

800-933-3401 or 414-382-6000

www.alverno.edu

HERITAGE COLLEGE

Minority and nontraditional-age men and women might be very interested in Heritage College in Toppenish, Washington. Heritage is an entire school tailored to the special needs of rural and isolated peoples, such as itinerant farm workers and Native Americans. With a commitment to serving this constituency, Heritage offers a low student-teacher ratio, committed faculty, and a student body that is likely to be making significant sacrifices to pursue an education. The school promotes "a Christian philosophy which recognizes the unique dignity of each human person." There is no cynicism or nihilism here, no one angry at the world because they lack meaning in their lives, no rows of Porches and BMWs in the parking lots.

Heritage College is located within the Yakama Indian Reservation. It has cooperative ventures with the Yakama Nation, Yakama Indian Nation Tribal Headquarters, Yakama Tribal School, Yakama Nation Natural Resources Division, Yakama Cultural Museum and Library, and the Tribal Administrator's Office.

Heritage College

3240 Fort Road

Toppenish, WA 98948

509-865-2244

www.heritage.edu

Nontraditional? Over 25? Over 40? Over X? Considering college? Check out Carole S. Fungaroli's *Traditional Degrees for Nontraditional Students* (Farrar, Straus & Giroux, 2000). She comes to the conclusion that it's never too late to go to college or pursue advanced education, and that latecomers are benefited in every aspect of their lives (career, personal, social). Finally, check out *Bears' Guide to Earning Degrees by Distance Learning* (Ten Speed Press, 1999), which identifies all types of degree completion and distance learning programs. If you're three units shy of finishing a bachelor's, even if it's been twenty years, the solution is in *Bears' Guide.* One nice thing about *Bears' Guide,* it differentiates cleanly between diploma mills and legitimate, accredited options.

Major universities and commuter campuses often serve the needs of nontraditional students very well. On almost any campus in the nation, the average GPA for older students is higher than that for traditional-age students. The average age of the entire student body at a major state university or commuter campus is often closer to thirty than to twenty, and with the other nontraditional and graduate students, you will see plenty of people in their forties, fifties, and beyond.

New College in Sarasota, Florida, and **Marlboro College** in Marlboro, Vermont, also seem to do well by nontraditional age students; the greater maturity and self-directedness that comes with age are an advantage in these challenging programs.

Also, see the list of Tribal, Indian, and Native American Colleges on p. 242 and the list of Hispanic Colleges, on p. 232.

And finally, you should know about **Florida Atlantic University's Lifelong Learning Society**, "the nation's largest university-based educational program for seniors." Offering a wide range of minicourses every week, this program is available on seven campuses in Florida. Call 561-297-3171 for more information.

MORE COOL IDEAS: SPECIALTY SCHOOLS

Here are a few specialty schools that may be of interest to you:

- **National Labor College,** Washington, DC
- **Philadelphia College of Textiles and Sciences,** Philadelphia, Pennsylvania
- **Institute of Textile Technology,** Charlottesville, Virginia
- **The Institute of Paper Science and Technology,** Atlanta, Georgia
- **The College of Insurance,** New York, New York
- **John Jay College of Criminal Justice,** New York, New York

"History of Rock Music" ranks among the most popular music courses offered at UNC-Chapel Hill. Associate professor John Covach wears his Fender Stratocaster in the classroom and jams along with some of his students on tunes from Elvis Presley, Jimi Hendrix, the Beach Boys, and others. Covach also teaches "The Beatles, Psychedelia, and the British Invasion" and a seminar just for freshmen entitled "Rock and Roll Music: The First Wave, 1955–64."

COMPUTER GAME STUDIES

By the time you read this sentence, the University of California, Irvine, will launch a new academic concentration in gaming studies, courtesy of The Interdisciplinary Gaming Studies Program. So if you've spent years perfecting your touch at Blasto! or whatever, you can apply that skill in college while you learn about the cultural impact of computerized games, the computer science behind special effects, and the demographics and psychographics of players. The program will install its own game room on campus, complete with state-of-the-art game stations. According to the *Wall Street Journal* (24 February 2000), computer games are a $7.45 billion business, about the same size as the domestic in-theater movie ticket sales, and growing rapidly. When virtual reality becomes a reality, graduates of this program will be poised to rule the world, or at least some version of it.

INTERPRETING AND TRANSLATING

The Monterey Institute of International Studies is primarily a graduate school, but it does have twenty undergraduates and is seeking to add more. This is one of the only institutions on U.S. soil to train live interpreters and translators, including those working in technical and scientific areas.

Monterey Institute of
International Studies
425 Van Buren
Monterey, CA 93940
408-647-4100
www.miis.edu

One of the older democracies in the world is the Cherokee Nation. Early European settlers could not understand their form of government, and referred to the Cherokee leaders as kings and chiefs. There never was, not even once, any person who could be called a Cherokee Princess, even though several are buried in graves so marked by romanticizing Europeans.

ART

Try these schools:

- **Rhode Island School of Design,** Providence, Rhode Island
- **California Institute of the Arts** (aka Cal Arts), Valencia, California
- **Parson's School of Design,** New York, New York
- **The School of the Art Institute of Chicago,** Chicago, Illinois
- **San Francisco Art Institute,** San Francisco, California
- **Cooper Union,** New York, New York

MUSIC

Try these schools:

- **The Juilliard School,** New York, New York
- **Oberlin College,** Oberlin, Ohio
- **Lawrence University,** Appleton, Wisconsin
- **Illinois Wesleyan University,** Bloomington, Illinois

Or check out these guides dedicated to arts and music schools: Peterson's *Professional Degree Programs in the Visual and Performing Arts* (Peterson's, 1995), or Carole J. Everett's *The Performing Arts Major's College Guide* (IDG Books Worldwide, 1998).

COOKING

The culinary arts might be the perfect direction for you to head in.

Academy of Culinary Arts
Indiana University of Pennsylvania
125 South Gilpin Street
Punxsutawney, PA 15767
800-438-6424 or 814-938-1159
www.iup.edu/cularts

California Culinary Academy
625 Polk Street
San Francisco, CA 94102
800-229-2433 or 415-771-3500
www.baychef.com

Kansas State University in Manhattan, Kansas, has a major in baking science.

**The Cambridge School of
Culinary Arts**
2020 Massachusetts Avenue
Cambridge, MA 02140-2104
617-354-2020
www.cambridgeculinary.com

**The Cooking & Hospitality Institute
of Chicago**
361 West Chestnut
Chicago, IL 60610
312-944-0882
www.chicnet.org

Culinary Academy of Long Island
141 Post Avenue
Westbury, NY 11590
516-876-8888
www.culinaryacademyli.com

**Culinary Arts Institute at The
Mississippi University for Women**
302 15th Street
South Columbus, MS 39701
662-241-7472
www.muw.edu/interdisc

**Culinary Institute of America
(aka CIA)**
433 Albany Post Road
Hyde Park, NY 12538
914-452-9600
www.ciachef.edu

Florida Culinary Institute
2400 Metro Centre Boulevard
West Palm Beach, FL 33407
800-TOP-Chef or 561-688-2001
www.floridaculinary.com

French Culinary Institute
462 Broadway
New York, NY 10013
888-FCI-CHEF or 212-219-8890
www.frenchculinary.com

**International Institute of
Culinary Arts**
100 Rock Street
Fall River, MA 02720
888-383-2665 or 508-675-9305
www.iica.com

New England Culinary Institute
250 Main Street
Montpelier, VT 05602
802-223-6324
www.neculinary.com

San Francisco Baking Institute
390 Swift Avenue, #13
South San Francisco, CA 94080
650-589-5784
www.sfbi.com

While we're on the subject of food: Why are there 10 hot dogs in a pack, and 8 hot dog buns in a pack?

School of Culinary Arts

Baltimore International College

17 Commerce Street

Baltimore, MD 21202-3230

410-752-4710

www.bic.edu/admissions/cularts.html

Western Culinary Institute

1201 S.W. 12th, Suite 100

Portland, OR 97201

800-666-0312 or 503-223-2245

www.westernculinary.com

AUCTIONEERING

Want to go to school for nine days and learn the high art of auctioneering? The Missouri Auction School could be for you. The oldest and largest auction school in the world, it has trained students from Great Britain to Japan, and claims "an international reputation for producing top auctioneers in all fields." The Missouri Auction School trained its first students in 1905, and it's still going strong today. You can learn from the pros about your special areas of interest during in-depth workshops on antiques, autos, real estate, art, machinery and equipment, livestock, business liquidations, and more.

The Missouri Auction School

213 South Fifth Street

St. Joseph, Missouri 64501

800-835-1955 or 816-279-7117

MODERN RAILROADING

The Modoc Railroad Academy in remote and beautiful Alturas, California, offers training for students who want "to enter the field of modern railroading." Railroad staffs are quite old, on average. While railroads have updated their technologies and are moving record amounts of freight, massive waves of retirement are expected to rock the industry in the next few years. "They anticipate more than 100,000 job openings in the next ten years," according to the Modoc Railroad Academy. The Academy

Virginia Polytechnic Institute and State University, aka Virginia Tech, has a Navy A-6 Flight Simulator as well as its own airport. Embry-Riddle has a Boeing 737-300 Flight Simulator. Purdue claims it has two. Many of the other aeronautical universities have simulators and training planes. (See p. 190. Of course the Air Force Academy has real planes, and lots of them.)

offers an eight-week intensive course leading to entry-level employability. This is a hands-on course, with real railroads, engines, tracks, and, they promise, whistles. It is approved by the Railroad Educational Training Association.

The Modoc Railroad Academy

2001 Railroad

Alturas, California 96101

530-233-5515

COMEDY SCHOOL

Or, for something totally different, why not go to school to learn to be a stand-up comic. The Humber Comedy Center offers a one-year, comprehensive training program in comedy at The American Comedy Institute in New York City or at Humber College in Toronto, Canada. It has an impressive board of advisors: Steve Allen (chairman), Anne Beatts, Irvin Arthur, Mark Breslin, Joe Flaherty, Bruce Jay Friedman, Eugene Levy, Rick Moranis, Jack Rollins, Perry Rosemond, George Shapiro, Dave Thomas.

The Humber Comedy Center's
American Comedy Institute

1600 Broadway, Suite 614

New York, NY 10019

212-247-5555

www.comedyinstitute.com

The Humber Comedy Center
Humber College

205 Humber College Boulevard

Toronto, ON M9W 5L7

Canada

416-675-3111

www.humberc.on.ca/~comedy

At the age of fifteen, John Goddard prepared a list of lifetime goals, 127 of them in all. He wanted to explore the Nile, the Amazon, and the Congo; study native cultures in Brazil, Borneo, Kenya, and Australia; climb the Matterhorn and Mt. Ararat; explore the Great Barrier Reef and the Red Sea; and retrace the steps of Marco Polo and Alexander the Great, and write at least one book. He did all these by the time he was in his thirties. Read about it in his book *Kayaks Down the Nile* (Brigham Young University Press, 1979). Maybe you should make a list of life goals now too.

AMERICORPS

Maybe you shouldn't go to college right away at all. Americorps accepts students right out of high school for terms of service from nine months to two years. Call 1-800-AMERICORPS or surf to www.americorps.org. You need to check out the Americorps program you're interested in carefully, however, as they are all different and can change radically from year to year. You'll have to live on almost nothing, cash-wise, but you'll gain a lump sum upon completion that can be applied to college tuition. Meanwhile, you can work on the environment or fight poverty or preserve the legacy of this and past generations.

TAKE A YEAR OFF

There's a Web site dedicated to structured time off run by Bob Gilpin out of Milton, Massachusetts. Call 617-698-8977 or 617-696-6297 or surf to www.timeoutassociates.com. You can learn about such opportunities as teaching in Kenya, apprenticing to a glassblower in San Francisco, and serving as a production slave on documentaries in New York. Bob told me he has thousands of such opportunities catalogued, and he works with students and their families to find the right one, sign them up, and oversee the transition. He charges a consultation fee, but for those families that can afford it, he's the known source for this type of thing. For a book on the subject, see Colin Hall and Ron Lieber's *Taking Time Off: Inspiring Stories of Students Who Enjoyed Successful Breaks from College and How You Can Plan Your Own* (Noonday Press, 1996).

SEMESTER AT SEA

Semester at Sea (SAS) accepts students who have completed "at least one full-time semester of college." Although students complete twelve credit hours per semester in SAS, several have told me that this is more like an adventure vacation than a semester at college. It's also pretty expensive at $15,550 single with portal, and a "full financial aid" rate of $4,975. (If you are in need of full financial assistance, where in the heck are you going to come up with $4,975???) Also, going abroad can be dangerous, even under the best-run programs. Check out www.cherese.org, although in all fairness, you can get hit by a bus on your way to church.

Semester at Sea

University of Pittsburgh

811 William Pitt Union

Pittsburgh, PA 15260

800-854-0195 or 412-648-7490

shipboard@sas.ise.pitt.edu

www.studyabroad.com

www.semesteratsea.com

As an alternate source, check out:

Sea Education Association

P.O. Box 6

Woods Hole, MA 02540

800-552-3633

www.seaeducation.org

www.sea.edu

MORE UNUSUAL CLASSES, MAJORS, AND PROGRAMS

- **The Center for Really Neat Research,** Syracuse University, Syracuse, New York
- **The Center for the Study of Popular Television,** Syracuse University
- **Ranch Management,** Texas Christian University, Fort Worth
- **Peace and Conflict Studies,** University of California, Berkeley
- **The Family Violence Education and Research Center,** SUNY Stony Brook
- **Math Ecology,** University of Tennessee, Knoxville
- **Energetic Materials Research and Testing Center** (that means explosives, folks), New Mexico Tech, Socorro, New Mexico
- **The National Superconducting Cyclotron Laboratory**, Michigan State University, East Lansing
- **Equestrian Studies**, Salem-Teikyo University, Salem, West Virginia

What are diploma mills? They are nonaccredited "colleges" and "universities" that grant degrees for a fee. Sometimes the "student" doesn't have to do any work at all, and sometimes no matter what they turn in it receives the same marks. Recently, a very famous, best-selling author was revealed to have "earned" his doctorate from one of these. He's on TV every day referred to as "Dr. _____." How embarrassing!

On the other hand, an honorary doctorate is a degree awarded to someone who a university admires, respects, or wants to curry the favor of. There's nothing wrong with an honorary doctorate. It's an honor to receive one. However, an honorary doctorate is not and has never been the same thing as an earned doctorate.

The Rev. Theodore M. Hesburgh, C.S.C., president emeritus of the University of Notre Dame, has received 141 honorary degrees, more than anyone else in the world. He has been honored because of his tireless service to others. He deserves the recognition. How admirable!

- **National Labor College,** Silver Spring, Maryland (an AFL-CIO affiliate where you can learn organizing, labor law, and the history of the labor movement)

- **Surf Camp,** Orange County Marine Institute (not to be confused with the Surf Science Technology Degree Program at Plymouth University, in England, U.K.)

- **The National Center for Bioethics in Research and Healthcare,** Tuskegee University, Tuskegee, Alabama

- **The School of Leadership Studies,** University of Richmond, Richmond, Virginia

- **Pornography (COL 289),** Wesleyan University, Middletown, Connecticut ("indefinitely suspended" as of summer 2000)

- **The Center for Nonproliferation Studies,** Monterey Institute of International Studies, Monterey, California

- **The *Simpsons* Sitcom as Social Satire,** University of California, Berkeley

Chapter Eleven

MEN'S, WOMEN'S, AND MINORITY-FOCUSED COLLEGES

The rationale for attending a men's, women's, or minority-focused institution was presented on p. 47. Also, read the essay in this chapter by Amelia R. Shelby, who explains why she went from an Ivy League school to an historically Black college for graduate school. Her rationale would apply to everyone who has done well but wondered what it would be like to be in the majority for a change. One warning about some of the schools listed in this chapter: Some schools that have traditionally served certain constituencies no longer have very impressive percentages of those populations. In other words, you could go to a school that claims to focus on you, and find you're still a minority. And finally, it can be a great idea to apply to some men's, women's or minority-focused institutions as part of your college choice process, even if you haven't ever thought about this option before. Students at these schools are passionate about them, and that's a clear sign that they have something special to offer.

WHY I *FINALLY* CHOSE TO ATTEND AN HISTORICALLY BLACK COLLEGE

by Amelia R. Shelby, Howard University

Having attended a predominately white secondary school and college, I have come to appreciate my experience at an African-American medical school even more (Howard University, College of Medicine). Although I don't regret the academic choices I have made over the years, I still wonder how my life might have been different if I had gone to an African-American college during those very formative years of my life. Attending African-American universities provides unique opportunities to discover one's own potential without the burden and responsibility tied to the politics of good race relations.

College is a time for discovering one's identity separate from the world you've always known. Like many ambitious young women, I wanted to go to the "best" school that accepted me and found myself at Columbia University in New York City. It was there that I made the realization that "best" is a relative term, and what is best for my high school classmates was not the best for me. I had much in common with my new classmates, but I was constantly reminded of how different I felt in a predominantly white school. In a desperate attempt to reconnect with my own culture I sought out the African-American community on campus. I participated in every campus group that dedicated itself to promoting self-knowledge in the students of color. It was a very important time in my life, but I also found myself investing much of my time to making my school aware that African-American students existed and that we wanted to know about our own history also.

It became perfectly obvious that at Columbia, I could be a talented Black student, but as an African-American at an African-American college, I could rise above labels and excel based on my own talents. Having grown up in a mixed middle-class neighborhood in the Midwest, I was sheltered from the ugly face of racism. I had a large and close-knit extended family and we were known in our community. All of these factors gave me a strong sense of identity and security. However, when I became old enough to go away to school, my world began to change. Like many African-American families in the 1980s, we moved to the suburbs, which was less integrated than the old neighborhood, and I attended a private school. Suddenly I was surrounded by people who drew their opinions about African-Americans from *The Cosby Show* and other equally distorted images available to mainstream Americans through the media. I made friends and became more comfortable with my surroundings, but I still couldn't shake the feeling that I was some kind of an ambassador for—or representative of—the entire black race. If there was a discussion in class about racism, the teacher asked my opinion. If there was a discussion of rap music in the lunchroom, my classmates asked about my musical tastes. I was in the position of educating my teachers, my peers, and my friends, about a culture that I myself knew less and less about. Just as a patient is best treated by the physician who knows him best, so is an African-American student best taught by individuals with whom the student shares a common history.

LIST OF HISTORICALLY BLACK COLLEGES

An "H" by the name refers to the college as being an historically and presently predominantly Black one, and it will probably remain so. A "P" by the name indicates that the college may or may not have been historically Black, although it is predominantly Black at present, but the college also has at some point opened attendance to students of all races and may or may not be actively recruiting those students. Be aware that some of these institutions are as much as 70 percent white, in spite of these designations. Also, several of these institutions consistently rank near the top for total student debt at date of graduation, so ask pointed and comparative questions about financial aid before deciding which historically Black college may be right for you.

Alabama A & M University - H
4107 Meridian Street
Normal, AL 35762
205-851-5000
www.aamu.edu

Alabama State University - P
915 South Jackson Street
Montgomery, AL 36104
334-229-4291
www.alasu.edu

Alcorn State University - H
1000 ASU Drive
Alcorn State, MS 39096-7500
800-222-6790 or 601-877-6100
www.alcorn.edu

Barber-Scotia College - P
145 Cabarnus Avenue, West
Concord, NC 28025
704-789-2902
www.barber-scotia.edu

Benedict College - P
1600 Harden Street
Columbia, SC 29204
803-256-4220
bchome.benedict.edu

Bennett College - H
(all women, United Methodist)
900 East Washington Street
Greensboro, NC 27401
800-413-5323 or 336-273-4431
www.bennett.edu

Bethune-Cookman College - H

640 Drive Mary McLeod

Bethune Boulevard

Daytona Beach, FL 32114-3099

800-448-0228 or 904-255-1401

www.bethune.cookman.edu

Bowie State University - P

14000 Jericho Park Road

Bowie, MD 20715-9465

301-464-3000

www.bowiestate.edu

Cheyney University

of Pennsylvania - H

Cheyney & Creek Roads

Cheyney, PA 19319-0200

800-223-3608 or 610-399-2000

www.cheyney.edu

Claflin College - P

700 College Avenue, NE

Orangeburg, SC 29115

800-922-1276 or 803-535-5097

www.scicu.org/claflin/cchome.htm

Coppin State College - P

2500 West North Avenue

Baltimore, MD 21216

410-383-5400

www.coppin.edu

Delaware State University - H

1200 North DuPont Highway

Dover, DE 19901-2277

302-739-4904

www.dsc.edu

Dillard University - H

2601 Gentilly Boulevard

New Orleans, LA 70122

800-216-6637 or 504-283-8822

www.dillard.edu

Edward Waters College - H

(African Methodist Episcopal)

1658 Kings Road

Jacksonville, FL 32209

904-366-2715

www.ewc.edu

For a scholarly review of the experiences of four thousand Black students at both historically Black colleges and at predominantly white colleges, see if you can find a copy of Walter R. Allen's *College in Black and White: African American Students in Predominately White and Historically Black Public Universities* (SUNY Press, 1991).

> **It must be borne in mind that the tragedy in life doesn't lie in not reaching your goal. The tragedy lies in having no goal to reach. It isn't a calamity to die with dreams unfulfilled, but it is a calamity not to dream. It is not a disaster to be unable to capture your ideal, but it is a disaster to have no ideal to capture. It is not a disgrace not to reach the stars, but it is a disgrace to have no stars to reach for. Not failure, but low aim is sin.**

—Dr. Benjamin E. Mays, president emeritus, Morehouse College

Fayetteville State University - P
1200 Murchison Road
Fayetteville, NC 28301-4298
910-486-1474
www.uncfsu.edu

Fisk University - H
1000 17th Avenue, North
Nashville, TN 37208
800-443-FISK or 615-329-8500
www.fisk.edu

Florida Memorial College - P
15800 N.W. 42nd Avenue
Miami, FL 33054
305-626-3750
www.fmc.edu

Grambling State University - P
P.O. Drawer 28
Grambling, LA 71245
318-274-2233
www.gram.edu

Hampton University - H
Hampton, VA 23668
800-737-7778 or 757-727-5328
www.hamptonu.edu

Howard University - H
2400 Sixth Street, NW
Washington, DC 20059
202-806-6100
www.howard.edu

Huston-Tillotson College - P
900 Chicon Street
Austin, TX 78702
512-505-3028
www.htc.edu

Jackson State University - P
1400 J.R. Lynch Street
Jackson, MS 39217
800-848-6817 or 601-968-2121
www.jsums.edu

Kentucky State University - P
400 East Main Street
Frankfort, KY 40601
800-325-1716 or 502-227-6000
www.kysu.edu

Langston University - H
Langston, OK 73050
405-466-2231
www.lunet.edu

LeMoyne-Owen College - H
807 Walker Avenue
Memphis, TN 38126
901-774-9090
www.lemoyne-owen.edu

Lincoln University - H
820 Chestnut Street
Jefferson City, MO
800-521-5052 or 573-681-5000
www.lincolnu.edu

Lincoln University - H

1570 Baltimore Pike

Lincoln University, PA 19352

610-932-8300

www.lincoln.edu

Livingstone College - P

701 West Monroe Street

Salisbury, NC 28144

800-835-3435 or 704-638-5500

www.livingstone.edu

Mary Holmes College - H

P.O. Drawer 1257

Highway 50 West

West Point, MS 39773-1257

www.maryholmes.edu

Meharry Medical College - H

1005 Drive D. B. Todd, Jr., Boulevard

Nashville, TN 37208-3599

615-327-6223

www.mmc.edu

Morehouse College - H

(all men)

830 Westview Drive, SW

Atlanta, GA 30314

800-851-1254 or 404-681-2800

www.morehouse.edu

Morris Brown College - P

643 Martin Luther King, Jr. Drive, NW

Atlanta, GA 30314

404-220-0152

www.morrisbrown.edu

Morris College - P

North Main Street

Sumter, SC 29150

888-778-1345 or 803-775-9371

www.icusc.org/morrise/mchome.htm

Norfolk State University - P

700 Park Avenue

Norfolk, VA 23504

757-823-8600

www.nsu.edu

North Carolina Central University - H

1801 Fayetteville Street

Durham, NC 27707

919-560-6100

www.nccu.edu

Oakwood College - H

(7th Day Adventist)

7000 Adventist Boulevard

Huntsville, AL 35896

800-824-5312

www.oakwood.edu

> **When house and land are gone and spent, Then learning is most excellent.**
>
> —*Samuel Foote*

Paine College - P
1235 15th Street
Augusta, GA 30901-3182
706-821-8320
www.paine.edu

Paul Quinn College - H
3837 Simpson Stuart Road
Dallas, TX 75241
800-237-2648 or 214-376-1000
www.pqc.edu

Saint Augustine's College - P
1315 Oakwood Avenue
Raleigh, NC 27610-2298
919-516-4012
www.st-aug.edu

Shaw University - H
118 East South Street
Raleigh, NC 27601
919-546-8275
www.shawu.edu

Spelman College - H
350 Spelman Lane, SW
Atlanta, GA 30314
800-982-2411 or 404-681-3643
www.spelman.edu

Stillman College - P
3600 Stillman Boulevard
Tuscaloosa, AL 35401
205-366-8817
www.stillman.edu

Talladega College - H
627 West Battle Street
Talladega, AL 35160
800-633-2440 or 256-362-0206
www.talladega.edu

Tougaloo College - H
500 West County Line Road
Tougaloo, MS 39174
800-424-2566
www.tougaloo.edu

Tuskegee University - H
Tuskegee, AL 36088
800-622-6531 or 334-727-8011
www.tusk.edu

Voorhees College - P
1411 Voorhees Road
Denmark, SC 29042
800-446-3351 or 803-793-3351
www.voorhees.edu

Wilberforce University - H
1055 North Bickett Road
Wilberforce, OH 45384
937-376-2911
www.wilberforce.edu

Wiley College - H

711 Wiley Avenue

Marshall, TX 75670

903-927-3235

www.wiley.edu

Xavier University - H (Catholic)

7325 Palmetto Street

New Orleans, LA 70125

504-483-7388

www.xula.edu

THE UNITED NEGRO COLLEGE FUND (UNCF) MEMBER INSTITUTIONS

Barber-Scotia College

145 Cabarrus Avenue, West

Concord, NC 28025

704-789-2902

www.barber-scotia.edu

Benedict College

Harden and Blanding Streets

Columbia, SC 29204

803-253-5143

bchome.benedict.edu

Bennett College

900 E. Washington Street

Greensboro, NC 27401

800-413-5323 or 336-273-4431

www.bennett.edu

Bethune-Cookman College

640 Dr. Mary McLeod

Bethun Boulevard

Daytona Beach, FL 32114-3099

800-448-0228 or 904-255-1401

www.bethune.cookman.edu

Claflin College

700 College Avenue, NE

Orangeberg, SC 29115

800-922-1276

www.scicu.org/claflin/cchome.htm

Clark Atlanta University

240 James P. Brawley Drive, SW

Atlanta, GA 30314

404-880-6605

www.cau.edu

Dillard University

2601 Gentilly Boulevard

New Orleans, LA 70122

800-216-6637

www.dillard.edu

Edward Waters College

1658 Kings Road

Jacksonville, FL 32209

904-366-2715

www.ewc.edu

> **"You enter to learn, but you go forth to serve."**
>
> —*Jim Mayo, regional director, United Negro College Fund*

Fisk University

1000 17th Avenue, North

Nashville, TN 37208

800-443-FISK or 615-329-8500

www.fisk.edu

Florida Memorial College

15800 N.W. 42nd Avenue

Miami, FL 33054

305-626-3750

www.fmc.edu

Huston-Tillotson College

900 Chicon Street

Austin, TX 78702

512-505-3028

www.htc.edu

Interdenominational Theological Center

700 Martin Luther King, Jr. Drive, SW

Atlanta, GA 30314

404-527-7790

Jarvis Christian College

U.S. Highway 80

Hawkins, TX 75765

903-769-5741

www.jarvis.edu

Johnson C. Smith University

100 Beatties Ford Road

Charlotte, NC 28216

800-782-7303 or 704-378-1000

www.jcsu.edu

Lane College

545 Lane Avenue

Jackson, TN 38301

800-390-7533 or 901-426-7500

www.lane-college.edu

LeMoyne-Owen College

807 Walker Avenue

Memphis, TN 38126

800-737-7778

www.lemoyne-owen.edu

Confronted by a player with four Fs and one D, Shelby Metcalf, basketball coach at Texas A&M, is purported to have said, "Son, looks to be like you're spending too much time on one subject."

Richard Lederer, humorist

Livingstone College

701 West Monroe Street

Salisbury, NC 28144

800-835-3435

www.livingstone.edu

Miles College

5500 Myron Massey Boulevard

Birmingham, AL 35064

800-445-0708 or 205-929-1000

www.miles.edu

Morehouse College

830 Westview Drive, SW

Atlanta, GA 30314

800-851-1254 or 404-681-2800

www.morehouse.edu

Morris College

North Main Street

Sumter, SC 29150

888-778-1345 or 803-775-9371

www.icusc.org/morris/mchome.htm

Morris Brown College

643 Martin Luther King, Jr. Drive, NW

Atlanta, GA 30314

404-220-0152

www.morrisbrown.edu

Oakwood College

7000 Adventist Boulevard

Huntsville, AL 35896

800-358-3978 or 256-726-7000

www.oakwood.edu

Paine College

1235 15th Street

Augusta, GA 30901-3182

706-821-8320

www.paine.edu

Paul Quinn College

3837 Simpson Stuart Road

Dallas, TX 75241

800-237-2648 or 214-376-1000

www.pqc.edu

Philander Smith College

812 W. 13th Street

Little Rock, AR 72202

501-370-5221

www.philander.edu

Rust College

150 Rust Avenue

Holly Springs, MS 38635

601-252-8000

www.centurytel.net/rust

> **The future was and remains the quintessential American art form. Other nations sit back and let their futures happen; we construct ours.**
>
> *—Prof. David Gelernter, Yale University*

Saint Augustine's College

1315 Oakwood Avenue

Raleigh, NC 27610-2298

919-516-4012

www.st-aug.edu

Spelman College

350 Spelman Lane, SW

Atlanta, GA 30314

800-982-2411 or 404-681-3643

www.spelman.edu

Saint Paul's College

406 Windsor Avenue

Lawrenceville, VA 23868

800-678-7071 or 804-848-4268

www.utoledo.edu/~wfraker/stpaul.html

Stillman College

3600 Stillman Boulevard

Tuscaloosa, AL 35401

205-366-8817

www.stillman.edu

Shaw University

118 E. South Street

Raleigh, NC 27601

919-546-8275

www.shawu.edu

Talladega College

627 W. Battle Street

Talladega, AL 35160

800-633-2440

www.talladega.edu

Faculty from Harvard University give out the Ig Nobel, an award for "Research which Cannot or Should Not Be Reproduced." Recent categories and winners: **Chemistry**, to a Japanese researcher who invented an infidelity-detection spray for wives to spray on their husbands' underwear; **Medicine**, to a Norwegian doctor who did an in-depth study of urine sample containers; **Peace**, to the South African entrepreneurs who invented a flamethrowing anti-carjacking device that burns would-be carjackers alive. In years past, the award was given out by Nobel prizewinners, of which Harvard has plenty.

While we're on this topic, the Nobel Prize is named after Alfred Bernhard Nobel, the inventor of dynamite and other explosives used in war. The Rhodes Scholarship is named after Cecil Rhodes, a ruthless colonialist who consolidated 95 percent of the world's diamond production by working Black South African laborers under slave conditions. One of his dreams was to recover the American colonies for Great Britain. And Duke University, Durham, North Carolina, is named after James B. Duke, the American tobacconist who controlled over 90 percent of the world tobacco market at one time. If you ever strike it rich under questionable circumstances, launch a scholarship or fund a university and in no time people will speak your name with reverence. It is clear that Bill Gates has every intention of doing this. In a hundred years, being a Gates Scholar will be the height of accomplishment, the greatest of scholastic honors.

Tougaloo College

500 West County Line Road

Tougaloo, MS 39174

888-424-2566

www.tougaloo.edu

Wilberforce University

1055 North Bickett Road

Wilberforce, OH 45384

937-376-2911

www.wilberforce.edu

❞I cannot live without books.❞

—Thomas Jefferson

Tuskegee University

Tuskegee, AL 36088

800-622-6531 or 334-727-8011

www.tusk.edu

Wiley College

711 Wiley Avenue

Marshall, TX 75670

903-927-3235

www.wiley.edu

Virginia Union University

1500 N. Lombardy Street

Richmond, VA 23220

804-257-5855

www.vuu.edu

Xavier University

7325 Palmetto Street

New Orleans, LA 70125

504-483-7388

www.xula.edu

Voorhees College

1411 Voorhees Road

Denmark, SC 29042

800-446-3351 or 803-793-3351

www.voorhees.edu

Bill Gates was a college dropout (Harvard). Michael Dell was a college dropout (University of Texas, Austin). Steve Jobs was a college dropout (Reed). On the other hand, Bill Clinton was a top student, and became a Rhodes Scholar. George Washington, Andrew Jackson, Martin Van Buren, Zachary Taylor, Millard Fillmore, Abraham Lincoln, Andrew Johnson, Grover Cleveland, and Harry Truman never went to college at all. Thomas Jefferson started a college, the University of Virginia, which he called an "Academical Village."

This is a very diverse collection of schools, including some that are overwhelmingly Hispanic, and others that merely have Hispanic/Latino Studies programs.

Contents of this list were gathered from the Web site of the White House Initiative on Educational Excellence for Hispanic Americans at the U.S. Department of Education (www.ed.gov/offices/OIIA/Hispanic) and from MOLIS-Minority On-Line Information Service (www.sciencewise.com/molis).

Adams State College
208 Edgemont Boulevard
Alamosa, CO 81101
800-824-6494 or 719-589-7011
www.adams.edu

American University of Puerto Rico
Road #2, KM14
Bayamon, PR 00960
787-798-2022
www.aupr.edu

Atlantic College
Box 1774
Guaynabo, PR 00970
787-720-1022

Barry University
11300 N.E. Second Avenue
Miami Shores, FL 33161
305-899-3000
www2.barry.edu

In Puerto Rico, faculty members, intellectuals, poets, and artistes from all over the island gather annually at the grave of painter and poet Roberto Alberty Torres, known the world over as Boquio. The event is called Baquinoquio. They toast Boquio and then pour drinks on his grave. They tell Boquio stories, many of which leave the crowd nodding and saying, "Sí, es Boquio." They recite epic poems in his honor, and they sing songs of praise. On the walk to the cemetery rows of cars will be parked with the trunks open, and in each trunk is a tub of ice, and in each tub is every kind of alcoholic drink, all for anyone who might pass by and all in honor of Boquio. Boquio was an original. He used to stop cars in the street, and yell at the drivers. "What are you doing? Get out! Walk!" Boquio was a college professor for fifteen minutes before the administration realized what a mistake they had made. The dean of the faculty of the Universidad de Puerto Rico was walking across campus one day, and saw Boquio staring up into a tree and talking to himself. Deciding to investigate, he came up to Boquio and looked up into the tree, too. He found the tree full of students. "What are you doing?" he demanded. "Well," said Boquio, "you cannot expect them to understand a tree from down *here*."

Bayamon Central University

Avenida Zaya Verde Urb. La Milagrosa

Bo. Hato Tejas

Bayamon, PR 00960

787-786-3030

www.ucb.edu.pr

Boricua College

3755 Broadway

New York, NY 10032

212-694-1000

California State University -
Bakersfield

9001 Stockdale Highway

Bakersfield, CA 93311

805-664-2011

www.csubak.edu

California State University -
Dominquez Hills

1000 East Victoria Street

Carson, CA 90747

310-243-3300

www.csudh.edu

California State University -
Fresno

5241 North Maple Avenue

Fresno, CA 93740

209-278-4240

www.csufresno.edu

California State University -
Los Angeles

5151 State University Drive

Los Angeles, CA 90032

323-343-3000

www.calstatela.edu

California State University -
Northridge

18111 Nordhoff Street

Northridge, CA 91330

818-677-1200

www.csun.edu

California State University -
San Bernardino

5500 University Parkway

San Bernardino, CA 92407

909-880-5000

www.csusb.edu

Caribbean Center for Advanced Stud-
ies - Miami Institute of Psychology

8180 N.W. 36th Street, Second Floor

Miami, FL 33166

305-593-1223

www.mip.ccas.edu

Caribbean Center for Advanced
Studies - San Juan Campus

Tanca Street, #151

San Juan, PR 00902-3711

787-725-6500

www.prip.ccas.edu

> **It's what we think we know already that often prevents us from learning.**
>
> —*Claude Bernard, French physiologist*

Caribbean University - Bayamon Campus
P.O. Box 493
Bayamon, PR 00960-0493
787-780-0070
www.caribbean.edu

City College, City University of New York
160 Convent Avenue
New York, NY 10031
212-650-7000
www.ccny.cuny.edu

College of Aeronautics
La Guardia Airport
Flushing, NY 11371
718-429-6600
www.aero.edu

The College of Santa Fe
1600 St. Michael's Drive
Santa Fe, NM 87501
800-456-2673 or 505-473-6011
www.csf.edu

Conservatory of Music of Puerto Rico
350 Rafael Lamar Street
San Juan, PR 00918
787-751-0160

Eastern New Mexico University
1200 West University
Portales, NM 88130
800-367-3668 or 505-562-1011
www.enmu.edu

Florida International University
11200 S.W. Eighth Street
Miami, FL 33199
305-348-2000
www.fiu.edu

Heritage College
3240 Fort Road
Toppenish, WA 98948
509-865-2244
www.heritage.edu

Inter American University of Puerto Rico
Aguadilla Campus
Barrio Corrales
Sector Calero
Aguadilla, PR 00605
787-891-0925
www.interaguadilla.edu

Inter American University
of Puerto Rico
Arecibo Campus
Carretera #2, Km. 80.4
Bo. San Daniel
Sector Las Canelas
Arecibo, PR 00614
787-878-5475
www.arecibo.inter.edu

Inter American University
of Puerto Rico
Barranquitas Campus
Bo. Helechal, Carr. 156
Intersección 719
Barranquitas, PR 00794
787-857-4040
www.inter.edu

Inter American University
of Puerto Rico
Bayamon Campus
Carretera 830 #500
Bo. Cerro Gordo
Bayamon, PR 00970
787-279-1912
www.bc.inter.edu

Inter American University
of Puerto Rico
Fajardo Campus Calle
Union-Batey Central
Carr. 195
Fajardo, PR 00738
787-863-2390
www.inter.edu

Inter American University
of Puerto Rico
Guayama Campus, Bo. Machete
Carr. 744, Km 1.2
Guayama, PR 00785
787-864-2222
www.inter.edu/guayama

Inter American University
of Puerto Rico
Metropolitan Campus, Carretera 1,
Km 16.3
Esq. Calle Francisco Sein
Río Piedras, PR 00919
787-250-1912
www.metro.inter.edu

Inter American University
of Puerto Rico
Ponce Campus
Bo. Sabanetas, Carr. 1
Mercedita Station
Mercedita Ponce, PR 00715
787-284-1912
www.inter.edu/programponce.html

John Jay College of Criminal Justice-City University of New York
899 Tenth Avenue
New York, NY 10019
212-237-8000
www.jjay.cuny.edu

Mercy College
555 Broadway
Dobbs Ferry, NY 10522
914-693-4500
www.mercynet.edu

Mount St. Mary's College
12001 Chalon Road
Los Angeles, CA 90049
310-954-4015
www.msmc.la.edu

The National Hispanic University
14271 Story Road
San Jose, CA 95127
408-254-6900
www.nhu.edu

New Mexico Highlands University
National Avenue
Las Vegas, NM 87701
505-454-2711
www.nmhu.edu

New Mexico State University
University Avenue
Las Cruces, NM 88003
800-662-6678 or 505-646-0111
www.nmsu.edu

Northeastern Illinois University
5500 North St. Louis Avenue
Chicago, IL 60625
773-583-4050
www.neiu.edu

Our Lady of the Lake University
411 S.W. 24th Street
San Antonio, TX 78207
210-434-6711
www.ollusa.edu

In spite of alarmist media, violent crime is way down on campuses nationwide. However, arrests for drug and alcohol violations are way up. It might be a good idea to take those campus drug and alcohol policies seriously, and be particularly careful to avoid large, outdoor parties that look like they may be getting out of hand. Arrests can result in a permanent legal record, possible academic suspension, or even a rescission of your financial aid. "Students are definitely being more careful about where they drink. They're saying, 'I don't need the infraction, so I'm going to stay inside and not cause trouble.'" (*Chronicle of Higher Education,* 28 May 1999) By the way, policies that rescind financial aid as a penalty for rowdiness are blatantly discriminatory against poor and middle class students, while allowing more affluent students to rack up more infractions before facing any real penalty.

**Pontifical Catholic University
of Puerto Rico**
Arecibo Campus
Arecibo, PR 00613
787-881-1212
www.pucpr.edu

**Pontifical Catholic University
of Puerto Rico**
Guayama Campus
5 South Palmer Street
Guayama, PR 00784
787-864-0550
www.pucpr.edu

**Pontifical Catholic University
of Puerto Rico**
Mayagüez Campus
482 South Post Street
Mayagüez, PR 00681
787-834-5151
www.pucpr.edu

**Pontifical Catholic University
of Puerto Rico**
Ponce Campus 2250
Avenida Las Americas
Ponce, PR 00731
787-841-2000
www.pucpr.edu

Saint Augustine College
1333-45 West Argyle Street
Chicago, IL 60640
773-878-8756

Saint Mary's University
One Camino Santa Maria
San Antonio, TX 78228
210-436-3126
www.stmarytx.edu

Saint Peter's College
2641 Kennedy Boulevard
Jersey City, NJ 07306
888-SPC-9933 or 201-915-9000
www.spc.edu

Saint Thomas University
16400 N.W. 32nd Avenue
Miami, FL 33054
305-625-6000
www.stu.edu

San Diego State University
5500 Campanile Drive
San Diego, CA 92182
858-594-5200
www.sdsu.edu

St. Edward's University
3001 South Congress Avenue
Austin, TX 78704
512-448-8500
www.stedwards.edu

**❝Finding
out who you
are is the
whole point of
the human
experience.❞**

—Anna Quindlen

Sul Ross State University
Highway 90
Alpine, TX 79832
915-837-8011
www.sulross.edu

Texas A & M International University
5201 University Boulevard
Laredo, TX 78041
956-326-2001
www.tamiu.edu

**Texas A & M University
at Corpus Christi**
6300 Ocean Drive
Corpus Christi, TX 78412
512-994-5700
www.tamucc.edu

**Texas A & M University
at Kingsville**
955 West University Boulevard
Kingsville, TX 78363
361-593-2111
www.tamuk.edu

**Universidad Adventista
de las Antillas**
Carr. 106 Km 2.2 Int
Mayagüez, PR 00680
787-834-9595
www.uaa.edu

Universidad Metropolitana
Avenida Ana G. Mendez
Km. 0.3
Cupey Bajo, PR 00928
787-766-1717
www.suagm.edu/UMET/main/default.htm

**Universidad Politecnica
de Puerto Rico**
377 Ponce de León Avenue
San Juan, PR 00919
787-754-8000
www.pupr.edu

Universidad del Turabo
Carretera 189
Km. 3.3
Gurabo, PR 00778
787-743-7979
www.suagm.edu

University of Houston - Downtown
One Main Street
Houston, TX 77002
713-221-8000
www.dt.uh.edu

University of the Incarnate Word
4301 Broadway
San Antonio, TX 78209
210-829-6000
www.uiw.edu

University of La Verne

1950 Third Street

La Verne, CA 91750

909-593-3511

www.ulaverne.edu

University of Miami

1262 Memorial Drive

Coral Gables, FL 33124

305-284-2211

www.miami.edu

University of New Mexico

Mesa Vista 3080

Albuquerque, NM 87131

505-277-0111

www.unm.edu

University of Puerto Rico

Aguadilla Regional College

Calle Belt

Aguadilla, PR 00604

787-890-2681

www.upr.edu

University of Puerto Rico

Arecibo Technological University College

Carretera Núm. 953, Km. 0.8

Arecibo, PR 00613

787-878-2830

www.upr.edu

University of Puerto Rico

Bayamon University College

#170 Carretera 174

Minillas Industrial Park

Bayamon, PR 00959

787-786-2885

www.cutb.upr.clu.edu

University of Puerto Rico

Cayey University College

Avenida Antonio R. Barceló

Cayey, Puerto Rico 00736

787-738-2161

www.cuc.upr.clu.edu

Q. Is it more prestigious to be a tenured professor or a famous actor?

A. Actors tell stories that serve a function. We go through things for people. Historically, that's what plays do. You go to the theater and you have that catharsis because there's a heroic or nonheroic figure going through these things that speak to you in some way, and you are involved and feel vital, and maybe you learn, but at least you have an experience because we all can't go through these heroic things. . . . That's a great service. . . . If I were a teacher at Yale, I'd be teaching people who are already really well educated. You're not really saving anybody.

—David Duchovny of The X Files *in a* Movieline *interview*

University of Puerto Rico

Humacao University College

Bo. Tejas

Humacao, PR 00791

787-850-0000

www.upr.clu.edu

University of Puerto Rico

Mayagüez Campus

Carretera Núm. 2, Calle Post

Mailing address: c/o P.O. Box 5000

Mayagüez, Puerto Rico 00681

787-832-4040

www.w3rum.upr.clu.edu

University of Puerto Rico

Medical Sciences Campus

Centro Médico

Río Piedras, Puerto Rico

Mailing address: c/o P.O. Box 365067

San Juan, PR 00936

787-758-2525

www.rcm.upr.edu

University of Puerto Rico

Ponce Technological University College

Avenida Santiago de los Caballeros

Esquina By-Pass

Ponce, PR 00732

787-844-8181

www.upr.clu.edu

University of Puerto Rico

Río Piedras Campus

Avenida Ponce de León

Parada 38

Río Piedras, PR

Mailing address: c/o P.O. Box 23300

San Juan, PR 00931

787-764-0000

www.upracd.upr.clu.edu:9090

University of the Sacred Heart

Rosales esquina San Antonio

Pda. 26 1/2

San Juan, PR 00911

787-728-1515

www.sagrado.edu

News Flash: WASP males are underrepresented at some elite universities. For example, at Harvard, one in five is a non-Jewish European-American male. In the general population in the United States and Canada, more than one in three is a non-Jewish European-American male. On this same issue, certain smaller liberal arts schools have ignored their own failure to attract a diverse student body. Some good small colleges are white, white, white. If this matters to you, be sure to inquire about it.

(Source: U. S. News & World Report, *29 March 1999)*

The University of Texas at Arlington

701 South Nedderman

Arlington, TX 76019

817-272-2011

www.uta.edu

The University of Texas at Austin

One South Mall

Austin, TX 78705

512-471-3434

www.utexas.edu

**The University of Texas
at Brownsville - Texas
Southmost College**

80 Fort Brown

Brownsville, TX 78520

956-544-8200

www.utb.edu

The University of Texas at Dallas

2601 North Floyd Road

Richardson, TX 75083

972-883-2111

www.ut.dallas.edu

The University of Texas at El Paso

500 West University Avenue

El Paso, TX 79968

915-747-5000

www.utep.edu

Western New Mexico University

1000 West College Avenue

Silver City, NM 88062

800-222-9668 or 505-538-6238

www.wnmu.edu

Whittier College

13406 East Philadelphia Street

Whittier, CA 90608

562-907-4200

www.whittier.edu

Woodbury University

7500 Glen Oaks Boulevard

Burbank, CA 91510

818-767-0888

www.woodburyu.edu

❝ **We fear
things in
proportion to
our ignorance
of them.** ❞

—Livy

Two Facts You Should Know

1. Your IQ will actually go up while you are in college, if you pick a demanding college.

2. People with higher IQs have more sex than people with lower IQs.

A majority of these colleges do not grant bachelor's degrees, only associates degrees. Contents of this list were gathered from the American Indian Higher Education Consortium (www.aihec.org) and the WWW Virtual Library-American Indians: Index of Native American Resources on the Internet (www.hanksville.org/NAresources) Web sites.

American Indian College of the Assemblies of God
10020 North 15th Avenue
Phoenix, AZ 85021
602-944-3335

American Indian Institute
The University of Oklahoma, College of Continuing Education
555 Constitution Street, Suite 237
Norman, OK 73072-7820
405-325-4127
www.occe.ou.edu./aii.html

Bay Mills Community College
12214 West Lake Shore Drive
Brimley, MI 49715
906-248-3354
www.bmcc.org

Blackfeet Community College
U.S. Highway 89
Browning, MT 59417
406-338-7755

Cankdeska Cikana Community College
101 College Drive
Fort Totten, ND 58335
701-766-4415
www.little-hoop.cc.nd.us

College of the Menominee Nation
Highway 4755
Keshena, WI 54135
715-799-4921
www.menominee.edu

Crownpoint Institute of Technology
Lowerpoint Road
Crownpoint, NM 87313
505-786-4100
www.cit.cc.nm.us

D-Q University
Road 31
Davis, CA 95617
530-758-0470
www.dqu.cc.ca.us

Diné College
Route 12 at Highway 64
Tsaile, AZ 86556
520-724-6669
www.ncc.cc.nm.us

Dull Knife Memorial College
100 College Drive
Lame Deer, MT 59043
406-477-6215
www.dkmc.cc.mt.us

**Fond du Lac Tribal and
Community College**
2101 14th Street
Cloquet, MN 55720
218-879-0800
www.fdl.cc.mn.us

Fort Belknap College
Highways 2 and 66
Harlem, MT 59526
406-353-2607
www.montana.edu/~wwwse/fbc/fbc.html

Fort Berthold Community College
220 Eighth Avenue North
New Town, ND 58763
701-627-4738
www.fbcc.bia.edu

Fort Peck Community College
Highway 2 East
Poplar, MT 59255
406-768-5551
www.fpcc.cc.mt.us

**Gabriel Dumont Institute of Native
Studies and Applied Research**
505 23rd Street East
Saskatoon, SK S7K 4K7
Canada
306-934-4941
www.gdins.org

Haskell Indian Nations University
155 Indian Avenue
Lawrence, KS 66046
785-749-8497
www.haskell.edu

Institute of American Indian Arts
1600 St. Michael's Drive
Santa Fe, NM 87504
505-988-6463
www.iaiancad.org

**Keweenaw Bay Ojibwa
Community College**
107 Bear Town Road
Baraga, MI 49908
906-353-8161

> ❝ **Eighty percent of success is showing up.** ❞
>
> —*Woody Allen*

Lac Courte Oreilles Ojibwa Community College
13466 West Trepania Road
Hayward, WI 54843
715-634-4790
www.lco-college.edu

Leech Lake Tribal College
Route 3
Cass Lake, MN 56633
218-335-2828
www.lltc.org

Little Big Horn College
1 Forest Lane
Crow Agency, MT 59022
406-638-2228
main.lbhc.cc.mt.us

Little Priest Tribal College
601 East College Drive
Winnebago, NE 68071
402-878-2380
www.lptc.cc.ne.us

Native American Educational Services (NAES) College
2838 West Peterson Avenue
Chicago, IL 60659
773-761-5000
www.naes.indian.com

Nebraska Indian Community College
College Hill Road
Macy, NE 68071
402-837-5078

Northwest Indian College
2522 Kwina Road
Bellingham, WA 98226
360-676-2772
www.nwic.edu

Oglala Lakota College
Piya Wiconi Road
Kyle, SD 57752
605-455-2321
www.olc.edu

Red Crow Community College
Junction 505 West
Cardston, AB TOI 1YO
Canada
403-737-2400

Salish Kootenai College
52000 Highway 93
Pablo, MT 59855
406-675-4800
www.skc.edu

Saskatchewan Indian

Federated College

118 College West

University of Regina

Regina, SK S4S 0A2

Canada

306-584-8333

www.sifc.edu

Si Tanka College

435 North Elm

Eagle Butte, SD 57625

605-964-6044

www.sitanka.org

Sinte Gleska University

Spotted Trail Drive

Rosebud, SD 57570

605-747-2263

www.sinte.indian.com

Sisseton Wahpeton

Community College

Old Agency

Agency Village, SD 57262

605-698-3966

swcc.cc.sd.us/cc.htm

Sitting Bull College

1341 92nd Street

Fort Yates, ND 58538

701-854-3861

Southwestern Indian

Polytechnic Institute

9169 Coors Road, NW

Albuquerque, NM 87184

505-897-2347

www.sipi.bia.edu

MASCOTS

The coolest mascot in the U.S. and Canada is, without a doubt, the Banana Slug, which guides the University of California, Santa Cruz sports teams into battle. The ass from Colorado College of Mines, which they gracefully refer to as a donkey or occasionally even try to pass off as a mule, is another nominee. This rivals Virginia Tech's Hokie Bird, which is actually a turkey. The ugliest is—and there may be some debate here—the Stanford tree, which looks like an oddly shaped Christmas present wrapped by someone's drunken uncle. It is absolutely incomprehensible that anyone would guess what this visual abomination might depict. Another favorite of mine, on the weirdness scale, is Oglethorpe University's Stormy Petrel, *Thalassidroma wilsonii*, a tough and oily seabird with a unique quality: when dried you can light one on fire and use it as a torch. Then, there's always the University of California, Irvine's fighting Anteaters.

Stone Child College
Rocky Boy Route
Box Elder, MT 59521
406-395-4313

Turtle Mountain Community College
BIA #7, North
Belcourt, ND 58316
701-477-7862
www.turtle-mountain.cc.nd.us

United Tribes Technical College
3315 University Drive
Bismarck, ND 58504
701-255-3285
www.united-tribes.tec.nd.us

**White Earth Tribal and
Community College**
210 Main Street South
Mahnomen, MN 56557
218-935-0417

Also note that Heritage College and Prescott College have close ties to Native American Nations, and both train teachers to the standard state teaching credential in Native American settings.

Sometimes an otherwise distinguished university has an event attached to it that it really wishes would just go away. The University of Michigan's HashBash is such an event. Started years before Nancy Reagan dreamed up that brilliant slogan, "Just Say No," it has become an institution in its own right. The HashBash happens on the first Saturday of April and is sponsored by the Michigan chapter of NORML. The event entails a rally on the Diag at "high noon," with much open-air burning of Rastafarian-size marijuana cigars. Along with speakers for the reform of marijuana laws, featured guests often include people from *High Times* magazine, eighty-year-old glaucoma grandmas protesting for access to medical marijuana, such dope luminaries as Tommy Chong of the renowned Cheech & Chong, and general mayhem. There are peripheral events to the actual rally, such as hippie drum circles all over town, special events at nightclubs, a preponderance of house parties in the evening, and people generally smoking pot everywhere. There is a large influx of people from out of town. The next day everyone goes back to class, and starts studying as hard as before, because you can't make it at the University of Michigan without studying hard, even if you have to study with red eyes.

Similarly, Vassar College's Queer Association has had dibs on the best party of the year, the HomoHop, a "celebration of sexuality and pleasure," which the administration had been uneasy with for years. Recently the sponsors of the HomoHop decided to end the tradition (for now, anyway) due to excessive drinking by straight people. For more entertaining news, also see the box on Nude Olympics and Naked Soccer on p. 289 and p. 314.

Alverno College
3400 South 43rd Street
Milwaukee, WI 53234-3922
800-933-3401 or 414-382-6000
www.alverno.edu

Barnard College at Columbia University
3009 Broadway
New York, NY 10027
212-854-5262
www.barnard.columbia.edu

Bennett College
(historically Black)
900 East Washington Street
Greensboro, NC 27401
800-413-5323 or 336-273-4431
www.bennett.edu

Brenau University
One Centennial Circle
Gainesville, GA 30501
770-534-6299
www.brenau.edu

Bryn Mawr College
101 North Merion Avenue
Bryn Mawr, PA 19010-2899
800-BMC-1885 or 610-526-5000
www.brynmawr.edu

Carlow College
3333 Fifth Avenue
Pittsburgh, PA 15213
412-578-6000
www.carlow.edu

Cedar Crest College
100 College Drive
Allentown, PA 18104-6196
800-360-1222 or 610-437-4471
www.cedarcrest.edu

Chatham College
Woodland Road
Pittsburgh, PA 15232
412-365-1100
www.chatham.edu

College of Notre Dame of Maryland
4701 North Charles Street
Baltimore, MD 21210
410-435-0100
www.ndm.edu

Columbia College
1301 Columbia College Drive
Columbia, SC 29203
803-786-3012
www.collacoll.edu

> **"A ship in port is safe, but that's not what ships are built for."**
>
> *—Grace Murray Hopper, mathematician*

Converse College

580 East Main Street

Spartanburg, SC 29302

864-596-9040

www.converse.edu

Emmanuel College

400 The Fenway

Boston, MA 02115

617-277-9340

www.emmanuel.edu

Hollins University

7916 Williamson Road

Roanoke, VA 24020

800-456-9595or 540-362-6000

www.hollins.edu

Judson College

302 Bibb Street

Marion, AL 36756

334-683-5100

www.judson.edu

Mary Baldwin College

Frederick and New Streets

Staunton, VA 24401

800-468-2262 or 540-887-7000

www.mbc.edu

Marymount College

100 Marymount Avenue

Tarrytown, NY 10591-3796

800-724-4312 or 914-631-3200

www.marymt.edu

Midway College

512 East Stephens Street

Midway, KY 40347-1120

800-755-0031 or 606-846-4421

www.midway.edu

Mills College

5000 MacArthur Boulevard

Oakland, CA 94613-1301

800-87-MILLS or 510-430-2255

www.mills.edu

The lifetime value of a high school diploma is $1,057,500. The lifetime value of a bachelor's degree is $1,535,100. The lifetime value of a master's degree is $1,795,800. The lifetime value of a Ph.D. is $2,074,800. The lifetime value of a medical degree is $5,810,000. Education creates social and financial mobility in our society. The U.S. Bureau of Labor Statistics tracks income by thousands of categories, and education is one of the few that show up as a lockstep indicator of income. (All figures in 1995 dollars based on average earnings times potential years of employment and assuming no compounding.)

Mississippi University for Women

1100 College Street

Columbus, Mississippi 39701

877-GO2-THEW or 662-329-4720

www.muw.edu

Moore College of Art & Design

Twentieth Street and The Parkway

Philadelphia, PA 19103-1179

800-523-2025 or 215-568-4515

www.moore.edu

Mount Holyoke College

50 College Street

South Hadley, MA 01075

413-538-2000

www.mtholyoke.edu

Mount Mary College

2900 North Menomonee River Parkway

Milwaukee, WI 53222

414-258-4810

www.mtmary.edu

Mount St. Mary's College

12001 Chalon Road

Los Angeles, CA 90049

310-954-4015

www.msmc.la.edu

Notre Dame College

4545 College Road

South Euclid, OH 44121

216-381-1680

www.ndc.edu

Peace College

15 East Peace Street

Raleigh, NC 27604-1194

800-PEACE-47 or 919-508-2000

www.peace.edu

Pine Manor College

400 Heath Street

Chestnut Hill, MA 02467

800-PMC-1357 or 617-731-7000

www.pmc.edu

Randolph-Macon Woman's College

2500 Rivermont Avenue

Lynchburg, VA 24503-1526

804-947-8100

www.rmwc.edu

Regis College

235 Wellesley Street

Weston, MA 02193

617-893-1820

www.regis.edu

> **Every time I catch myself saying, 'Oh no, you shouldn't try that,' I think, 'Yes, I *should*.'**
>
> —*Erica Jong*

> **I think the girl who is able to earn her own living and pay her way should be as happy as anybody on Earth.**
>
> —*Susan B. Anthony*

One of the world's largest collections of newspaper cartoons, comic books, and cartoon art is housed at the Michigan State University Library Special Collections Department.

Saint Mary-of-the-Woods College

3301 St. Mary's Road

St. Mary-of-the-Woods, IN 47876

812-535-5151

woods.smwc.edu

Salem College

Winston-Salem, NC 27108

800-327-2536 or 910-721-2600

www.salem.edu

Simmons College

300 The Fenway

Boston, MA 02115-5898

800-345-8468 or 617-521-2000

www.simmons.edu

Smith College

(Has scholarship for mature women 24+)

Elm Street

Northampton, MA 01063

413-584-2700

www.smith.edu

Stephens College

1200 East Broadway

Columbia, MO 65215

800-876-7207 or 573-442-2211

www.stephens.edu

Stern College for Women at Yeshiva University

(Jewish)

500 West 185th Street

New York, NY 10033-3299

www.yu.edu/stern.html

Sweet Briar College

Sweet Briar, VA 24595

804-381-6100

www.sbc.edu

Trinity College

125 Michigan Avenue, NE

Washington, DC 20017-1094

800-492-6882 or 202-884-9000

www.trinitydc.edu

Ursuline College

2550 Lander Road

Pepper Pike, OH 44124

440-449-4200

www.en.com/ursweb

Playboy once ran an "article" on Women of the Women's Colleges. It was, predictably, controversial. There was no shortage of women to pose, and women to protest. I'm not sure what this means, but there's plenty to deconstruct here. Cultural anthropology, anyone?

Wellesley College

106 Central Street

Wellesley, MA 02481

617-235-0320

www.wellesley.edu

Wells College

Aurora, NY 13026

800-952-9355 or 315-364-3265

www.wells.edu

Wesleyan College

4760 Forsyth Road

Macon, GA 31210-4462

912-477-1110

www.wesleyan-college.edu

William Smith College

639 Main Street

Geneva, NY 14456

315-781-3700

www.hws.edu

THE MEN'S COLLEGES

Deep Springs College

Off California Highway 168

HC72, Box 45001

Dyer, NV 89010-9803

760-872-2000

www.deepsprings.edu

Hampden-Sydney College

College Road

Hampden-Sydney, VA 23943-0667

800-755-0733 or 804-223-6000

www.hsc.edu

Hobart College

639 South Main Street

Geneva, NY 14456

315-781-3700

www.hws.edu

Morehouse College

(Black college)

830 Westview Drive SW

Atlanta, GA 30314

800-851-1254 or 404-681-2800

www.morehouse.edu

Saint John's University

(Catholic)

Collegeville, MN 56321

320-363-2011

www.csbjsu.edu

Wabash College

301 W. Wabash Avenue

Crawfordsville, IN 47933-0352

765-361-6100

www.wabash.edu

❝ I am always more interested in what I am about to do than in what I have already done. ❞

—*Rachel Carson, environmentalist*

Chapter Twelve

EVERY ACCREDITED FOUR-YEAR

BACHELOR'S DEGREE-GRANTING COLLEGE

IN THE UNITED STATES AND CANADA

WHAT DOES "ACCREDITED" MEAN?
WHY DOES IT MATTER?

When looking for the right college to attend, as a student or parent, you might ask yourself, "How do I know if this college is going to provide an actual education?" or "What are the standards by which I can judge a college's commitment to academic quality?" It may seem that in today's competitive market a college can pop up out of anywhere and start teaching what they choose. These are all valid concerns that you share with the higher education community.

In order to address these concerns, regional, national, and specialized accrediting associations provide a voluntary, nongovernmental review process that is carried out by the college itself and a board of educational peers. In order to establish itself as a valid and recognized institution of learning, a college or university puts itself through this accrediting process. *If an institution is not accredited, graduate schools and employers may not recognize its degrees.*

The majority of institutions are accredited by a regional accrediting association. The United States has been split up into six areas with six different associations. A smaller percentage of institutions receive their accreditation from a national or specialized accrediting association depending on their educational focus. The accreditation process is one in which, according to the Council for Higher Education Accreditation (CHEA), "the faculty, administrators, and staff of the institution or academic program conduct a self-study using the accrediting association's set of expectations about quality as their guide. A team of peers [from within the higher education system that are] selected by the accrediting association reviews the evidence, visits the campus to interview faculty and staff, and writes a report of its assessment." (Source: "About CHEA" at the CHEA Web site: www.chea.org) This report is then presented to a commission within the accrediting association that reviews the information and issues a judgment as to whether the institution shall receive accreditation. Accreditation is not a one-time event; it is an ongoing process with evaluations taking place every five to ten years.

In turn, the accrediting associations go through a similar review process in a similar time frame made by the core organization of this accrediting process, the Council for Higher Education Accreditation. CHEA is a respected nonprofit organization within the higher education community. It has been the independent voice for setting standards of academic quality, accountability, and accreditation, and for communicating with the Department of Education. Its mission is to ensure quality and accountability of learning institutions, to help set higher education policy with the federal government, and to communicate with and educate institutions and individuals within the higher education community. It is continuously researching and evaluating new ways to achieve and ensure the quality of our higher education institutions, those that you or your child would like to attend.

All institutions listed in the college directory have been accredited by one of the following associations. Should you have any concerns about a college, find out which association granted its accreditation and call them. If you have any general questions about the accreditation process, you can contact CHEA or try their Web site for information and links to other higher education organizations.

Disclaimer!

Part I: We have made every effort to identify every accredited institution at the time this book went to press. However, it is entirely possible that an institution may have become accredited after this book went to press, or we may have missed an accredited institution through error on our part or on the part of the accrediting authorities, or there may be an accrediting authority that is unknown to us but carries weight for a certain type of institution. If you do *not* find an institution on these lists, it does not mean, necessarily, that it is not accredited by a reputable accrediting authority. Inquire with the institution in question. If you *do* find an institution on the following lists, it means it was accredited by one or more of the following authorities at the time this book went to press.

Part II: Finally, we would be remiss if we did not state forcefully that the institutions listed herein are of vastly differing missions and quality. Just because an institution is accredited does not in and of itself mean that it will provide the quality and type of education that you seek.

Council for Higher Education Accreditation
One Dupont Circle NW, Suite 510
Washington, DC 20036
202-955-6126
www.chea.org

> It is not the critic who counts, not the person who points out how the strong one stumbles or where the doer of deeds could have done them better. The credit belongs to the one who is actually in the arena, whose face is marred by dust and sweat and blood, who strives valiantly, who errs and comes up short again and again, because there is no effort without error and shortcomings, who knows the greatest devotion, who spends himself in a worthy cause, who at the best knows in the end the high achievement of triumph and who at worst, if he fails while daring greatly, knows his place shall never be with those timid and cold souls who know neither victory nor defeat.

—*Theodore Roosevelt*

Middle States Association of Colleges and Schools (MSA)

Commission on Institutions of Higher Education

3624 Market Street

Philadelphia, PA 19104-2680

215-662-5606

www.msache.org

New England Association of Schools and Colleges

Commission on Institutions of Higher Education

209 Burlington Road

Bedford, MA 07130-1433

781-271-0022

www.neasc.org/contents.htm#commis

North Central Association of Colleges and Schools

Commission on Institutions of Higher Education

30 North LaSalle, Suite 2400

Chicago, IL 60602-2504

312-263-0456

www.ncacihe.org

Northwest Association of Schools and Colleges

Commission on Colleges

11130 N.E. 33rd Place, Suite 120

Bellevue, WA 98004

425-827-2005

Southern Association of Colleges and Schools

Commission on Colleges

1866 Southern Lane

Decatur, GA 30033-4097

800-248-7701 or 404-679-4500

www.sacs.org

Western Association of Schools and Colleges

Accrediting Commission for Senior Colleges and Universities

985 Atlantic Avenue, Suite 100

Alameda, CA 94501

510-748-9001

www.wascweb.org

"The way I see it, if you want the rainbow, you gotta put up with the rain."

—*Dolly Parton*

NATIONAL AND SPECIALIZED ACCREDITATION ASSOCIATIONS

Accrediting Association of Bible Colleges (AABC)

Commission on Accreditation

5890 Semoran Boulevard

Orlando, FL 32822

407-207-0808

www.aabc.org

Distance Education and Training Council (DETC)

1601 Eighteenth Street, NW

Washington, DC 20009-2529

202-234-5100

www.detc.org

Accrediting Council for Independent Colleges and Schools (ACICS)

750 First Street, NE Suite 980

Washington, DC 20002-4241

202-336-6780

www.acics.org

Association of Advanced Rabbinical and Talmudic Schools

175 Fifth Avenue, Room 711

New York, NY 10010

212-477-0950

Association of Theological Schools in the United States and Canada (ATS)

10 Summit Park Drive

Pittsburgh, PA 15275-1103

412-788-6505

www.ats.edu

INTERNATIONAL STUDENTS

The United States Department of Education does not publish a guide for international students, but most colleges and universities have a staff member who is responsible for serving as a liaison to international students. Call or e-mail the admissions office of any institution for more information. In the United States, international tuition is usually the same as the out-of-state tuition for public universities, and the same as everyone else for private universities. United States government funding in most cases is not available for foreign students. For more information:

U.S. Department of Education · 400 Maryland Avenue, SW · Washington, DC 20202-0498

800-USA-LEARN · CustomerService@inet.ed.gov · www.ed.gov

> **"We can be absolutely certain only about things we do not understand."**
>
> *—Eric Hoffer, the "long-shoreman philosopher" of the San Francisco labor days*

A

Abilene Christian University
1600 Campus Court
Abilene, TX 79699
915-674-2000
www.acu.edu

Abilene Intercollegiate School of Nursing
2149 Hickory
Abilene, TX 79601
915-672-2441

Academy of Art College
79 New Montgomery
San Francisco, CA 94105
415-274-2200
www.academyart.edu

Adams State College
208 Edgemont Boulevard
Alamosa, CO 81101
800-824-6494 or 719-589-7011
www.adams.edu

Adelphi University
South Avenue
Garden City, NY 11530
516-877-3000
www.adelphi.edu

Adrian College
110 South Madison Street
Adrian, MI 49221
800-877-2246 or 517-265-5161
www.adrian.edu

The Advertising Arts College
10025 Mesa Rim Road
San Diego, CA 92121
858-546-0602
www.taac.edu

Agnes Scott College
141 East College Avenue
Decatur, GA 30030
404-638-6000
www.agnesscott.edu

Al Collins Graphic Design School
1140 South Priest Drive
Tempe, AZ 85281
602-966-3000
www.alcollins.com

Alabama Agricultural & Mechanical University
4107 Meridian Street
Normal, AL 35762
256-851-5000
www.aamu.edu

Alabama State University
915 South Jackson Street
Montgomery, AL 36104
334-229-4100
www.alasu.edu

Alaska Bible College
College Road
Glennallen, AK 99588
907-822-3201
www.akbible.edu

Alaska Pacific University
4101 University Drive
Anchorage, AK 99508
907-561-1266
www.alaskapacific.edu

Albany College of Pharmacy of Union University
106 New Scotland Avenue
Albany, NY 12208
518-445-7200
www.acp.edu

Albany State University
504 College Drive
Albany, GA 31705
912-430-4600
www.asurams.edu

Albertson College of Idaho
2112 Cleveland Boulevard
Caldwell, ID 83605
208-459-5334
www.acofi.edu

Albertus Magnus College
700 Prospect Street
New Haven, CT 06511
203-773-8550
www.albertus.edu

Albion College
611 East Porter
Albion, MI 49224
517-629-1000
www.albion.edu

Albright College
Thirteenth and Bern Streets
Reading, PA 19612
610-921-2381
www.albright.edu

Alcorn State University
1000 ASU Drive
Alcorn State, MS 39096
800-222-6790 or 601-877-6100
www.alcorn.edu

Alderson-Broaddus College
500 College Hill
Philippi, WV 26416
304-457-1700
www.ab.edu

Alfred University
Saxon Drive
Alfred, NY 14802
607-871-2111
www.alfred.edu

Alice Lloyd College
100 Purpose Road
Pippa Passes, KY 41844
606-368-2101
www.aliceloyd.edu

Allegheny College
520 North Main Street
Meadville, PA 16335
814-332-3100
www.alleg.edu

Allegheny University of the Health Sciences
Broad and Vine Streets
Philadelphia, PA 19102
215-762-7000
www.asri.edu

Allen College
1825 Logan Avenue
Waterloo, IA 50703
319-235-3545
www.allencollege.edu

LOOKING FOR AN INTERESTING SPORT TO PURSUE IN COLLEGE?

The University of Missouri at Rolla has a mine-rescue team. The team competes against corporate mine-rescue teams, as there are no other collegiate mine-rescue teams.

New Mexico Tech has its very own, fully operational mine in the Magdalena Mountains near the Socorro campus. Students enrolled in mineral engineering gain "hands-on" experience.

Allen University
1530 Harden Street
Columbia, SC 29204
803-254-4165
www.scicu.org/allen/auhome.htm

**Allentown College
of St. Francis de Sales**
2755 Station Avenue
Center Valley, PA 18034
610-282-1100
www.allencol.edu

Alma College
614 West Superior Street
Alma, MI 48801
517-463-7111
www.alma.edu

Alvernia College
400 St. Bernardine Street
Reading, PA 19607
610-796-8200
www.alvernia.edu

Alverno College
3400 South 43rd Street
Milwaukee, WI 53234-3922
800-933-3401 or 414-382-6000
www.alverno.edu

Amber University
1700 Eastgate Drive
Garland, TX 75041
972-279-6511
www.amberu.edu

American Academy of Art
332 South Michigan Avenue
Chicago, IL 60604
312-461-0600
www.aaart.edu

American Baptist College
1800 Baptist World Center Drive
Nashville, TN 37207
615-228-7877

**American College of Prehospital
Medicine**
365 Canal Street
New Orleans, LA 70130
504-561-6543
www.acpm.edu

**American Indian College of the
Assemblies of God**
10020 North 15th Avenue
Phoenix, AZ 85021
602-944-3335

The trustees of Alma College in Michigan ran a full page ad in the *Chronicle of Higher Education:* "How do you measure quality in a college or university?" They cited five key factors:

1. Strong faculty mentoring

2. Collaborative research opportunities

3. Engaged learning

4. Global awareness

5. Service learning

None of these important items is easy to measure, which is why college rankings tend to focus on things that are easy to measure, like endowments. I once saw an editor from a national magazine try to defend the criteria they use to rank colleges. He said, and this is a literal quote: "We don't know what goes on in the classroom. We don't have any way to measure that."

The American Intercontinental University
3330 Peachtree Road, NE
Atlanta, GA 30326
404-231-9000
www.aiuniv.edu

American International College
1000 State Street
Springfield, MA 01109
413-737-7000
www.aic.edu

American Military University
9104-P Manassas Drive
Manassas, VA 22111
703-330-5398
www.amunet.edu

The American University
4400 Massachusetts Avenue, NW
Washington, DC 20016
202-885-1000
www.american.edu

American University of Puerto Rico
Road #2, KM14
Bayamon, PR 00960
787-798-2022
www.aupr.edu

Amherst College
South Pleasant Street
Amherst, MA 01002
413-542-2000
www.amherst.edu

Anderson College
316 Boulevard
Anderson, SC 29621
864-231-2000
www.anderson-college.edu

Anderson University
1100 East Fifth Street
Anderson, IN 46012
765-649-9071
www.anderson.edu

Andrew Jackson University
10 Old Montgomery Highway
Birmingham, AL 35209
205-871-9288
www.aju.edu

Andrews University
U.S. 31
Berrien Springs, MI 49104
616-471-7771
www.andrews.edu

CoOl ScHoLaRsHiP!

The Mr. and Mrs. Frederick Beckley Scholarship, more commonly known as the Left-Handed Scholarship, was first awarded at Juniata College in Huntington, Pennsylvania, in 1979. Mrs. Beckley, a former Juniata student, met her husband, Frederick, while playing tennis at the college in 1919, their freshman year. The two were paired because both were left-handed. They married in 1924, and later established the unusual scholarship targeting the 10 percent of the population often slighted in a right-handed society. The Beckley Award is open to any Juniata student who demonstrates financial need as well as academic promise. The only stipulation is that the student must be left-handed.

Angelo State University
2601 West Avenue North
San Angelo, TX 76901
915-942-2073
www.angelo.edu

Anna Maria College
50 Sunset Lane
Paxton, MA 01612
508-849-3300
www.anna-maria.edu

Antioch College (part of the Antioch University System)
795 Livermore Street
Yellow Springs, OH 45387
937-767-7331
www.antioch-college.edu

Antioch University
150 East South College Street
Yellow Springs, OH 45387
937-767-6494
www.antioch.edu

Appalachian Bible College
100 North Sand Branch Road
Bradley, WV 25818
304-877-6428
www.appbibco.edu

Appalachian State University
River Street
Boone, NC 28608
828-262-2000
www.appstate.edu

Aquinas College
1607 Robinson Road
Grand Rapids, MI 49506
800-678-9593 or 616-459-8281
www.aquinas.edu

Aquinas College
4210 Harding Road
Nashville, TN 37205
615-297-7545
www.aquinas-tn.edu

Concerned that students have lost the art of presenting an idea well, some schools have begun to teach you know, like, "speaking," across the curriculum. Schools that were mentioned in articles about the new speaking-intensive curriculum include:

- Mary Washington College in Virginia
- Stanford University in California
- Smith College in Massachusetts
- The University of Pennsylvania
- Mount Holyoke College in Massachusetts
- DePauw University in Indiana
- Butler University in Indiana
- The College of William and Mary in Virginia
- The University of Richmond in Virginia
- The University of Utah
- Allegheny College in Pennsylvania
- Hamilton College in New York
- North Carolina State University
- Central College in Iowa
- Hamline University in Minnesota

I attended classes at one of the top large universities in the nation. The students were like sheep. They wrote down anything the professor said. They never asked questions, and they never, never, never challenged the professor. In the seminar format of some smaller colleges, you get "speaking" in every single class, even mathematics.

Arizona Bible College
1718 West Maryland Avenue
Phoenix, AZ 85015
602-242-6400

Arizona State University
Forest Avenue
Tempe, AZ 85287
480-965-9011
www.asu.edu

Arizona State University West
4701 West Thunderbird Road
Phoenix, AZ 85069
602-543-5500
www.west.asu.edu

Arkansas Baptist College
1600 Dr. Martin Luther King, Jr., Drive
Little Rock, AR 72202
501-372-6883

Arkansas State University
2105 East Aggie Road
Jonesboro, AR 72401
870-972-2100
www.astate.edu

Arkansas Tech University
Coliseum Drive
Russellville, AR 72801
501-968-0389
www.atu.edu

Arlington Baptist College
3001 West Division Street
Arlington, TX 76012
817-461-8741
www.abconline.edu

Armstrong Atlantic State University
11935 Abercorn Street
Savannah, GA 31419
912-927-5211
www.armstrong.edu

Armstrong University
1608 Webster Street
Oakland, CA 94612
510-835-7900
www.armstrong-u.edu

Art Academy of Cincinnati
1125 Saint Gregory Street
Cincinnati, OH 45202
513-721-5205
www.artacademy.edu

Art Center College of Design
1700 Lida Street
Pasadena, CA 91109
626-396-2200
www.artcenter.edu

The Art Institute of Atlanta
6600 Peachtree Dunwoody Road
100 Embassy Row
Atlanta, GA 30328
404-266-1341
www.aia.aii.edu

Art Institute of Fort Lauderdale
1799 S.E. 17th Street
Fort Lauderdale, FL 33316
954-463-3000
www.aifl.edu

Art Institute of Southern California
2222 Laguna Canyon Road
Laguna Beach, CA 92651
949-376-6000
www.aisc.edu

The Art Institutes of Portland
2000 S.W. Fifth Avenue
Portland, OR 97201
503-228-6528
www.aii.eduPortland.html

> **Eighty-seven percent of all statistics are made up on the spot.**
>
> —*Research assistant*

**The Art Institutes International
at San Francisco (formerly Louise
Salinger Academy of Fashion)**
101 Jessie Street
San Francisco, CA 94105
415-974-6666

Asbury College
One Macklem Drive
Wilmore, KY 40390
606-858-3511
www.asbury.edu

Ashland University
401 College Avenue
Ashland, OH 44805
419-289-4142
www.ashland.edu

Assumption College
500 Salisbury Street
Worcester, MA 01615
508-752-5615
www.assumption.edu

Athens State University
300 North Beaty Street
Athens, AL 35611
205-233-8100
www.athens.edu

Atlanta Christian College
2605 Ben Hill Road
East Point, GA 30344
404-761-8861
www.acc.edu

Atlanta College of Art
1280 Peachtree Street, NE
Atlanta, GA 30309
404-733-5001
www.aca.edu

Atlantic College
Box 1774
Guaynabo, PR 00970
787-720-1022

Atlantic Union College
338 Main Street
South Lancaster, MA 01561-1000
508-368-2000
www.atlanticuc.edu

Auburn University Montgomery
7300 University Drive
Montgomery, AL 36124
334-244-3000
www.aum.edu

Audrey Cohen College
75 Varick Street
New York, NY 10013
212-343-1234
www.audrey-cohen.edu

Augsburg College
2211 Riverside Avenue
Minneapolis, MN 55454
612-330-1024
www.augsburg.edu

Augusta State University
2500 Walton Way
Augusta, GA 30904
706-737-1440
www.aug.edu

Augustana College
639 38th Street
Rock Island, IL 61201
800-798-8100 or 309-794-7000
www.augustana.edu

Augustana College
2001 South Summit Avenue
Sioux Falls, SD 57197
800-727-2844 or 605-336-4111
inst.augie.eduindex.html

Aurora University
347 South Gladstone Avenue
Aurora, IL 60506
630-892-6431
www.aurora.edu

Austin College
900 North Grand Avenue
Sherman, TX 75090
903-813-2000
www.austinc.edu

Austin Peay State University
601 College Street
Clarksville, TN 37040
931-648-7011
www.apsu.edu

Averett College
420 West Main Street
Danville, VA 24541
804-791-5600
www.averett.edu

Avila College
11901 Wornall Road
Kansas City, MO 64145
816-942-8400
www.avila.edu

Azusa Pacific University
901 East Alosta
Azusa, CA 91702
626-969-3434
wwwapu.edu

B

Babson College
231 Forest Street
Babson Park, MA 02157
800-488-3696 or 617-235-1200
www.babson.edu

Baker College of Auburn Hills
1500 University Drive
Auburn Hills, MI 48326
810-340-0600
www.baker.edu

Baker College of Cadillac
9600 East 13th Street
Cadillac, MI 49601
616-775-8458
www.baker.edu

Baker College of Flint
1050 West Bristol Road
Flint, MI 48507
810-767-7600
www.baker.edu

Baker College of Jackson
2800 Springport Road
Jackson, MI 49202
517-789-6123
www.baker.edu

Baker College of Mount Clemens
34950 Little Mack Avenue
Clinton Township, MI 48035
810-791-6610
www.baker.edu

Baker College of Muskegon
123 East Apple Avenue
Muskegon, MI 49442
616-726-4904
www.baker.edu

Baker College of Owosso
1020 South Washington Street
Owosso, MI 48867
517-723-5251
www.baker.edu

Baker College of Port Huron
3403 Lapeer Road
Port Huron, MI 48060
810-985-7000
www.baker.edu

Baker University
606 West Eighth Street
Baldwin City, KS 66006
785-594-6451
www.bakeru.edu

Listen to Babson College radio at www.radio.babson.edu

Baldwin-Wallace College
275 Eastland Road
Berea, OH 44017
440-826-2900
www.baldwinw.edu

Ball State University
2000 University Avenue
Muncie, IN 47306
765-289-1241
www.bsu.edu

Baltimore Hebrew University
5800 Park Heights Avenue
Baltimore, MD 21215
410-578-6900
www.bhu.edu

Baltimore International College
17 Commerce Street
Baltimore, MD 21202
410-752-4710
www.bic.edu

Baptist Bible College
628 East Kearney Street
Springfield, MO 65803
417-268-6000
www.seebbc.edu

Baptist Bible College & Seminary
538 Venard Road
Clarks Summit, PA 18411
717-586-2400
www.bbc.edu

**Baptist Missionary Association
Theological Seminary**
1530 East Pine Street
Jacksonville, TX 75766
903-586-2501

Barat College
700 East Westleigh Road
Lake Forest, IL 60045
847-234-3000
www.barat.edu

Barber-Scotia College
145 Cabarrus Avenue, West
Concord, NC 28025
704-789-2902
www.barber-scotia.edu

Barclay College
607 North Kingman
Haviland, KS 67059
316-862-5252
www.barclaycollege.edu

Bard College
P.O. Box 5000
Annandale-on-Hudson, NY 12504-5000
914-758-6822
www.bard.edu

Barnard College
3009 Broadway
New York, NY 10027
212-854-5262
www.barnard.edu

Barry University
11300 N.E. Second Avenue
Miami Shores, FL 33161
305-899-3000
www2.barry.edu

Bartlesville Wesleyan College
2201 Silver Lake Road
Bartlesville, OK 74006
918-335-6200
www.bwc.edu

Ball State University in Indiana recently gave a desktop computer and a color printer to its top incoming freshmen.

(Source: Wall Street Journal, 31 March 1999)

Barton College
400 Atlantic Christian College Drive
Wilson, NC 27893
252-399-6300
www.barton.edu

Bastyr University
14500 Juanita Drive NE
Bothell, WA 98011
425-823-1300
www.bastyr.edu

Bates College
2 Andrews Road
Lewiston, ME 04240
207-786-6255
www.bates.edu

Bay Path College
588 Longmeadow Street
Longmeadow, MA 01106
413-567-0621
www.baypath.edu

Bayamon Central University
Avenuenida Zaya Verde Urb. La Mila-grosa
Bo. Hato Tejas
Bayamon, PR 00960
787-786-3030
www.ucb.edu.pr

Baylor University
M. P. Daniel Esplanade
Waco, TX 76798
800-BAYLOR-U or 254-710-1811
www.baylor.edu

Beaver College
450 South Easton Road
Glenside, PA 19038
215-572-2900
www.beaver.edu

Becker College
61 Sever Street
Worcester, MA 01615
508-791-9241
www.becker.edu

Belhaven College
1500 Peachtree Street
Jackson, MS 39202
601-968-5928
www.belhaven.edu

Bellarmine College
2001 Newburg Road
Louisville, KY 40205
502-452-8211
www.bellarmine.edu

Bellevue University
1000 Galvin Road, South
Bellevue, NE 68005
402-291-8100
www.bellevue.edu

Bellin College of Nursing
725 South Webster Avenue
Green Bay, WI 54305
920-433-3560
www.bellin.org/bcn

Every St. Patrick's Day, Bates College students cut a hole in the ice of Lake Andrews and go swimming. There is a Dip Master, "a student annually appointed grand-poobah of the polar plunge," who cuts the hole with the same ax that has been used forever for this purpose. At 11:30 P.M. those who dip gather in the basement of Smith South Hall to read from the *Dip Book,* which includes a ritual reading of the names of all Dip Masters past.

Belmont Abbey College
100 Belmont-Mt. Holly Road
Belmont, NC 28012
704-825-6700
www.belmontabbeycollege.edu

Belmont University
1900 Belmont Boulevard
Nashville, TN 37212
615-460-6000
www.belmont.edu

Beloit College
700 College Street
Beloit, WI 53511
608-363-2000
www.beloit.edu

Bemidji State University
1500 Birchmont Drive, NE
Bemidji, MN 56601
218-755-2000
www.bemidji.msus.edu

Benedict College
1600 Harden Street
Columbia, SC 29204
803-256-4220
www.benedict.edu

Benedictine College
1020 North Second Street
Atchison, KS 66002
913-367-5340
www.benedictine.edu

Benedictine University
5700 College Road
Lisle, IL 60532
630-829-6000
www.ben.edu

Bennett College
900 East Washington Street
Greensboro, NC 27401
800-413-5323 or 336-273-4431
www.bennett.edu

Bennington College
Route 67A
Bennington, VT 05201
802-442-5401
www.bennington.edu

Bentley College
175 Forest Street
Waltham, MA 02154
617-891-2000
www.bentley.edu

Berea College
101 Chestnut Street
Berea, KY 40403
800-326-5948 or 606-986-9341
www.berea.edu

Berean University
1445 Boonville Avenue
Springfield, MO 65802
417-862-9533
www.berean.edu

Berkeley College of New York City
3 East 43rd Street
New York, NY 10017
212-986-4343
www.berkeleycollege.edu

Berklee College of Music
1140 Boylston Street
Boston, MA 02215
617-266-1400
www.berklee.edu

Students at Bethany College in West Virginia have the Buffalo River running right alongside campus. During the warmer months, a favorite student outing is to go tubing, floating downstream on large inner tubes.

Bernard M. Baruch College-City University of New York
17 Lexington Avenue
New York, NY 10010
212-802-2000
www.baruch.cuny.edu

Berry College
2277 Martha Berry Boulevard, NE
Mount Berry, GA 30149
706-232-5374
www.berry.edu

Beth Medrash Govoha
617 Sixth Street
Lakewood, NJ 08701
732-367-1060

Bethany College
800 Bethany Drive
Scotts Valley, CA 95066
408-438-3800
wwwbethany.edu

Bethany College
421 North First Street
Lindsborg, KS 67456
785-227-3311
www.bethanylb.edu

Bethany College
Route 67
Bethany, WV 26032
304-829-7000
info.bethany.wvnet.edu

Bethel College
1001 West McKinley Avenue
Mishawaka, IN 46545
219-259-8511
www.bethel-in.edu

Bethel College
300 East 27th Street
North Newton, KS 67117
316-283-2500
www.bethelks.edu

Bethel College
3900 Bethel Drive
St. Paul, MN 55112
612-638-6400
www.bethel.edu

Bethel College
325 Cherry Avenue
McKenzie, TN 38201
901-352-4000
www.bethel-college.edu

Bethune-Cookman College
640 Dr. Mary McLeod
Bethune Boulevard
Daytona Beach, FL 32114-3099
800-448-0228 or 904-255-1401
www.bethune.cookman.edu

Biola University
13800 Biola Avenue
La Mirada, CA 90639
562-903-6000
www.biola.edu

Birmingham-Southern College
900 Arkadelphia Road
Birmingham, AL 35254
205-226-4600
www.bsc.edu

Black Forest Hall
2787 Quick Road
Harbor Springs, MI
616-526-7066

Black Hills State University
1200 University Avenue
Spearfish, SD 57799
605-642-6011
www.bhsu.edu

Blackburn College
700 College Avenue
Carlinville, IL 62626
217-854-3231
www.blackburn.edu

❝ Twenty years from now you will be more disappointed by the things you didn't do than by the ones you did. ❞

—*Mark Twain*

**Blessing-Rieman College
of Nursing**
Broadway at 11th Street
Quincy, IL 62301
217-228-5520
www.brcn.edu

Bloomfield College
467 Franklin Street
Bloomfield, NJ 07003
973-748-9000
www.bloomfield.edu

**Bloomsburg University
of Pennsylvania**
400 East Second Street
Bloomsburg, PA 17815
717-389-4000
www.bloomu.edu

Blue Mountain College
201 West Main
Blue Mountain, MS 38610
601-685-4771
www.bmc.edu

Bluefield College
3000 College Drive
Bluefield, VA 24605
540-356-3682
www.bluefield.edu

Bluefield State College
219 Rock Street
Bluefield, WV 24701
800-654-7798 or 304-327-4000
www.bluefield.wvnet.edu

Bluffton College
280 West College Avenue
Bluffton, OH 45817
800-488-3257 or 419-358-3000
www.bluffton.edu

GOLF COURSES

Many colleges have golf courses near campus, for example, Reed College in Portland, Oregon, is right next door to an eighteen-hole city course. Reedies tend not to be the golfing type, but I hear there used to be a team of Reed duffers calling themselves the "Slasher 500." These schools have courses on campus or on university property:

- Bucknell University, Lewisburg, Pennsylvania
- Furman University, Greenville, South Carolina
- Jacksonville University, Jacksonville, Florida
- Kansas State University (also has a PGA-approved course in golf course management), Manhattan
- Michigan State, East Lansing (has two golf courses)
- Michigan Tech, Houghton, Michigan
- Purdue University, West Lafayette, Indiana (has two golf courses)
- St. Francis College, Loretto, Pennsylvania
- University of North Carolina, Chapel Hill
- Virginia Polytechnic Institute, aka Virginia Tech, Blacksburg

But that's nothing. New Mexico Tech hosts the ultimate golf challenge, the notorious and nefarious Elfego Baca Shoot, a novelty long-distance hole played from the top of Socorro Peak to a green located three miles away. Each summer, some of the hardiest golfers in the country tee off on this par ∞ hole.

Boise Bible College
8695 Marigold Street
Boise, ID 83714
208-376-7731
netnow.micron.net/~boibible

Boise State University
1910 University Drive
Boise, ID 83725
208-385-1491
www.boisestate.edu

The Boston Conservatory
8 The Fenway
Boston, MA 02215
617-536-6340
www.bostonconservatory.edu

Boston University
147 Bay State Road
Boston, MA 02215
617-353-2000
www.bu.edu

Boricua College
3755 Broadway
New York, NY 10032
212-694-1000

Boston Architectural Center
320 Newbury Street
Boston, MA 02115
617-536-3170
www.the-bac.edu

Boston College
140 Commonwealth Avenue
Chestnut Hill, MA 02467
800-360-2522 or 617-552-8000
www.bc.edu

Bowdoin College
5700 College Station
Brunswick, ME 04011
207-725-3000
www.bowdoin.edu

Bowie State University
14000 Jericho Park Road
Bowie, MD 20715
301-464-3000
www.bowiestate.edu

Bowling Green State University
Bowling Green, OH 43403
419-372-2531
www.bgsu.edu

 **The life which is unexamined is not worth living.**

—*Plato*

Bradford College
320 South Main Street
Bradford, MA 01835
978-372-7161
www.bradford.edu

Bradley University
1501 West Bradley Avenue
Peoria, IL 61625
309-676-7611
www.bradley.edu

Brandeis University
415 South Street
Waltham, MA 02454
781-736-3000
www.brandeis.edu

Briar Cliff College
3303 Rebecca Street
Sioux City, IA 51104
712-279-5321
www.briar-cliff.edu

Briarcliffe College
1055 Stewart Avenue
Bethpage, NY 11714
516-470-6000
www.bcl.org

Bridgewater College
402 East College Street
Bridgewater, VA 22812
540-828-8000
www.bridgewater.edu

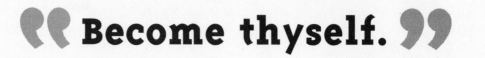

"Become thyself."
—*Nietzsche*

Brenau University
One Centennial Circle
Gainesville, GA 30501
770-534-6299
www.brenau.edu

Brescia University
717 Frederica Street
Owensboro, KY 42301
502-685-3131
www.brescia.edu

Brevard College
400 North Broad Street
Brevard, NC 28712
704-883-8292
www.brevard.edu

Brewton-Parker College
Highway 280
Mount Vernon, GA 30445
912-583-2241
www.bpc.edu

Bridgewater State College
Cedar and Grove Streets
Bridgewater, MA 02325
508-697-1200
www.bridgew.edu

Brigham Young University
Campus Drive
Provo, UT 84602
801-378-4636
www.byu.edu

**Brigham Young University,
Hawaii Campus**
55-220 Kulanui Street
Oahu, HI 96762
808-293-3211
www.byuh.edu

**Brooklyn College-City University
of New York**
2900 Bedford Avenue
Brooklyn, NY 11210
718-951-5000
www.brooklyn.cuny.edu

Brooks Institute of Photography
801 Alston Road
Santa Barbara, CA 93108
805-966-3888
www.brooks.edu

Brown University
45 Prospect Street
Providence, RI 02912
401-863-1000
www.brown.edu

Bryan College
P.O. Box 7000
Dayton, TN 37321
423-775-2041
www.bryan.edu

Bryant College
1150 Douglas Pike
Smithfield, RI 02917
401-232-6000
www.bryant.edu

**Bryn Athyn College of the
New Church**
P.O. Box 717
Bryn Athyn, PA 19009
215-947-4200
www.newchurch.edu

Bryn Mawr College
101 North Merion Avenue
Bryn Mawr, PA 19010-2899
800-BMC-1885 or 610-526-5000
www.brynmawr.edu

Bucknell University
Dent Drive
Lewisburg, PA 17837
570-523-1271
www.bucknell.edu

Buena Vista University
610 West Fourth Street
Storm Lake, IA 50588
800-383-2821 or 712-749-2103
www.bvu.edu

Burlington College
95 North Avenue
Burlington, VT 05401
802-862-9616
www.burlcol.edu

Butler University
4600 Sunset Avenue
Indianapolis, IN 46208
800-368-6852 or 317-940-8000
www.butler.edu

C

**Cabarrus College
of Health Sciences**
431 Copperfield Boulevard, NE
Concord, NC 28025
704-783-1555

Cabrini College
610 King Of Prussia Road
Radnor, PA 19087
610-902-8100
www.cabrini.edu

Caldwell College
9 Ryerson Avenue
Caldwell, NJ 07006
973-618-3000
www.caldwell.edu

California Baptist College
8432 Magnolia Avenue
Riverside, CA 92504
909-343-4213

**" Man is the
measure of all
things. "**

—Protagorus

California College of Arts & Crafts
5212 Broadway
Oakland, CA 94618
510-594-3600
www.ccac-art.edu

**California College
for Health Sciences**
222 West 24th Street
National City, CA 91950
619-477-4800
www.cchs.edu

**California College
of Podiatric Medicine**
1210 Scott Street
San Francisco, CA 94115
415-563-8070
www.ccpm.edu

California Institute of the Arts
24700 McBean Parkway
Valencia, CA 91355
805-255-1050
www.calarts.edu

**California Institute of Integral
Studies**
(offers one-year completion of B.A. program for adults)
9 Peter Yorke Way
San Francisco, CA 94109
415-575-6100
www.ciis.edu

**California Institute of Technology
(Caltech)**
1200 East California Boulevard
Pasadena, CA 91125
626-395-6811
www.caltech.edu

California Lutheran University
60 West Olsen Road
Thousand Oaks, CA 91360
805-492-2411
www.clunet.edu

California Maritime Academy
200 Maritime Academy Drive
Vallejo, CA 94590
800-561-1945 or 707-654-1000
www.csum.edu

**California National University
for Advanced Studies**
16909 Parthemia Street
North Hills, CA 91343
805-756-1111
www.cnuas.edu

**California State Polytechnic
University - Pomona**
3801 West Temple Avenue
Pomona, CA 91768
909-869-7659
www.csupomona.edu

**California State Polytechnic
University - San Luis Obispo**
Perimeter Street
San Luis Obispo, CA 93407
805-756-1111
www.calpoly.edu

**California State University -
Bakersfield**
9001 Stockdale Highway
Bakersfield, CA 93311
805-664-2011
www.csubak.edu

California State University - Chico
First and Normal Streets
Chico, CA 95929
530-898-6101
www.csuchico.edu

**California State University -
Dominquez Hills**
1000 East Victoria Street
Carson, CA 90747
310-243-3300
www.csudh.edu

California State University - Fresno
5241 North Maple Avenue
Fresno, CA 93740
209-278-4240
www.csufresno.edu

California State University - Fullerton
Nutwood Avenue
Fullerton, CA 92634
714-278-2300
www.fullerton.edu

California State University - Hayward
25800 Carlos Bee Boulevard
Hayward, CA 94542
510-885-3000
www.csuhayward.edu

California State University - Long Beach
1250 Bellflower Boulevard
Long Beach, CA 90840
562-985-4111
www.csulb.edu

California State University - Los Angeles
5151 State University Drive
Los Angeles, CA 90032
323-343-3000
www.calstatela.edu

California State University - Northridge
18111 Nordhoff Street
Northridge, CA 91330
818-677-1200
www.csun.edu

California State University - Sacramento
6000 J Street
Sacramento, CA 95819
916-278-6011
www.csus.edu

California State University - San Bernardino
5500 University Parkway
San Bernardino, CA 92407
909-880-5000
www.csub.edu

California State University - San Marcos
333 South Twin Oaks Valley Road
San Marcos, CA 92096
760-750-4000
www.csusm.edu

California State University - Stanislaus
801 West Monte Vista Avenue
Turlock, CA 95382
209-667-3082
www.csustan.edu

California University of Pennsylvania
250 University Avenue
California, PA 15419
724-938-4000
www.cup.edu

Calumet College of Saint Joseph
2400 New York Avenue
Whiting, IN 46394
219-473-7770
www.ccsj.edu

> **What is reality, anyway? Nothing but a collective hunch.**
>
> —*Jane Wagner, comedy writer (in San Francisco Chronicle, 17 January 2000)*

Amelia Earhart was a career counselor at Purdue University from 1935 to 1937.

> **❝It ain't so much the things we don't know that get us in trouble. It's the things we know that ain't so.❞**
>
> —*Artemus Ward*

Calvary Bible College
15800 Calvary Road
Kansas City, MO 64147
816-322-0110
www.calvary.edu

Calvin College
3201 Burton Street, SE
Grand Rapids, MI 49546
800-688-0122 or 616-957-6000
www.calvin.edu

Cambridge College
1000 Massachusetts Avenue
Cambridge, MA 02138
800-877-GRAD or 617-868-1000
www.cambridge.edu

Cameron University
2800 West Gore Boulevard
Lawton, OK 73505
580-581-2200
www.cameron.edu

Campbell University
56 Main Street
Buies Creek, NC 27506
910-893-1200
www.campbell.edu

Campbellsville University
One University Drive
Campbellsville, KY 42718
502-465-5000
www.campbellsvil.edu

Canisius College
2001 Main Street
Buffalo, NY 14208
716-883-7000
www.canisius.edu

Capital University
2199 East Main Street
Columbus, OH 43209
800-289-6289 or 614-236-6011
www.capital.edu

Capitol College
11301 Springfield Road
Laurel, MD 20708
301-369-2800
www.capitol-college.edu

Cardinal Stritch University
6801 North Yates Road
Milwaukee, WI 53217
800-347-8822 or 414-410-4000
www.stritch.edu

Caribbean Center for Advanced Studies-Miami Institute of Psychology
8180 N.W. 36th Street, Second Floor
Miami, FL 33166
305-593-1223
www.mip.ccas.edu

Caribbean Center for Advanced Studies
San Juan Campus
Tanca Street, #151
San Juan, PR 00902-3711
787-725-6500
www.prip.ccas.edu

Caribbean University - Bayamon Campus
P.O. Box 493
Bayamon, PR 00960-0493
787-780-0070
www.caribbean.edu

Carleton College
One North College Street
Northfield, MN 55057
507-646-4000
www.carleton.edu

Carlow College
3333 Fifth Avenue
Pittsburgh, PA 15213
412-578-6000
www.carlow.edu

Carnegie Mellon University
5000 Forbes Avenue
Pittsburgh, PA 15213
412-268-2000
www.cmu.edu

Carroll College
1601 North Benton Avenue
Helena, MT 59625
406-447-4401
www.carroll.edu

Carroll College
100 North East Avenue
Waukesha, WI 53186
800-227-7655 or 262-547-1211
www.cc.edu

Carson-Newman College
1646 Russell Avenue
Jefferson City, TN 37760
423-471-4000
www.cn.edu

Carthage College
2001 Alford Park Drive
Kenosha, WI 53140
414-551-8500
www.carthage.edu

Case Western Reserve University
10900 Euclid Avenue
Cleveland, OH 44106
800-444-6984 or 216-368-2000
www.cwru.edu

Castleton State College
Seminary Street
Castleton, VT 05735
802-468-5611
www.csc.vsc.edu

Catawba College
2300 West Innes Street
Salisbury, NC 28144
704-637-4111
www.catawba.edu

The Catholic University of America
620 Michigan Avenue, NE
Washington, DC 20064
202-319-5000
www.cua.edu

Cazenovia College
22 Sullivan Street
Cazenovia, NY 13035
315-655-8283
www.cazcollege.edu

Cedar Crest College
100 College Drive
Allentown, PA 18104-6196
800-360-1222 or 610-437-4471
www.cedarcrest.edu

Cedarville College
P.O. Box 601
Cedarville, OH 45314
800-766-2211 or 937-766-2211
www.cedarville.edu

Centenary College
400 Jefferson Street
Hackettstown, NJ 07840
908-852-1400
www.centenarycollege.edu

Centenary College of Louisiana
2911 Centenary Boulevard
Shreveport, LA 71134
318-869-5011
www.centenary.edu

> **It is absolutely frightening to realize that half the people in the country have below average intelligence.**
>
> —*Clyde Watkins, capitalist*

A Carnegie Foundation for the Advancement of Teaching report says, "The failure of research universities seems most serious in conferring degrees upon inarticulate students."

(*Source:* Chronicle of Higher Education, *26 March 1999*)

The Center for Creative Studies College of Art & Design
245 East Kirby Street
Detroit, MI 48202
313-664-7400
www.ccscad.edu

Central Baptist College
1501 College Avenue
Conway, AR 72032
501-329-6872
ww.cbc.edu

Central Bible College
3000 North Grant Avenue
Springfield, MO 65803
417-833-2551
www.cbcag.edu

Central Christian College
1200 South Main
McPherson, KS 67460
316-241-0723
www.centralcollege.edu

Central Christian College of the Bible
911 Urbandale Drive, East
Moberly, MO 65270
816-263-3900
www.cccb.edu

Central College
812 University
Pella, IA 50219
515-628-9000
www.central.edu

Central Connecticut State University
1615 South Stanley Street
New Britain, CT 06050
860-832-3200
www.ccsu.ctstateu.edu

Central Methodist College
411 Central Methodist Square
Fayette, MO 65248
660-248-3391
www.cmc.edu

Central Michigan University
Mount Pleasant, MI 48859
517-774-4000
www.cmich.edu

Central Missouri State University
South Street
Warrensburg, MO 64093
660-543-4111
www.cmsu.edu

Central State University
1400 Brush Row Road
Wilberforce, OH 45384
937-376-6011

Some small universities achieve a nice balance, with the attention and atmosphere of a small school with some of the programs only a large institution could offer. For example, Central Washington University in Ellensburg offers students an opportunity to do real research at the undergraduate level, uses a team-based approach to teaching, and has two unusual programs: Resource Management, including environmental, water, and public lands use issues important to all Western states, and the Primatology Center, offering an undergraduate major of primate studies. Ellensburg is nice, too, with a mellow personality all its own. If primates are your thing, there is also a Primate Colony at Bucknell University, offering an undergraduate degree program in animal behavior.

Central Washington University
400 East Eighth Avenue
Ellensburg, WA 98926
509-963-1111
www.cwu.edu

Centre College
600 West Walnut Street
Danville, KY 40422
606-238-5200
www.centre.edu

Chadron State College
1000 Main Street
Chadron, NE 69337
308-432-6000
www.csc.edu

Chaminade University of Honolulu
3140 Waialae Avenue
Honolulu, HI 96816
808-735-4711
www.chaminade.edu

Champlain College
163 South Willard Street
Burlington, VT 05402
802-860-2700
www.champlain.edu

Chaparral College
4585 East Speedway Boulevard
Tucson, AZ 85712
520-327-6866
www.chap-col.edu

Chapman University
333 North Glassell Street
Orange, CA 92866
714-997-6815
www.chapman.edu

**Charles R. Drew University
of Medicine & Science**
1731 East 120th Street
Los Angeles, CA 90059
213-563-4800
www.cdrew.edu

Charleston Southern University
9200 University Boulevard
Charleston, SC 29423
803-863-7000
www.csuniv.edu

Charter Oak State College
66 Cedar Street
Newington, CT 06111
860-666-4595
www.cosc.edu

Chatham College
Woodland Road
Pittsburgh, PA 15232
412-365-1100
www.chatham.edu

Chestnut Hill College
9601 Germantown Avenue
Philadelphia, PA 19118
215-248-7000
www.chc.edu

Cheyney University of Pennsylvania
Cheyney and Creek Roads
Cheyney, PA 19319-0200
800-223-3608 or 610-399-2000
www.cheyney.edu

> **Creative minds have always been known to survive any kind of bad training.**
>
> —Anna Freud (in *Great Quotes from Great Women*)

Around Danville, Kentucky, you will see an odd code painted on buildings: C6-H0. This commemorates a 1921 football game between Centre College and Harvard, which Centre won 6-0. It was, at the time, Harvard's first loss in five years. Twenty-nine years later the Associated Press called this game "the sports upset of the first half-century." Now you know.

> ## Life is either a daring adventure, or nothing.
>
> *—Helen Keller*

Chicago State University
9501 South King Drive
Chicago, IL 60628
773-995-2000
www.csu.edu

Chowan College
200 Jones Drive
Murfreesboro, NC 27855
919-398-4101
www.chowan.edu

The Christendom College
134 Christendom Drive
Front Royal, VA 22630
540-636-2900
www.christendom.edu

Christian Brothers University
650 East Parkway South
Memphis, TN 38104
901-321-3000
www.cbu.edu

Christian Heritage College
2100 Greenfield Drive
El Cajon, CA 92019
619-441-2200
www.christianheritage.edu

Christopher Newport University
1 University Place
Newport News, VA 23606
757-594-7100
www.cnu.edu

**Cincinnati Bible College
& Seminary**
2700 Glenway Avenue
Cincinnati, OH 45204
513-244-8100
www.cincybible.edu

**Cincinnati College
of Mortuary Science**
645 West North Bend Road
Cincinnati, OH 45224
513-761-2020
www.ccms.edu

Circleville Bible College
1476 Lancaster Pike
Circleville, OH 43113
740-474-8896
www.biblecollege.edu

The Citadel
171 Moultrie Street
Charleston, SC 29409
803-953-5000
www.citadel.edu

The City College
City University of New York
160 Convent Avenue
New York, NY 10031
212-650-7000
www.ccny.cuny.edu

City College of Colorado Springs
6050 Erin Park Drive, Suite 250
Colorado Springs, CO 80918
719-532-1234

City University
335 116th Avenue, SE
Bellevue, WA 98004
425-637-1010
www.cityu.edu

Claflin College
700 College Avenue, NE
Orangeburg, SC 29115
800-922-1276 or 803-535-5097
www.scicu.org/claflin/cchome.htm

More than three out of five college students change their major at least once before graduating and, as noted elsewhere, one in four does not return after the freshman year.

Claremont McKenna College
500 East Ninth Street
Claremont, CA 91711
909-621-8111
www.mckenna.edu

Clarion University of Pennsylvania
840 Wood Street
Clarion, PA 16214
814-226-2000
www.clarion.edu

Clark Atlanta University
240 James P. Brawley Drive, SW
Atlanta, GA 30314
404-880-6605
www.cau.edu

Clark University
950 Main Street
Worcester, MA 01610
508-793-7711
www.clarku.edu

Clarke College
1550 Clarke Drive
Dubuque, IA 52001
319-588-6300
www.clarke.edu

Clarkson College
101 South 42nd Street
Omaha, NE 68131
800-647-5500 or 402-552-3100
www.clarksoncollege.edu

Clarkson University
8 Clarkson Avenue
Potsdam, NY 13699
315-268-6400
www.clarkson.edu

Clayton College and State University
5900 North Lee Street
Morrow, GA 30260
770-961-3400
www.clayton.edu

Clear Creek Baptist Bible College
300 Clear Creek Road
Pineville, KY 40977
606-337-3196
www.ccbbc.edu

Clearwater Christian College
3400 Gulf-to-Bay Boulevard
Clearwater, FL 34619
727-726-1153
www.clearwater.edu

Cleary College
2170 Washtenaw Avenue
Ypsilanti, MI 48197
800-686-1883 or 517-548-3670
www.cleary.edu

Clemson University
North Palmetto Boulevard
Clemson, SC 29634
864-656-3311
www.clemson.edu

Cleveland Chiropractic College
590 North Vermont Avenue
Los Angeles, CA 90004
213-660-6166
www.clevelandchiropractic.edu

Cleveland Chiropractic College
6401 Rockhill Road
Kansas City, MO 64131
800-274-0617 or 816-501-0100
www.clevelandchiropractic.edu

Cleveland College of Jewish Studies
26500 Shaker Boulevard
Beachwood, OH 44122
216-464-4050
www.ccjs.edu

Cleveland Institute of Art
11141 East Boulevard
Cleveland, OH 44106
216-421-7000
www.cia.edu

> **There were two things I had a right to: liberty and death. If I could not have one, I would have the other, for no man should take me alive.**
>
> —Harriet Tubman

Cleveland Institute of Music
11021 East Boulevard
Cleveland, OH 44106
216-791-5000
www.cim.edu

Cleveland State University
East 24th Street and Euclid Avenue
Cleveland, OH 44115
216-687-2000
www.csuohio.edu

Clinch Valley College of The University of Virginia
One College Avenue
Wise, VA 24293
540-328-0100
www.clinch.edu

Coastal Carolina University
755 Highway 544
Conway, SC 29528
803-347-3161
www.coastal.edu

Coe College
1220 First Avenue, NE
Cedar Rapids, IA 52402
319-399-8000
www.coe.edu

Cogswell Polytechnic College
1175 Bordeaux Drive
Sunnyvale, CA 94089
408-541-0100
www.cogswell.edu

Coker College
300 East College Avenue
Hartsville, SC 29550
843-383-8000
www.coker.edu

Colby College
4000 Mayflower Hill
Waterville, ME 04901
207-872-3000
www.colby.edu

Colby-Sawyer College
100 Main Street
New London, NH 03257
603-526-2010
www.colby-sawyer.edu

Colegio Biblico Pentecostal
Carretera 848 Entrada los Marq
St. Just, PR 00978
787-257-7373

Colegio Universitario del Este
Carolina, PR 00983-2010
787-257-7373
www.suagm.eduCUE/main/default.htm

Coleman College
7380 Parkway Drive
La Mesa, CA 91942
619-465-3990
www.coleman.edu

Colgate University
13 Oak Drive
Hamilton, NY 13346
315-824-1000
www.colgate.edu

College of Aeronautics
La Guardia Airport
Flushing, NY 11371
718-429-6600
www.aero.edu

College of the Atlantic
105 Eden Street
Bar Harbor, ME 04609
800-528-0025 or 207-288-5015
www.coa.edu

College of Charleston
66 George Street
Charleston, SC 29424
803-953-5507
www.cofc.edu

College of the Holy Cross
One College Street
Worcester, MA 01610
508-793-2011
www.holycross.edu

College of Insurance
101 Murray Street
New York, NY 10007
212-962-4111
www.tci.edu

College of Lifelong Learning, University System of New Hampshire
125 North State Street
Concord, NH 03301
603-228-3000
usnh.unh.edu

College Misericordia
301 Lake Street
Dallas, PA 18612
717-674-6400
www.miseri.edu

College of Mount Saint Joseph
5701 Delhi Road
Cincinnati, OH 45233
800-654-9314 or 513-244-4200
www.msj.edu

College of Mount Saint Vincent
6301 Riverdale Avenue
Riverdale, NY 10471
718-405-3200
www.cmsv.edu

The College of New Jersey
2000 Pennington Road
Ewing, NJ 08628
609-771-1855
www.tcnj.edu

College of New Rochelle
29 Castle Place
New Rochelle, NY 10805
914-632-5300
www.cnr.edu

College of Notre Dame
1500 Ralston Avenue
Belmont, CA 94002
650-593-1601
www.cnd.edu

College of Notre Dame of Maryland
4701 North Charles Street
Baltimore, MD 21210
410-435-0100
www.ndm.edu

> **I'm just an average citizen.**
>
> —*Rosa Parks*

College of Our Lady of the Elms
291 Springfield Street
Chicopee, MA 01013
413-594-2761
www.elms.edu

College of the Ozarks
Opportunity Avenue
Point Lookout, MO 65726
800-222-0525 or 417-334-6411
www.cofo.edu

College of Saint Benedict
37 South College Avenue
Saint Joseph, MN 56374
320-363-5505
www.csbsju.edu

College of Saint Catherine
2004 Randolph Avenue
St. Paul, MN 55105
612-690-6000
www.stkate.edu

College of Saint Elizabeth
2 Convent Road
Morristown, NJ 07960
973-605-7000
www.st-elizabeth.edu

College of Saint Mary
1901 South 72nd Street
Omaha, NE 68104
800-926-5534 or 402-399-2400
www.csm.edu

The College of Saint Rose
432 Western Avenue
Albany, NY 12203
518-454-5111
www.strose.edu

College of Saint Scholastica
1200 Kenwood Avenue
Duluth, MN 55811
800-447-5444 or 218-723-6000
www.css.edu

The College of Saint Thomas More
3013 Lubbock Avenue
Fort Worth, TX 76109
817-923-8459
www.cstm.edu

The College of Santa Fe
1600 St. Michael's Drive
Santa Fe, NM 87501
800-456-2673 or 505-473-6011
www.csf.edu

College of the Southwest
6610 Lovington Highway
Hobbs, NM 88240
800-530-4400 or 505-392-6561
www.csw.edu

College of St. Joseph
71 Clement Road
Rutland, VT 05701
802-773-5900
www.csj.edu

College of Staten Island - City University of New York
2800 Victory Boulevard
Staten Island, NY 10314
718-982-2000
www.csi.cuny.edu

College of Visual Arts
344 Summit Avenue
St. Paul, MN 55102
800-766-6067 or 612-224-3416
www.cvs.edu

Phi Beta Kappa was founded at the College of William and Mary in Williamsburg, VA, December 5, 1776. Only Phi Beta Kappans can nominate students for inclusion in Phi Beta Kappa. This is an honor, but it is a separate designation from graduating "with honors."

The College of West Virginia
609 South Kanawha Street
Beckley, WV 25802
304-253-7351
www.cwv.edu

The College of William and Mary
P.O. Box 8795
Williamsburg, VA 23187-8795
757-221-4000
www.wm.edu

College of Wooster
1189 Beall Avenue
Wooster, OH 44691
330-263-2311
www.wooster.edu

Colorado Christian University
180 South Garrison Street
Lakewood, CO 80226
800-443-2484 or 303-202-0100
www.ccu.edu

Colorado College
14 East Cache la Poudre Street
Colorado Springs, CO 80903
719-389-6000
www.coloradocollege.edu

Colorado School of Mines
1500 Illinois Street
Golden, CO 80401
800-446-9488 or 303-273-3000
www.mines.edu

Colorado State University
College Avenue
Fort Collins, CO 80523
970-491-6211
www.colostate.edu

Colorado Technical University
4435 North Chestnut Street
Colorado Springs, CO 80907
719-598-0200
www.colotechu.edu

Columbia College
1001 Rogers Street
Columbia, MO 65216
800-231-2391 or 573-875-8700
www.ccis.edu

Columbia College
Carretera 183, KM 1.7
Caguas, PR 00726
787-743-4041

Columbia College
1301 Columbia College Drive
Columbia, SC 29203
803-786-3012
www.collacoll.edu

Columbia College Chicago
600 South Michigan Avenue
Chicago, IL 60605
312-663-1600
www.colum.edu

Columbia College Hollywood
18618 Oxnard Street
Tarzana, CA 91356
818-345-8414
www.columbiacollege.edu

Columbia College of Nursing
2121 East Newport Avenue
Milwaukee, WI 53211
414-961-3500

❝I've experienced more discrimination as a woman than as a Black person.❞

—Shirley Chisholm, U.S. Congresswoman from New York

A photograph of a jackalope is enameled into the floor in the hallway of an engineering building at Colorado School of Mines.

> **Those who cannot remember the past are condemned to repeat it.**
>
> *—George Santayana*

Columbia International University
7435 Monticello Road
Columbia, SC 29230
803-754-4100
www.ciu.edu

Columbia Union College
7600 Flower Avenue
Takoma Park, MD 20912
301-891-4000
www.cuc.edu

Columbia University
2960 Broadway
New York, NY 10027-6902
212-854-1754
www.columbia.edu

Columbus College of Art & Design
107 North Ninth Street
Columbus, OH 43215
614-224-9101
www.ccad.edu

Columbus State University
4225 University Avenue
Columbus, GA 31907
706-568-2001
www.colstate.edu

Commonwealth International University
2520 Fifth Avenue, South
Billings, MT 59101
406-256-1000
www.commonwealth.edu

Community Hospital of Roanoke Valley College of Health Sciences
920 South Jefferson Street
Roanoke, VA 24031
540-985-8483

Conception Seminary College
Federal Highway 136 & State Highway VV
Conception, MO 64433
660-944-2218

Concord College
Vermillion Street
Athens, WV 24712
304-384-3115
www.concord.edu

Concordia College
1804 Green Street
Selma, AL 36701
334-874-5700
higher-ed.lcms.org/selma.htm

Concordia College
4090 Geddes Road
Ann Arbor, MI 48105
734-995-7300
www.ccaa.edu

Concordia College
901 South Eighth Street
Moorhead, MN 56562
218-299-4000
www.cord.edu

Concordia College
800 North Columbia Avenue
Seward, NE 68434
800-535-5494 or 402-643-3651

Concordia College
171 White Plains Road
Bronxville, NY 10708
914-337-9300
www.concordia-ny.edu

Concordia University
1530 Concordia, West
Irvine, CA 92612
949-854-8002
www.cui.edu

Concordia University
7400 Augusta Street
River Forest, IL 60305
708-771-8300
www.curf.edu

Concordia University
275 North Syndicate Street
St. Paul, MN 55104
612-641-8278
www.csp.edu

Concordia University
2811 N.E. Holman Street
Portland, OR 97211
503-288-9371
www.cu-portland.edu

Concordia University at Austin
3400 Interstate 35, North
Austin, TX 78705
512-452-7661
www.concordia.edu

Concordia University Wisconsin
12800 North Lake Shore Drive
Mequon, WI 53097
414-243-5700
www.cuw.edu

Connecticut College
270 Mohegan Avenue
New London, CT 06320
860-447-1911
camel.conncoll.edu

**Conservatory of Music
of Puerto Rico**
350 Rafael Lamar Street
San Juan, PR 00918
787-751-0160

Converse College
580 East Main Street
Spartanburg, SC 29302
864-596-9000
www.converse.edu

**The Cooper Union for the
Advancement of Science & Art**
30 Cooper Square
New York, NY 10003
212-254-6300
www.cooper.edu

Coppin State College
2500 West North Avenue
Baltimore, MD 21216
410-383-5910
www.coppin.edu

Corcoran College of Art
500 17th Street, NW
Washington, DC 20006
202-639-1800
www.corcoran.edu

Cornell College
600 First Street, West
Mount Vernon, IA 52314
800-747-1112 or 319-895-4000
www.cornell-iowa.edu

Cornell University
410 Thurston Avenue
Ithaca, NY 14850-2488
607-255-2000
www.cornell.edu

> ❝ **How do we judge the quality of an undergraduate institution? We look at the athletic program. We have found an inverse relationship between the quality of a school's intercollegiate sports program and the quality of its academic program.** ❞
>
> —*Yale Law School recruiter, perhaps in jest, perhaps not*

College athletic programs long predate the professional leagues that dominate our culture and our televisions today. For example, Campbell Soup's cans are designed to match the colors of the Cornell football team from the 1800s.

(Source: L. M. Boyd)

Cornerstone College & Grand Rapids Baptist Seminary
1001 East Beltline Avenue, NE
Grand Rapids, MI 49505
616-949-5300
www.cornerstone.edu

Cornish College of the Arts
710 East Roy Street
Seattle, WA 98102
206-726-5000
www.cornish.edu

Covenant College
14049 Scenic Highway
Lookout Mountain, GA 30750
706-820-1560
www.covenant.edu

Creighton University
2500 California Plaza
Omaha, NE 68178
402-280-2700
www.creighton.edu

Crichton College
6655 Winchester Road
Memphis, TN 37175
901-367-9800
www.crichton.edu

Criswell College, The
4010 Gaston Avenue
Dallas, TX 75246
214-821-5433
www.criswell.edu

Crown College
6425 County Road 30
St. Bonifacius, MN 55375
612-446-4100
www.crown.edu

Crown College
8739 South Hosmer Street
Tacoma, WA 98444
509-359-2201

Culinary Institute of America
433 Albany Post Road
Hyde Park, NY 12538
914-452-9600
www.ciachef.edu

Culver-Stockton College
One College Hill
Canton, MO 63435
217-231-6000
www.culver.edu

Cumberland College
6190 College Station Drive
Williamsburg, KY 40769
606-549-2200
www.cumber.edu

Cumberland University
One Cumberland Square
Lebanon, TN 37087
615-444-2562
www.cumberland.edu

Curry College
1071 Blue Hill Avenue
Milton, MA 02186
617-333-0500
www.curry.edu:8080

The Curtis Institute of Music
1726 Locust Street
Philadelphia, PA 19103
215-893-5252
www.curtis.edu

D

Daemen College
4380 Main Street
Amherst, NY 14226
716-839-3600
www.daemen.edu

Dakota State University
820 North Washington
Madison, SD 57042
605-256-5111
www.dsu.edu

Dakota Wesleyan University
1200 West University Avenue
Mitchell, SD 57301
605-995-2600
www.dwu.edu

Dallas Baptist University
3000 Mountain Creek Parkway
Dallas, TX 75211
214-333-7100
www.dbu.edu

Dallas Christian College
2700 Christian Parkway
Dallas, TX 75234
972-241-3371
www.popi.net/dcc

Dalton State College
213 North College Drive
Dalton, GA 30720
706-272-4438
www.peachnet.dalton.edu

Dana College
2848 College Drive
Blair, NE 68008
402-426-9000
www.dana.edu

Daniel Webster College
20 University Drive
Nashua, NH 03063
603-883-3556
www.dwc.edu

Dartmouth College
East Wheelock Street
Hanover, NH 03755
603-646-1110
www.dartmouth.edu

Davenport College of Business
415 East Fulton Street
Grand Rapids, MI 49503
800-632-9569 or 616-451-3511
www.davenport.edu

David Lipscomb University
3901 Granny White Pike
Nashville, TN 37204
615-269-1000
www.dlu.edu

David N. Myers College
112 Prospect Avenue, SE
Cleveland, OH 44115
216-696-9000
www.dnmyers.edu

Davidson College
Main and Griffith Streets
Davidson, NC 28036
704-892-2000
www.davidson.edu

> **Be nice to your college counselors. Remember, we write your recommendations.**
>
> —*A college counselor*

The Nude Olympics are a tradition at Princeton University. Students meet at midnight on the eve of the first good snow for a "nude frolic." Several other Northeastern universities have the same tradition, and it is unclear where the tradition began. Each claims to be the originator of the practice. Even Davidson College in North Carolina has a nude frolic on the eve of the first big snow, and also claims to be the school that invented it.

Davis and Elkins College
100 Campus Drive
Elkins, WV 26241
800-624-3157 or 304-637-1900
www.dne.edu

Deaconess College of Nursing
6150 Oakland Avenue
St. Louis, MO 63139
314-768-3044

Deep Springs College
Off California Highway 168
Deep Springs, California
Mailing address: c/o HC72 Box 45001
Dyer, NV 89010-9803
760-872-2000
www.deepsprings.edu

The Defiance College
701 North Clinton Street
Defiance, OH 43512
419-784-4010
www.defiance.edu

Delaware State University
1200 North Dupont Highway
Dover, DE 19901-2277
302-739-4904
www.dsc.edu

Delaware Valley College of Science & Agriculture
700 East Butler Avenue
Doylestown, PA 18901
215-345-1500
www.devalcol.edu

Delta State University
Highway 8, West
Cleveland, MS 38733
601-846-3000
www.deltast.edu

Denison University
100 South Road
Granville, OH 43023
800-336-4766 or 740-587-0810
www.denison.edu

Denver Technical College
925 South Niagara Street
Denver, CO 80224
303-329-3000
www.dtc.edu

DePaul University
25 East Jackson
Chicago, IL 60604
312-362-8300
www.depaul.edu

DePauw University
313 South Locust Street
Greencastle, IN 46135
765-658-4800
www.depauw.edu

Design Institute of San Diego
8555 Commerce Avenue
San Diego, CA 92121
858-566-1200
www.disd.edu

Detroit College of Business
4801 Oakman Boulevard
Dearborn, MI 48126
313-581-4400
www.dcb.edu

> **A quitter never wins— and a winner never quits.**
>
> —*The locker room mantra*

The last unbeaten-, untied-, and unscored-upon collegiate football team in the nation was the 1933 team from DePauw University, Greencastle, Indiana. Theirs was football's version of a perfect season. Oddly enough, just the prior year Colgate University's team was also unbeaten, untied, and unscored upon. It hasn't happened lately.

DeVry Institutes of Technology
One Tower Lane, Suite 1000
Oakbrook Terrace, IL 60181
630-571-7700
www.devry.edu

Dickinson College
College and Louther Streets
Carlisle, PA 17013
717-243-5121
www.dickinson.edu

Dickinson State University
Eighth Avenue West and Third Street
West
Dickinson, ND 58601
800-227-2507 or 701-227-2507
www.dsu.nodak.edu

Dillard University
2601 Gentilly Boulevard
New Orleans, LA 70122
800-216-6637 or 504-283-8822
www.dillard.edu

Divine Word College
102 Jacoby Drive, SW
Epworth, IA 52045
319-876-3353
www.dillard.edu

Doane College
1014 Boswell Avenue
Crete, NE 68333
800-333-6263 or 402-826-2161
www.doane.edu

**Dr. William M. Scholl College
of Podiatric Medicine**
1001 North Dearborn Street
Chicago, IL 60610
312-280-2880
www.scholl.edu

Dominican College of Blauvelt
470 Western Highway
Orangeburg, NY 10962
914-359-7800
www.dc.edu

Dominican College of San Rafael
50 Acacia Street
San Rafael, CA 94901
415-457-4440
www.dominican.edu

**Dominican School of Philosophy
and Theology**
2401 Ridge Road
Berkeley, CA 94709
510-849-2030
www.dspt.edu

> ❝ **Do not worry about
> your difficulties in
> mathematics; I can assure
> you that mine are
> still greater.** ❞
>
> —*Albert Einstein*

WINTER SPORTS, ANYONE?

Reed College has a college-owned ski cabin on historic Mt. Hood, which boasts at least theoretical twelve-month skiing, although I've heard the surface quality is poor in the summer. Michigan Tech (Houghton, Michigan) has 200 inches of snow a year, its own cross-country ski trails, and its own ski run, Mont Ripley Ski Hill, "the steepest in the Midwest!" Students engineer giant snow and ice sculptures just like those in Fairbanks, Alaska. Michigan Tech also features sled-dog races. Students pull the sleds and the dogs' job is to stay put and ride. Colorado Mountain College has a course in "Ski-Area Operations," which entails, you guessed it, lots of skiing.

Dominican University
7900 West Division Street
River Forest, IL 60305
708-366-2490
www.dom.edu

Dordt College
498 Fourth Avenue NE
Sioux Center, IA 51250
712-722-6000
www.dordt.edu

Dowling College
Idle Hour Boulevard
Oakdale, NY 11769
516-244-3000
www.dowling.edu

Drake University
2507 University Avenue
Des Moines, IA 50311
800-443-7253 or 515-271-2191
www.drake.edu

Drew University
36 Madison Avenue
Madison, NJ 07940
973-408-3000
www.drew.edu

Drexel University
3141 Chestnut Street
Philadelphia, PA 19104
215-895-2000
www.drexel.edu

Drury College
900 North Benton
Springfield, MO 65802
417-873-7879
www.drury.edu

Duke University
2138 Campus Drive
Durham, NC 27708
919-684-8111
www.duke.edu

Educational consulting companies help colleges and universities recruit students. They design the look and the content of the slick brochures you get in the mail, do focus surveys on the exact wording of the letters you get from presidents and deans, and provide a range of demographic and psychographic analyses used to strategize the entire process. They are also very expensive, and only the largest and best-funded, and the most desperate, institutions can afford to retain them every year. (The Robert E. Cook Honors College at IUP brags in their viewbook that it is an entirely homegrown product, designed and written by currently enrolled students. It *is* different.)

You may not realize this, but these consultants may know much more about you than you know about yourself. Schools and their consultants know your age, your address, your social security number, your GPA, your ACT and SAT scores, the number of times you've visited which schools, your career interests, the matriculation patterns of past graduates of your high school, and the credit histories and estimated income of your parents. They even use this data to manipulate financial aid offers to keep each offer at the minimum needed to recruit each type of student.

Interestingly enough, if you are a nontraditional student—say you dropped out of school or worked for a year after graduating or went to high school abroad—they won't know about you at all. So while colleges are busy fighting for the attention of the traditional student, the nontraditional student is operating in a vacuum. Both types of students need to do their own research and, most of all, *their own thinking,* to find the school where they will thrive and grow the most. Don't let a marketing company tell you to go to Lower Slobavia University just because they get paid a bonus for your enrollment.

Duquesne University
600 Forbes Avenue
Pittsburgh, PA 15282
412-396-6000
www.duq.edu

D'Youville College
320 Porter Avenue
Buffalo, NY 14201
716-881-3200
www.dyc.edu

E

Earlham College
801 National Road, West
Richmond, IN 47374
765-983-1200
www.earlham.edu

East Carolina University
East Fifth Street
Greenville, NC 27858
252-328-6131
www.ecu.edu

East Central University
Twelfth and Francis Streets
Ada, OK 74820
580-332-8000
www.ecok.edu

East Coast Bible College
6900 Wilkinson Boulevard
Charlotte, NC 28214
704-394-2307
www.ecbc.edu

**East Stroudsburg University
of Pennsylvania**
200 Prospect Street
East Stroudsburg, PA 18301
717-422-3545
www.esu.edu

East Tennessee State University
University Parkway
Johnson City, TN 37614
423-439-4213
www.etsu.edu

East Texas Baptist University
1209 North Grove Street
Marshall, TX 75670
903-935-7963
www.etbu.edu

Eastern College
1300 Eagle Road
St. Davids, PA 19087
610-341-5803
www.eastern.edu

**Eastern Connecticut State
University**
83 Windham Street
Willimantic, CT 06226
860-465-5000
www.ecsu.ctstateu.edu

Eastern Illinois University
600 Lincoln Avenue
Charleston, IL 61920
217-581-5000
www.eiu.edu

Eastern Kentucky University
521 Lancaster Avenue
Richmond, KY 40475
606-622-1000
www.eku.edu

Eastern Mennonite University
1200 Park Road
Harrisonburg, VA 22802
540-432-4000
www.emu.edu

Eastern Michigan University
202 Welch Hall
Ypsilanti, MI 48197
734-487-1849
www.emich.edu

Eastern Nazarene College
23 East Elm Avenue
Quincy, MA 02170
617-773-6350
www.enc.edu

Eastern New Mexico University
1200 West University
Portales, NM 88130
800-367-3668 or 505-562-2121
www.enmu.edu

Eastern Oregon University
1410 L Avenue
La Grande, OR 97850
541-962-3511
www.eou.edu

Eastern Washington University
526 Fifth Street
Cheney, WA 99004
509-359-6200
www.ewu.edu

East-West University
816 South Michigan Avenue
Chicago, IL 60605
312-939-0111
www.eastwest.edu

Eckerd College
4200 54th Avenue, South
St. Petersburg, FL 33711
813-867-1166
www.eckerd.edu

Edgewood College
855 Woodrow Street
Madison, WI 53711
800-444-4861 or 608-257-4861
www.edgewood.edu

Edinboro University of Pennsylvania
Edinboro, PA 16444
814-732-2000
www.edinboro.edu

Edward Waters College
1658 Kings Road
Jacksonville, FL 32209
904-355-3030
www.ewc.edu

Electronic Data Processing College
48 Betances Street
San Sebastian, PR 00755
809 896-2137

Elizabeth City State University
1704 Weeksville Road
Elizabeth City, NC 27909
252-335-3400
www.ecsu.edu

Elizabethtown College
One Alpha Drive
Elizabethtown, PA 17022
717-361-1000
www.etown.edu

Elmhurst College
190 Prospect Avenue
Elmhurst, IL 60126
630-617-3500
www.elmhurst.edu

Elmira College
One Park Place
Elmira, NY 14901
607-735-1800
www.elmira.edu

Pre-Med? At Elizabethtown College in Elizabethtown, Pennsylvania, undergraduates get to work on cadavers.

Elon College
Haggard Avenue
Elon College, NC 27244
336-584-2200
www.elon.edu

Embry-Riddle Aeronautical University
600 South Clyde Morris Boulevard
Daytona Beach, FL 32114
904-226-6000
www.embryriddle.edu

Embry-Riddle Aeronautical University
3200 Willow Creek Road
Prescott, AZ 86301
800-888-3728 or 520-708-3728
www.pr.erau.edu

Emerson College
100 Beacon Street
Boston, MA 02116
617-578-8500
www.emerson.edu

Emmanuel College
P.O. Box 129
Franklin Springs, GA 30639
706-245-7226
www.emmanuel-college.edu

Emmanuel College
400 The Fenway
Boston, MA 02115
617-277-9430
www.emmanuel.edu

Emmaus Bible College
2570 Asbury Road
Ankeny, IA 52001
319-588-8000
www.emmaus.edu

Emory & Henry College
One Garnand Avenue
Emory, VA 24327
540-944-4121
www.ehc.edu

Emory University
1380 South Oxford Road, NE
Atlanta, GA 30322
404-727-6123
www.emory.edu

Emporia State University
1200 Commercial Street
Emporia, KS 66801
316-343-1200
www.emporia.edu

> " Even in some of the more affluent public high schools, budget cuts have decimated counseling staff. In too many others, counselors are really social workers, forced to spend most of their time on school violence, unwanted pregnacies, alcoholism, and other problems—with college counseling lost in the shuffle. "
>
> —*Bill Paul (in the* Chronicle of Higher Education*)*

You may need a better dictionary. The spelling checkers and thesauri on most word processing programs are no substitute for a dictionary at your side while you write. I recommend *The American Heritage Dictionary of the English Language*. Some features that set it apart: word histories, describing some of the more interesting etymologies; usage notes, addressing questions of convention vs. "rule" lexicography, among other things; great descriptions of the origins of the letters of the alphabet; and proper names from history and geography. It also passes the "atheist and expletives" test. If you want to know the quality of any dictionary, look up "atheist" and all your favorite expletives. Go ahead. See for yourself. If you check carefully, I think you will find that *American Heritage* designed page breaks so that more expletives would show up as headings. Check it out. I am not kidding.

Endicott College
376 Hale Street
Beverly, MA 01915
508-927-0585
www.endicott.edu

Erskine College
Two Washington Street
Due West, SC 29639
864-379-2131
www.erskine.edu

Escuela de Artes Plasticas de Puerto Rico
Apartado 1112
San Juan, PR 00902
787-725-8120

Eugene Bible College
2155 Bailey Hill Road
Eugene, OR 97405
541-485-1780
www.ebc.edu

Eureka College
300 East College Avenue
Eureka, IL 61530
309-467-3721
www.eureka.edu

Evangel University
1111 North Glenstone Avenue
Springfield, MO 65802
417-865-2811
www.evangel.edu

Evergreen State College
2700 Evergreen Parkway
Olympia, WA 98505
360-866-6000
www.evergreen.edu

F

Fairfield University
1073 North Benson Road
Fairfield, CT 06430
203-254-4000
www.fairfield.edu

Fairleigh Dickinson University
1000 River Road
Teaneck, NJ 07666
201-692-2000
www.fdu.edu

Fairmont State College
1201 Locust Avenue
Fairmont, WV 26554
304-367-4000
www.fscwv.edu

Faith Baptist Bible College
1900 N.W. Fourth Street
Ankeny, IA 50021
515-964-0601

Fashion Institute of Technology
Seventh Avenue at 27th Street
New York, NY 10001
212-217-7999
www.fitnyc.suny.edu

Faulkner University
5345 Atlanta Highway
Montgomery, AL 36109
205-272-5820
www.faulkner.edu

Fayetteville State University
1200 Murchison Road
Fayetteville, NC 28301
910-486-1111
www.uncfsu.edu

Felician College
262 South Main Street
Lodi, NJ 07644
201-778-1190
www.felician.edu

Ferris State University
1349 Cramer Circle
Big Rapids, MI 49307
616-592-2100
www.ferris.edu

Ferrum College
Route 40 West
Ferrum, VA 24088
540-365-2121
www.ferrum.edu

Fisk University
1000 17th Avenue North
Nashville, TN 37208
800-443-FISK or 615-329-8500
www.fisk.edu

Fitchburg State College
160 Pearl Street
Fitchburg, MA 01420
978-345-2151
www.fsc.edu

Five Towns College
305 North Service Road
Dix Hills, NY 11746
516-424-7000
www.ftc.edu

Flagler College
74 King Street
St. Augustine, FL 32085
904-829-6481
www.flagler.edu

Florida Agricultural & Mechanical University
South Martin Luther King Boulevard
Tallahassee, FL 32307
850-599-3000
www.famu.edu

Florida Atlantic University
777 Glades Road
Boca Raton, FL 33431
561-297-3000
www.fau.edu

Florida Baptist Theological College
5400 College Drive
Graceville, FL 32440
850-263-3261
www.fbtc.edu

Florida Christian College
1011 Bill Beck Boulevard
Kissimmee, FL 34744
407-847-8966
www.fcc.edu

Florida College
119 Glen Arven Avenue
Temple Terrace, FL 33617
813-899-5131
www.flcoll.edu

Florida Gulf Coast University
10501 FGCU Boulevard, South
Fort Myers, FL 33965
800 590-3428 or 941-590-1000
www.fgcu.edu

Florida Hospital College of Health Sciences
800 Lake Estelle Drive
Orlando, FL 32803
407-895-7747

Florida Institute of Technology
150 West University Boulevard
Melbourne, FL 32901
407-674-8000
www.fit.edu

Florida International University
11200 S.W. Eighth Street
Miami, FL 33199
305-348-2000
www.fiu.edu

Florida Memorial College
15800 N.W. 42nd Avenue
Miami, FL 33054
305-626-3600
www.fmc.edu

> **It is not enough to have a good mind. The main thing is to use it well.**
>
> —*René Descartes*

Florida Metropolitan University System - Fort Lauderdale College
1040 Bayview Drive
Fort Lauderdale, FL 33304
954-568-1600
www.cci.edufmu/784ftlauderdale/
fftlauderdale.htm

Florida Metropolitan University System - Orlando College, North
5421 Diplomat Circle
Orlando, FL 32810
407-628-5870
www.cci.edufmu/767orlandonorth/
forlandonorth.htm

Florida Metropolitan University System - Tampa College - Pinellas
2471 McMullen Booth Road, Suite 200
Clearwater, FL 34619
727-725-2688
www.cci.edufmu/763tampapinellas/
ftampapinellas.htm

Florida Metropolitan University System - Tampa College
3319 West Hillsborough Avenue
Tampa, FL 33614
813-879-6000
www.cci.edufmu/762tampa/
ftampa.htm

Florida Southern College
111 Lake Hollingsworth Drive
Lakeland, FL 33801
941-680-4111
www.flsouthern.edu

Florida State University
Tallahassee, FL 32306
850-644-2525
www.fsu.edu

Fontbonne College
6800 Wydown Boulevard
St. Louis, MO 63105
314-862-3456
www.fontbonne.edu

Fordham University
Lincoln Center
113 West 60 Street
New York, NY 10023
800-FORDHAM or 212-636-6000
www.fordham.edu

Fort Hays State University
600 Park Street
Hays, KS 67601
785-628-4000
www.fhsu.edu

Fort Lewis College
1000 Rim Drive
Durango, CO 81301
970-247-7100
www.fortlewis.edu

Fort Valley State University
1005 State University Drive
Fort Valley, GA 31030
912-825-6315
www.fvsu.edu

Framingham State College
100 State Street
Framingham, MA 01701
508-626-1220
www.framingham.edu

Francis Marion University
Highway 327
Florence, SC 29501
803-661-1362
www.fmarion.edu

Approximately 70 percent of incoming freshmen go to a college they've never even seen.

Franciscan University of Steubenville
1235 University Boulevard
Steubenville, OH 43952
740-283-3771
www.franuniv.edu

Frank Lloyd Wright School of Architecture
Taliesin West
Scottsdale, AZ 85261
602-860-2700
www.taliesin.edu

Franklin College of Indiana
501 East Monroe Street
Franklin, IN 46131
317-738-8000
www.franklincoll.edu

Franklin Institute of Boston
41 Berkeley Street
Boston, MA 02116
617-423-4630
www.franklin-fib.edu

Franklin & Marshall College
P.O. BOX 3003
Lancaster, PA 17604-3003
717-291-3911
www.fandm.edu

Franklin Pierce College
College Road
Rindge, NH 03461
603-899-5111
www.fpc.edu

Franklin University
201 South Grant Avenue
Columbus, OH 43215
614-341-6300
www.franklin.edu

Free Will Baptist Bible College
3606 West End Avenue
Nashville, TN 37205
615-844-5000
www.fwbbc.edu

Freed-Hardeman University
158 East Main Street
Henderson, TN 38340
901-989-6000
www.fhu.edu

Fresno Pacific University
1717 South Chestnut Avenue
Fresno, CA 93702
559-453-2000
www.fresno.edu

Friends University
2100 University
Wichita, KS 67213
800-794-6945 or 316-261-5800
www.friends.edu

> **To ridicule philosophy is really to philosophize.**
>
> *—Pascal*

THAT GREAT SIFTING AND WINNOWING

"Whatever may be the limitations which trammel inquiry elsewhere, we believe that the great state university of Wisconsin should ever encourage that continual and fearless sifting and winnowing by which alone the truth can be found."

-University of Wisconsin, Madison, Board of Regents Report, 1894

Frostburg State University
101 Braddock Road
Frostburg, MD 21532
301-687-4000
www.frostburg.edu

Furman University
3300 Poinsett Highway
Greenville, SC 29613
864-294-2000
www.furman.edu

G

Gallaudet University
800 Florida Avenue, NE
Washington, DC 20002
202-651-5000
www.gallaudet.edu

Gannon University
109 University Square
Erie, PA 16541-0001
814-871-7000
www.gannon.edu

Gardner-Webb University
College Avenue
Boiling Springs, NC 28017
704-434-2361
www.gardner-webb.edu

Geneva College
3200 College Avenue
Beaver Falls, PA 15010
412-846-5100
www.geneva.edu

George Fox University
414 North Meridian Street
Newberg, OR 97132
503-538-8383
www.georgefox.edu

George Mason University
4400 University Drive
Fairfax, VA 22030
703-993-1000
www.gmu.edu

George Washington University
2121 I Street, NW
Washington, DC 20052
202-994-4949
www.gwu.edu

Georgetown College
400 East College Street
Georgetown, KY 40324
502-863-8000
www.georgetowncollege.edu

Georgetown University
37th & O Streets, NW
Washington, DC 20057
202-687-0100
www.georgetown.edu

Georgia Baptist College of Nursing
274 Boulevard, Northeast
Atlanta, GA 30312
404-265-4512
www.gbcn.edu

THE HOOFERS

In 1931 the University of Wisconsin Memorial Union sponsored a skiing club, called the Hoofers. From this humble beginning began one of the most intense—and occasionally, rabble-rousing—of college outdoor activities clubs in the nation. Hoofers are outdoor fun enthusiasts nonpareil, climbing the highest mountains, helicopter skiing, canoeing, horseback riding, you name it, and are often photographed in flagrante delicto with a cold beer in one hand. It is a great honor to be a Hoofer.

Georgia College and State
University
Campus Box 97
Milledgeville, GA 31061-0490
912-445-5004
www.gcsu.edu

Georgia Institute of Technology
225 North Avenue, NW
Atlanta, GA 30332
404-894-2000
www.gatech.edu

Georgia Southern University
P.O. Box 8055
Statesboro, GA 30460-8055
912-681-5611
www.gasou.edu

Georgia Southwestern State
University
800 Wheatley Street
Americus, GA 31709
912-928-1279
www.gsw.edu

Georgia State University
University Plaza
Atlanta, GA 30303
404-651-2000
www.gsu.edu

Georgian Court College
900 Lakewood Avenue
Lakewood, NJ 08701
908-364-2200
www.georgian.edu

Gettysburg College
300 North Washington Street
Gettysburg, PA 17325
717-337-6000
www.gettysburg.edu

Glenville State College
200 High Street
Glenville, WV 26351
304-462-7361
www.glenville.wvnet.edu

God's Bible School and College
1810 Young Street
Cincinnati, OH 45210
513-721-7944

Goddard College
123 Pitkin Place
Plainfield, VT 05667
802-454-8311
www.goddard.edu

Golden Gate University
536 Mission Street
San Francisco, CA 94105
415-442-7000
www.ggu.edu

Goldey-Beacom College
4701 Limestone Road
Wilmington, DE 19808
302-998-8814
goldey.gbc.edu

Gonzaga University
502 East Boone Avenue
Spokane, WA 99258
509-328-4220
www.gonzaga.edu

Gordon College
255 Grapevine Road
Wenham, MA 01984
978-927-2300
www.gordonc.edu

Goshen College
1700 South Main Street
Goshen, IN 46526
219-535-7000
www.goshen.edu

Goucher College
1021 Dulaney Valley Road
Baltimore, MD 21204
410-337-6000
www.goucher.edu

Governors State University
University Drive
University Park, IL 60466
708-534-5000
www.govst.edu

Grace Bible College
1011 Aldon Street SW
Grand Rapids, MI 49509
616-538-2330
www.gbcol.edu

Grace College and Seminary
200 Seminary Drive
Winona Lake, IN 46590
219-372-5100
www.grace.edu

Grace University
1311 South Ninth Street
Omaha, NE 68108
402-449-2800
www.graceu.edu

Graceland College
700 College Avenue
Lamoni, IA 50140
800-346-9209 or 515-784-5000
www.graceland.edu

Grambling State University
403 Main Street
Grambling, LA 71245
318-247-3811
www.gram.edu

Grand Canyon University
3300 West Camelback Road
Phoenix, AZ 85017
800-800-9776 or 602-249-3300
www.grand-canyon.edu

Grand Valley State University
One Campus Drive
Allendale, MI 49401
616-895-6611
www.gvsu.edu

Grand View College
1200 Grandview Avenue
Des Moines, IA 50316
800-444-6083 or 515-263-2800
www.gvc.edu

Grantham College of Engineering
34641 Grantham College Road
Slidell, LA 70469
504-649-4191
www.grantham.edu

Gratz College
Old York Road and Melrose Avenue
Melrose Park, PA 19027
215-635-7300
www.gratzcollege.edu

Great Lakes Christian College
6211 West Willow Highway
Lansing, MI 48917
517-321-0242
www.glcc.edu

Great Lakes Maritime Academy
Northwestern Michigan College
1701 East Front Street
Traverse City, MI 49686
800-748-0566 x1200 or 231-922-1200
www.nmc.edu~maritime

Green Mountain College
One College Circle
Poultney, VT 05764
802-287-9313
www.greenmtn.edu

Greensboro College
815 West Market Street
Greensboro, NC 27401
910-272-7102
www.gborocollege.edu

Greenville College
315 East College Avenue
Greenville, IL 62246
618-664-1840
www.greenville.edu

Grinnell College
1213 Sixth Avenue
Grinnell, IA 50112
515-269-4000
www.grinnell.edu

Grove City College
100 Campus Drive
Grove City, PA 16127
412-458-2000
www.gcc.edu

Guilford College
5800 West Friendly Avenue
Greensboro, NC 27410
910-316-2000
www.guilford.edu

Gustavus Adolphus College
800 West College Avenue
St. Peter, MN 56082
507-933-8000
www.gustavus.edu

Gwynedd-Mercy College
1325 Sumneytown Pike
P.O. Box 901
Gwynedd Valley, PA 19437
215-646-7300
www.gmc.edu

H

Hamilton College
198 College Hill Road
Clinton, NY 13323
315-859-4104
www.hamilton.edu

Hamilton Technical College
1011 East 53rd Street
Davenport, IA 52807
319-386-3570
www.vca1.com/hamiltontech

Hamline University
1536 Hewitt Avenue
St. Paul, MN 55104
651-523-2800
www.hamline.edu

Hampden-Sydney College
College Road
Hampden-Sydney, VA 23943
800-755-0733 or 804-223-6000
www.hsc.edu

Hampshire College
893 West Street
Amherst, MA 01002
413-549-4600
www.hampshire.edu

Hampton University
Hampton, VA 23668
757-727-5328
www.hamptonu.edu

> **I hold it, that a little rebellion, now and then, is a good thing, and as necessary in the political world as storms in the physical.**
>
> *—Thomas Jefferson*

When Phil Wood was a student at Occidental College in Southern California, there was a twenty-four-hour poker game that went on uninterrupted for years. Although the games were illegal, Dean Culley was known to help out more than one poker loser with a few bucks until brighter days. Phil Wood now owns Ten Speed Press, publisher of this guide. Many people consider publishing a gamble, too. Mr. Wood uses the skills he gained in these poker games to negotiate tough deals with authors and booksellers. Not all learning goes on in the classroom.

Hannibal-LaGrange College
2800 Palmyra Road
Hannibal, MO 63401
573-221-3675
www.hlg.edu

Hanover College
P.O. BOX 108
Hanover, IN 47243
812-866-7000
www.hanover.edu

Hardin-Simmons University
2200 Hickory Street
Abilene, TX 79698
915 670-1000
www.hsutx.edu

Harding University
900 East Center Avenue
Searcy, AR 72149
800-477-4407 or 501-279-4274
www.harding.edu

**Harrington Institute
of Interior Design**
410 South Michigan Avenue
Chicago, IL 60605
312-939-4975
www.interiordesign.edu

Harris-Stowe State College
3026 Laclede Avenue
St. Louis, MO 63103
314-340-3366
www.hssc.edu

Hartwick College
4020 West Street
Oneonta, NY 13820
607-431-4200
www.hartwick.edu

Harvard University
Massachusetts Hall
Cambridge, MA 02138
617-495-1000
www.harvard.edu

Harvey Mudd College
301 East 12th Street
Claremont, CA 91711
909-621-8120
www.hmc.edu

Haskell Indian Nations University
155 Indian Avenue
Lawrence, KS 66046
785-749-8497
www.haskell.edu

Hastings College
800 Turner Avenue
Hastings, NE 68902
402-463-2402
www.hastings.edu

Haverford College
370 Lancaster Avenue
Haverford, PA 19041
610-896-1000
www.haverford.edu

Hawaii Pacific University
1166 Fort Street Mall
Honolulu, HI 96813
808-544-0200
www.hpu.edu

Brain twister: A business executive travels from London to New York, then falls asleep in the limousine ride to his hotel. When he wakes up, his watch is missing. He hails a cop, accusing the limousine driver of stealing his watch. The driver claims he just coincidentally owns the same type of Rolex. The exec says, "No, you stole my watch and I can prove it." How did he prove it?

Hebrew College
43 Hawes Street
Brookline, MA 02146
617-232-8710
shamash.org/hc

Hebrew Theological College
7135 Carpenter Road
Skokie, IL 60077
847-982-2500
www.htcnet.edu

Hebrew Union College -
Jewish Institute of Religion
3077 University Avenue
Los Angeles, CA 90007
213-749-3424
www.huc.edu

Heidelberg College
310 East Market Street
Tiffin, OH 44883
419-448-2000
www.heidelberg.edu

Hellenic College - Holy Cross Greek
Orthodox School of Theology
50 Goddard Avenue
Brookline, MA 02146
617-731-3500
www.hchc.edu

Henderson State University
1100 Henderson Street
Arkadelphia, AR 71999
870-230-5000
www.hsu.edu

Hendrix College
1601 Harkrider Street
Conway, AR 72032
501-329-6811
www.hendrix.edu

Henry Cogswell College
2802 Wetmore Avenue
Everett, WA 98201
425-258-3351
www.henrycogswell.edu

Herbert H. Lehman College -
City University of New York
250 Bedford Park Boulevard West
Bronx, NY 10468-1589
212-960-8000
www.lehman.cuny.edu

Heritage College
3240 Fort Road
Toppenish, WA 98948
509-865-2244
www.heritage.edu

The Herman M. Finch University
of Health Sciences
The Chicago Medical School
3333 Green Bay Road
North Chicago, IL 60064
847-578-3000
www.finchcms.edu

Hesser College
3 Sundial Avenue
Manchester, NH 03103
603-668-6660
www.hesser.edu

High Point University
833 Montlieu Avenue
High Point, NC 27262
910-841-9000
www.highpoint.edu

Hilbert College
5200 South Park Avenue
Hamburg, NY 14075
716-649-7900
www.hilbert.edu

> " Education has produced a vast population able to read but unable to distinguish what is worth reading. "
>
> —*G. M. Trevelyan*

Hillsdale College
33 East College Avenue
Hillsdale, MI 49242
517-437-7341
www.hillsdale.edu

Holy Family College
Grant and Frankford Avenues
Philadelphia, PA 19114
215-637-7700
www.hfc.edu

Hiram College
P.O. Box 67
Hiram, OH 44234
330-569-3211
www.hiram.edu

Holy Names College
3500 Mountain Boulevard
Oakland, CA 94619
510-436-1000
www.hnc.edu

❝ But it does move! ❞

—Galileo

Hobart & William Smith Colleges
639 South Main Street
Geneva, NY 14456
315-789-5500
www.hws.edu

Home Study International
12501 Old Columbia Pike
Silver Spring, MD 20914
301-680-6570
www.hsi.edu

Hobe Sound Bible College
11298 S.E. Gomez Avenue
Hobe Sound, FL 33455
561-546-5534
www.hsbc.edu

Hood College
401 Rosemont Avenue
Frederick, MD 21701
301-663-3131
www.hood.edu

Hofstra University
1000 Fulton Avenue
Hempstead, NY 11550
516-463-6600
www.hofstra.edu

Hope College
141 East 12th Street
Holland, MI 49422
616-395-7000
www.hope.edu

Hollins University
7916 Williamson Road
Roanoke, VA 24020
800-456-9595 or 540-362-6000
www.hollins.edu

Hope International University
2500 East Nutwood Avenue
Fullerton, CA 92831
714-879-3901
www.hiu.edu

Holy Apostles College and Seminary
33 Prospect Hill Road
Cromwell, CT 06416
860-632-3000
www.holy-apostles.org

Houghton College
One Willard Avenue
Houghton, NY 14744
716-567-9200
www.houghton.edu

Houston Baptist University
7502 Fondren Road
Houston, TX 77074
281-649-3000
www.hbu.edu

Howard Payne University
1000 Fisk Avenue
Brownwood, TX 76801
915-646-2502
www.hputx.edu

Howard University
2400 Sixth Street, NW
Washington, DC 20059
202-806-2500
www.howard.edu

Humboldt State University
One Harpst Street
Arcata, CA 95521
707-826-3011
www.humboldt.edu

Humphreys College
6650 Inglewood Avenue
Stockton, CA 95207
209-478-0800
www.humphreys.edu

Hunter College - City University of New York
695 Park Avenue
New York, NY 10021
212-772-4000
www.hunter.cuny.edu

Huntingdon College
1500 East Fairview Avenue
Montgomery, AL 36106
334-833-4222
www.huntingdon.edu

Huntington College
2303 College Avenue
Huntington, IN 46750
219-356-6000
www.huntington.edu

Husson College
One College Circle
Bangor, ME 04401
207-941-7988
www.husson.edu

Huston-Tillotson College
900 Chicon Street
Austin, TX 78702
512-505-3000
www.htc.edu

I

Idaho State University
741 South Seventh Avenue
Pocatello, ID 83209
208-236-0211
www.isu.edu

Illinois College
1101 West College Street
Jacksonville, IL 62650
217-245-3000
www.ic.edu

Illinois College of Optometry
3241 South Michigan Avenue
Chicago, IL 60616
312-225-1700
www.ico.edu

> **❝ I never let schooling get in the way of my education. ❞**
>
> —*Mark Twain*

Worried about boozing in your dorm? Pick a drug-alcohol-nicotine-free dorm. Many campuses have them now, so inquire. Or go to Centre College in Danville, Kentucky. It's smack in the middle of a dry county.

The Illinois Institute of Art
350 North Orleans
Chicago, IL 60654
312-280-3500
www.alia.aii.edu

Illinois Institute of Technology
10 West 33rd Street
Chicago, IL 60616
312-567-3000
www.iit.edu

Illinois State University
1000 Illinois State University
Normal, IL 61790
309-438-2111
www.ilstu.edu

Illinois Wesleyan University
P.O. Box 2900
Bloomington, IL 61702
309-556-1000
www.iwu.edu

Immaculata College
1145 King Road, P.O. Box 300
Immaculata, PA 19345-0300
610-647-4400
www.immaculata.edu

Indiana Institute of Technology
1600 East Washington Boulevard
Fort Wayne, IN 46803
800-937-2448 or 219-422-5561
www.indtech.edu

Indiana State University
200 North Seventh Street
Terre Haute, IN 47809
812-237-6311
www.indstate.edu

Indiana University Bloomington
107 S. Indiana Avenue
Bloomington, IN 47405-7000
812-855-4848
www.iub.edu

Indiana University East
2325 North Chester Boulevard
Richmond, IN 47374
317-973-8200
www.iue.indiana.edu

Indiana University at Kokomo
2400 South Washington Street
Kokomo, IN 46904
765-455-9200
www.iuk.indiana.edu

Indiana University Northwest
3400 Broadway
Gary, IN 46408
219-980-6500
www.iun.indiana.edu

Indiana University of Pennsylvania
Indiana, PA 15705
412-357-2100
www.iup.edu

Indiana University - Purdue University at Fort Wayne
2101 Coliseum Boulevard East
Fort Wayne, IN 46805
219-481-6100
www.ipfw.edu

Indiana University - Purdue University at Indianapolis
355 North Lansing
Indianapolis, IN 46202
317-274-5555
www.iupui.edu

Indiana University South Bend
1700 Mishawaka Avenue
South Bend, IL 46634
219-237-4111
www.iusb.edu

Indiana University Southeast
4201 Grant Line Road
New Albany, IN 47150
812-941-2000
www.ius.indiana.edu

Indiana Wesleyan University
4201 South Washington Street
Marion, IN 46953
800-332-6901 or 765-677-2138
www.indwes.edu

Institute for Christian Studies
1909 University Avenue
Austin, TX 78705
512-476-2772
www.ics.edu

Institute of Computer Technology
3200 Wilshire Boulevard, No. 400
Los Angeles, CA 90010
213-381-3333
www.ict.college

**Inter American University
of Puerto Rico**
Aguadilla Campus
Barrio Corrales
Sector Calero
Aguadilla, PR 00605
787-891-0925
www.interaguadilla.edu

**Inter American University
of Puerto Rico**
Arecibo Campus
Carretera #2, Km. 80.4
Bo. San Daniel
Sector Las Canelas
Arecibo, PR 00614
787-878-5475
www.arecibo.inter.edu

**Inter American University
of Puerto Rico**
Barranquitas Campus
Bo. Helechal, Carr. 156
Intersección 719
Barranquitas, PR 00794
787-857-4040
www.inter.edu

**Inter American University
of Puerto Rico**
Bayamon Campus
Carretera 830 #500
Bo. Cerro Gordo
Bayamon, PR 00970
787-279-1912
bc.inter.edu

**Inter American University
of Puerto Rico**
Fajardo Campus
Calle Union-Batey Central
Carr. 195
Fajardo, PR 00738
787-863-2390
www.inter.edu

**Inter American University
of Puerto Rico**
Guayama Campus
Bo. Machete
Carr. 744, Km 1.2
Guayama, PR 00785
787-864-2222
www.inter.edu/guayama

**Inter American University
of Puerto Rico**
Metropolitan Campus
Carretera 1, Km 16.3
Esq. Calle Francisco Sein
Río Piedras, PR 00919
787-250-1912
www.metro.inter.edu

**Inter American University
of Puerto Rico**
Ponce Campus
Bo. Sabanetas, Carr. 1
Mercedita Station
Mercedita Ponce, PR 00715
787-284-1912
www.inter.edu/programponce.html

> **“Much learning doth make thee mad.”**
>
> —*The Acts of the Apostles*
> *26:24*

> **No, I'm no enemy to learning; it hurts not me.**
>
> *—William Congreve*

Interior Designers Institute
1061 Camelback Road
Newport, CA 92660
714-675-4451

International Academy of Design
5225 Memorial Highway
Tampa, FL 33634
813-881-0007
www.academy.edu

International Academy of Merchandising and Design
One North State Street, No. 400
Chicago, IL 60602
312-541-3910
www.iamd.edu

International Bible College
3625 Helton Drive
Florence, AL 35630
205-766-6610
www.i-b-c.edu

International Business College
3811 Illinois Road
Fort Wayne, IN 46804
219-432-8702
www.bradfordschools.com

International College
2654 East Tamiami Trail
Naples, FL 34112
941-774-4700
www.internationalcollege.edu

International Fine Arts College
1737 North Bayshore Drive
Miami, FL 33132
305-373-4684
www.ifac.edu

Iona College
715 North Avenue
New Rochelle, NY 10801
914-633-2000
www.iona.edu

Iowa State University
Ames, IA 50011
515-294-2042
www.iastate.edu

Iowa Wesleyan College
601 North Main Street
Mount Pleasant, IA 52641
319-385-8021
www.iwc.edu

Ithaca College
Route 96B
Ithaca, NY 14850
607-274-3013
www.ithaca.edu

ITT Technical Institute - Anaheim
525 North Muller Avenue
Anaheim, CA 92801
714-535-3700
www.itt-tech.edu

ITT Technical Institute - Boise
12302 West Explorer Drive
Boise, ID 83713
208-322-8844
www.itt-tech.edu

ITT Technical Institute - Earth City
13505 Lakefront Drive
Earth City, MO 63045
314-298-2212
www.itt-tech.edu

ITT Technical Institute - Fort Wayne
4919 Coldwater Road
Fort Wayne, IN 46825
219-484-4107
www.itt-tech.edu

ITT Technical Institute - Greenfield
6300 West Layton Avenue
Greenfield, WI 53220
414-282-9494
www.itt-tech.edu

ITT Technical Institute - Indianapolis
9511 Angola Court
Indianapolis, IN 46268
317-875-8640
www.itt-tech.edu

ITT Technical Institute - Knoxville
10208 Technology Drive
Knoxville, TN 37919
423-671-2800
www.itt-tech.edu

ITT Technical Institute - Maitland
2600 Lake Lucien Drive, Suite 140
Maitland, FL 32751
407-660-2900
www.itt-tech.edu

ITT Technical Institute - Murray
920 West LeVoy Drive
Murray, UT 84123
801-263-3313
www.itt-tech.edu

ITT Technical Institute - Nashville
441 Donelson Pike
Nashville, TN 37214
615-889-8700
www.itt-tech.edu

ITT Technical Institute - Newburgh
10999 Stahl Road
Newburgh, IN 47630
812-858-1600
www.itt-tech.edu

ITT Technical Institute - Phoenix
4837 East McDowell Road
Phoenix, AZ 85008
602-252-2331
www.itt-tech.edu

ITT Technical Institute - Rancho Cordova
10863 Gold Center Drive
Rancho Cordova, CA 95670
916-851-3900
www.itt-tech.edu

ITT Technical Institute - San Bernardino
630 East Brier Drive, Suite 150
San Bernardino, CA 92408
909-889-3800
www.itt-tech.edu

ITT Technical Institute - San Diego
9680 Granite Ridge Drive
San Diego, CA 92123
619-571-8500
www.itt-tech.edu

ITT Technical Institute - Seattle
12720 Gateway Drive, Suite 100
Seattle, WA 98168
206-244-3300
www.itt-tech.edu

ITT Technical Institute - Sylmar
12669 Encinitas Avenue
Sylmar, CA 91342
818-364-5151
www.itt-tech.edu

A "legacy" is a student related to one or more alumni of a school. Legacies *always* get preferential admissions treatment. One technical college in the Old South puts colored dots on your admissions folder for every alumna/us who writes a recommendation letter for you. I've seen folders covered up in dots. A graduate student analyzed this legacy preference at Ivy League schools, and found it to be worth 15 percent of the total admission decision. My informal surveys of admissions deans suggest it is much more important than that! Now that's a different kind of affirmative action.

ITT Technical Institute - Tampa
4809 Memorial Highway
Tampa, FL 33634
813-885-2244
www.itt-tech.edu

ITT Technical Institute - Thornton
500 East 84th Avenue
Thornton, CO 80228
303-288-4488
www.itt-tech.edu

**ITT Technical Institute -
West Covina**
1530 West Cameron Avenue
West Covina, CA 91790
626-960-8681
www.itt-tech.edu

J

Jackson State University
1400 J. R. Lynch Street
Jackson, MS 39217
800-848-6817 or 601-968-2121
www.jsums.edu

Jacksonville State University
700 North Pelham Road, North
Jacksonville, AL 36265
205-782-5781
www.jsu.edu

Jacksonville University
2800 University Boulevard North
Jacksonville, FL 32211
904-744-3950
www.ju.edu

James Madison University
800 South Main Street
Harrisonburg, VA 22807
540-568-6211
www.jmu.edu

Jamestown College
6000 College Lane
Jamestown, ND 58405
800-336-2554 or 701-252-3467
www.jc.edu

Jarvis Christian College
U.S. Highway 80
Hawkins, TX 75765
903-769-5741
www.jarvis.edu

**Jewish Hospital College of Nursing
& Allied Health**
306 South Kingshighway Boulevard
St. Louis, MO 63110
314-454-7055

**Jewish Theological Seminary
of America**
3080 Broadway
New York, NY 10027
212-678-8000
www.jtsa.edu

John Brown University
200 West University Street
Siloam Springs, AR 72761
501-524-9500
www.jbu.edu

John Carroll University
20700 North Park Boulevard
University Heights, OH 44118
216-397-1886
www.jcu.edu

John F. Kennedy University
12 Altarinda Road
Orinda, CA 94563
925-254-0200
www.jfku.edu

John Jay College of Criminal Justice - City University of New York
899 Tenth Avenue
New York, NY 10019
212-237-8000
www.jjay.cuny.edu

John Wesley College
2314 North Centennial Street
High Point, NC 27265
336-889-2262
www.johnwesley.edu

Johns Hopkins University
34th & Charles Streets
Baltimore, MD 21218
410-516-8068
www.jhu.edu

Johnson Bible College
7900 Johnson Drive
Knoxville, TN 37998
423-573-4517
www.jbc.edu

Johnson C. Smith University
100 Beatties Ford Road
Charlotte, NC 28216
800-782-7303 or 704-378-1000
www.jcsu.edu

Johnson State College
337 College Hill
Johnson, VT 05656
802-635-2356
www.jsc.vsc.edu

Johnson & Wales University
8 Abbott Park Place
Providence, RI 02903
401-598-1000
www.jwu.edu

Joint Military Intelligence College
Defense Intelligence Analysis Center
200 MacDill Boulevard
Washington, DC 20340
202-231-3344
www.dia.mil

Leon Botstein, president of Simon's Rock College of Bard and president of Bard College, believes that the last two years of high school should be abolished. He says students are bored and unchallenged, and should go on to some type of job training or university after their sophomore year.

Jones College
5353 Arlington Expressway
Jacksonville, FL 32211
904-743-1122
www.jones.edu

Jones International University
9697 East Mineral Circle
Englewood, CO 80155
303-784-8045
www.jonesinternational.edu

Judson College
302 Bibb Street
Marion, AL 36756
334-683-5100
www.judson.edu

Judson College
1151 North State Street
Elgin, IL 60123
847-695-2500
www.judson-il.edu

The Juilliard School
60 Lincoln Center Plaza
New York, NY 10023
212-799-5000
www.juilliard.edu

Juniata College
1700 Moore Street
Huntingdon, PA 16652
814-641-3000
www.juniata.edu

K

Kalamazoo College
1200 Academy Street
Kalamazoo, MI 49006
616-337-7000
www.kzoo.edu

Kansas City Art Institute
4415 Warwick Boulevard
Kansas City, MO 64111
816-561-4852
www.kcai.edu

Kansas State University
17th & Anderson Streets
Manhattan, KS 66506
785-532-6011
www.ksu.edu

Many schools have a tradition of having a midnight yell sometime during finals week. One interesting thing about this tradition is that each school thinks their yell is a unique practice. Like the Nude Olympics at midnight on the night of the first snow, several schools also claimed to "own" this finals-week yell tradition. In a recent year, UCLA's yell got out of hand, with students burning furniture and breaking car windows. It is not clear how this helps with finals. And Princeton's Nude Olympics recently got out of hand, as well, with the president of the university vowing to shut down the practice. The students of Princeton are probably smart enough to lay low for a year or two before bringing back the venerable frolic. That always leaves the University of Michigan's Naked Mile, and Luther College's Naked Soccer. At Luther College (Decorah, Iowa), students gather for Naked Soccer at 2 A.M. on a night between final exams and graduation. The administration is busy trying to stamp out the practice, as it is "not consistent with a church-related college," says associate dean for student life, Robert A. Felde (as quoted in the *Chronicle of Higher Education*, 11 February 2000). Perhaps you can start your own "tradition" wherever you go to college. Since students roll over every four years, it only takes a couple of years to create a tradition, and conversely, it may only take a couple of years to stamp out a tradition, as well.

Kansas Wesleyan University
100 East Claflin
Salina, KS 67401
800-874-1154 or 785-827-5541
www.kwu.edu

Kean University
1000 Morris Avenue
Union, NJ 07083
908-527-2000
www.kean.edu

Keene State College
229 Main Street
Keene, NH 03435
603-352-1909
www.keene.edu

Kendall College
2408 Orrington Avenue
Evanston, IL 60201
847-866-1300
www.kendall.edu

Kendall College of Art & Design
111 Division Avenue, North
Grand Rapids, MI 49503
800-676-2787 or 616-451-2787
www.kcad.edu

Kennesaw State University
1000 Chastain Road
Kennesaw, GA 30144
770-882-2911
www.kennesaw.edu

Kent State University
Kent, OH 44242
330-672-3000
www.kent.edu

Kentucky Christian College
100 Academy Parkway
Grayson, KY 41143
606-474-3000
www.kcc.edu

Kentucky Mountain Bible College
855 Kentucky Highway 541
Vancleve, KY 41385
606-666-5000
www.kmbc.edu

Kentucky State University
400 East Main Street
Frankfort, KY 40601
800-325-1716 or 502-227-6000
www.kysu.edu

Kentucky Wesleyan College
3000 Frederica Street
Owensboro, KY 42302
502-926-3111
www.kwc.edu

Kenyon College
College Park Street
Gambier, OH 43022-9623
740-427-5000
www.kenyon.edu

Kettering College of Medical Arts
3737 Southern Boulevard
Kettering, OH 45429
937-296-7218
www.kcma.edu

Kettering University
1700 West Third Avenue
Flint, MI 48504
810-762-9500
www.kettering.edu

> **Beware that you do not lose the substance by grasping at the shadow.**
>
> —*Aesop*

Unusual gifts appear to be common at Juniata College. In 1957, the late Col. Will Judy, Chicago publisher of *Dog World Magazine*, provided funds for a room in Juniata's Lesher Hall in honor of his "titian-tressed" wife. The room is designated for red-headed students only.

Keuka College
East Bluff Drive
Keuka Park, NY 14478
315-536-4411
www.keuka.edu

King College
1350 King College Road
Bristol, TN 37620
423-968-1187
www.king.edu

King's College
133 North River Street
Wilkes-Barre, PA 18711
717-826-5900
www.kings.edu

Knox College
2 East South Street
Galesburg, IL 61401
309-341-7000
www.knox.edu

Kutztown University of Pennsylvania
Kutztown, PA 19530
610-683-4000
www.kutztown.edu

L

La Roche College
9000 Babcock Boulevard
Pittsburgh, PA 15237
412-367-9300
www.laroche.edu

La Salle University
1900 West Olney Avenue
Philadelphia, PA 19141
215-951-1000
www.lasalle.edu

La Sierra University
4700 Pierce Street
Riverside, CA 92515
909-785-2000
www.lasierra.edu

Laboratory Institute of Merchandising
12 East 53rd Street
New York, NY 10022
212-752-1530
www.limcollege.edu

Lafayette College
Easton, PA 18042
610-330-5000
www.lafayette.edu

LaGrange College
601 Broad Street
LaGrange, GA 30240
706-882-2911
www.lgc.edu

Lake Erie College
391 West Washington Street
Painesville, OH 44077
440-352-3361
www.lakeerie.edu

Lake Forest College
555 North Sheridan Road
Lake Forest, IL 60045
847-234-3100
www.lfc.edu

Lake Superior State University
650 West Easterday Avenue
Sault Suite Marie, MI 49783
906-632-6841
www.lssu.edu

Lakeland College
P.O. Box 359
Sheboygan, WI 53082
920-565-2111
www.lakeland.edu

Lakeview College of Nursing
903 North Logan Avenue
Danville, IL 61832
217-443-5238
www.lakeviewcol.edu

Lamar University
4400 Martin Luther King, Jr., Parkway
Beaumont, TX 77710
409-880-8185
www.lamar.edu

Lambuth University
705 Lambuth Boulevard
Jackson, TN 38301
901-425-2500
www.lambuth.edu

Lancaster Bible College
901 Eden Road
Lancaster, PA 17601
717-569-7071
www.lbc.edu

Lander University
320 Stanley Avenue
Greenwood, SC 29649
864-388-8400
www.lander.edu

Lane College
545 Lane Avenue
Jackson, TN 38301
800-390-7533 or 901-426-7500
www.lane-college.edu

Langston University
Langston, OK 73050
405-466-3207
www.lunet.edu

Lasell College
1844 Commonwealth Avenue
Newton, MA 02166
617-243-2000
www.lasell.edu

Lawrence Technological University
21000 West Ten Mile Road
Southfield, MI 48075
800-225-5588 or 284-204-4000
www.ltu.edu

Lawrence University
P.O. Box 599
Appleton, WI 54912
920-832-7000
www.lawrence.edu

Le Moyne College
1419 Salt Springs Road
Syracuse, NY 13214
315-445-4100
www.lemoyne.edu

Lebanon Valley College
101 North College Avenue
Annville, PA 17003
717-867-6100
www.lvc.edu

Lee University
1120 North Ocoee Street
Cleveland, TN 37320
423-614-8000
www.leeuniversity.edu

Lees-McRae College
P.O. Box 128
Banner Elk, NC 28604-0128
800-280-4562 or 828-898-5241
www.lmc.edu

Lehigh University
27 Memorial Drive, West
Bethlehem, PA 18015
610-758-3000
www.lehigh.edu

Steven Spielberg was turned down when he applied to film school. Eduardo Sanchez and Daniel Myrick, directors of the phenomenally successful movie *The Blair Witch Project,* went to film school at the University of Central Florida, approximately three thousand miles away from Hollywood.

LeMoyne-Owen College
807 Walker Avenue
Memphis, TN 38126
800-737-7778 or 901-774-9090
www.lemoyne-owen.edu

Lenoir-Rhyne College
Seventh Avenue & Eighth Street, NE
Hickory, NC 28603
828-328-1741
www.lrc.edu

Lesley College
29 Everett Street
Cambridge, MA 02138
617-868-9600
www.lesley.edu

LeTourneau University
2100 Mobberly Avenue
Longview, TX 75607
903-233-3000
www.letu.edu

Lewis and Clark College
0615 S.W. Palatine Hill Road
Portland, OR 97219
503-768-7200
www.lclark.edu

Lewis University
Route 53
Romeoville, IL 60441
815-838-0500
www.lewisu.edu

Lewis-Clark State College
500 Eighth Avenue
Lewiston, ID 83501
208-799-5272
www.lcsc.edu

Liberty University
1971 University Boulevard
Lynchburg, VA 24502
804-582-2000
www.liberty.edu

L.I.F.E. Bible College
1100 Covina Boulevard
San Dimas, CA 91773
909-599-5433
www.lifebible.edu

Life University
1269 Barclay Circle
Marietta, GA 30060
770-424-0554
www.life.edu

Limestone College
1115 College Drive
Gaffney, SC 29340
864-489-7151
www.limestone.edu

**Lincoln Christian College
and Seminary**
100 Campus View Drive
Lincoln, IL 62656
217-732-3168
www.lccs.edu

Lincoln University
281 Masonic Avenue
San Francisco, CA 94118
415-221-1212
www.lincolnuca.edu

Lincoln University
820 Chestnut Street
Jefferson City, MO 65102
800-521-5052 or 573-681-5000
www.lincolnu.edu

Lincoln University
1570 Old Baltimore Pike
Lincoln University, PA 19352
610-932-8300
www.lincoln.edu

Lindenwood University
209 South Kingshighway Boulevard
St. Charles, MO 63301
314-949-2000
www.lindenwood.edu

> **Every time a child says, 'I don't believe in fairies,' there's a little fairy somewhere that falls down dead.**
>
> *—Sir James Barrie*

Lindsey Wilson College
210 Lindsey Wilson Street
Columbia, KY 42728
502-384-2126
www.lindsey.edu

Linfield College
900 S.E. Baker
McMinnville, OR 97128
503-434-2200
www.linfield.edu

Livingstone College
701 West Monroe Street
Salisbury, NC 28144
800-835-3435 or 704-638-5500
www.livingstone.edu

**Lock Haven University
of Pennsylvania**
Lock Haven, PA 17745
717-893-2011
www.lhup.edu

Logan College of Chiropractic
1851 Schoettler Road
Chesterfield, MO 63006
800-782-3344 or 636-227-2100
www.logan.edu

Loma Linda University
Loma Linda, CA 92350
909-824-4300
www.llu.edu

Long Island University
700 Northern Boulevard
Brookville, NY 11548
516-299-2501
www.liu.edu

Longwood College
201 High Street
Farmville, VA 23909
804-395-2000
www.lwc.edu

Loras College
1450 Alta Vista
Dubuque, IA 52001
800-245-6727 or 319-588-7103
www.loras.edu

Los Angeles College of Chiropractic
16200 East Amber Valley Drive
Whittier, CA 90604
562-947-2700
www.lacc.edu

Louisiana College
1140 College Drive
Pineville, LA 71359
318-487-7011
www.lacollege.edu

Louisiana State University
Baton Rouge, LA 70803
225-388-3202
www.lsu.edu

**Louisiana State University
Medical Center**
433 Bolivar Street
New Orleans, LA 70112
504-568-4808
www.lsumc.edu

**Louisiana State University at
Shreveport**
One University Place
Shreveport, LA 71115
318-797-5000
www.lsus.edu

Louisiana Tech University
P.O. Box 3178
Ruston, LA 71272
318-257-0211
www.latech.edu

Lourdes College
6832 Convent Boulevard
Sylvania, OH 43560
419-885-3211
www.lourdes.edu

> ❝ If one will begin with certainties, one shall end in doubts; but one if one will be content to begin with doubts, one shall end in certainties. ❞
>
> —*Francis Bacon*

Loyola College, Baltimore
4501 North Charles Street
Baltimore, MD 21210
410-617-2000
www.loyola.edu

Loyola Marymount University
7900 Loyola Boulevard
Los Angeles, CA 90045
310-338-2700
www.lmu.edu

Loyola University, Chicago
6525 North Sheridan Road
Chicago, IL 60626
773-274-3000
www.luc.edu

Loyola University, New Orleans
6363 St. Charles Avenue
New Orleans, LA 70118
504-865-2011
www.loyno.edu

Lubbock Christian University
5601 19th Street
Lubbock, TX 79407
806-796-8800
www.lcu.edu

Luther College
700 College Drive
Decorah, IA 52101
319-387-2000
www.luther.edu

Lutheran Bible Institute of Seattle
4221 228th Avenue, SE
Issaquah, WA 98027
425-392-0400
www.lbi.edu

Lycoming College
700 College Place
Williamsport, PA 17701
717-321-4000
www.lycoming.edu

Lynchburg College
1501 Lakeside Drive
Lynchburg, VA 24501
804-544-8100
www.lynchburg.edu

Lyndon State College
1001 College Road
Lyndonville, VT 05851
802-626-6200
www.lsc.vsc.edu

Lynn University
3601 North Military Trail
Boca Raton, FL 33431
561-994-0770
www.lynn.edu

Lyon College
2300 Highland Road
Batesville, AR 72503
870-793-9813
www.lyon.edu

M

Macalester College
1600 Grand Avenue
St. Paul, MN 55105
612-696-6000
www.macalester.edu

MacMurray College
447 East College Avenue
Jacksonville, IL 62650
217-479-7025
www.mac.edu

Macon State College
100 College Station Drive
Macon, GA 31206
912-471-2800
www.maconstate.edu

Madonna University
36600 Schoolcraft Road
Livonia, MI 48150
800-852-4951 or 734-432-5300
www.munet.edu

Magnolia Bible College
822 South Huntington
Kosciusko, MS 39090
601-289-2896
www.mbc.org

**Maharishi University
of Management**
1000 North Fourth Street
Fairfield, IA 52557
515-472-7000
www.mum.edu

Maine College of Art
97 Spring Street
Portland, ME 04101
207-775-3052
www.meca.edu

Maine Maritime Academy
Pleasant Street
Castine, ME 04420
800-227-8465 or 207-326-4311
www.mainemaritime.edu

Malone College
515 25th Street, NW
Canton, OH 44709
330-471-8100
www.malone.edu

Manchester College
604 College Avenue
North Manchester, IN 46962
219-982-5000
www.manchester.edu

Manhattan Christian College
1415 Anderson Avenue
Manhattan, KS 66502
785-539-3571
www.mccks.edu

Manhattan College
Manhattan College Parkway
Riverdale, NY 10471
718-862-8000
www.manhattan.edu

Manhattan School of Music
120 Claremont Avenue
New York, NY 10027
212-749-2802
www.msmnyc.edu

Manhattanville College
2900 Purchase Street
Purchase, NY 10577
914-694-2200
www.mville.edu

**Mansfield University
of Pennsylvania**
Mansfield, PA 16933
717-662-4000
www.mnsfld.edu

Maranatha Baptist Bible College
745 West Main Street
Watertown, WI 53094
800-622-2947 or 920-261-9300
www.mbbc.edu

Marian College
3200 Cold Spring Road
Indianapolis, IN 46222
317-955-6000
www.marian.edu

Marian College of Fond du Lac
45 South National Avenue
Fond du Lac, WI 54935
800-262-7426 or 920-923-7600
www.mariancollege.edu

Marietta College
215 Fifth Street
Marietta, OH 45750
740-376-4643
www.marietta.edu

Marist College
290 North Road
Poughkeepsie, NY 12601
914-575-3000
www.marist.edu

> **At Mansfield University of Pennsylvania, a young woman who killed herself in the 1930s after being jilted by a boyfriend, reportedly still haunts North Hall. Since then, students have told of seeing her ghost, carrying a candle that eerily lights her face.**
>
> —*USA Today*

The most popular T-shirt at MIT right now is "Everything I ever needed to know I learned from *Star Trek*."

Marlboro College
South Road
Marlboro, VT 05344
800-257-4333 or 802-257-4333
www.marlboro.edu

Marquette University
530 North 16th Street
Milwaukee, WI 53233
800-222-6544 or 414-288-7223
www.marquette.edu

Mars Hill College
124 Cascade Street
Mars Hill, NC 28754
704-689-1111
www.mhc.edu

Marshall University
400 Hal Greer Boulevard
Huntington, WV 25755
800-642-3463 or 304-696-3170
www.marshall.edu

Martin Luther College
1995 Luther Court
New Ulm, MN 56073
507-354-8221
www.mlc-wels.edu

Martin Methodist College
433 West Madison Street
Pulaski, TN 38478
931-363-9804
www.martinmethodist.edu

Martin University
2171 Avondale Place
Indianapolis, IN 46218
317-543-3235
www.martin.edu

Mary Baldwin College
Frederick and New Streets
Staunton, VA 24401
800-468-2262 or 540-887-7000
www.mbc.edu

Mary Washington College
1301 College Avenue
Fredericksburg, VA 22401
540-654-1000
www.mwc.edu

Marycrest International University
1607 West 12th Street
Davenport, IA 52804
319-326-9512
www.mcrest.edu

Marygrove College
8425 West McNichols Road
Detroit, MI 48221
313-864-8000
www.marygrove.edu

The Maryland Institute College of Art
1300 West Mt. Royal Avenue
Baltimore, MD 21217
410-669-9200
www.mica.edu

Marylhurst University
17600 Pacific Highway 43
Marylhurst, OR 97036
503-636-8141
www.marylhurst.edu

Marymount College
100 Marymount Avenue
Tarrytown, NY 10591-3796
800-724-4312 or 914-631-3200
www.marymt.edu

Marymount Manhattan College
221 East 71st Street
New York, NY 10021
212-517-0400
marymount.mmm.edu

Marymount University
2807 North Glebe Road
Arlington, VA 22207
703-522-5600
www.marymount.edu

Maryville College
502 East Lamar Alexander Parkway
Maryville, TN 37804
423-981-8000
www.maryvillecollege.edu

Maryville University of Saint Louis
13550 Conway Road
St. Louis, MO 63141
314-529-9300
www.maryvillestl.edu

Marywood University
2300 Adams Avenue
Scranton, PA 18509
717-348-6231
www.marywood.edu

Massachusetts College of Art
621 Huntington Avenue
Boston, MA 02115
617-232-1555
www.massart.edu

**Massachusetts College
of Liberal Arts**
375 Church Street
North Adams, MA 01247
413-662-5000
www.cs.nasc.mass.edu

**Massachusetts College of Pharmacy
& Allied Health Sciences**
179 Longwood Avenue
Boston, MA 02115
617-732-2880
www.mcp.edu

**Massachusetts Institute of
Technology**
77 Massachusetts Avenue
Cambridge, MA 02139
617-253-1000
www.mit.edu

Massachusetts Maritime Academy
101 Academy Drive
Buzzards Bay, MA 02532
800-544-3411 or 508-830-5000
www.mma.mass.edu

The Master's College and Seminary
21716 West Placerita Canyon Road
Santa Clarita, CA 91321
800-568-6248 or 805-259-3540
www.masters.edu

Mayville State University
330 Third Street, NE
Mayville, ND 58257
701-786-2301
www.masu.nodak.edu

McIntosh College
23 Cataract Avenue
Dover, NH 03820
603-742-1234
www.mcintosh.dover.nh.us

McKendree College
701 College Road
Lebanon, IL 62254
618-537-4481
www.mckendree.edu

McMurry University
South 14th Street and Sayles Boulevard
Abilene, TX 79697
915-691-6200
www.mcm.edu

I'm told that there is a U.S.-based university with a major in bagpipe. I cannot discover which it is. Perhaps you've heard it?

McNeese State University
4100 Ryan Street
Lake Charles, LA 70609
318-475-5000
www.mcneese.edu

McPherson College
1600 East Euclid
McPherson, KS 67460
316-241-0731
www.mcpherson.edu

Medaille College
18 Agassiz Circle
Buffalo, NY 14214
716-884-3281
www.medaille.edu

Medcenter One College of Nursing
512 North Seventh Street
Bismarck, ND 58501
701-323-6271
www.medcenterone.com/nursing/
nursing.htm

**Medgar Evers College -
City University of New York**
1650 Bedford Avenue
Brooklyn, NY 11225
718-270-4900
www.mec.cuny.edu

Medical College of Georgia
1120 15th Street
Augusta, GA 30912
706-721-0211
www.mcg.edu

**Medical University
of South Carolina**
171 Ashley Avenue
Charleston, SC 29425
803-792-2300
www.musc.edu

Memphis College of Art
Overton Park
1930 Poplar Avenue
Memphis, TN 38104
901-726-4085
www.mca.edu

Menlo College
1000 El Camino Real
Atherton, CA 94027
650-688-3753
www.menlo.edu

**Mennonite College of Nursing
at Illinois State University**
804 North East Street
Bloomington, IL 61701
309-829-0715
www.ilstu.eduHome96/MCN/mcn.htm

Mercer University
1400 Coleman Avenue
Macon, GA 31207
912-752-2700
www.mercer.edu

Mercy College
555 Broadway
Dobbs Ferry, NY 10522
914-693-4500
www.mercynet.edu

Mercy College of Health Sciences
928 Sixth Avenue
Des Moines, IA 50309
515-643-6601
www.mchs.edu

Mercyhurst College
501 East 38th Street
Erie, PA 16546
814-824-2000
www.mercyhurst.edu

Meredith College
3800 Hillsborough Street
Raleigh, NC 27607-5298
919-829-8600
www.meredith.edu

Merrimack College
315 Turnpike Street
North Andover, MA 01845
508-837-5000
shiva.merrimack.edu

Mesa State College
1170 Elm Street
Grand Junction, CO 81502
970-248-1020
www.mesastate.edu

Messiah College
Grantham, PA 17027
717-766-2511
www.messiah.edu

Methodist College
5400 Ramsey Street
Fayetteville, NC 28311
910-630-7000
www.methodist.edu

**Metropolitan College
of Court Reporting**
4640 East Elwood Street
Phoenix, AZ 85040
602-955-5900

**Metropolitan College
of Court Reporting**
2201 San Pedro Street, NE
Albuquerque, NM 87110
505-888-3400

**Metropolitan State College
of Denver**
1006 11th Street
Denver, CO 80217
303-556-2400
www.mscd.edu

Metropolitan State University
700 East Seventh Street
St. Paul, MN 55106
612-772-7777
www.metrostate.edu

Miami University
Oxford, OH 45056
513-529-1809
www.muohio.edu

Michigan State University
East Lansing, MI 48824
517-355-1855
www.msu.edu

Michigan Technological University
1400 Townsend Drive
Houghton, MI 49931
906-487-1885
www.mtu.edu

Mid-America Bible College
3500 S.W. 119th Street
Oklahoma City, OK 73170
405-691-3800
www.mabc.edu

MidAmerica Nazarene University
2030 East College Way
Olathe, KS 66062
913-782-3750
www.mnu.edu

Mid-Continent Baptist Bible College
99 Powell Road, East
Mayfield, KY 42066
502-247-8521

Middle Tennessee State University
1301 East Main Street
Murfreesboro, TN 37132
615-898-2300
www.mtsu.edu

> Read not to contradict and confute, nor to believe and take for granted, nor to find talk and discourse, but to weigh and consider.
>
> —*Francis Bacon*

Middlebury College
Route 30
Middlebury, VT 05753
802-443-5000
www.middlebury.edu

Midland Lutheran College
900 North Clarkson Street
Fremont, NE 68025
800-642-8382 or 402-721-5480
www.mlc.edu

Midway College
512 East Stephens Street
Midway, KY 40347-1120
800-755-0031 or 606-846-4421
www.midway.edu

Midwestern State University
3410 Taft Boulevard
Wichita Falls, TX 76308
940-397-4000
www.mwsu.edu

Midwestern University
555 31st Street
Downers Grove, IL 60515
630-969-4400
www.midwestern.edu

Miles College
5500 Myron Massey Boulevard
Birmingham, AL 35064
800-445-0708 or 205-929-1000
www.miles.edu

Millersville University of Pennsylvania
P.O. Box 1002
Millersville, PA 17551-0302
717-872-3011
www.millersv.edu

Milligan College
P.O. Box 500
Milligan College, TN 37682
423-461-8700
www.milligan.edu

Millikin University
1184 West Main Street
Decatur, IL 62522
217-424-6211
www.millikin.edu

Mills College
5000 MacArthur Boulevard
Oakland, CA 94613-1301
800-87-MILLS or 510-430-2255
www.mills.edu

Millsaps College
1701 North State Street
Jackson, MS 39210
601-974-1000
www.millsaps.edu

Milwaukee Institute of Art & Design
273 East Erie Street
Milwaukee, WI 53202
414-276-7889
www.miad.edu

Milwaukee School of Engineering
1025 North Broadway
Milwaukee, WI 53202
414-277-7100
www.msoe.edu

According to a study reported in the *Wall Street Journal* (13 September 1999), 77 percent of college students expect to become millionaires in their lifetimes. Interesting, but unlikely.

Minneapolis College of Art & Design
2501 Stevens Avenue South
Minneapolis, MN 55404
612-874-3700
www.mcad.edu

Minnesota Bible College
920 Mayowood Road SW
Rochester, MN 55902
507-288-4563
www.mnbc.edu

Minnesota State University - Mankato
South Road and Ellis Avenue
Mankato, MN 56002
800-722-0544 or 507-389-6767
www.mankato.msus.edu

Minot State University
500 University Avenue, West
Minot, ND 58707
701-858-3000
www.misu.nodak.edu

Mississippi College
200 West College Street
Clinton, MS 39058
601-925-3000
www.mc.edu

Mississippi State University
P.O. Box 5325
Mississippi State, MS 39762
601-325-2213
www.msstate.edu

Mississippi University for Women
1100 College Street
Columbus, MS 39701
877-GO2-THEW or 662-329-4750
www.muw.edu

Mississippi Valley State University
14000 Highway 82, West
Itta Bena, MS 38941
601-254-3997
www.mvsu.edu

Missouri Baptist College
One College Park Drive
St. Louis, MO 63141
314-434-1115
www.mobap.edu

Missouri Southern State College
3950 East Newman Road
Joplin, MO 64801
417-624-8181
www.mssc.edu

Missouri Technical School
1167 Corporate Lake Drive
St. Louis, MO 63132
314-569-3600
www.motech.edu

Missouri Valley College
500 East College Drive
Marshall, MO 65340
660-831-4000
www.moval.edu

When you get on an airplane and read the safety information card in the seat back in front of you, what is the logic behind this sentence: "If you are sitting in an exit row and you cannot understand this card or cannot see well enough to follow these instructions, please tell a crew member"? Also, why are instructions in Braille provided at drive-through bank ATMs?

> [Liberal arts] colleges, in providing teaching models that merit study by others, in encouraging faculty-student collaboration of a kind not common in other intellectual settings, offer a distinct alternative to the forms of instruction common in larger institutions. If, in addition, they are able to show the self-discipline that allows them to emphasize certain subjects, leaving others to the more specialized universities, they accept the proposition that there is not a single road for all undergraduate colleges to follow. "

—Stephen R. Graubard, editor (in "Distinctively American: The Residential Liberal Arts Colleges," Daedulus 128, no. 1 [1999])

Missouri Western State College
4525 Downs Drive
St. Joseph, MO 64507
816-271-4200
www.mwsc.edu

Molloy College
1000 Hempstead Avenue
Rockville Centre, NY 11571
516-678-5000
www.molloy.edu

Monmouth College
700 East Broadway
Monmouth, IL 61462
309-457-2311
www.monm.edu

Monmouth University
Norwood and Cedar Avenues
West Long Branch, NJ 07764
732-571-3400
www.monmouth.edu

Montana State University - Billings
1500 North 30th Street
Billings, MT 59101
406-657-2011
www.msubillings.edu

Montana State University - Bozeman
P.O. Box 172180
Bozeman, MT 59717-2180
406-994-0211
www.montana.edu

Montana State University - Northern
P.O. Box 7751
Havre, MT 59501
800-662-6132 or 406-265-3700
www.nmclites.edu

Montana Tech of The University of Montana
1300 West Park Street
Butte, MT 59701
406-496-4101
www.mtech.edu

Montclair State University
Valley Road and Normal Avenue
Upper Montclair, NJ 07043
973-655-4000
www.montclair.edu

Monterey Institute of International Studies
425 Van Buren
Monterey, CA 93940
408-647-4100
www.miis.edu

Montreat College
310 Gaither Circle
Montreat, NC 28757
828-669-8011
www.montreat.edu

Montserrat College of Art
23 Essex Street
Beverly, MA 01915
508-922-8222
www.montserrat.edu

Movie star Bruce Willis studied drama at Montclair State College in New Jersey.

Moody Bible Institute
820 North LaSalle Boulevard
Chicago, IL 60610
312-329-4000
www.moody.edu

Moore College of Art & Design
The Parkway at 20th Street
Philadelphia, PA 19103-1179
800-523-2025 or 215-568-4515
www.moore.edu

Moorhead State University
1104 Seventh Avenue South
Moorhead, MN 56563
218-236-2011
www.moorhead.msus.edu

Moravian College
1200 Main Street
Bethlehem, PA 18018
610-861-1300
www.moravian.edu

Morehead State University
150 University Boulevard
Morehead, KY 40351
606-783-2221
www.morehead-st.edu

Morehouse College
830 Westview Drive, SW
Atlanta, GA 30314
800-851-1254 or 404-681-2800
www.morehouse.edu

Morgan State University
1700 East Spring Lane
Baltimore, MD 21251
410-319-3333
www.morgan.edu

Morningside College
1501 Morningside Avenue
Sioux City, IA 51106
800-831-0806 or 712-274-5000
www.morningside.edu

Morris Brown College
643 Martin Luther King, Jr. Drive, NW
Atlanta, GA 30314
404-220-0152
www.morrisbrown.edu

Morris College
North Main Street
Sumter, SC 29150
888-778-1345 or 803-775-9371
www.icusc.org/morris/mchome.htm

TOP TEN COLLEGES AND UNIVERSITIES ACCORDING TO A RANKING BASED ON LAISSEZ-FAIRE PRINCIPLES

Harvard University

Brown University

Princeton University

Stanford University

Yale University

California Institute of Technology

Massachusetts Institute of Technology

Dartmouth College

Amherst College

Columbia University

(Source: "A New Ranking of American Colleges on Laissez-Faire Principles, 1999–2000" www.stanford.edu/~jerfox/laissez-faire-1999-2000.txt)

Morrison College - Reno
140 Washington Street
Reno, NV 89503
702-323-4145
www.morrison.edu

Mount Aloysius College
7373 Admiral Peary Highway
Cresson, PA 16630
814-886-4131
www.mtaloy.edu

Mount Angel Seminary
1 Abbey Drive
St. Benedict, OR 97373
503-845-3951

Mount Carmel College of Nursing
127 South Davis Avenue
Columbus, OH 43222
614-234-5800
www.mccn.edu

Mount Holyoke College
50 College Street
South Hadley, MA 01075
413-538-2000
www.mtholyoke.edu

Mount Ida College
777 Dedham Street
Newton Centre, MA 02459
617-928-4500
www.mountida.edu

Mount Marty College
1105 West Eighth Street
Yankton, SD 57078
800-658-4552 or 605-668-1514
www.mtmc.edu

Mount Mary College
2900 North Menomonee River Parkway
Milwaukee, WI 53222
414-258-4810
www.mtmary.edu

Mount Mercy College
1330 Elmhurst Drive, NE
Cedar Rapids, IA 52402
319-363-8213
www.mtmercy.edu

Mount Olive College
634 Henderson Street
Mount Olive, NC 28365
919-658-2502
www.mountolive.edu

Mount Saint Clare College
400 North Bluff Boulevard
Clinton, IA 52732
319-242-4023
www.clare.edu

Mount Saint Mary College
330 Powell Avenue
Newburgh, NY 12550
914-561-0800
www.msmc.edu

Mount St. Mary's College
12001 Chalon Road
Los Angeles, CA 90049
310-954-4015
www.msmc.la.edu

**Mount Saint Mary's College
& Seminary**
16300 Old Emmitsburg Road
Emmitsburg, MD 21727
301-447-6122
www.msmary.edu

Mount Senario College
1500 College Avenue West
Ladysmith, WI 54848
715-532-5511
www.mscfs.edu

Mount Sinai School of Medicine
One Gustave L. Levy Place
New York, NY 10029
212-241-6500
www.mssm.edu

Mount Union College
1972 Clark Avenue
Alliance, OH 44601
330-821-5320
www.muc.edu

Mount Vernon Nazarene College
800 Martinsburg Road
Mount Vernon, OH 43050
740-397-9000
www.mvnc.edu

Muhlenberg College
2400 Chew Street
Allentown, PA 18104
610-821-3100
www.muhlenberg.edu

Multnomah Bible College
8435 N.E. Glisan Street
Portland, OR 97220
503-255-0332
www.multnomah.edu

Murray State University
One Murray Street
Murray, KY 42071
502-762-3011
www.murraystate.edu

Muskingum College
163 Stormont Drive
New Concord, OH 43762
740-826-8211
www.muskingum.edu

N

Naropa University
213 Arapahoe Avenue
Boulder, CO 80302
800-772-6951 or 303-444-0202
www.naropa.edu

National American University
321 Kansas City Street
Rapid City, SD 57701
605-394-4800
www.nationalcollege.edu

National College of Chiropractic
200 East Roosevelt Road
Lombard, IL 60148
630-629-2000
www.national.chiropractic.edu

The National Hispanic University
14271 Story Road
San Jose, CA 95127
408-254-6900
www.nhu.edu

National University
11255 North Torrey Pines Road
La Jolla, CA 92037
858-642-8000
www.nu.edu

National-Louis University
2840 Sheridan Road
Evanston, IL 60201
847-475-1100
www.nl.edu

**Native American Educational
Services (NAES) College**
2838 West Peterson Avenue
Chicago, IL 60659
773-761-5000
www.naes.indian.com

Naval Postgraduate School
One University Circle
Monterey, CA 93943
408-656-2441
www.nps.navy.mil

Nazarene Bible College
1111 Academy Park Loop
Colorado Springs, CO 80910
719-596-5110
www.nbc.edu

Nazareth College of Rochester
4245 East Avenue
Rochester, NY 14618
716-389-2525
www.naz.edu

Nebraska Christian College
1800 Syracuse Street
Norfolk, NE 68701
402-379-5000
www.nechristian.edu

Nebraska Methodist College of Nursing & Allied Health
8501 West Dodge Road
Omaha, NE 68114
402-354-4984
www.methodistcollege.edu

Nebraska Wesleyan University
5000 St. Paul Avenue
Lincoln, NE 68504
402-466-2371
www.nebrwesleyan.edu

Neumann College
One Neumann Drive
Aston, PA 19014
610-459-0905
www.neumann.edu

New College of California
50 Fell Street
San Francisco, CA 94102
415-241-1300
www.newcollege.edu

New College of the University of South Florida
5700 North Tamiami Trail
Sarasota, FL 34243-2197
941-359-4269
www.newcollege.usf.edu

New England College
26 Bridge Street
Henniker, NH 03242
603-428-2211
www.nec.edu

New England College of Optometry
424 Beacon Street
Boston, MA 02115
617-266-2030
www.ne-optometry.edu

New England Conservatory of Music
290 Huntington Avenue
Boston, MA 02115
617-262-1120
www.newenglandconservatory.edu

New England Institute of Technology
2500 Post Road
Warwick, RI 02886
401-739-5000
www.neit.edu

New England School of Art and Design/Suffolk University
81 Arlington Street
Boston, MA 02116
617-536-0383
www.suffolk.edu/nesad

New Hampshire College
2500 North River Road
Manchester, NH 03104
603-668-2211
wwwnhc.edu

New Jersey City University
2039 Kennedy Boulevard
Jersey City, NJ 07305
201-200-2000
www.njcu.edu

There is nothing quite so important in the education of a scientist as reading a forty-year-old science textbook.

New Jersey Institute of Technology
University Heights
Newark, NJ 07102
973-596-3000
www.njit.edu

New Mexico Highlands University
Box 9000
Las Vegas, NM 87701
505-454-2711
www.nmhu.edu

**New Mexico Institute of Mining
& Technology**
901 LeRoy Place
Socorro, NM 87801
505-835-5500
www.nmt.edu

New Mexico State University
University Avenue
Las Cruces, NM 88003
800-662-6678 or 505-646-0111
www.nmsu.edu

New School University
66 West 12th Street
New York, NY 10011
212-229-5600
www.newschool.edu

New York City Technical College
300 Jay Street
Brooklyn, NY 11201
718-260-5000
www.nyctc.cuny.edu

New York Institute of Technology
Northern Boulevard
Old Westbury, NY 11568
516-686-7516
www.nyit.edu

New York School of Interior Design
170 70th Street
New York, NY 10021
212-472-1500
www.nysid.edu

New York University
70 Washington Square, South
New York, NY 10012
212-998-1212
www.nyu.edu

Newberry College
2100 College Street
Newberry, SC 29108
803-276-5010
www.newberry.edu

Newbury College
129 Fisher Avenue
Brookline, MA 02146
800-NEW-BURY or 617-730-7007
www.newbury.edu

Newman University
3100 McCormick Avenue
Wichita, KS 67213
800-736-7585 or 316-942-4291
www.newmanu.edu

Psychoneuroimmunology is a new field. Perhaps you would be interested in it. It's the study of how the brain wards off illness. The power of positive thinking is, in fact, real, but how does it work? No one knows, but those in psychoneuroimmunology are trying to find out.

Newschool of Architecture
1249 F Street
San Diego, CA 92101
858-235-4100
www.newschoolarch.edu

Niagara University
Niagara University, NY 14109
716-285-1212
www.niagara.edu

Nicholls State University
Thibodaux, LA 70310
504-446-8111
www.nich.edu

Nichols College
Dudley, MA 01571
508-943-1560
www.nichols.edu

Norfolk State University
700 Park Avenue
Norfolk, VA 23504
757-823-8600
www.nsu.edu

North Carolina Agricultural &
Technical State University
1601 East Market Street
Greensboro, NC 27411
336-334-7500
www.ncat.edu

North Carolina Central University
1801 Fayetteville Street
Durham, NC 27707
919-560-6100
www.nccu.edu

North Carolina School of the Arts
1533 South Main Street
Winston-Salem, NC 27117
336-770-3399
www.ncarts.edu

North Carolina State University
Raleigh, NC 27695
919-515-2011
www.ncsu.edu

North Carolina Wesleyan College
3400 North Wesleyan Boulevard
Rocky Mount, NC 27804
919-985-5100
www.ncwc.edu

North Central Bible College
910 Elliot Avenue, South
Minneapolis, MN 55404
612-332-3491
www.northcentral.edu

North Central College
30 North Brainard Street
Naperville, IL 60566
630-637-5100
www.noctrl.edu

North Central University
910 Elliot Avenue South
Minneapolis, MN 55404
612-332-3491
www.northcentral.eduncu.htm

North Dakota State University
1301 University Drive
Fargo, ND 58105
701-231-8011
www.ndsu.nodak.edu

"The truly disadvantaged student is the child of a soccer mom, shuttled from one scheduled activity to another," says *Newsweek* magazine, in an article on how college admission really works. The point: It's really hard to stand out in this crowd of good kids with good grades and all the right activities.

North Georgia College & State University
Dahlonega, GA 30597
706-864-1400
www.ngcsu.edu

North Greenville College
P.O. Box 1892
Tigerville, SC 29688
864-977-7000
www.ngc.edu

North Park University
3225 West Foster Avenue
Chicago, IL 60625
773-244-6200
www.northpark.edu

Northeast Louisiana University
700 University Avenue
Monroe, LA 71209
318-342-1000
www.nlu.edu

Northeastern Illinois University
5500 North St. Louis Avenue
Chicago, IL 60625
773-583-4050
www.neiu.edu

Northeastern State University
600 North Grand Avenue
Tahlequah, OK 74464
918-456-5511
www.nsuok.edu

Northeastern University
360 Huntington Avenue
Boston, MA 02115
617-373-2000
www.neu.edu

Northern Arizona University
Flagstaff, AZ 86011
888-667-3628 or 520-523-6602
www.nau.edu

Northern Illinois University
De Kalb, IL 60115
815-753-0446
www.niu.edu

Northern Kentucky University
Nunn Drive
Highland Heights, KY 41099
606-572-5100
www.nku.edu

Northern Michigan University
1401 Presque Isle Avenue
Marquette, MI 49855
906-227-1000
www.nmu.edu

Northern State University
1200 South Jay Street
Aberdeen, SD 57401
605-626-3011
www.northern.edu

Northland College
1411 Ellis Avenue
Ashland, WI 54806
715-682-1699
www.northland.edu

Northwest Christian College
828 East 11th Avenue
Eugene, OR 97401
541-343-1641
www.nwcc.edu

Northwest College of Art
16464 State Highway 305
Poulsbo, WA 98370
360-779-9993
www.nca.edu

Northwest College of the Assemblies of God
5520 108th Avenue, NE
Kirkland, WA 98083
425-822-8266

Teach them what has been said in the past, for there is none born wise.

—*Ptahhotpe (about 4,350 years ago)*

Northwest Missouri State University
800 University Drive
Maryville, MO 64468
660-562-1110
www.nwmissouri.edu

Northwest Nazarene University
623 Holly Street
Nampa, ID 83686
208-467-8011
www.nnc.edu

Northwestern College
3003 North Snelling Avenue
St. Paul, MN 55113
612-631-5100
www.nwc.edu

Northwestern College of Chiropractic
2501 West 84th Street
Bloomington, MN 55431
612-888-4777
www.nwhealth.edunwchiro

Northwestern College of Iowa
101 Seventh Street SW
Orange City, IA 51041
712-737-7000
www.nwciowa.edu

Northwestern Oklahoma State University
709 Oklahoma Boulevard
Alva, OK 73717
580-327-1700
www.nwalva.edu

Northwestern Polytechnic University
117 Fourier Avenue
Fremont, CA 94539
510-657-5911
www.npu.edu

Northwestern State University
College Avenue
Natchitoches, LA 71497
318-357-6361
www.nsula.edu

Northwestern University
633 Clark Street
Evanston, IL 60208
847-491-3741
www.nwu.edu

Northwood University
3225 Cook Road
Midland, MI 48640
517-837-4200
www.northwood.edu

Norwich University
158 Harron Drive
Northfield, VT 05663
802-485-2000
www.norwich.edu

Notre Dame College
2321 Elm Street
Manchester, NH 03104
603-669-4298
www.notredame.edu

Notre Dame College
4545 College Road
South Euclid, OH 44121
216-381-1680
www.ndc.edu

Nova Southeastern University
3301 College Avenue
Fort Lauderdale, FL 33314
954-475-7300
www.nova.edu

Nyack College
1 South Boulevard
Nyack, NY 10960
914-358-1710
www.nyackcollege.edu

O

Oak Hills Christian College
1600 Oak Hills Road, SW
Bemidji, MN 56601
218-751-8670
www.oakhills.edu

Oakland City University
143 North Lucretia Street
Oakland City, IN 47660
800-737-5125 or 812-749-1231
www.oak.edu

Oakland University
Walton and Squirrel Roads
Rochester, MI 48309
248-370-2100
www.oakland.edu

Oakwood College
7000 Adventist Boulevard
Huntsville, AL 35896
800-358-3978 or 256-726-7000
www.oakwood.edu

Oberlin College
70 North Professor Street
Oberlin, OH 44074
440-775-8121
www.oberlin.edu

Occidental College
1600 Campus Road
Los Angeles, CA 90041
323-259-2500
www.oxy.edu

Oglala Lakota College
Piya Wiconi Road
Kyle, SD 57752
605-455-2321
www.olc.edu

Oglethorpe University
4484 Peachtree Road, NE
Atlanta, GA 30319
404-261-1441
www.oglethorpe.edu

Ohio Dominican College
1216 Sunbury Road
Columbus, OH 43219
614-253-2741
www.odc.edu

Ohio Northern University
525 South Main Street
Ada, OH 45810
419-772-2000
www.onu.edu

Ohio State University
190 North Oval Drive
Columbus, OH 43210
614-292-6446
www.osu.edu

Ohio University
Athens, OH 45701
740-593-1000
www.ohiou.edu

Ohio Valley College
4501 College Parkway
Parkersburg, WV 26101
304-485-7384
www.ovc.edu

Ohio Wesleyan University
61 South Sandusky Street
Delaware, OH 43015
740-368-2000
www.owu.edu

Check out this honor system: Students at Oberlin College can check out a variety of paintings to hang in their dorm rooms. The rental fee is $5 per semester. Among the collection are four original Picassos. None of the paintings has ever been lost or damaged.

Oklahoma Baptist University
500 West University
Shawnee, OK 74801
405-275-2850
www.okbu.edu

Oklahoma Christian University of Science & Arts
2501 East Memorial Road
Oklahoma City, OK 73136
405-425-5000
www.oc.edu

Oklahoma City University
2501 North Blackwelder Avenue
Oklahoma City, OK 73106
405-521-5000
www.okcu.edu

Oklahoma Panhandle State University
P.O. Box 430
Goodwell, OK 73939
580-349-2611
www.opsu.edu

Oklahoma State University
Office of Admissions
324 Student Union
Stillwater, OK 74078-1012
405-744-5000
pio.okstate.edu

Old Dominion University
5215 Hampton Boulevard
Norfolk, VA 23529
757-683-3000
www.odu.edu

Olivet College
320 South Main Street
Olivet, MI 49076
616-749-7000
www.olivetnet.edu

Olivet Nazarene University
One University Avenue
Bourbonnais, IL 60914-2271
815-939-5011
www.olivet.edu

"Kirk" copyright © Kirk Anderson. All Rights Reserved. Reprinted with permission.

O'More College of Design
423 South Margin Street
Franklin, TN 37065
615-794-4254
www.omorecollege.edu

Oral Roberts University
7777 South Lewis Avenue
Tulsa, OK 74171
918-495-6161
www.oru.edu

Oregon Health Sciences University
3181 S.W. Sam Jackson Park Road
Portland, OR 97201
503-494-7878
www.ohsu.edu

Oregon Institute of Technology
3201 Campus Drive
Klamath Falls, OR 97601
541-885-1900
www.oit.edu

Oregon State University
Corvallis, OR 97331
541-737-2111
www.orst.edu

Otis College of Art and Design
9045 Lincoln Boulevard
Westchester, CA 90045
310-665-6800
www.otisart.edu

Ottawa University
1001 South Cedar Street
Ottawa, KS 66067
913-242-5200
www.ottawa.edu

COUNSELORS ARE OVERWORKED, UNDERFUNDED

"The most frequently mentioned problem (by 16% of the respondents) was the lack of sufficient time to get to know students, to engage in creative planning with students, and to carry out effective college counseling. Other identified problems included (1) the need to help expand student horizons (to consider more college options, to think more independently, to reach higher, etc.); (2) insufficient financial resources, resulting in small staffs, student/counselor ratios that are too high, and small operating budgets; (3) student apathy and indifference toward taking responsibility, meeting deadlines, etc., (4) the counselors' difficulty in keeping up to date with financial aid developments, college admissions requirements, career information, etc.; and (5) too many responsibilities for counselors, including many non-counseling duties, such as managing student discipline and doing clerical work. . . . Students who need effective college counseling the most—those who are from low income families and attend public schools where a small percentage of classmates go on to college—are helped the least."

-David R. Holmes, Herbert F. Dalton, Jr., David G. Erdmann, Thomas C. Hayden, and Alton O. Roberts in Frontiers of Possibility (The National College Counseling Project sponsored by the National Association for College Admissions Counseling; Burlington, VT: The Instructional Development Center, University of Vermont, 1986)

Otterbein College
102 West College Avenue
Westerville, OH 43081
800-488-8144 or 614-823-1500
www.otterbein.edu

Ouachita Baptist University
410 Ouachita
Arkadelphia, AR 71998
870-245-5000
www.obu.edu

Our Lady of the Holy Cross College
4123 Woodland Drive
New Orleans, LA 70131
504-394-7744
www.olhcc.edu

Our Lady of the Lake College
5345 Brittany Drive
Baton Rouge, LA 70808
504-768-1700
www.ololcollege.edu

Our Lady of the Lake University
411 S.W. 24th Street
San Antonio, TX 78207
210-434-6711
www.ollusa.edu

Ozark Christian College
1111 North Main Street
Joplin, MO 64801
417-624-2518
www.occ.edu

P

Pace University
One Pace Plaza
New York, NY 10038
212-346-1200
www.pace.edu

Pacific Lutheran University
South 121st Street
Tacoma, WA 98447
253-531-6900
www.plu.edu

Pacific Northwest College of Art
1219 S.W. Park Avenue
Portland, OR 97208
503-226-4391
www.pnca.edu

Pacific Oaks College
5 Westmoreland Place
Pasadena, CA 91103
626-397-1300
www.pacificoaks.edu

Pacific States University
1516 South Western Avenue
Los Angeles, CA 90006
213-731-2383
www.psuca.edu

Pacific Union College
One Angwin Avenue
Angwin, CA 94508
707-965-6311
www.puc.edu

Food service at undergraduate institutions used to resemble those at hospitals and prisons. Although they lacked flavor and choice, they did have one advantage: They served meals planned and balanced by nutritionists. There has been a revolution in college food services away from viewing students as wards of the institution and toward viewing them as discriminating consumers. College food services today resemble, more than anything else, the food court at a mall. Nutritionally, it's a disaster. But students are happier about it by far.

Pacific University
2043 College Way
Forest Grove, OR 97116
503-357-6151
www.pacificu.edu

Paier College of Art
20 Forham Avenue
Hamden, CT 06517
203-287-3032
www.paierart.edu

Paine College
1235 15th Street
Augusta, GA 30901
706-821-8200
www.paine.edu

Palm Beach Atlantic College
901 South Flagler Drive
West Palm Beach, FL 33416
561-803-2000
www.pbac.edu

Palmer College of Chiropractic
1000 Brady Street
Davenport, IA 52803
800-722-2586 or 319-884-5656
www.palmer.edu

Park College
8700 River Park Drive
Parkville, MO 64152
816-741-2000
www.park.edu

Parker College of Chiropractic
2500 Walnut Hill Lane
Dallas, TX 75229
972-438-6932
www.parkercc.edu

Patten College
2433 Coolidge Avenue
Oakland, CA 94601
510-533-8300
www.patten.edu

Paul Quinn College
3837 Simpson Stuart Road
Dallas, TX 75241
800-237-2648 or 214-376-1000
www.pqc.edu

Paul Smith's College
Route 86 and 30
Paul Smiths, NY 12970
518-327-6000
www.paulsmiths.edu

Peace College
15 East Peace Street
Raleigh, NC 27604
800-PEACE-47 or 919-508-2000
www.peace.edu

Peirce College
1420 Pine Street
Philadelphia, PA 19102
215-545-6400

Pennsylvania College of Optometry
8360 Old York Road
Elkins Park, PA 19027
214-780-1400
www.pco.edu

Pennsylvania College of Technology
One College Avenue
Williamsport, PA 17701
717-326-3761
www.pct.edu

Pennsylvania State University
201 Old Main
University Park, PA 16804
814-865-4700
www.psu.edu

Pepperdine University
24255 Pacific Coast Highway
Malibu, CA 90263
310-456-4000
www.pepperdine.edu

Peru State College
600 Hoyt Street
Peru, NE 68421
402-872-3815
www.peru.edu

Pfeiffer University
Route 52
Misenheimer, NC 28109
704-463-1360
www.pfeiffer.edu

Philadelphia College of Bible
200 Manor Avenue
Langhorne, PA 19047
215-752-5800
www.pcb.edu

Philadelphia College of Textiles and Science
Schoolhouse Lane and Henry Avenue
Philadelphia, PA 19144
215-951-2700
www.philacol.edu

Philander Smith College
812 West 13th Street
Little Rock, AK 72202
501-375-9845
www.philander.edu

Piedmont Bible College
716 Franklin Street
Winston-Salem, NC 27101
336-725-8344
www.pbc.edu

Piedmont College
165 Central Avenue
Demorest, GA 30535
706-778-3000
www.piedmont.edu

Pikeville College
214 Sycamore Street
Pikeville, KY 41501
606-432-9200
www.pc.edu

Pine Manor College
400 Heath Street
Chestnut Hill, MA 02467
800-PMC-1357 or 617-731-7000
www.pmc.edu

Pittsburg State University
1701 South Broadway
Pittsburg, KS 66762
316-231-7000
www.pittstate.edu

Pitzer College
1050 North Mills Avenue
Claremont, CA 91711
909-621-8000
www.pitzer.edu

Plymouth State College
17 High Street
Plymouth, NH 03264
603-535-5000
www.plymouth.edu

For most families, college is the second largest purchase they will ever make. If there are more than one child, the family's combined college expenses will exceed the cost of its house. This is obviously a very important decision, requiring research and weighing more than one factor. Be aware of your family's sacrifices to send you to the college of your choice. Be grateful, and strive to make the investment worthwhile.

Point Loma Nazerene University
3900 Lomaland Drive
San Diego, CA 92106
858-849-2200
www.ptloma.edu

Point Park College
201 Wood Street
Pittsburgh, PA 15222
412-391-4100
www.ppc.edu

Polytechnic University
Six MetroTech Center
Brooklyn, NY 11201
718-260-3600
www.poly.edu

Pomona College
550 North College Avenue
Claremont, CA 91711
909-621-8131
www.pomona.edu

Pontifical Catholic University of Puerto Rico
Arecibo Campus
Arecibo, PR 00613
787-881-1212
www.pucpr.edu

Pontifical Catholic University of Puerto Rico
Guayama Campus
5 South Palmer Street
Guayama, PR 00784
787-864-0550
www.pucpr.edu

Pontifical Catholic University of Puerto Rico
Mayagüez Campus
482 South Post Street
Mayagüez, PR 00681
787-834-5151
www.pucpr.edu

Pontifical Catholic University of Puerto Rico
Ponce Campus
2250 Avenida Las Americas
Ponce, PR 00731
787-841-2000
www.pucpr.edu

Pontifical College of Josephinum
7625 North High Street
Columbus, OH 43235
614-885-5585
www.pcj.edu

Portland State University
P.O. Box 751
Portland, OR 97207
503-725-3000
www.pdx.edu

Practical Bible College
400 Riverside Drive
Bible School Park, NY 13737
607-729-1581
www.lakenet.org/~pbc

Prairie View A & M University
P.O. Box 4019
Prairie View, TX 77446
409-857-3311
www.pvamu.edu

Pratt Institute
200 Willoughby Avenue
Brooklyn, NY 11205
718-636-3600
www.pratt.edu

Presbyterian College
South Broad Street
Clinton, SC 29325
864-833-2820
www.presby.edu

Prescott College
220 Grove Avenue
Prescott, AZ 86301
520-778-2090
www.prescott.edu

Presentation College
1500 North Main Street
Aberdeen, SD 57401
605-225-1634
www.presentation.edu

Princeton University
Princeton, NJ 08544
609-258-3000
www.princeton.edu

Principia College
One Maybeck Place
Elsah, IL 62028
800-277-4648 or 618-374-2131
www.prin.edu

Providence College
549 River Avenue
Providence, RI 02918
401-865-1000
www.providence.edu

Puget Sound Christian College
410 Fourth Avenue, North
Edmonds, WA 98020
425-775-8686

Purdue University
West Lafayette, IN 47907
765-494-4600
www.purdue.edu

Purdue University Calumet
2200 169th Street
Hammond, IN 46323
219-989-2993
www.calumet.purdue.edu

Purdue University North Central
1401 South U.S. Highway 421
Westville, IN 46391
219-785-5200
www.purduenc.edu

Q

Queens College
1900 Selwyn Avenue
Charlotte, NC 28274
704-337-2200
www.queens.edu

Queens College - City University of New York
65-30 Kissena Boulevard
Flushing, NY 11367
718-997-5000
www.qc.edu

Quincy University
1800 College Avenue
Quincy, IL 62301
217-222-8020
www.quincy.edu

Fred Hargadon, dean of admissions at Princeton, presides over a process that admits approximately one out of ten applicants. He has been known to say to parents that if he were to lose the entire admitted freshman class, he could create a statistically identical class from rejected applicants. There is a book out on him and the Princeton admissions process that generated major buzz in publishing circles: *Getting In*, by William Henry Paul (Perseus, 1997). It describes, in great detail, the application experiences of actual students, not to be confused with *Getting In* by James Finney Boylan (Warner Books, 1998), a hilarious novel about the experiences of a small group of students and their parents as they take "the college tour" in a Winnebago.

Quinnipiac College
275 Mt. Carmel Avenue
Hamden, CT 06518
203-288-5251
www.quinnipiac.edu

R

Rabbi Jacob Joseph School
One Plainfield Avenue
Edison, NJ 08817
732-985-6533

Rabbinical College of America
226 Sussex Avenue
Morristown, NJ 07960
201-267-9404
www.rca.edu

Radcliffe Institute for Advanced Studies
10 Garden Street
Cambridge, MA 02138
617-495-8601
www.radcliffe.edu

Radford University
801 Norwood Street
Radford, VA 24142
540-831-5000
www.runet.edu

Ramapo College of New Jersey
505 Ramapo Valley Road
Mahwah, NJ 07430
201-529-7500
www.ramapo.edu

Randolph-Macon College
204 Henry Street
Ashland, VA 23005
804-798-8372
www.rmc.edu

Randolph-Macon Woman's College
2500 Rivermont Avenue
Lynchburg, VA 24503-1526
804-947-8100
www.rmwc.edu

Reed College
3203 S.E. Woodstock Boulevard
Portland, OR 97202
503-771-1112
www.reed.edu

Reformed Bible College
3333 East Beltline, NE
Grand Rapids, MI 49525
616-222-3000
www.reformed.edu

Regent University
1000 Regent University Drive
Virginia Beach, VA 23464
800-373-5504 or 757-226-4127
www.regent.edu

Regents College of the University of the State of New York
7 Columbia Circle
Albany, NY 12203
518-464-8500
www.regents.edu

A swim test is required to graduate from Principia College, on the banks of the Mississippi River. No swim, no pass. I guess they don't want their graduates to drown in the river.

MORE ON MASCOTS

The largest and heaviest mascot of any school is Purdue University's Boilermaker Special, a replica of a steam locomotive and coal tender built onto a heavy truck frame. Before becoming the Boilermakers, Purdue teams were known variously as Haymakers, Railsplitters, Sluggers, and The Cornfield Sailors.

Regis College
235 Wellesley Street
Weston, MA 02193
617-893-1820
www.regis.edu

Regis University
3333 Regis Boulevard
Denver, CO 80221
303-458-4100
www.regis.edu

Reinhardt College
7300 Reinhardt College Circle
Waleska, GA 30183
770-720-5600
www.reinhardt.edu

Rensselaer Polytechnic Institute
110 Eighth Street
Troy, NY 12180
518-276-6000
www.rpi.edu

Research College of Nursing
2316 East Meyer Boulevard
Kansas City, MO 64132
816-276-4700

Rhode Island College
600 Mount Pleasant Avenue
Providence, RI 02908
401-456-8090
www.ric.edu

Rhode Island School of Design
2 College Street
Providence, RI 02903
401-454-6402
www.risd.edu

Rhodes College
2000 North Parkway
Memphis, TN 38112
901-843-3000
www.rhodes.edu

Rice University
(formal title is William Marsh Rice)
6100 South Main Street
Houston, TX 77005
713-527-8101
www.rice.edu

**Richard Stockton College
of New Jersey**
P.O. Box 195
Pomona, NJ 08240
609-652-1776
www.stockton.edu

Rider University
2083 Lawrenceville Road
Lawrenceville, NJ 08648
609-896-5000
www.rider.edu

Ringling School of Art & Design
2700 North Tamiami Trail
Sarasota, FL 34234
941-351-5100
www.rsad.edu

U.S. Senator Blanche L. Lincoln writes letters to prospectives on behalf of her alma mater, Randolph-Macon Woman's College. She credits her education at Randolph-Macon for helping launch her career, which led her to become the youngest woman ever elected to the U.S. Senate: "This uncommon college will give you much more than academic skills. The liberal arts and sciences curriculum will give you versatility and adaptability. The Honor Code will give you proof of the value of honesty and integrity. The experience will empower you to succeed throughout your life."

Ripon College
300 Seward Street
Ripon, WI 54971
920-748-8115
www.ripon.edu

Rivier College
420 South Main Street
Nashua, NH 03060
603-888-1311
www.rivier.edu

Roanoke Bible College
714 First Street
Elizabeth City, NC 27909
919-334-2070
www.roanokebible.edu

Roanoke College
221 College Lane
Salem, VA 24153
540-375-2500
www.roanoke.edu

The Robert E. Cook Honors College
at Indiana University of Pennsylvania
290 Pratt Street
Indiana, PA 15705
800-487-9122 or 724-357-4971
www.iup.edu/honors/

Robert Morris College
401 South State Street
Chicago, IL 60605
312-935-6600
www.rmcil.edu

Robert Morris College
881 Narrows Run Road
Moon Township, PA 15108
412-262-8200
www.robert-morris.edu

Roberts Wesleyan College
2301 Westside Drive
Rochester, NY 14624
716-594-6000
www.roberts.edu

Rochester College
800 West Avon Road
Rochester Hills, MI 48307
800-521-6010 or 248-218-2000
www.rc.edu

Rochester Institute of Technology
One Lomb Memorial Drive
Rochester, NY 14623
716-475-2411
www.rit.edu

Rockford College
5050 East State Street
Rockford, IL 61108
815-226-4000
www.rockford.edu

Rockhurst College
1100 Rockhurst Road
Kansas City, MO 64110
816-501-4000
www.rockhurst.edu

Rocky Mountain College
1511 Poly Drive
Billings, MT 59102
800-877-6259 or 406-657-1000
www.rocky.edu

**Rocky Mountain College
of Art and Design**
6878 East Evans Avenue
Denver, CO 80224
303-753-6046
www.rmcad.edu

Roger Williams University
One Old Ferry Road
Bristol, RI 02809
401-253-1040
www.rwu.edu

Rollins College
1000 Holt Avenue
Winter Park, FL 32789
407-646-2000
www.rollins.edu

> **One finds many companions for food and drink, but in a serious business one's companions are few.**
>
> —*Theognis*

Roosevelt University
430 South Michigan Avenue
Chicago, IL 60605
312-341-3500
www.roosevelt.edu

Rose-Hulman Institute of Technology
5500 Wabash Avenue
Terre Haute, IN 47803
800-248-7448 or 812-877-1511
www.rose-hulman.edu

Rosemont College
1400 Montgomery Avenue
Rosemont, PA 19010
610-527-0200
www.rosemont.edu

Rowan University
201 Mullica Hill Road
Glassboro, NJ 08028
609-256-4000
www.rowan.edu

Rush University
600 South Paulina
Chicago, IL 60612
312-942-7120
www.rushu.rush.edu

Rust College
150 Rust Avenue
Holly Springs, MS 38635
601-252-8000
www.centurytel.net/rust

Rutgers University - Camden
311 North Fifth Street
Camden, NJ 08102
609-225-6095
www.camden.rutgers.edu

Rutgers University - Newark
15 Washington Street
Newark, NJ 07102
973-648-1766
www.newark.rutgers.edu

Rutgers University - University College New Brunswick
83 Somerset Street
New Brunswick, NJ 08901
732-932-7461
ucnb.rutgers.edu

S

Sacred Heart Major Seminary
2701 Chicago Boulevard
Detroit, MI 48206
313-883-8500
www.ichange.net/~shms1

Sacred Heart University
5151 Park Avenue
Fairfield, CT 06432
203-371-7999
www.sacredheart.edu

The Sage Colleges
45 Ferry Street
Troy, NY 12180
518-270-2000
www.sage.edu

Saginaw Valley State University
7400 Bay Road
University Center, MI 48710
517-790-4000
www.svsu.edu

Rutgers, the State College of New Jersey, was originally known as Queen's College, holding its first classes in a tavern in New Brunswick in 1771.

Saint Ambrose University
518 West Locust Street
Davenport, IA 52803
319-383-8700
www.sau.edu

Saint Andrews Presbyterian College
1700 Dogwood Mile
Laurinburg, NC 28352
910-277-5000
www.sapc.edu

Saint Anselm College
100 St. Anselm Drive
Manchester, NH 03102
603-641-7000
www.anselm.edu

Saint Anthony College of Nursing
5658 East State Street
Rockford, IL 61108
815-395-5091

Saint Augustine College
1333-45 West Argyle Street
Chicago, IL 60640
773-878-8756

Saint Augustine's College
1315 Oakwood Avenue
Raleigh, North Carolina 27610-2298
919-516-4000
www.st-aug.edu

Saint Francis College
Franciscan Way
Loretto, PA 15940
814-472-3000
www.sfcpa.edu

Saint Francis Medical Center College of Nursing
511 N.E. Greenleaf Street
Peoria, IL 61603
309-655-2201
www.sfmccon.edu

Saint John's Seminary College
5118 Seminary Road
Camarillo, CA 93012
805-482-2755
www.west.net/~sjsc

Saint John's University
Collegeville, MN 56321
320-363-2011
www.csbsju.edu

Saint Joseph College
1678 Asylum Avenue
Fairfield, CT 06432
860-232-4571
www.sjc.edu

Saint Joseph Seminary College
75376 River Road
St. Benedict, LA 70457
504-892-1800

Saint Joseph's College
US Highway 231
Rensselaer, IN 47978
219-866-6000
www.saintjoe.edu

Saint Joseph's College
245 Clinton Avenue
Brooklyn, NY 11205
718-636-6800
www.sjcny.edu

Saint Joseph's College of Maine
278 Whites Bridge Road
Standish, ME 04084
207-892-6766
www.sjcme.edu

Saint Joseph's University
5600 City Line Avenue
Philadelphia, PA 19131
610-660-1000
www.sju.edu

Saint Leo University
33701 State Road 52
Saint Leo, FL 33574
352-588-8200
www.saintleo.edu

Saint Louis Christian College
1360 Grandview Drive
Florissant, MO 63033
314-837-6777
www.slcc4ministry.edu

Saint Louis College of Pharmacy
4588 Parkview Place
St. Louis, MO 63110
314-367-8700
www.stlcop.edu

Saint Louis University
221 North Grand Boulevard
St. Louis, MO 63103
314-977-2222
www.slu.edu

Saint Luke's College
4426 Wornall Road
Kansas City, MO 64111
816-932-2233
www.saint-lukes.org/about/slc

Saint Martin's College
5300 Pacific Avenue SE
Lacey, WA 98503
360-491-4700
www.stmartin.edu

Saint Mary College
4100 South Fourth Street
Leavenworth, KS 66048
913-758-6102
www.smcks.edu

Saint Mary-of-the-Woods College
3301 St. Mary's Road
St. Mary-of-the-Woods, IN 47876
812-535-5151
www.smwc.edu

Saint Mary's College
Notre Dame, IN 46556
219-284-4000
www.saintmarys.edu

Saint Mary's College
3535 Indian Trail
Orchard Lake, MI 48324
810-683-0508

Saint Mary's College of California
1928 St. Mary's Road
Moraga, CA 94575
925-631-4000
www.stmarys-ca.edu

Saint Mary's Seminary & University
5400 Roland Avenue
Baltimore, MD 21210
410-864-4000
www.stmarys.edu

Saint Mary's University
One Camino Santa Maria
San Antonio, TX 78228
210-436-3011
www.stmarytx.edu

Saint Mary's University of Minnesota
700 Terrace Heights
Winona, MN 55987
800-635-5987 or 507-452-4430
www.smumn.edu

Saint Meinrad College
Indiana Highway 62
St. Meinrad, IN 47577
812-357-6611
www.saintmeinrad.edu

Saint Michael's College
Winooski Park
Colchester, VT 05439
802-655-2000
www.smcvt.edu

Saint Norbert College
100 Grant Street
De Pere, WI 54115
800-236-4878 or 920-337-3181
www.snc.edu

Saint Paul's College
406 Windsor Avenue
Lawrenceville, VA 23868
800-678-7071 or 804-848-4268
www.saintpauls.edu

Saint Peter's College
2641 Kennedy Boulevard
Jersey City, NJ 07306
888-SPC-9933 or 201-915-9000
www.spc.edu

Saint Thomas University
16400 N.W. 32nd Avenue
Miami, FL 33054
305-625-6000
www.stu.edu

Saint Vincent College
300 Fraser Purchase Road
Latrobe, PA 15650
800-SVC-5549 or 724-539-9761
www.stvincent.edu

Saint Xavier University
3700 West 103rd Street
Chicago, IL 60655
312-298-3000
www.sxu.edu

Salem College
Winston-Salem, NC 27108
800-327-2536 or 910-721-2600
www.salem.edu

Salem State College
352 Lafayette Street
Salem, MA 01970
508-741-6000
www.salem.mass.edu

Salem-Teikyo University
241 East Main Street
Salem, WV 26426
304-782-5011
www.salem-teikyo.wvnet.edu

Salisbury State University
1101 Camden Avenue
Salisbury, MD 21801
410-543-6000
www.ssu.umd.edu

MOUNTAIN DAY

Each year, students, faculty, and staff at Juniata College in Huntington, Pennsylvania, anxiously await the crisp, cool mornings, the sunny afternoons, and the lovely display of autumn color in the central Pennsylvania mountains. All of these signs mean Mountain Day can't be far away. That's the day the college president cancels classes and closes the entire college down, so faculty, staff, and students can head for the wilderness. Only the president knows when Mountain Day will be, and it is rumored he never decides in advance. The tradition harkens back to 1878, when students avoided a smallpox outbreak by hiding for six weeks in a cabin in the woods. On Mountain Day, Juniatians head to a mountain park to play football, tug-of-war, volleyball, and more, and eat an impromptu feast provided by the college.

Salish Kootenai College
52000 Highway 93
Pablo, MT 59855
406-675-4800
www.skc.edu

Salve Regina University
100 Ochre Point Avenue
Newport, RI 02840
401-847-6650
www.salve.edu

Sam Houston State University
1700 Sam Houston Avenue
Huntsville, TX 77341
409-294-1111
www.shsu.edu

Samford University
800 Lakeshore Drive
Birmingham, AL 35229
205-870-2011
www.samford.edu

Samuel Merritt College
370 Hawthorne Avenue
Oakland, CA 94609
510-869-6511
www.samuelmerritt.edu

San Diego State University
5500 Campanile Drive
San Diego, CA 92182
858-594-5200
www.sdsu.edu

San Francisco Art Institute
800 Chestnut Street
San Francisco, CA 94133
415-771-7020
www.sfai.edu

**San Francisco Conservatory
of Music**
1201 Ortega Street
San Francisco, CA 94122
415-564-8086
www.sfcm.edu

San Francisco State University
1600 Holloway Avenue
San Francisco, CA 94132
415-338-1111
www.sfsu.edu

San Jose Christian College
790 South 12th Street
San Jose, CA 95108
408-293-9058
www.sjchristiancol.edu

San Jose State University
One Washington Square
San Jose, CA 95192
408-924-1000
www.sjsu.edu

Santa Clara University
500 El Camino Real
Santa Clara, CA 95053
408-554-4764
www.scu.edu

Sarah Lawrence College
One Meadway
Bronxville, NY 10708
914-337-0700
www.slc.edu

**The Savannah College
of Art & Design**
342 Bull Street
Savannah, GA 31402
912-525-5000
www.scad.edu

Savannah State University
3219 College Street
Savannah, GA 31404
912-356-2187
www.savstate.edu

Schiller International University
453 Edgewater Drive
Dunedin, FL 34698
813-736-5082
www.schiller.edu

School for International Training
Kipling Road, P.O. Box 676
Brattleboro, VT 05302-0676
802-257-7751
www.sit.edu

School of The Art Institute of Chicago
37 South Wabash Avenue
Chicago, IL 60603
312-899-5219
www.artic.edusaic

School of Visual Arts
209 East 23rd Street
New York, NY 10010
212-592-2000
www.schoolofvisualarts.edu

Schreiner College
2100 Memorial Boulevard
Kerrville, TX 76059
830-896-5411
www.schreiner.edu

Scripps College
1030 North Columbia Avenue
Claremont, CA 91711
909-621-8224
www.scrippscol.edu

Seattle Pacific University
3307 Third Avenue, West
Seattle, WA 98119
206-281-2000
www.spu.edu

Seattle University
Twelfth Avenue and East Columbia
Street
Seattle, WA 98122
206-296-6000
www.seattleu.edu

Seton Hall University
400 South Orange Avenue
South Orange, NJ 07079
973-761-9000
www.shu.edu

Seton Hill College
Seton Hill Drive
Greensburg, PA 15601
724-834-2200
www.setonhill.edu

Sewanee, The University of the South
735 University Avenue
Sewanee, TN 37383
931-598-1000
www.sewanee.edu

Shaw University
118 East South Street
Raleigh, NC 27601
919-546-8200
www.shawu.edu

Shawnee State University
940 Second Street
Portsmouth, OH 45662
740-354-3205
www.shawnee.edu

Cooper Union has an unusual admissions practice. They send applicants a project to complete under a tight deadline. No cookie cutter essay will cut it for Cooper Union. Oh, by the way, Cooper Union is free. See more on p. 182.

Sheldon Jackson College
801 Lincoln Street
Sitka, AK 99835
907-747-5222
www.sheldonjackson.edu

Shenandoah University
1460 University Drive
Winchester, VA 22601
540-665-4500
www.su.edu

Shepherd College
Shepherdstown, WV 25443
800-344-5231 or 304-876-5000
www.shepherd.edu

Shimer College
438 North Sheridan Road
Waukegan, IL 60079
847-623-8400
www.shimer.edu

**Shippensburg University
of Pennsylvania**
1871 Old Main Road
Shippensburg, PA 17257
717-532-9121
www.ship.edu

Shorter College
315 Shorter Avenue
Rome, GA 30165
706-291-2121
www.shorter.edu

Siena College
515 Loudon Road
Loudonville, NY 12211
518-783-2300
www.siena.edu

Siena Heights University
1247 East Siena Heights Drive
Adrian, MI 49221
517-263-0731
www.sienahts.edu

Sierra Nevada College
800 College Drive
Incline Village, NV 89450
775-831-1314
www.sierranevada.edu

Silver Lake College
2406 South Alverno Road
Manitowoc, WI 54220
800-236-4752 or 920-684-6691
www.sl.edu

Simmons College
300 The Fenway
Boston, MA 02115-5898
800-345-8468 or 617-521-2000
www.simmons.edu

Simon's Rock College of Bard
84 Alford Road
Great Barrington, MA 01230
413-528-0771
www.simons-rock.edu

Simpson College
2211 College View Drive
Redding, CA 96003
916-224-5600
www.simpsonca.edu

Simpson College
701 North C Street
Indianola, IA 50125
515-961-6251
www.simpson.edu

In a recent survey, 70 percent of smokers said they'd like to quit.

Sinte Gleska University
Spotted Trail Drive
Rosebud, SD 57570
605-747-2263
www.sinte.indian.com

**Sistema Universitario
Ana G. Mendez**
Colegio Universitario del Este
Carretera 190
Avenuenida Principal Sabana
Barrio Sabana Abajo
Carolina, PR 00983
787-257-7373
www.suagm.eduCUE/main/default.htm

**Sistema Universitario
Ana G. Mendez**
Universidad Metropolitana Avenuenida
Ana G. Mendez
Km. 0.3
Cupey Bajo, PR 00928
787-766-1717
www.suagm.eduUMET/main/default.htm

**Sistema Universitario
Ana G. Mendez**
Universidad del Turabo
Carretera 189
Km 3.3
Gurabo, PR 00778
787-743-7979
www.suagm.eduUT/main/default.htm

Skidmore College
815 North Broadway
Saratoga Springs, NY 12866
518-584-5000
www.skidmore.edu

Slippery Rock University
300 Old Main Street
Slippery Rock, PA 16057
412-738-0512
www.sru.edu

Smith College
Elm Street
Northampton, MA 01063
413-584-2700
www.smith.edu

Sojourner-Douglass College
500 North Caroline Street
Baltimore, MD 21205
410-276-0306
host.sdc.edu

Sonoma State University
1801 East Cotati Avenue
Rohnert Park, CA 94928
707-664-2192
www.sonoma.edu

South Carolina State University
300 College Avenue, NE
Orangeburg, SC 29117
803-536-7000
www.scsu.edu

South College
709 Mall Boulevard
Savannah, GA 31406
912-691-6000
www.southcollege.edu

**South Dakota School
of Mines & Technology**
501 East St. Joseph Street
Rapid City, SD 57701
605-394-2256
www.sdsmt.edu

In a recent survey, 70 percent of attorneys said they'd like to quit.

South Dakota State University
Box 2201
Brookings, SD 57007
605-688-4121
www.sdstate.edu

Southeast College of Technology
828 Downtowner Loop West
Mobile, AL 36609
334-343-8200
home.earthlink.net/~sctech/index.html

Southeast Missouri State University
One University Plaza
Cape Girardeau, MO 63701
573-651-2000
www.semo.edu

Southeastern Baptist College
4229 Highway 15, North
Laurel, MS 39440
601-426-6346

**Southeastern Baptist
Theological Seminary**
222 North Wingate Street
Wake Forest, NC 27588
919-556-3101
www.sebts.edu

Southeastern Bible College
3001 Highway 280, East
Birmingham, AL 35243
205-970-9200
www.sebc.edu

**Southeastern College of the
Assemblies of God**
1000 Longfellow Boulevard
Lakeland, FL 33801
941-667-5000
www.secollege.edu

Southeastern Louisiana University
Western Avenue
Hammond, LA 70402
504-549-2000
www.selu.edu

**Southeastern Oklahoma State
University**
Durant, OK 74701
580-924-0121
www.sosu.edu

Southeastern University
501 I Street, SW
Washington, DC 20024
202-488-8162
www.seu.edu

Southern Adventist University
4881 Taylor Circle
Collegedale, TN 37315
423-238-2111
www.southern.edu

Southern Arkansas University
East Lane Drive
Magnolia, AR 71753
800-332-7286 or 870-235-4000
www.saumag.edu

Southern California College
55 Fair Drive
Costa Mesa, CA 92626
714-556-3610
www.sccu.edu

**Southern California College
of Optometry**
2575 Yorba Linda Boulevard
Fullerton, CA 92631
714-870-7226
www.scco.edu

**Southern California Institute
of Architecture**
5454 Beethoven Street
Los Angeles, CA 90066
310-574-1123
www.sciarc.edu

Southern Christian University
1200 Taylor Road
Montgomery, AL 36117
334-277-2277
www.southernchristian.edu

Southern Connecticut State University
501 Crescent Street
New Haven, CT 06515
203-392-5200
www.scsu.ctstateu.edu

Southern Illinois University Carbondale
Carbondale, IL 62901
618-453-2121
www.siu.edusiuc

Southern Illinois University Edwardsville
Edwardsville, IL 62026
618-692-2000
www.siue.edu

Southern Methodist University
6425 Boaz Street
Dallas, TX 75275
214-768-2000
www.smu.edu

Southern Nazarene University
6729 N.W. 39th Expressway
Bethany, OK 73008
405-789-6400
www.snu.edu

Southern Oregon University
1250 Siskiyou Boulevard
Ashland, OR 97520
541-552-6113
www.sou.edu

Southern Polytechnic State University
1100 South Marietta Parkway
Marietta, GA 30060
770-528-7281
www.spsu.edu

Southern University and Agricultural & Mechanical College at Baton Rouge
G. Leon Netterville Drive
Baton Rouge, LA 70813
504-771-4500
www.subr.edu

Southern University at New Orleans
6400 Press Drive
New Orleans, LA 70126
504-286-5000
www.suno.edu

SUICIDE AND THE SMALLER COLLEGE

The national suicide rate for Americans age fifteen to twenty-four is 1.1 per 10,000 per annum. So, for any seven liberal arts colleges with 1,500 students each, it would be absolutely normal for one of them to have a suicide in any given year. However, on the specific campus that has the suicide, the event has magnified impact due to the small size of the institution. Parents may wonder if the school is providing a nurturing and protective environment. Student peers may wonder if they missed the warning signs that could have saved their friend. And the administration may worry about getting an undeserved reputation while they also worry about liability. Every suicide is a tragedy, but a unique event at a small school should not be blown out of proportion.

Southern Utah University
351 West Center
Cedar City, UT 84720
435-586-7706
www.suu.edu

Southern Vermont College
982 Foothills Road
Bennington, VT 05201
802-442-5427
www.svc.edu

Southern Wesleyan University
907 Wesleyan Drive
Central, SC 29630
864-639-2453
www.swu.edu

Southwest Baptist University
1600 University Avenue
Bolivar, MO 65613
417-326-5281
www.sbuniv.edu

Southwest Missouri State University
901 South National Avenue
Springfield, MO 65804
417-836-5000
www.smsu.edu

Southwest State University
1501 State Street
Marshall, MN 56258
800-642-0684 or 507-537-7021
www.southwest.msus.edu

Southwest Texas State University
601 University Drive
San Marcos, TX 78666
512-245-9111
www.swt.edu

Southwestern Adventist University
100 Hillcrest Drive
Keene, TX 76059
817-645-3921
www.swau.edu

Southwestern Assemblies of God University
1200 Sycamore Street
Waxahachie, TX 75165
972-937-4010
www.sagu.edu

Southwestern Baptist Theological Seminary
2001 West Seminary Drive
Fort Worth, TX 76122
817-923-1921
www.swbts.edu

Southwestern Christian College
200 Bowser Circle
Terrell, TX 75160
972-524-3341

Southwestern College
2625 East Cactus Road
Phoenix, AZ 85032
800-247-2697 or 602-992-6101
www.southwesterncollege.edu

Southwestern College
100 College Street
Winfield, KS 67156
316-221-4150
www.sckans.edu

Southwestern College of Christian Ministries
7210 N.W. 39th Expressway
Bethany, OK 73008
405-789-7661
www.sccm.edu

Southwestern Oklahoma State University
100 Campus Drive
Weatherford, OK 73096
580-772-6611
www.swosu.edu

Southwestern University
1001 East University Avenue
Georgetown, TX 78627
512-863-6511
www.southwestern.edu

Spalding University
851 South Fourth Street
Louisville, KY 40203
502-585-9911
www.spalding.edu

Spelman College
350 Spelman Lane, SW
Atlanta, GA 30314
800-982-2411 or 404-681-3643
www.spelman.edu

Spring Arbor College
106 East Main Street
Spring Arbor, MI 49283
517-750-1200
www.arbor.edu

Spring Hill College
4000 Dauphin Street
Mobile, AL 36608
334-380-4000
www.shc.edu

Springfield College
263 Alder Street
Springfield, MA 01109
413-748-3000
www.spfldcol.edu

St. Bonaventure University
Route 417
St. Bonaventure, NY 14778
716-375-2000
www.sbu.edu

St. Charles Borromeo Seminary
100 East Wynnewood Road
Wynnewood, PA 19096
610-667-3394

St. Cloud State University
720 Fourth Avenue South
St. Cloud, MN 56301
320-255-0121
www.stcloudstate.edu

St. Edward's University
3001 South Congress Avenue
Austin, TX 78704
512-448-8500
www.stedwards.edu

St. Francis College
180 Remsen Street
Brooklyn, NY 11201
718-522-2300
www.stfranciscollege.edu

St. Gregory's University
1900 West MacArthur
Shawnee, OK 74801
405-878-5100
www.sgc.edu

St. Hyacinth College and Seminary
66 School Street
Granby, MA 01033
413-467-7191

St. John Fisher College
3690 East Avenue
Rochester, NY 14618
716-385-8000
www.sjfc.edu

St. John Vianney College Seminary
2900 S.W. 87th Avenue
Miami, FL 33165
305-223-4561

St. John's College
421 North Ninth Street
Springfield, IL 62702
217-525-5628

> **Common sense is not so common.**
>
> —*Voltaire*

St. John's College
60 College Avenue
Annapolis, MD 21404
410-263-2371
www.sjca.edu

St. John's College
1160 Camino Cruz Blanca
Santa Fe, NM 87501
505-984-6000
www.sjcsf.edu

St. John's Seminary
127 Lake Street
Brighton, MA 02135
617-254-2610

St. John's University
8000 Utopia Parkway
Jamaica, NY 11439
718-990-6161
www.stjohns.edu

St. Lawrence University
23 Romoda Drive
Canton, NY 13617
315-229-5011
www.stlawu.edu

St. Mary's College of Maryland
18952 E. Fisher Road
St. Mary's City, MD 20686
301-862-0200
www.smcm.edu

St. Olaf College
1520 St. Olaf Avenue
Northfield, MN 55057
507-646-2222
www.stolaf.edu

St. Thomas Aquinas College
125 Route 340
Sparkill, NY 10976
914-398-4000
www.stac.edu

Stanford University
Stanford, CA 94305
650-723-2300
www.stanford.edu

State University of New York at Albany
1400 Washington Avenue
Albany, NY 12222
518-442-3300
www.albany.edu

State University of New York at Binghamton
P.O. Box 6000
Binghamton, NY 13902-6000
607-777-2000
www.binghamton.edu

State University of New York at Brockport
350 New Campus Drive
Brockport, NY 14420
716-395-2211
www.brockport.edu

Stanford University and the University of California, Berkeley have a longstanding athletic rivalry, which is odd for two schools whose primary mission is, without question, academics. This rivalry has led to stolen mascots and icons, pranks, and sharp verbal exchanges, some of it demonstrating a sharp wit. For example, on Saturday, February 19, 2000, the men's basketball team at the University of California, Berkeley (known the world over as "Cal") lost to Stanford, 101-50, the worst point-spread loss in the history of Cal basketball. The next week at Cal the *Daily Californian* carried this headline: "The Cal men's basketball team makes history at Stanford." That oughta show 'em!

**State University of New York
at Buffalo**
Flint Road
Buffalo, NY 14260
716-645-2000
www.buffalo.edu

**State University of New York
Buffalo State College**
1300 Elmwood Avenue
Buffalo, NY 14222
716-878-4000
www.buffalostate.edu

**State University of New York
College at Cortland**
P.O. Box 2000
Cortland, NY 13045
607-753-4712
www.cortland.edu

**State University of New York
at Farmingdale**
Route 110
Farmingdale, NY 11735-1021
516-420-2000
www.farmingdale.edu

**State University of New York
at Fredonia**
Fredonia, NY 14063
716-673-3111
www.fredonia.edu

**State University of New York
at Geneseo**
One College Circle
Geneseo, NY 14454
716-245-5501
www.geneseo.edu

**State University of New York
at New Paltz**
75 South Manheim Boulevard
New Paltz, NY 12561
914-257-2121
www.newpaltz.edu

**State University of New York
College at Old Westbury**
Route 107
Old Westbury, NY 11568
516-876-3000
www.oldwestbury.edu

**State University of New York
College at Oneonta**
Rovine Parkway
Oneonta, NY 13820
607-436-3500
www.oneonta.edu

**State University of New York
at Oswego**
Route 104
Oswego, NY 13126
315-341-2500
www.oswego.edu

Every college has its legends. When I was visiting Reed, someone told me there was a car buried under the new library wing. I assumed it was an urban legend, but I managed to find and interview several students who swear they were actually there that fateful Saturday night in 1987 when, the day before graduation, over twenty students rolled Mark Verna's '78 MG into the pit that was to become the basement of the new library wing. They dug a hole, buried the car, and put the dirt back. On Sunday they graduated, and on Monday the construction crews poured concrete forever over the entombed auto. Kilian Kerwin was there and claims to have the gas cap from the car. Dave Conlin was there. J. J. Haapala has photos to prove it. Poor Mr. Verna was in Europe at the time.

Nothing endures but change.

—*Heraclitus*

State University of New York at Plattsburgh
101 Broad Street
Plattsburgh, NY 12901
518-564-2000
www.plattsburgh.edu

State University of New York at Stony Brook
Nicolls Road
Stony Brook, NY 11794
516-689-6000
www.sunysb.edu

State University of New York Cobleskill College of Agriculture & Technology
Route 7
Cobleskill, NY 12043
518-234-5011
www.cobleskill.edu

State University of New York College at Potsdam
44 Pierrepont Avenue
Potsdam, NY 13676
315-267-2000
www.potsdam.edu

State University of New York College of Environmental Science and Forestry
One Forestry Drive
Syracuse, NY 13210
315-470-6500
www.esf.edu

State University of New York College of Technology at Alfred
Alfred, NY 14802
607-587-4111
www.alfredtech.edu

State University of New York College of Technology at Delhi
Delhi, NY 13753
607-746-4000
www.delhi.edu

State University of New York Empire State College
One Union Avenue
Saratoga Springs, NY 12866
518-587-2100
www.esc.edu

State University of New York Health Science Center at Brooklyn
450 Clarkson Avenue
Brooklyn, NY 11203
718-270-1000
www.hscbklyn.edu

State University of New York Institute of Technology at Utica/Rome
Campus Drive
Utica, NY 13504
315-792-7100
www.sunyit.edu

State University of New York Maritime College
6 Pennyfield Avenue
Throggs Neck, NY 10465
718-409-7200
www.sunymaritime.edu

State University of New York Purchase College
735 Anderson Hill Road
Purchase, NY 10577
914-251-6000
www.purchase.edu

State University of New York Upstate Medical University
750 East Adams Street
Syracuse, NY 13210
315-464-5275
www.hscsyr.edu

State University of West Georgia
1600 Maple Street
Carrollton, GA 30118
770-836-6500
www.westga.edu

Stephen F. Austin State University
1936 North Street
Nacogdoches, TX 75962
409-468-2011
www.sfasu.edu

Stephens College
1200 East Broadway
Columbia, MO 65215
800-876-7207 or 573-442-2211
www.stephens.edu

Sterling College
Cooper at Broadway
Sterling, KS 67579
316-278-2173
www.sterling.edu

Sterling College
16 Sterling Drive
Craftsbury Common, VT 05827
800-648-3591 or 802-586-7711
www.sterlingcollege.edu

Stetson University
421 North Woodland Boulevard
DeLand, FL 32720
904-822-7000
www.stetson.edu

Stevens Institute of Technology
Castle Point on the Hudson
Hoboken, NJ 07030
201-216-5100
www.stevens-tech.edu

Stillman College
3600 Stillman Boulevard
Tuscaloosa, AL 35401
205-349-4240
www.stillman.edu

Stonehill College
320 Washington Street
North Easton, MA 02357
508-238-1081
www.stonehill.edu

Strayer University
1025 15th Street, NW
Washington, DC 20005
202-408-2400
www.strayer.edu

Suffolk University
41 Temple Street
Boston, MA 02114
617-723-4700
www.suffolk.edu

Sul Ross State University
P.O. Box C-114
Alpine, TX 79832
915-837-8011
www.sulross.edu

❝When you apply to my school, you're not just applying to my school. You're also applying to New York City. I had a guy from Kentucky who went barefoot and rode a Harley-Davidson motorcycle, and he fit in perfectly, while I had a guy from New Jersey that seemed to have a 'Kick me' sign on him. He was mugged every week. It's not where you're from that matters, but who you are.❞

—Director of Admissions, off the record, for a New York City university

---

The world's largest shovel collection is right on campus at Stonehill College in Eaton, Massachusetts. There are twenty-five silver-plated shovels, and special models of all sizes and great ingenuity to handle everything from coffee beans to sludge to dandelions. Stonehill once had a cattle graveyard on campus, and somewhere there's still a bronze marker for one "Queen of the East," a celebrated guernsey. Lest you think Stonehill too quirky, you should know that it has a high freshman retention rate and graduation rate so students must be very happy there.

Sullivan College
3101 Bardstown Road
Lousiville, KY 40205
502-456-6504
www.sullivan.edu

Suomi College
601 Quincy Street
Hancock, MI 49930
800-682-7604 or 906-487-7274
www.suomi.edu

Susquehanna University
514 University Avenue
Selinsgrove, PA 17870
717-374-0101
www.susqu.edu

Swarthmore College
500 College Avenue
Swarthmore, PA 19081
610-328-8000
www.swarthmore.edu

Sweet Briar College
Sweet Briar, VA 24595
804-381-6100
www.sbc.edu

Syracuse University
300 Tolley
Syracuse, NY 13244
315-443-1870
www.syr.edu

T

Tabor College
400 South Jefferson
Hillsboro, KS 67063
316-947-3121
www.tabor.edu

Talladega College
627 West Battle Street
Talladega, AL 35160
800-633-2440 or 256-362-0206
www.talladega.edu

Talmudic University of Florida
1910 Alton Road
Miami Beach, FL 33139
305-534-7050
www.talmudicu.edu

Talmudical Academy of New Jersey
Route 524
Adelphia, NJ 07710
732-431-1600

Tampa Technical Institute
2410 East Busch Boulevard
Tampa, FL 33612
813-935-5700
www.tampatech.edu

Tarleton State University
1333 West Washington Street
Stephenville, TX 76402
254-968-9000
www.tarleton.edu

Taylor University
236 West Reade Avenue
Upland, IN 46989
765-998-2751
www.tayloru.edu

Teikyo Loretto Heights University
3001 South Federal Boulevard
Denver, CO 80236
303-937-4200
www.tlhu.edu

Teikyo Post University
800 Country Club Road
Waterbury, CT 06708
203-596-4500
www.teikyopost.edu

Temple University
Broad and Montgomery Streets
Philadelphia, PA 19122
215-204-7000
www.temple.edu

Tennessee State University
3500 John A. Merritt Boulevard
Nashville, TN 37209
615-963-5000
www.tnstate.edu

Tennessee Technological University
Box 5006
Cookeville, TN 38505
615-372-3101
www.tntech.edu

Tennessee Temple University
1815 Union Avenue
Chattanooga, TN 37404
423-493-4100
www.tntemple.edu

Tennessee Wesleyan College
204 College Street
Athens, TN 37371
423-745-7504
www.tnwc.edu

Texas A & M International University
5201 University Boulevard
Laredo, TX 78041
956-326-2001
www.tamiu.edu

Texas A & M University
University Drive
College Station, TX 77843
409-845-3211
www.tamu.edu

Texas A & M University - Commerce
Commerce, TX 75429
903-886-5102
www.tamu-commerce.edu

Texas A & M University - Corpus Christi
6300 Ocean Drive
Corpus Christi, TX 78412
512-994-5700
www.tamucc.edu

Texas A & M - Galveston
200 Seawolf Parkway
Galveston, TX 77553
800-850-6376 or 409-740-4400
www.tamug.tamu.edu

Texas A & M University - Kingsville
Kingsville, TX 78363
512-593-2111
www.tamuk.edu

Texas A & M University System Health Science Center
College Station, TX 77840
409-845-7743

Texas A & M University - Texarkana
Texarkana, TX 75505
903-838-6514
www.tamut.edu

Texas Chiropractic College
5912 Spencer Highway
Pasadena, TX 77505
281-487-1170
www.txchiro.edu

Texas Christian University
2800 South University Drive
Fort Worth, TX 76129
817-257-7000
www.tcu.edu

Texas Lutheran University
1000 West Court Street
Seguin, TX 78155
830-372-8000
www.txlutheran.edu

Texas Southern University
3100 Cleburne Street
Houston, TX 77004
713-313-7011
www.tsu.edu

Texas Tech University
Brownfield Highway
Lubbock, TX 79409
806-742-2011
www.texastech.edu

Texas Tech University Health Sciences Center
3601 Fourth Street
Lubbock, TX 79430
806-743-3111
www.ttuhsc.edu

Texas Wesleyan University
1201 Wesleyan Street
Fort Worth, TX 76105
817-531-4444
www.txwesleyan.edu

Texas Woman's University
Denton, TX 76204
940-898-2000
www.twu.edu

Thiel College
75 College Avenue
Greenville, PA 16125
724-589-2000
www.thiel.edu

Thomas Aquinas College
10000 North Ojai Road
Santa Paula, CA 93060
805-525-4417
www.thomasaquinas.edu

Thomas College
1501 Millpond Road
Thomasville, GA 31792
912-226-1621
www.thomascollege.edu

Thomas College
180 West River Road
Waterville, ME 04901
207-873-0771
www.thomas.edu

Thomas Edison State College
101 West State Street
Trenton, NJ 08608
609-984-1100
www.tesc.edu

Thomas Jefferson School of Law
2121 San Diego Avenue
San Diego, CA 92110
858-297-9700
www.jeffersonlaw.edu

Thomas Jefferson University
11th and Walnut Streets
Philadelphia, PA 19107
215-955-6000
www.tju.edu

Thomas More College
333 Thomas More Parkway
Crestview Hills, KY 41017
606-341-5800
www.thomasmore.edu

The Thomas More College of Liberal Arts
Six Manchester Street
Merrimack, NH 03054
603-880-8308
www.thomasmorecollege.edu

Tiffin University
155 Miami Street
Tiffin, OH 44883
419-447-6442
www.tiffin.edu

The average number of children by a married faculty member at Thomas Aquinas College is 5.3. "I'd have to think that must put us at the top of some survey or another," says the college's general counsel. For more on Thomas Aquinas, see p.204.

Toccoa Falls College
Toccoa Falls, GA 30598
706-886-6831
www.toccoafalls.edu

Tougaloo College
500 West County Line Road
Tougaloo, MS 39174
888-424-2566 or 601-977-7700
www.tougaloo.edu

Touro College
27 West 23rd Street
New York, NY 10010
212-463-0400
www.touro.edu

Towson University
8000 York Road
Towson, MD 21252
410-830-2000
www.towson.edu

Transylvania University
300 North Broadway
Lexington, KY 40508
606-233-8300
www.transy.edu

Trevecca Nazarene University
333 Murfreesboro Road
Nashville, TN 37210
615-248-1200
www.trevecca.edu

Trinity Bible College
50 South Sixth Avenue
Ellendale, ND 58436
701-349-3621
www.tbc2day.edu

Trinity Christian College
6601 West College Drive
Palos Heights, IL 60463
708-597-3000
www.trnty.edu

Trinity College
300 Summit Street
Hartford, CT 06106
860-297-2000
www.trincoll.edu

Trinity College
125 Michigan Avenue, NE
Washington, DC 20017
800-492-6882 or 202-884-9000
www.trinitydc.com

> **One's character is one's fate.**
>
> *—Heraclitus*

There *is* a college out there for you, whoever you are. If you haven't found it yet, keep looking. For example, The National Technical Institute for the Deaf at the Rochester Institute of Technology provides a top-quality education in technical and professional studies for deaf and hard of hearing students. The program employs more than 100 full-time interpreters to assist students, who study, live, and socialize right along with the other 12,000 students on the Rochester campus. The program has a 95 percent employment rate for its graduates. Another special feature: the opportunity to do research at the International Center for Hearing and Speech Research.

National Technical Institute for the Deaf • Rochester Institute of Technology
Lyndon Baines Johnson Building • 52 Lomb Memorial Drive • Rochester, New York 14623-5604
716-475-6906 (voice/TTY) • www.rit.edu/418www/new/NTID.html

Trinity College
208 Colchester Avenue
Burlington, VT 05401
802-658-0337
www.trinityvt.edu

Trinity College of Florida
2430 Trinity Oaks Boulevard
New Port Richey, FL 33465
727-376-6911
www.trinitycollege.edu

Trinity College of Nursing
555 Sixth Street, Suite 300
Moline, IL 61265
309-757-2093
www.trinityqc.com

Trinity International University
2065 Half Day Road
Deerfield, IL 60015
847-945-8800
www.tiu.edu

Trinity Lutheran College
4221 228th Avenue SE
Issaquah, WA 98029
800-843-5659 or 425-392-0400
www.tlc.edu

Trinity University
715 Stadium Drive
San Antonio, TX 78212
210-736-7011
www.trinity.edu

Tri-State University
1 University Avenue
Angola, IN 46703
219-665-4100
www.tristate.edu

Troy State University
University Avenue
Troy, AL 36082
334-670-3000
www.troyst.edu

Troy State University Dothan
3601 U.S. Highway 231, North
Dothan, AL 36304
334-983-6556
www.tsud.edu

**Troy State University
in Montgomery**
231 Montgomery Street
Montgomery, AL 36103
334-834-1400
www.tsum.edu

COLLEGE PLANNING DIFFERS BY FAMILY INCOME

Lower income families and upper income families have entirely different concerns when it comes to college planning and college counseling. Lower income families want to know how to pay for college, and if they can pay for college at all. That is their number one concern, eclipsing all others. Upper income families want to know how to improve their students' chances of getting into the most competitive colleges. They want to know what techniques or tips or angles will give their students the biggest "boost" over equally prepared competitors. This results in too-high placement of upper income students, relative to their abilities, and too low placement of lower income students, relative to their abilities. All too seldom, at either end of the scale, is the number one concern to find a good match between a student's preparation and interests and a college or university's greatest institutional strengths. Whether you are wealthy or not, brilliant or not, your first concern should be to find a college or university where you will be truly happy and thrive.

Truman State University
101 East Normal Street
Kirksville, MO 63501
660-785-4000
www.truman.edu

Tufts University
Medford, MA 02155
617-628-5000
www.tufts.edu

Tulane University
6823 St. Charles Avenue
New Orleans, LA 70118
504-865-5000
www.tulane.edu

Tusculum College
60 Shiloh Road
Greeneville, TN 37743
423-636-7300
www.tusculum.edu

Tuskegee University
Tuskegee, AL 36088
800-622-6531 or 334-727-8011
www.tusk.edu

U

Union College
310 College Street
Barbourville, KY 40906
606-546-4151
www.unionky.edu

Union College
3800 South 48th Street
Lincoln, NE 68506
402-488-2331
www.ucollege.edu

Union College
Schenectady, NY 12308
518-388-6000
www.union.edu

The Union Institute
440 East McMillan Street
Cincinnati, OH 45206
513-861-6400
www.tui.edu

Union University
2447 Highway 45 By-Pass
1050 Union University Drive
Jackson, TN 38305
901-668-1818
www.uu.edu

United States Air Force Academy
2304 Cadet Drive
Colorado Springs, CO 80840
719-333-1110
www.usafa.af.mil

United States Coast Guard Academy
31 Mohegan Avenue
New London, CT 06320
860-444-8444
www.cga.edu

Every student at the United States Coast Guard Academy lives in the same dorm, Chase Hall. Chase Hall contains a barbershop, a post office, bookstore, uniform store, dry cleaners, and two shooting ranges.

A school's reputation doesn't always match the reality at that school. Several years ago Tulane University in New Orleans thought it was getting too much of a reputation as a party school, so it studied its own students' alcohol consumption. Here's what they found: consumption well below the national average. An administrator told me: "You can't make it at Tulane if you party a lot. This is way too difficult a school to have lived up to its image, but because we're here in New Orleans we got painted with the same brush." Yes, Mardi Gras is wild, but that's one day a year. At Tulane, you can expect to be studying for most of the other 364.

United States International University
10455 Pomerado Road
San Diego, CA 92131
858-271-4300
www.usiu.edu

United States Merchant Marine Academy
300 Steamboat Road
Kings Point, NY 11024
800-732-6267 or 516-773-5000
www.usmma.edu

United States Military Academy
Stony Lonesome Road
West Point, NY 10996
914-938-4200
www.usma.edu

United States Naval Academy
121 Blake Road
Annapolis, MD 21402
410-293-1000
www.nadn.navy.mil

Unity College in Maine
Unity, ME 04988
207-948-3131
www.unity.edu

Universidad Adventista de las Antillas
Carr. 106 Km 2.2 Int
Mayagüez, PR 00680
787-834-9595
www.uaa.edu

Universidad Politecnica de Puerto Rico
377 Ponce de León Avenue
San Juan, PR 00919
787-754-8000
www.pupr.edu

University of Advancing Computer Technology
2625 West Baseline Road
Tempe, AZ 85283
602-383-8228
www.uact.edu

The University of Akron
302 East Buchtel Avenue
Akron, OH 44325
330-972-7111
www.uakron.edu

The University of Alabama
Campus Drive
Tuscaloosa, AL 35487
205-348-6010
www.ua.edu

The University of Alabama at Birmingham
701 South 20th Street
Birmingham, AL 35294
205-934-4011
www.uab.edu

The University of Alabama in Huntsville
301 Sparkman Drive
Huntsville, AL 35899
256-890-6120
www.uah.edu

University of Alaska - Anchorage
3211 Providence Drive
Anchorage, AK 99508
907-786-1437
www.uaa.alaska.edu

University of Alaska - Fairbanks
College Road
Fairbanks, AK 99775
907-474-7112
www.uaf.edu

"One who learns must suffer."

—Aeschylus

University of Alaska - Southeast
11120 Glacier Highway
Juneau, AK 99801
907-465-6509
www.jun.alaska.edu

University of Arizona
East University Boulevard
Tucscon, AZ 85721
520-621-5511
www.arizona.edu

**University of Arkansas
at Fayetteville**
Fayetteville, AR 72701
501-575-2000
www.uark.edu

**University of Arkansas
at Little Rock**
2801 South University Avenue
Little Rock, AR 72204
501-569-3200
www.ualr.edu

**University of Arkansas
at Monticello**
Highway 425
Monticello, AR 71655
870-367-6811
www.uamont.edu

University of Arkansas at Pine Bluff
1200 North University Drive
Pine Bluff, AR 71601
800-264-8272 or 870-543-8470
www.uapb.edu

**University of Arkansas
for Medical Sciences**
4301 West Markham Street
Little Rock, AR 72205
501-686-5000
www.uams.edu

University of the Arts
320 South Broad Street
Philadelphia, PA 19102
215 875-4800
www.uarts.edu

University of Baltimore
1420 North Charles Street
Baltimore, MD 21201
410-837-4200
www.ubalt.edu

University of Bridgeport
380 University Avenue
Bridgeport, CT 06602
203-576-4665
www.bridgeport.edu

University of California, Berkeley
Berkeley, CA 94720
510-642-6000
www.berkeley.edu

University of California, Davis
One Shields Avenue
Davis, CA 95616
530-752-1011
www.ucdavis.edu

University of California, Irvine
Irvine, CA 92697
949-824-5011
www.uci.edu

The student union at the University of Colorado at Boulder has a dining room named after Alferd Packer, a notorious Wild West cannibal. Here's another trivia item: In Boulder, and only in Boulder, the University of Colorado is known as C.U.

In 1900 the *Ladies Home Journal* spearheaded a national crusade to outlaw homework, claiming that it damaged children's health. They ran a series of tirades against it for over a decade, with expert testimony from doctors, educators, and priests, all of whom agreed that homework is counterproductive at best, and most likely downright dangerous for children.

University of California, Los Angeles
405 Hilgard Avenue
Los Angeles, CA 90095
310-825-5754
www.ucla.edu

University of California, Riverside
900 University Avenue
Riverside, CA 92521
909-787-1012
www.ucr.edu

University of California, San Diego
9500 Gilman Drive
La Jolla, CA 92093
619-534-2230
www.ucsd.edu

**University of California,
San Francisco**
513 Parnassus Avenue
San Francisco, CA 94143
415-476-9000
www.ucsf.edu

**University of California,
Santa Barbara**
552 University Road
Santa Barbara, CA 93106
805-893-8000
www.ucsb.edu

University of California, Santa Cruz
1156 High Street
Santa Cruz, CA 95064
408-459-2058
www.ucsc.edu

University of Central Arkansas
201 Donaghey Avenue
Conway, AR 72035
501-450-5000
www.uca.edu

University of Central Florida
4000 Central Florida Boulevard
Orlando, FL 32816
407-823-2000
www.ucf.edu

University of Central Oklahoma
100 North University Drive
Edmond, OK 73034
405-341-2980
www.ucok.edu

University of Central Texas
1901 Clear Creek Road
Killeen, TX 76540
254-721-5000
www.tarleton.educenter

TOP TEN COLLEGES WITH "SUBSTANTIAL PROPORTIONALITY" FOR WOMEN'S ATHLETIC PROGRAMS AS DEFINED BY TITLE IX

Creighton University	Vanderbilt University	Drexel University
USAF Academy	USN Academy	Manhattan College
Yale University	North Carolina State University	Georgia Institute of Technology
USM Academy		

(Source: Jim Naughton "Women's Teams in NCAA's Division I See Gains in Participation and Budgets," The Chronicle of Higher Education, *[3 April 1998])*

The University of Charleston
2300 MacCorkle Avenue
Charleston, WV 25304
304-357-4800
www.uchaswv.edu

University of Chicago
5801 South Ellis Avenue
Chicago, IL 60637
773-702-1234
www.uchicago.edu

University of Cincinnati
2624 Clifton Avenue
Cincinnati, OH 45221
513-556-2201
www.uc.edu

University of Colorado at Boulder
Boulder, CO 80309
303-492-1411
www.colorado.edu

**University of Colorado
at Colorado Springs**
1420 Austin Bluffs Parkway
Colorado Springs, CO 80918
800-990-8227 or 719-262-3000
www.uccs.edu

University of Colorado at Denver
1250 14th Street
Denver, CO 80217
303-556-2400
www.cudenver.edu

**University of Colorado Health
Sciences Center**
4200 East Ninth Avenue
Denver, CO 80262
303-372-0000
www.uchsc.edu

University of Connecticut
352 Mansfield Road
Storrs, CT 06269
860-486-2000
www.uconn.edu

**University of Connecticut
Health Center**
263 Farmington Avenue
Farmington, CT 06032
860-679-2000
www.uchc.edu

The University of Dallas
1845 East Northgate Drive
Irving, TX 75062
972-721-5000
www.udallas.edu

University of Dayton
300 College Park
Dayton, OH 45469
937-229-1000
www.udayton.edu

University of Delaware
Newark, DE 19716
302-831-2000
www.udel.edu

> **Until higher education for the most ambitious youth in American society is seen as something other than credentialing—providing a certificate that the individual will be able to exchange for something called a job—the joys and necessities of learning will be rendered in a debased coinage. The best of America's liberal arts colleges recognize that their so-called product is something other than a negotiable instrument designed to guarantee employment.**
>
> *—Stephen R. Graubard, editor (in "Distinctively American: The Residential Liberal Arts Colleges," Daedalus 128, no. 1 [1999])*

Question from the University of Chicago admissions forms: "Given the probability that the federal tax code, nondairy creamer, Dennis Rodman and the art of mime all came from outer space, name something else that has extraterrestrial origins and defend your hypothesis."

University of Denver
2199 South University Boulevard
Denver, CO 80208
800-525-9495 or 303-871-2000
www.du.edu

University of Detroit Mercy
4001 West McNichols Road
Detroit, MI 48219
313-993-1000
800-635-5020
www.udmercy.edu

University of the District of Columbia
4200 Connecticut Avenue, NW
Washington, DC 20008
202-274-5100
www.udc.edu

**University of Dubuque, College
of Liberal Arts**
2000 University Avenue
Dubuque, IA 52001
319-589-3223
www.dbq.edu

University of Evansville
1800 Lincoln Avenue
Evansville, IN 47722
800-423-8633 or 812-479-2000
www.evansville.edu

University of Findlay
1000 North Main Street
Findlay, OH 45840
419-424-8313
www.findlay.edu

University of Florida
S.W. 13th Street
Gainesville, FL 32611
352-392-3261
www.ufl.edu

The University of Georgia
456 East Broad Street
Athens, GA 30602
706-542-3000
www.uga.edu

University of Great Falls
1301 20th Street South
Great Falls, MT 59405
406-791-8610
www.ugf.edu

University of Guam
UOG Station
Mangilao, Guam 96923
671-735-2201
www.uog.edu

University of Hartford
200 Bloomfield Avenue
West Hartford, CT 06117
860-768-4100
www.hartford.edu

TOP TEN MOST INNOVATIVE AND/OR UNORTHODOX COLLEGES

Reed College

Antioch College

Marlboro College

University of California, Santa Cruz

Pitzer College

Sarah Lawrence College

Eugene Lange College of the New
    School for Social Research

Bard College

Cornell College

Deep Springs College

(Source: The Insider's Guide to the Colleges, *25th ed., St. Martin's Griffin, 1998)*

University of Hawaii at Hilo
200 West Kawili Street
Hilo, HI 96720
808-974-7444
www2.hawaii.edu~uhhilo

University of Hawaii at Manoa
2444 Dole Street
Honolulu, HI 96822
808-956-8207
www.hawaii.edu

University of Hawaii - West Oahu
96-129 Ala Ike
Pearl City, HI 96782
808-453-6179
www.uhwo.hawaii.edu

University of Houston - Clear Lake
2700 Bay Area Boulevard
Houston, TX 77058
281-283-7600
www.cl.uh.edu

University of Houston - Downtown
One Main Street
Houston, TX 77002
713-221-8000
www.dt.uh.edu

University of Houston - University Park
4800 Calhoun
Houston, TX 77204
713-743-1000
www.uh.edu

University of Houston - Victoria
2506 East Red River
Victoria, TX 77901
512-576-3151
www.vic.uh.edu

University of Idaho
Moscow, ID 83844
208-885-6326
www.uidaho.edu

University of Illinois at Chicago
601 South Morgan Street
Chicago, IL 60607
312-996-7000
www.uic.edu

University of Illinois at Springfield
P.O. Box 19243
Springfield, IL 62794-9243
217-206-6600
www.uis.edu

University of Illinois at Urbana-Champaign
901 West Illinois Street
Champaign, IL 61820
217-333-1000
www.uiuc.edu

University of the Incarnate Word
4301 Broadway
San Antonio, TX 78209
210-829-6000
www.uiw.edu

The University of Indianapolis
1400 East Hanna Avenue
Indianapolis, IN 46227
317-788-3368
www.uindy.edu

University of Iowa
Jefferson Street
Iowa City, IA 52242
319-335-3500
www.uiowa.edu

University of Judaism
15600 Mulholland Drive
Los Angeles, CA 90077
310-476-9777
www.uj.edu

> **There is only one good, knowledge, and one evil, ignorance.**
>
> —*Socrates*

University of Kansas
Fifteenth and Iowa Streets
Lawrence, KS 66045
785-864-2700
www.ukans.edu

University of Kansas Medical Center
3901 Rainbow Boulevard
Kansas City, KS 66160
913-588-1401
www.kumc.edu

University of Kentucky
Lexington, KY 40506
606-257-9000
www.uky.edu

University of La Verne
1950 Third Street
La Verne, CA 91750
909-593-3511
www.ulaverne.edu

The University of Louisiana at Lafayette
104 University Circle
Lafayette, LA 70504
337-482-1000
www.usl.edu

The University of Louisiana at Monroe
700 University Avenue
Monroe, LA 71209
800-372-5127 or 318-342-5252
www.nlu.edu

University of Louisville
2301 South Third Street
Louisville, KY 40292
502-852-5555
www.louisville.edu

University of Maine
107 Maine Avenue
Orono, ME 04469
207-581-1110
www.umaine.edu

University of Maine at Augusta
46 University Drive
Augusta, ME 04330
207-621-3403
www.uma.maine.edu

University of Maine at Farmington
86 Maine Street
Farmington, ME 04938
207-778-7256
www.umf.maine.edu

University of Maine at Fort Kent
25 Pleasant Street
Fort Kent, ME 04743
207-834-7500
www.umfk.maine.edu

University of Maine at Machias
Nine O'Brien Avenue
Machias, ME 04654
207-255-1210
www.umm.maine.edu

University of Maine at Presque Isle
181 Maine Street
Presque Isle, ME 04769
207-768-9525
www.umpi.maine.edu

University of Mary
7500 University Drive
Bismarck, ND 58504
701-255-7500
www.umary.edu

University of Mary Hardin-Baylor
900 College Street
Belton, TX 76513
254-295-8642
www.umhb.edu

University of Maryland at Baltimore
520 West Lombard Street
Baltimore, MD 21201
410-706-3100
www.umaryland.edu

University of Maryland -
Baltimore County
1000 Hilltop Circle
Baltimore, MD 21250
410-455-1000
www.umbc.edu

University of Maryland -
College Park
Route 1, Baltimore Boulevard
College Park, MD 20742
301-405-1000
www.umd.edu

University of Maryland -
Eastern Shore
Backbone Road
Princess Anne, MD 21853
410-651-2200
www.umes.edu

University of Maryland
University College
University Boulevard at Adelphi Road
College Park, MD 20742
301-985-7000
www.umuc.edu

University of Massachusetts
at Amherst
Amherst, MA 01003
413-545-0111
www.umass.edu

University of Massachusetts -
Boston
100 Morrisey Boulevard
Boston, MA 02125
617-287-6800
www.umb.edu

University of Massachusetts -
Dartmouth
285 Old Westport Road
North Dartmouth, MA 02747
508-999-8004
www.umassd.edu

University of Massachusetts -
Lowell
One University Avenue
Lowell, MA 01854
508-934-4000
www.uml.edu

University of Massachusetts
Medical School
55 Lake Avenue, North
Worcester, MA 01605
508-856-8100
www.umassmed.edu

TOP TEN PRIVATE, FOUR-YEAR UNDERGRADUATE COLLEGES AND UNIVERSITIES PRODUCING THE MOST PH.D.'S IN ALL FIELDS OF STUDY, 1920–1990

Reed College

Oberlin College

Wesleyan University

Swarthmore College

Smith College

Barnard College

Carleton College

Wellesley College

Pomona College

Amherst College

(Source: Baccalaureate Origins of Doctorate Recipients, *7th ed., Franklin & Marshall College, March 1993)*

**University of Medicine and
Dentistry of New Jersey**
65 Bergen Street
University Heights
Newark, NJ 07107
973-972-4300
www.umdnj.edushrpweb

The University of Memphis
Memphis, TN 38152
901-678-2000
www.memphis.edu

University of Miami
1252 Memorial Drive
Coral Gables, FL 33124
305-284-2211
www.miami.edu

University of Michigan
Ann Arbor, MI 48109
734-764-1817
www.umich.edu

University of Michigan - Dearborn
4901 Evergreen Road
Dearborn, MI 48128
313-593-5000
www.umd.umich.edu

University of Michigan - Flint
303 East Kearsley
Flint, MI 48502
810-762-3000
www.flint.umich.edu

University of Minnesota - Crookston
2900 University Avenue
Crookston, MN 56716
218-281-6510
www.crk.umn.edu

University of Minnesota - Duluth
10 University Drive
Duluth, MN 55812
218-726-8000
www.d.umn.edu

University of Minnesota - Morris
600 East Fourth Street
Morris, MN 56267
320-589-2211
www.mrs.umn.edu

**University of Minnesota -
Twin Cities**
100 Church Street, SE
Minneapolis, MN 55455
612-626-1616
www.umn.edutc

University of Mississippi
Fraternity Road
University, MS 38677
601-232-7211
www.olemiss.edu

**University of Mississippi
Medical Center**
2500 North State Street
Jackson, MS 39216
601-984-1000
www.umcnews.com

"It's easier to get into Heaven than an Ole Miss sorority." This is a well-known saying in Mississippi, where counselors put rejected young ladies on a suicide watch for as much as a month after rush. Ole Miss is the University of Mississippi in Oxford, Mississippi. Sorority Rush at Ole Miss has been studied by sociologists and anthropologists. Here's a trivia item: The University of Mississippi has the only legal marijuana fields in the country. Here's another: Centre College's student center in Danville, Kentucky, is a refurbished hemp warehouse.

University of Missouri - Columbia
Admissions-230 Jesse Hall
Columbia, MO 65211
573-882-2121
www.missouri.edu

University of Missouri - Kansas City
5100 Rockhill Road
Kansas City, MO 64110
816-235-1000
www.umkc.edu

University of Missouri - Rolla
1870 Miner Circle
Rolla, MO 65401
573-341-4114
www.umr.edu

University of Missouri - Saint Louis
8001 Natural Bridge Road
St. Louis, MO 63121
314-516-5000
www.umsl.edu

University of Mobile
5735 College Parkway
Mobile, AL 36663
334-675-5990
www.umobile.edu

University of Montana - Missoula
Missoula, MT 59812
406-243-2311
www.umt.edu

University of Montevallo
Station 6030
Montevallo, AL 35115
205-665-6000
www.montevallo.edu

University of Nebraska at Kearney
905 West 25th Street
Kearney, NE 68849
308-865-8441
www.unk.edu

University of Nebraska - Lincoln
Fourteenth and R Streets
Lincoln, NE 68588
402-472-7211
www.unl.edu

University of Nebraska
Medical Center
986810 Nebraska Medical Center
Omaha, NE 68198
402-559-4000
www.unmc.edu

University of Nebraska at Omaha
60th and Dodge
Omaha, NE 68182
402-554-2800
www.unomaha.edu

University of Nevada - Las Vegas
4505 Maryland Parkway
Las Vegas, NV 89154
702-895-3311
www.unlv.edu

University of Nevada - Reno
Reno, NV 89557
702-784-1110
www.unr.edu

University of New England
11 Hills Beach Road
Biddeford, ME 04005
207-283-0171
www.une.edu

❝Material objects are of two kinds, atoms and compounds of atoms. The atoms themselves cannot be swamped by any force, for they are preserved indefinitely by their absolute solidity.❞

—Lucretius

The University of Missouri-Rolla, has a half-scale replica Stonehenge, designed and built by students in 1984. The design may be ancient, but Rolla's stones were cut by waterjet technology.

University of New Hampshire
Durham, NH 03824
603-862-1234
www.unh.edu

University of New Haven
300 Orange Avenue
West Haven, CT 06516
203-932-7000
www.newhaven.edu

University of New Mexico
Albuquerque, NM 87131
505-277-0111
www.unm.edu

University of New Orleans
Lakefront
New Orleans, LA 70148
504-280-6000
www.uno.edu

University of North Alabama
Morrison Avenue
Florence, AL 35632
205-765-4100
www.una.edu

The University of North Carolina at Asheville
One University Heights
Asheville, NC 28804
828-251-6600
www.unca.edu

The University of North Carolina at Chapel Hill
Chapel Hill, NC 27599
919-962-2211
www.unc.edu

The University of North Carolina at Charlotte
9201 University City Boulevard
Charlotte, NC 28223
704-547-2000
www.uncc.edu

The University of North Carolina at Greensboro
1000 Spring Garden Street
Greensboro, NC 27402
336-334-5000
www.uncg.edu

The University of North Carolina of Pembroke
One University Drive
Pembroke, NC 28372
910-521-6000
www.uncp.edu

The University of North Carolina at Wilmington
601 South College Road
Wilmington, NC 28403
910-962-3000
www.uncwil.edu

University of North Dakota
University Avenue
Grand Forks, ND 58202
701-777-2011
www.und.edu

University of North Florida
4567 St. Johns Bluff Road South
Jacksonville, FL 32224
904-620-1000
www.unf.edu

> **We ought to live as though we'll die this night, and learn as though we were going to live forever.**
>
> —*Unknown*

The second largest college in North America is the University of Phoenix, with 55,000 students in ninety-six campuses nationwide. The Community College of the Air Force has even more, with 370,500 studying at locations around the world.

University of North Texas
1401 West Prairie
Denton, TX 76203
940-565-2000
www.unt.edu

University of Northern Colorado
501 20th Street
Greeley, CO 80639
970-351-1890
www.unco.edu

University of Northern Iowa
1222 West 27th Street
Cedar Falls, IA 50614
319-273-2311
www.uni.edu

University of Notre Dame
Notre Dame, IN 46556
219-631-5026
www.nd.edu

University of Oklahoma
660 Parrington Oval
Norman, OK 73019
405-325-0311
www.ou.edu

**University of Oklahoma Health
Sciences Center**
S. L. Young Boulevard
Oklahoma City, OK 73126
405-271-4000
www.uokhsc.edu

University of Oregon
Agate and 13th Streets
Eugene, OR 97403
541-346-3111
www.uoregon.edu

**University of Osteopathic Medicine
and Health Sciences**
3200 Grand Avenue
Des Moines, IA 50312
515-271-1400
www.uomhs.edu

University of the Ozarks
415 North College Avenue
Clarksville, AR 72830
501-979-1000
www.ozarks.edu

University of the Pacific
3601 Pacific Avenue
Stockton, CA 95211
209-946-2011
www.uop.edu

University of Pennsylvania
34th and Spruce Streets
Philadelphia, PA 19104
215-898-5000
www.upenn.edu

University of Phoenix
4615 East Elwood Street
Phoenix, AZ 85040
602-966-9577
www.uophx.edu

University of Pittsburgh
4200 Fifth Avenue
Pittsburgh, PA 15260
412-624-4200
www.pitt.edu

The University of Pittsburgh at Bradford has a stocked trout spring running through the campus called Tunungwant Creek. Students and faculty are often found fly fishing between classes. Catch and release, of course.

University of Portland
5000 North Willamette Boulevard
Portland, OR 97203
503-943-7911
www.up.edu

**University of Puerto Rico -
Aguadilla Regional College**
Calle Belt
Aguadilla, PR 00604
787-890-2681
www.upr.edu

**University of Puerto Rico - Arecibo
Technological University College**
Carretera Núm. 953
Km. 0.8
Arecibo, PR 00613
787-878-2830
www.upr.edu

**University of Puerto Rico -
Bayamon University College**
#170 Carretera 174
Minillas Industrial Park
Bayamon, PR 00959
787-786-2885
wwwcutb.upr.clu.edu

**University of Puerto Rico -
Carolina Regional College**
Carretera Núm. 887
Carolina, PR 00984
787-257-0000
www.upr.edu

**University of Puerto Rico -
Cayey University College**
Avenida Antonio R. Barceló
Cayey, Puerto Rico 00736
787-738-2161
www.cuc.upr.clu.edu

**University of Puerto Rico -
Humacao University College**
Bo. Tejas
Humacao, PR 00791
787-850-0000
www.upr.clu.edu

**University of Puerto Rico -
La Montaña Regional College**
Carretera Núm. 10
Km. 52.2
Utuado, PR 00641
787-894-2828
www.upr.edu

**University of Puerto Rico -
Mayagüez Campus**
Carretera Núm. 2
Calle Post
Mayagüez, Puerto Rico
Mailing address: c/o P.O. Box 5000
Mayagüez, Puerto Rico 00681
787-832-4040
w3rum.upr.clu.edu

**University of Puerto Rico -
Medical Sciences Campus**
Centro Médico
Río Piedras, Puerto Rico
Mailing address: c/o P.O. Box 365067
San Juan, PR 00936
787-758-2525
www.rcm.upr.edu

**University of Puerto Rico - Ponce
Technological University College**
Avenida Santiago de los Caballeros
Esquina By-Pass
Ponce, PR 00732
787-844-8181
www.upr.clu.edu

University of Puerto Rico - Río Piedras Campus
Avenida Ponce de León
Parada 38
Río Piedras, PR
Mailing address: c/o P.O. Box 23300
San Juan, PR 00931
787-764-0000
www.upracd.upr.clu.edu:9090

University of Puget Sound
1500 North Warner
Tacoma, WA 98416
206-756-3100
www.ups.edu

University of Redlands
1200 East Colton Avenue
Redlands, CA 92373
909-793-2121
www.redlands.edu

University of Rhode Island
75 Lower College Road
Kingston, RI 02881
401-874-2444
www.uri.edu

University of Richmond
28 Westhampton Way
Richmond, VA 23173
804-289-8000
www.richmond.edu

University of Rio Grande
Rio Grande, OH 45674
614-245-5353
www.urgrgcc.edu

University of Rochester
Rochester, NY 14627
716-275-2121
www.rochester.edu

University of the Sacred Heart
Rosales esquina San Antonio
Pda. 26 1/2
San Juan, PR 00911
787-728-1515
www.sagrado.edu

University of Saint Francis
500 North Wilcox Street
Joliet, IL 60435
815-740-3360
www.stfrancis.edu

University of Saint Francis
2701 Spring Street
Fort Wayne, IN 46808
800-729-4732 or 219-458-2451
www.sfc.edu

University of Saint Thomas
2115 Summit Avenue
St. Paul, MN 55105
612-962-5000
www.stthomas.edu

University of San Diego
5998 Alcala Park
San Diego, CA 92110
858-260-4600
www.acusd.edu

University of San Francisco
2130 Fulton Street
San Francisco, CA 94117
415-422-6136
www.usfca.edu

University of Science and Arts of Oklahoma
Seventeenth Street and Grand Avenue
Chickasha, OK 73018
405-224-3140
www.usao.edu

> **There is nothing so ridiculous but some philosopher has said it.**
>
> —*Cicero*

**University of the Sciences
in Philadelphia**
600 South 43rd Street
Philadelphia, PA 19104
215-596-8800
www.usip.edu

University of Scranton
Linden and Monroe Avenues
Scranton, PA 18510
570-941-7400
www.uofs.edu

University of Sioux Falls
1101 West 22nd Street
Sioux Falls, SD 57105
605-331-5000
www.thecoo.edu

University of the South (Sewanee)
735 University Avenue
Sewanee, TN 37383
800-522-2234 or 931-598-1000
www.sewanee.edu

University of South Alabama
307 University Boulevard
Mobile, AL 36688
334-460-6101
www.usouthal.edu

University of South Carolina
Columbia, SC 29208
803-777-7000
www.sc.edu

University of South Carolina - Aiken
471 University Parkway
Aiken, SC 29801
803-648-6851
www.usca.sc.edu

**University of South Carolina -
Spartanburg**
800 University Way
Spartanburg, SC 29303
864-503-5000
www.uscs.edu

University of South Dakota
414 East Clark Street
Vermillion, SD 57069
605-677-5011
www.usd.edu

University of South Florida
4202 East Fowler Avenue
Tampa, FL 33620
813-974-2154
www.usf.edu

University of Southern California
University Park Campus
Los Angeles, CA 90089
213-740-2311
www.usc.edu

University of Southern Colorado
2200 Bonforte Boulevard
Pueblo, CO 81001
719-549-2100
www.uscolo.edu

University of Southern Indiana
8600 University Boulevard
Evansville, IN 47712
812-464-8600
www.usi.edu

University of Southern Maine
96 Falmouth Street
Portland, ME 04104
207-780-4480
www.usm.maine.edu

**The University
of Southern Mississippi**
East Memorial Drive
Hattiesburg, MS 39406
601-266-4111
www.usm.edu

**"Education
is the best
provision for
old age."**

—Aristotle

University of Southwestern Louisiana
104 University Circle
Lafayette, LA 70504
318-482-1000
www.usl.edu

University of St. Thomas
3800 Montrose Boulevard
Houston, TX 77006
713-522-7911
www.stthom.edu

University of Tampa
401 West Kennedy Boulevard
Tampa, FL 33606
813-253-3333
www.utampa.edu

The University of Tennessee at Chattanooga
615 McCallie Avenue
Chattanooga, TN 37403
423-744-4111
www.utc.edu

The University of Tennessee at Knoxville
527 Andy Holt Tower
Knoxville, TN 37996
423-974-1000
www.utk.edu

The University of Tennessee at Martin
Martin, TN 38238
901-587-7000
www.utm.edu

The University of Tennessee at Memphis
800 Madison Avenue
Memphis, TN 38163
901-448-5500
www.utmem.edu

The University of Texas at Arlington
701 South Nedderman
Arlington, TX 76019
817-272-2011
www.uta.edu

The University of Texas at Austin
One South Mall
Austin, TX 78712
512-471-3434
www.utexas.edu

The University of Texas at Brownsville - Texas Southmost College
80 Fort Brown
Brownsville, TX 78520
956-544-8200
www.utb.edu

The Library at the University of Tennessee, Knoxville, has on exhibit a centaur skeleton from the centaur excavations at Volos. The exhibit shows the skeleton of a centaur along with a map of Greece, ceramics, and clay tablets, which are described as "the most extensive collection of centaurian literature in a library in the Eastern United States." Aubrey Mitchell, Associate Dean of Libraries, says, "This unique exhibit enables all visitors to Hodges Library an opportunity to link the distant past with the fast-changing present and to form opinions on how to better interpret the future. The library is pleased to have the exhibit." I have seen this with my own eyes, and if you get within a day's drive of Knoxville, this is very much worth the trip.

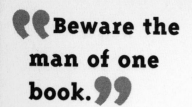

Beware the man of one book.

—Roman saying

The University of Texas at Dallas
2601 North Floyd Road
Richardson, TX 75083
972-883-2111
www.ut.dallas.edu

The University of Texas at El Paso
500 West University Avenue
El Paso, TX 79968
915-747-5000
www.utep.edu

The University of Texas Health Science Center at San Antonio
7703 Floyd Curl Drive
San Antonio, TX 78284
210 567-2000
www.uthscsa.edu

The University of Texas Houston Health Science Center
7000 Fannin Street
Houston, TX 77225
713-500-3333
www.uthouston.edu

The University of Texas Medical Branch at Galveston
300 University Boulevard
Galveston, TX 77555
409-772-1215
www.utmb.edu

The University of Texas - Pan American
1201 West University Drive
Edinburg, TX 78539
956-381-2011
www.panam.edu

The University of Texas of the Permian Basin
4901 East University Boulevard
Odessa, TX 79762
915-542-2020
www.utpb.edu

The University of Texas at San Antonio
6900 North Loop 1604 West
San Antonio, TX 78249
210-458-4011
ww.utsa.edu

The University of Texas Southwestern Medical Center at Dallas
5323 Harry Hines Boulevard
Dallas, TX 75235
214-648-3111
www.swmed.edu

The University of Texas at Tyler
3900 University Boulevard
Tyler, TX 75799
903-566-7000
www.uttyl.edu

University of Toledo
2801 West Bancroft Street
Toledo, OH 43606
419-530-2211
www.utoledo.edu

University of Tulsa
600 South College Avenue
Tulsa, OK 74104
918-631-2000
www.utulsa.edu

A study of binge drinking on Greek Row at the University of Washington came up with a surprise finding: Male "Greeks" were just as likely as female "Greeks" to have been "coerced" into unwanted sexual activity, and were more likely to have emotional trauma from the event. The study was conducted by the University of Washington Addictive Behaviors Research Center, and the results were published in *Sex Roles,* a quarterly academic journal.

University of Utah
110 Park
Salt Lake City, UT 84112
801-581-7200
www.utah.edu

University of Vermont
85 South Prospect Street
Burlington, VT 05405
802-656-3186
www.uvm.edu

University of the Virgin Islands
No. 2 John Brewers Bay
St. Thomas, VI 00802
340-776-9200
www.uvi.edu

University of Virginia
P.O. Box 400160
Charlottesville, VA 22904-4160
804-924-0311
www.virginia.edu

The University of Virginia's College at Wise
1 College Avenue
Wise, VA 24293
800-468-3412 or 540-328-0102
www.clinch.edu

University of Washington
Seattle, WA 98195
206-543-2100
www.washington.edu

The University of West Alabama
205 North Washington Street
Livingston, AL 35470
205-652-3400
www.westal.edu

The University of West Florida
11000 University Parkway
Pensacola, FL 32514
850-474-2000
www.uwf.edu

The University of West Los Angeles
1155 West Arbor Vitae Street
Inglewood, CA 90301
210-342-5225
www.uwla.edu

University of Wisconsin - Eau Claire
105 Garfield Avenue
Eau Claire, WI 54701
715-836-2637
www.uwec.edu

University of Wisconsin - Green Bay
2420 Nicolet Drive
Green Bay, WI 54311
920-465-2000
www.uwgb.edu

University of Wisconsin - La Crosse
1725 State Street
La Crosse, WI 54601
608-785-8000
perth.uwlax.edu

> ❝ Ah God! Had I but studied
> In the days of my foolish youth! ❞
>
> —*François Villon*

The University of Wisconsin, Madison, is the only campus in the nation with two daily student newspapers, *The Daily Cardinal*, launched in 1892, and the *Badger Herald*, a rightward-leaning paper launched in 1969 in reaction to the supposedly too leftward-leaning *Cardinal*. Thousands of left-wing student newspapers were launched in the sixties, but the *Badger Herald* was years ahead of the post-sixties resurgence of conservatism in America.

> **" Till women are more rationally educated, the progress in human virtue and improvement in knowledge must receive continual checks. "**
>
> —*Mary Wollstonecraft Shelley*

University of Wisconsin - Madison
500 Lincoln Drive
Madison, WI 53706
608-262-1234
www.wisc.edu

University of Wisconsin - Milwaukee
Downer Avenue and Kenwood Boulevard
Milwaukee, WI 53201
414-229-4331
www.uwm.edu

University of Wisconsin - Oshkosh
800 Algoma Boulevard
Oshkosh, WI 54901
920-424-1234
www.uwosh.edu

University of Wisconsin - Parkside
900 Wood Road
Kenosha, WI 53141
414-595-2345
www.uwp.edu

University of Wisconsin - Platteville
1 University Plaza
Platteville, WI 53818
608-348-1234
www.uwplatt.edu

University of Wisconsin - River Falls
410 South Third Street
River Falls, WI 54022
715-425-3201
www.uwrf.edu

University of Wisconsin - Stevens Point
2100 Main Street
Stevens Point, WI 54481
715-346-0123
www.uwsp.edu

University of Wisconsin - Stout
712 South Broadway
Menomonie, WI 54751
715-232-1431
www.uwstout.edu

University of Wisconsin - Superior
1800 Grand Avenue
Superior, WI 54880
715-394-8101
www.uwsuper.edu

University of Wisconsin - Whitewater
800 West Main Street
Whitewater, WI 53190
414-472-1918
www.uww.edu

University of Wyoming
Laramie, WY 82071
307-766-4121
www.uwyo.edu

Upper Iowa University
605 Washington Street
Fayette, IA 52142
319-425-5200
www.uiu.edu

Urbana University
579 College Way
Urbana, OH 43078
937-484-1301
www.urbana.edu

Ursinus College
P.O. Box 1000
Collegeville, PA 19426-1000
610-489-4111
www.ursinus.edu

Ursuline College
2550 Lander Road
Pepper Pike, OH 44124
440-449-4200
www.en.com/ursweb

Utah State University
Logan, UT 84322
735-797-1000
www.usu.edu

Utah Valley State College
800 West 1200 South
Orem, UT 84058
801-222-8000
www.uvsc.edu

Utica College of Syracuse University
1600 Burrstone Road
Utica, NY 13502
315-792-3111
www.ucsu.edu

V

Valdosta State University
1500 North Patterson Street
Valdosta, GA 31698
912-333-5952
www.valdosta.edu

Valley Forge Christian College
1401Charlestown Road
Phoenixville, PA 19460
610-935-0450
www.vfcc.edu

Valley City State University
101 College Street, SW
Valley City, ND 58072
800-532-8641 or 701-845-7122
www.vcsu.nodak.edu

Valparaiso University
Valparaiso, IN 46383
219-464-5000
www.valpo.edu

Vanderbilt University
2201 West End Avenue
Nashville, TN 37240
615-322-7311
www.vanderbilt.edu

Interested in big storms? Valparaiso University of Valparaiso, Indiana, has a storm chase program within its meteorology curriculum. Faculty and students chase storms full-time during the height of tornado season, ranging across the Plains states in scenes reminiscent of the 1990s movie *Twister.*

VanderCook College of Music
3140 South Federal Street
Chicago, IL 60616
800-448-2655 or 312-225-6288
www.mcs.net/~vcmusic

Vanguard University
55 Fair Drive
Costa Mesa, CA 92626
714-556-3610
www.vanguard.edu

Vassar College
124 Raymond Avenue
Poughkeepsie, NY 12604
914-437-7000
www.vassar.edu

Vennard College
P.O. Box 29
University Park, IA 52595
515-673-8391
www.vennard.edu

Vermont Technical College
Main Street
Randolph Center, VT 05061
802-728-1252
www.vtc.vsc.edu

Villa Julie College
1525 Green Spring Valley Road
Stevenson, MD 21153
410-486-7000
www.vjc.edu

Villanova University
800 Lancaster Avenue
Villanova, PA 19085
610-519-5000
www.villanova.edu

Virginia Commonwealth University
901 West Franklin Street
Richmond, VA 23284
804-828-0100
www.vcu.edu

Virginia Intermont College
1013 Moore Street
Bristol, VA 24201
540-669-6101
www.vic.edu

Virginia Military Institute
Lexington, VA 24450
540-464-7000
www.vmi.edu

**Virginia Polytechnic Institute
and State University**
Blacksburg, VA 24061
540-231-6000
www.vt.edu

CoOl BoOk AlErT!

Bears' Guide to Earning Degrees by Distance Learning by John Bear and Mariah Bear (Ten Speed Press, 1999)

This is a classic resource for anyone who wants to earn a college degree over the Internet, through evening and weekend classes, by passing exams, or through any of a number of other nontraditional methods. The book is revised often, so the information is always up-to-date and relevant. The fourteenth edition contains more than 2,000 schools and hundreds of online programs.

Virginia State University
1 Hayden Drive
Petersburg, VA 23806
804-524-5000
www.vsu.edu

Virginia Union University
1500 North Lombardy Street
Richmond, VA 23220
804-257-5855
www.vuu.edu

Virginia Wesleyan College
1584 Wesleyan Drive
Norfolk, VA 23502
757-455-3200
www.vwc.edu

Viterbo College
815 South Ninth Street
La Crosse, WI 54601
608-796-3000
www.viterbo.edu

Voorhees College
1411 Voorhees Road
Denmark, SC 29042
800-446-3351 or 803-793-3351
www.voorhees.edu

W

Wabash College
301 West Wabash Avenue
Crawfordsville, IN 47933-0352
765-361-6100
www.wabash.edu

Wadhams Hall Seminary-College
6866 State Highway 37
Ogdensburg, NY 13669
315-393-4231
www.wadhams.edu

Wagner College
Howard Avenue and Campus Road
Staten Island, NY 10301
718-390-3100
www.wagner.edu

Wake Forest University
1834 Wake Forest Road
Winston-Salem, NC 27106
336-759-5000
www.wfu.edu

Waldorf College
106 South Sixth Street
Forest City, IA 50436
515-582-2450
www.waldorf.edu

Walla Walla College
204 South College Avenue
College Place, WA 99324
509-527-2327
www.wwc.edu

**Walsh College of Accountancy
& Business Administration**
3838 Livernois Road
Troy, MI 48007
248-689-8282
www.walshcol.edu

Walsh University
2020 Easton Street, NW
North Canton, OH 44720
800-362-9846 or 330-499-7090
www.walsh.edu

Warner Pacific College
2219 S.E. 68th Avenue
Portland, OR 97215
503-775-4366
www.warnerpacific.edu

Warner Southern College
5301 U.S. Highway 27, South
Lake Wales, FL 33853
941-638-1426
www.warner.edu

Warren Wilson College
701 Warren Wilson Road
Asheville, NC 28815
704-298-3325
www.warren-wilson.edu

Wartburg College
222 Ninth Street, NW
Waverly, IA 50677
319-352-8200
www.wartburg.edu

Washburn University of Topeka
Seventeenth and College Streets
Topeka, KS 66621
785-231-1010
www.washburn.edu

Washington Bible College
6511 Princess Garden Parkway
Lanham, MD 20706
301-552-1400
www.bible.edu

Washington College
300 Washington Avenue
Chestertown, MD 21620
800-422-1782 or 410-778-2800
www.washcoll.edu

Washington and Jefferson College
60 South Lincoln Street
Washington, PA 15301
724-222-4400
www.washjeff.edu

Washington and Lee University
Lexington, VA 24450
540-463-8400
www.wlu.edu

Washington State University
Pullman, WA 99164
509-335-3564
www.wsu.edu

Washington University
One Brookings Drive
St. Louis, MO 63130
314-935-5000
www.wustl.edu

Wayland Baptist University
1900 West Seventh Street
Plainview, TX 79072
806-296-5521
www.wbu.edu

Wayne State College
1111 Main Street
Wayne, NE 68787
402-375-7000
www.wsc.edu

Wayne State University
656 West Kirby
Detroit, MI 48202
313-577-2424
www.wayne.edu

The vice president of academic affairs at Warren Wilson College, Virginia McKinley, Ph.D., writes a letter to all prospective freshmen, containing this advice:

"You are not expected to choose a major right away. In fact, I believe there is value in waiting for a while before you decide on a major. I encourage you to use your first two years in college to explore your interests and talents by taking a wide range of liberal arts area courses. That kind of exploration will help you find the area that is just right for you. Until you choose a major, you will have an academic advisor assigned to you who will help you make course selections and will provide general direction to your academic planning."

Waynesburg College
51 West College Street
Waynesburg, PA 15370
412-627-8191
www.waynesburg.edu

Webb Institute
Crescent Beach Road
Glen Cove, NY 11542
516-671-2213
www.webb-institute.edu

Webber College
Route 17
Babson Park, FL 33827
941-638-1431
www.webber.edu

Weber State University
3750 Harrison Boulevard
Ogden, UT 84408
801-626-6006
www.weber.edu

Webster University
470 East Lockwood Avenue
St. Louis, MO 63119
314-968-6900
www.webster.edu

Wellesley College
106 Central Street
Wellesley, MA 02481
781-283-1000
www.wellesley.edu

Wells College
Aurora, NY 13026
800-952-9355 or 315-364-3265
www.wells.edu

Wentworth Institute of Technology
550 Huntington Avenue
Boston, MA 02115
617-442-9010
www.wit.edu

Wesley College
120 North State Street
Dover, DE 19901
302-736-2300
www.wesley.edu

Wesley College
111 Wesley Circle
Florence, MS 39073
601-845-2265

Wesleyan College for Women
4760 Forsyth Road
Macon, GA 31210-4462
912-477-1110
www.wesleyan-college.edu

Wesleyan University
Church and High Streets
Middletown, CT 06457
860-685-2000
www.wesleyan.edu

**West Chester University
of Pennsylvania**
South High Street
West Chester, PA 19383
610-436-1000
www.wcupa.edu

West Liberty State College
P.O. Box 295
West Liberty, WV 26074
304-336-5000
www.wlsc.wvnet.edu

West Suburban College of Nursing
3 Erie Court
Oak Park, IL 60302
708-763-6530

West Texas A & M University
Fourth Avenue and 23rd Street
Canyon, TX 79016
806-656-2000
www.wtamu.edu

> **❝ Is to know the good to do the good?❞**
>
> —*Socrates*

> **These lands are ours. No one has a right to remove us, because we were the first owners. The Great Spirit above has appointed this place for us, on which to light our fires, and here we will remain. As to boundaries, the Great Spirit knows no boundaries, nor will his red children acknowledge any.**
>
> *—Tecumseh*

West Virginia State College
P.O. Box 1000
Institute, WV 25112
304-766-3000
www.wvsc.edu

West Virginia University
University Avenue
Morgantown, WV 26506
304-293-0111
www.wvu.edu

West Virginia University Institute of Technology
405 Fayette Pike
Montgomery, WV 25136
304-442-3071
wvit.wvnet.edu

West Virginia University at Parkersburg
300 Campus Drive
Parkersburg, WV 26101
304-424-8000
www.wvup.wvnet.edu

West Virginia Wesleyan College
59 College Avenue
Buckhannon, WV 26201
304-473-8000
www.wvwc.edu

Westbrook College of the University of New England
716 Stevens Avenue
Portland, ME 04103
207-797-7261
www.une.eduwc/history.html

Western Baptist College
5000 Deer Park Drive, SE
Salem, OR 97301
503-581-8600
www.wbc.edu

Western Carolina University
Cullowhee, NC 28723
704-227-7211
www.wcu.edu

Western Connecticut State University
181 White Street
Danbury, CT 06810
203-837-8200
www.wcsu.edu

Western Illinois University
One University Circle
Macomb, IL 61455
309-295-1414
www.wiu.edu

Western International University
9215 North Black Canyon Highway
Phoenix, AZ 85021
602-943-2311
www.wintu.edu

Western Kentucky University
One Big Red Way
Bowling Green, KY 42101
502-745-0111
www.wku.edu

Western Maryland College
Two College Hill
Westminster, MD 21157
410-848-7000
www.wmdc.edu

Western Michigan University
1201 Oliver Street
Kalamazoo, MI 49008
616-387-3530
www.wmich.edu

Western Montana College of The University of Montana
710 South Atlantic Street
Dillon, MT 59725
406-683-7151
www.wmc.edu

Western New England College
1215 Wilbraham Road
Springfield, MA 01119
413-782-3111
www.wnec.edu

Western New Mexico University
1000 West College Avenue
Silver City, NM 88062
800-222-9668 or 505-538-6238
www.wnmu.edu

Western Oregon University
345 North Monmouth Avenue
Monmouth, OR 97361
503-838-8000
www.wou.edu

Western State College of Colorado
Gunnison, CO 81231
800-876-5309 or 970-943-2114
www.western.edu

**Western State University College
of Law - Orange County**
1111 North State College Boulevard
Fullerton, CA 92831
714-738-1000
www.wsulaw.edu

**Western States Chiropractic
College**
2900 N.E. 132nd Avenue
Portland, OR 97230
503-256-3180
www.wschiro.edu

**Western University
of Health Sciences**
309 East Second Street
College Plaza
Pomona, CA 91766
909-623-6116
www.westernu.edu

Western Washington University
516 High Street
Bellingham, WA 98225
360-650-3350
www.wwu.edu

Westfield State College
577 Western Avenue
Westfield, MA 01086
413-568-3311
www.wsc.mass.edu

Westminster College
501 Westminster Avenue
Fulton, MO 65251
573-642-3361
www.westminster-mo.edu

Westminster College
319 South Market Street
New Wilmington, PA 16172
412-946-8761
www.westminster.edu

**Westminster College of
Salt Lake City**
1840 South 1300 East
Salt Lake City, UT 84105
801-484-7651
www.wcslc.edu

Westmont College
955 La Paz Road
Santa Barbara, CA 93108
805-565-6000
www.westmont.edu

Westwood College of Technology
7350 North Broadway
Denver, CO 80221
303-426-7000
www.westwood.edu

Wheaton College
501 East College Avenue
Wheaton, IL 60187
630-752-5000
www.wheaton.edu

Wheaton College
Norton, MA 02766
800-394-6003 or 508-285-7722
www.wheatonma.edu

Wheeling Jesuit University
316 Washington Avenue
Wheeling, WV 26003
304-243-2000
www.wju.edu

Wheelock College
200 The Riverway
Boston, MA 02215
617-734-5200
www.wheelock.edu

Whitman College
345 Boyer Avenue
Walla Walla, WA 99362
509-527-5111
www.whitman.edu

Whittier College
13406 East Philadelphia Street
Whittier, CA 90608
562-907-4200
www.whittier.edu

Whitworth College
300 West Hawthorne Road
Spokane, WA 99251
509-777-1000
www.whitworth.edu

Wichita State University
1845 Fairmont Street
Wichita, KS 67260
800-362-2594 or 316-978-3456
www.wichita.edu

Widener University
One University Place
Chester, PA 19013
610-499-4000
www.widener.edu

Wilberforce University
1055 North Bickett Road
Wilberforce, OH 45384
937-376-2911
www.wilberforce.edu

Wiley College
711 Wiley Avenue
Marshall, TX 75670
903-927-3235
www.wiley.edu

“I want to
seize fate by
the throat!”

—Beethoven

MADRIGAL DINNER AND DANCE

Each November, students at Juniata College in Huntington, Pennsylvania, camp out for more than a week to get preferential seating at the Madrigal Dinner and Dance, the only formal dance of the year. About half the student body attends, with preferred seating going out on a first-come, first-served basis. Students revel in making their wait as comfortable and elaborate as possible, erecting large tents and homemade wooden shelters, and bringing televisions, computers, and portable heaters with them. For twenty-five years the faculty and staff have shown their appreciation for the students by serving as the wait staff for this event. They have a similar dinner and dance at Reed College, complete with a boar's head and a medieval procession.

Wilkes University
170 South Franklin Street
Wilkes-Barre, PA 18766
717-408-5000
www.wilkes.edu

Willamette University
900 State Street
Salem, OR 97301
503-370-6300
www.willamette.edu

William Carey College
498 Tuscan Avenue
Hattiesburg, MS 39401
601-582-5051
www.wmcarey.edu

William Jewell College
500 College Hill
Liberty, MO 64068
816-781-7700
www.jewell.edu

**William Paterson University
of New Jersey**
300 Pompton Road
Wayne, NJ 07470
973-595-2000
www.wpunj.edu

William Penn College
201 Trueblood Avenue
Oskaloosa, IA 52577
515-673-1001
www.wmpenn.edu

William Tyndale College
35700 West Twelve Mile Road
Farmington Hills, MI 48331
248-553-7200
www.williamtyndale.edu

William Woods University
200 West 12th Street
Fulton, MO 65251
573-642-2251
www.williamwoods.edu

Williams Baptist College
201 Fulbright Avenue
Walnut Ridge, AR 72476
870-886-6741
www.wbcoll.edu

Williams College
Williamstown, MA 01267
413-597-3131
www.williams.edu

Wilmington College
320 Dupont Highway
New Castle, DE 19720
302-328-9401
www.wilmcoll.edu

Wilmington College
Wilmington, OH 45177
937-382-6661
www.wilmington.edu

Rutgers beat Princeton 6-4 in the first-ever intercollegiate football game on November 6, 1869. If you're really into sports trivia, here's another piece: The first forward pass was thrown at Ripon College, Ripon, Wisconsin, when Izzy Smith passed to left end Orin P. Ramsey in 1906. The huddle was also invented at Ripon, by weak-voiced quarterback Casey Finnegan, who was unable to call the play loud enough for the offensive side to hear from their positions. In 1997, Liz Heaston of Willamette University, Salem, Oregon, became the first female ever to play and score in an intercollegiate college football game, playing as a kicker on special teams; her uniform and shoes are in the College Football Hall of Fame in South Bend, Indiana.

Wilson College
1015 Philadelphia Avenue
Chambersburg, PA 17201
717-264-4141
www.wilson.edu

Wingate University
Campus Box 3059
Wingate, NC 28174
704-233-8000
www.wingate.edu

Winona State University
Sanborn and Main Streets
Winona, MN 55987
800-342-5978 or 507-457-5000
www.winona.msus.edu

Winona State University - Rochester Center
Highway 14, East
859 30th Avenue, SE
Rochester, MN 55904
507-285-7100
www.roch.edu

Winston-Salem State University
601 Martin Luther King, Jr. Drive
Winston-Salem, NC 27110
336-750-2000
www.wssu.edu

Winthrop University
701 Oakland Avenue
Rock Hill, SC 29733
803-323-2211
www.winthrop.edu

Wisconsin Lutheran College
8800 West Bluemound Road
Milwaukee, WI 53226
414-443-8800
www.wlc.edu

Wittenberg University
P.O. Box 720
Springfield, OH 45501
937-327-6231
www.wittenberg.edu

Wofford College
429 North Church Street
Spartanburg, SC 29303
864-597-4000
www.wofford.edu

Woodbury College
660 Elm Street
Montpelier, VT 05602
802-229-0516
www.woodbury-college.edu

Woodbury University
7500 Glen Oaks Boulevard
Burbank, CA 91510
818-767-0888
www.woodburyu.edu

Worcester Polytechnic Institute
100 Institute Road
Worcester, MA 01609
508-831-5000
www.wpi.edu

Worcester State College
486 Chandler Street
Worcester, MA 01602
508-793-8000
www.worc.mass.edu

World College
Lake Shores Plaza
5193 Shore Drive, Suite 105
Virginia Beach, VA 23455
757-464-4600
www.cie-wc.edu

Wright State University
3640 Colonel Glenn Highway
Dayton, OH 45435
937-775-3333
www.wright.edu

X

Xavier University
3800 Victor Parkway
Cincinnati, OH 45207
513-745-3000
www.xu.edu

Xavier University
7325 Palmetto Street
New Orleans, LA 70125
504-483-7411
www.xula.edu

Y

Yale University
New Haven, CT 06520
203-432-9300
www.yale.edu

Yeshiva Beth Yehuda - Yeshiva Gedolah of Greater Detroit
24600 Greenfield Street
Oak Park, MI 48237
810-968-3360

Yeshiva Ohr Elchonon-Chabad/West Coast Talmudic Seminary
7215 Waring Avenue
Los Angeles, CA 90046
213-937-3763

Yeshiva Toras Chaim Talmudic Seminary
1555 Stuart Street
Denver, CO 80204
303-629-8200
ourworld.compuserve.com/home-pages/adar_corp/yeshivat.htm

Yeshiva University
500 West 185th Street
New York, NY 10033
212-960-5400
www.yu.edu

York College
1125 East Eighth Street
York, NE 68467
402-363-5627
www.york.edu

> **An invasion of armies can be resisted, but not an idea whose time has come.**
>
> *—Victor Hugo*

CoOl BoOk AlErT!

Major in Success: Make College Easier, Fire Up Your Dreams, and Get a Very Cool Job
by Patrick Combs (Ten Speed Press, 2000)

This is a book that actually answers the important questions about being a successful student. How do you figure out what career you'd truly love? How do you pick the best major for you? How do you get and stay motivated? What are some short-cuts to success? How do you get past the fears that hold you back? What will give you a competitive edge? With so much at stake during your college years—career, success, happiness, your future—you need this smart, savvy, and inspiring book to ensure you excel. The author, Patrick Combs, put himself through college by managing a rock band, then went on to land a great job with Levi Strauss & Company. Now he works as a professional speaker, award-winning Webmaster, and author. The revised and updated third edition of this book was just released and it's even better than before. Check it out!

York College - City University of New York
94-20 Guy R. Brewer Boulevard
Jamaica, NY 11451
718-262-2000
www.york.cuny.edu

York College of Pennsylvania
Country Club Road
York, PA 17405
717-846-7788
www.ycp.edu

Youngstown State University
One University Plaza
Youngstown, OH 44555
330-742-3000
www.ysu.edu

❝ Life can only be understood backwards; but it must be lived forwards. ❞

—*Kierkegaard*

Canadian universities are quite reasonable in cost for the quality of the education available. Canada publishes a guide for foreign students, "Destination Canada: Information for International Students," available from:

Canadian Bureau for International Education/
Bureau canadien de l'éducation internationale
220 Laurier Avenue West, Suite 1100
Ottawa, ON K1P 5Z9
Canada
613-237-4820
info@cbie.ca
www.cbie.ca

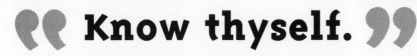

"Know thyself."
—Inscription at the Oracle at Delphi

The following is a directory of three- and four-year, degree-granting, recognized undergraduate educational institutions in Canada. It does not include distance-learning—only or purely theological institutions.

In the Canadian college/university system, a "college" is generally an institution that does not grant a degree, but provides professional diplomas. Most often it is the university that grants the undergraduate degree. However, many Canadian universities have affiliated colleges that reside somewhere nearby or on campus. Students can choose to attend these colleges with the ability to take classes at both their college and the affiliated university that will count toward a degree. Many of these colleges have specialties not offered at the university or other affiliated colleges. Sometimes these colleges will have the power to grant a degree, but most often they are granted by the affiliated university and signed by the chancellor of the college. I have included the recognized affiliated colleges at which a student can attend and achieve a degree.

A

Acadia University
Wolfville, NS B0P 1X0
Canada
902-585-1222
www.acadiau.ca

Alberta College of Art and Design
1407 14th Avenue NW
Calgary, AB T2N 4R3
Canada
403-284-7600
www.acad.ab.ca

Algoma University College
(affiliated with Laurentian University)
1520 Queen Street East
Sault Ste. Marie, ON P6A 2G4
Canada
705-949-2301
www.auc.on.ca

Athabasca University
One University Drive
Athabasca, AB T9S 3A3
Canada
780-675-6111
www.athabascau.ca

Atlantic School of Theology
640 Francklyn Street
Halifax, NS B3H 3B5
Canada
902-423-6939
www.astheology.ns.ca

Augustana University College
4901 46th Avenue
Camrose, AB T4V 2R3
Canada
800-661-8714 or 780-679-1100
www.augustana.ab.ca

B

Bishop's University
Lennoxville, QC J1M 1Z7
Canada
819-822-9600
www.ubishops.ca

Brandon University
270 18th Street
Brandon, MB R7A 6A9
Canada
204-728-9520
www.brandonu.ca

Brescia College at The University of Western Ontario
(women's college)
1285 Western Road
London, ON N6G 1H2
Canada
519-432-8353
www.uwo.ca/brescia

British Columbia Institute of Technology
3700 Willingdon Avenue
Burnaby, BC V5G 3H2
Canada
604-432-8419
www.bcit.bc.ca

Dropout rates have been increasing slightly for over a decade. Roughly one quarter of students do not return for the sophomore year. Many of them do return later, but that's still an amazing failure rate. One-fourth of students are so dissatisfied with their initial college experience that they opt out at the first opportunity.

Brock University
500 Glenridge Avenue
St. Catharines, ON L2S 3A1
Canada
905-688-5550
www.brocku.ca

C

Campion College at The University of Regina
3737 Wascana Parkway
Regina, SK S4S 0A2
Canada
306-586-4242
www.uregina.ca/campion

Canadian University College
235 College Avenue
College Heights, AB T4L 2E5
Canada
403-782-3381
www.cauc.ab.ca

Carleton University
1125 Colonel By-Drive
Ottawa, ON K1S 5B6
Canada
613-520-7400
www.carleton.ca

Collège Dominicain de Philosophie et de Théologie (French speaking)
96 Avenue Empress
Ottawa, ON K1R 7G2
Canada
613-233-5696
www.op.org/canada/college.htm

Collège Universitaire de Saint-Boniface (French speaking)
200 Avenue de la Cathédrale
Saint-Boniface, MB R2H 0H7
Canada
204-233-0210

Concord College
169 Riverton Avenue
Winnipeg, MB R2L 2E5
Canada
204-669-6583
www.concordcollege.mb.ca

Concordia University
1455 de Maisonneuve Ouest
Montréal, QC H3G 1M8
Canada
514-848-2668
www.concordia.ca

Concordia University College of Alberta
7128 Ada Boulevard NW
Edmonton, AB T5B 4E4
Canada
780-479-8481
www.concordia.edmonton.ab.ca

D

Dalhousie University
1236 Henry Street
Halifax, NS B3H 3J5
Canada
902-494-2211
www.dal.ca

DalTech at Dalhousie University
1236 Henry Street
Halifax, NS B3H 2J5
Canada
902-420-7980
www.dal.ca/daltech/index.html

E

Emily Carr Institute of Art and Design
1399 Johnston Street
Vancouver, BC V6H 3R9
Canada
604-844-3800
www.eciad.bc.ca

G

Grande Prairie Regional College
10726-106 Avenue
Grande Prairie, AB T8V 4C4
Canada
780-539-2911
www.gprc.ab.ca

H

Huntington University
(affiliated with Laurentian University)
935 Ramsey Lake Road
Sudbury, ON P3E 2C6
Canada
705-673-4126
www.laurentian.ca/www/huntington

Huron College at The University of Western Ontario
1349 Western Road
London, ON N6G 1H3
Canada
519-438-7224
www.uwo.ca/huron

K

King's College at The University of Western Ontario
266 Epworth Avenue
London, ON N6A 2M3
Canada
519-433-3491
www.uwo.ca/kings

CoOl BoOk AlErT!

Been There, Should've Done That by Suzette Tyler (Front Porch Press, 1997)

This collection of advice from upperclass students for incoming "frosh" is outstanding. It's one of those little books that is deceptively simple and profound at the same time. Although it's not aimed at top students, no student could fail to gain real advantage from reading this book after high school and before the first night in the frosh dorm. Tips on studying, ditching bad profs, negotiating with potentially insane roommates, to withdraw or not to withdraw, how and where to meet the sexually attractive, and preparing for life after college. By following the tips in this book, you won't get to senior year with that weird feeling, "Did I miss something?" Highly recommended.

The King's University College
9125 50th Street NW
Edmonton, AB T6B 2H3
Canada
780-465-3500
www.kingsu.ab.ca

Kwantlen University College
12666 72nd Avenue
Surrey, BC V3W 2M8
Canada
604-599-2000
www.kwantlen.bc.ca

L

Lakehead University
955 Oliver Road
Thunder Bay, ON P7B 5E1
Canada
807-343-8110
www.lakeheadu.ca

Laurentian University of Sudbury
935 Ramsey Lake Road
Sudbury, ON P3E 2C6
Canada
705-675-4843
www.laurentian.ca

Luther College at The University of Regina
3737 Wascana Parkway
Regina, SK S4S 0A2
Canada
306-585-5333
www.saskweb.com/luthercollege

M

Malaspina University College
900 Fifth Street
Nanaimo, BC V9R 5S5
Canada
250-755-8755
www.mala.bc.ca

Macdonald College Campus of McGill University
21111 Bord-du-Lac Road
Sainte-Anne-de-Bellevue, QC H9X 1C0
Canada
514-398-7710
www.agrenv.mcgill.ca

Marine Institute of Memorial University of Newfoundland
155 Ridge Road
St. Johns, NF A1C 5R3
Canada
800-563-5799
www.mi.mun.ca

McGill University
845 Sherbrooke Street West
Montréal, QC H3A 2T5
Canada
514-398-3910
www.mcgill.ca

McMaster University
1280 Main Street West
Hamilton, ON L8S 4L8
Canada
905-525-4600
www.mcmaster.ca

Memorial University of Newfoundland
St. John's, NF A1C 5S7
Canada
709-737-8262
www.mun.ca

Memorial University of Newfoundland - Sir Wilfred Grenfell College Campus
University Drive
Corner Brook, NF A2H 6P9
Canada
709-637-6200
www.swgc.mun.ca

> **A small daily task, if it be really daily, will beat the labors of a spasmodic Hercules.**
>
> —*Anthony Trollope*

> **In the fields of observa-
tion, chance favors only the
mind that is prepared.**
>
> —*Louis Pasteur*

**Menno Simons College of the
University of Winnipeg**
515 Portage Avenue
Winnipeg, MB R3B 2E9
Canada
204-786-9895
www.uwinnipeg.ca/~msc

Mount Allison University
65 York Street
Sackville, NB E0A 3C0
Canada
506-364-2269
www.mta.ca

Mount Royal College
4825 Richard Road SW
Calgary, AB T3E 6K6
Canada
403-240-6111
www.mtroyal.ab.ca

Mount Saint Vincent University
166 Bedford Highway
Halifax, NS B3M 2J6
Canada
902-457-6128
www.msvu.ca

N

Nipissing University
100 College Drive
North Bay, ON P1B 8L7
Canada
705-474-3450
www.unipissing.ca

**Northern Alberta Institute
of Technology**
11762 106th Street
Edmonton, AB T5G 2R1
Canada
780-471-6248
www.nait.ab.ca

Nova Scotia Agricultural College
21 Cox Road
Truro, NS B2N 5E3
Canada
902-893-6722
www.nsac.ns.ca

**Nova Scotia College of Art
and Design**
5163 Duke Street
Halifax, NS B3J 3J6
Canada
902-494-8129
www.nscad.ns.ca

O

Okanagan University College
1000 K.L.O. Road
Kelowna, BC V1Y 9K9
Canada
250-762-5445
www.okanagan.bc.ca

Q

Queen's University at Kingston
110 Alfred Street
Kingston, ON K7L 3N6
Canada
613-533-2218
www.info.queensu.ca

R

Redeemer College
777 Garner Road East
Ancaster, ON L9K 1J4
Canada
800-263-6467 or 905-648-2131
www.redeemer.on.ca

Royal Military College of Canada
17 Valour Street
Kingston, ON K7K 5L0
Canada
613-541-6000
www.rmc.ca

Royal Roads University
2005 Sooke Road
Victoria, BC V9B 5Y2
Canada
800-788-8028 or 250-391-2505
www.royalroads.ca

Ryerson Polytechnic University
350 Victoria Street
Toronto, ON M5B 2K3
Canada
416-979-5036
www.ryerson.ca

Saint Paul University
223 Main Street
Ottawa, ON K1S 1C4
Canada
613-236-1393
www.ustpaul.ca

**Saint Thomas More College at
The University of Saskatchewan**
1437 College Drive
Saskatoon, SK S7N 0W6
Canada
306-966-8900
www.usask.ca/stm

❝ Omit needless words. ❞

—William Strunk

S

Saint Francis Xavier University
West and St. Ninan Streets
Antigonish, NS B2G 2W5
Canada
902-867-2219
www.stfx.ca

Saint Jerome's University
Waterloo, ON N2L 3G3
Canada
519-884-8110
www.usjc.uwaterloo.ca

Saint Mary's University
923 Robie Street
Halifax, NS B3H 3C3
Canada
902-420-5415
www.stmarys.ca

Saint Thomas University
Fredericton, NB E3B 5G3
Canada
506-452-0532
www.stthomasu.ca

**Saskatchewan Indian Federated
College at The University of Regina**
3737 Wascana Parkway
Regina, SK S4S 0A2
Canada
306-584-8333
www.sifc.edu

Simon Fraser University
8888 University Drive
Burnaby, BC V5A 1S6
Canada
604-291-3224
www.sfu.ca

**Southern Alberta Institute
of Technology**
1301 16th Avenue NW
Calgary, AB T2M 0L3
Canada
403-284-7114
www.sait.ab.ca

T

Thornloe University
(affiliated with Laurentian University)
935 Ramsey Lake Road
Sudbury, ON P3E 2C6
Canada
705-673-1730
www.laurentian.ca

Trent University
1600 West Bank Drive
Peterborough, ON K9J 7B8
Canada
705-748-1215
www.trentu.ca

Trinity Western University
7600 Glover Road
Langley, BC V2Y 1Y1
Canada
800-468-6898 or 604-888-7511
www.twu.ca

U

Université de Hearst
(affiliated with Laurentian University)
60 9e Rue
Hearst, ON P0L 1N0
Canada
705-372-1781
www.univhearst.edu

Université Laval
(French speaking)
Québec City, QC G1K 7P4
Canada
418-656-2130
www.ulaval.ca

Université de Moncton
(French speaking)
165 Avenue Massey
Moncton, NB E1A 3E9
Canada
506-858-4129
www.umoncton.ca

Université de Montréal
(French speaking)
CP 6128, Succ Centre Ville
Montréal, QC H3C 3J7
Canada
514-343-6111
www.umontreal.ca

Modern taxonomy was standardized by Swedish botanist Carolus Linnaeus (1707–1778), who wanted a systematic way to name all the species newly discovered in the global explorations of his time. Every high school biologist can rattle off kingdom, phylum, class, order, family, genus, species. If you discover a species, you get to name it. Most are named after the discoverer, the place of discovery, or some physical attribute of the species itself. *Dicrotendipes thanatogratus*, a type of fly, is named after a band your parents might have been crazy about. Thanatogratus means "The Grateful Dead."

Université de Québec
(French speaking)
2875 Boulevard Laurier
Saint-Foy, QC G1V 2M3
Canada
418-657-3551
www.uquebec.ca

Université de Québec en Abitibi-Témiscamingue
(French speaking)
42 Monseigneur-Rhéaume est
CP 700
Rouyn, QC J9X 5E4
Canada
819-762-0971
www.uqat.uquebec.ca

Université de Québec à Chicoutimi
(French speaking)
555 Boulevard de l'Université
Chicoutimi, QC G7H 2B1
Canada
418-545-5011
www.uqac.uquebec.ca

Université de Québec à Hull
(French speaking)
CP 1250, Succursale 'B'
Hull, QC J8X 3X7
Canada
819-595-3900
www.uqah.uquebec.ca

Université de Québec à Montréal
(French speaking)
CP 8888, Surrcursale 'A'
Montréal, QC H3C 3P8
Canada
514-987-3000
www.uqam.ca

Université de Québec à Rimouski
(French speaking)
300 allée des Ursulines
Rimouski, QC G5L 3A1
Canada
418-723-1986
www.uqar.uquebec.ca

Université du Québec École Nationale d'Administration Publique
(French speaking)
945 rue Wolfe
Sainte-Foy, QC G1V 3J9
Canada
418-657-2489
www.enap.uquebec.ca

Université de Québec à Trois-Riviéres
(French speaking)
CP 500
Trois-Riviéres, QC G9A 5H7
Canada
819-376-5011
www.uqtr.uquebec.ca

Université Sainte-Anne
(French speaking)
Pointe-d'Église, NS B0W 1M0
Canada
902-769-2114
www.ustanne-59.ustanne.ednet.ns.ca

Université de Sherbrooke
(French speaking)
2500 Boulevard Université
Sherbrooke, QC J1K 2R1
Canada
819-821-7680
www.usherb.ca

University of Alberta
114th Street - 89th Avenue
Edmonton, AB T6G 2E2
Canada
780-492-3113
www.ualberta.ca

> **Until one is committed, there is hesitancy, the chance to draw back, always ineffectiveness, concerning all acts of initiative and creation. There is one elementary truth the ignorance of which kills countless ideas and splendid plans: that the moment one definitely commits oneself, then Providence moves, too. All sorts of things occur to help one that would never otherwise have occurred. A whole stream of events issues from the decision, raising in one's favor all manner of unforeseen incidents and meetings and material assistance which no one could have dreamed would have come one's way. Whatever you can do or dream you can, begin it. Boldness has genius, power and magic in it. Begin it now.**
>
> —*Johann Wolfgang von Goethe*

"Education is what survives when what has been learned has been for-gotten."

—B. F. Skinner

University of British Columbia
2016-1874 East Mall
Vancouver, BC V6T 1Z1
Canada
604-822-3014
www.ubc.ca

University of Calgary
2500 University Drive NW
Calgary, AB T2N 1N4
Canada
403-220-6645
www.ucalgary.ca

University College of Cape Breton
125 Grand Lake Road
Sydney, NS B1P 6L2
Canada
902-539-5300
www.uccb.ns.ca

University College of the Cariboo
900 McGill Road
Kamloops, BC V2C 5N3
Canada
250-828-5071
www.cariboo.bc.ca

University College of the Fraser Valley
33844 King Road, R.R. #2
Abbotsford, BC V2S 4N2
Canada
604-853-7441
www.ucfv.bc.ca

University of Guelph
50 Stone Road East
Guelph, ON N1G 2W1
Canada
519-821-2130
www.uoguelph.ca

University of King's College
6350 Coburg Road
Halifax, NS B3H 2A1
Canada
902-422-1271
www.ukings.ns.ca

University of Lethbridge
4401 University Drive
Lethbridge, AB T1K 3M4
Canada
403-320-5700
www.uleth.ca

Without question, one of the most unusual institutions of higher education in the United States is the Maharishi University of Management in Fairfield, Iowa. Founded in 1971 by Maharishi Mahesh Yogi as Maharishi International University, the school integrates meditation with a curriculum in the sciences, arts, humanities, business, engineering, and computer sciences. It changed its name in 1995 to Maharishi University of Management. The school is accredited by the Commission on Institutions of Higher Education of the North Central Association of Colleges and Schools, and offers bachelor's, master's, and doctoral degrees. It offers students "the knowledge and experience they need to successfully manage all areas of life—both personal and professional" and promises to develop your "consciousness and creativity." The school has in the past proposed to map the brain waves of presidential candidates to see which of them, if any, would be appropriate to occupy the White House.

Maharashi University of Management • 1000 North Fourth Street • Fairfield, Iowa 53557-1155
515-472-1110 • www.mum.edu/admissions

University of Manitoba
66 Chancellors Circle
Winnepeg, MB R3T 2N2
Canada
204-474-8808
www.umanitoba.ca

University of New Brunswick
3 Bailey Drive
Fredericton, NB E3B 5A3
Canada
506-453-4666
www.unb.ca

**University of Northern
British Columbia**
3333 University Way
Prince George, BC V2L 4Z9
Canada
888-419-5588 or 250-960-6305
www.unbc.edu

University of Ottawa
550 Cumberland Street
Ottawa, ON K1N 6N5
Canada
613-562-5800
www.uottawa.ca

University of Prince Edward Island
550 University Avenue
Charlottetown, PE C1A 4P3
Canada
902-566-0439
www.upei.ca

University of Regina
3737 Wascana Parkway
Regina, SK S4S 0A2
Canada
306-585-4591
www.uregina.ca

**University of Saint Michael's
College**
81 Saint Mary Street
Toronto, ON M5S 1J4
Canada
416-926-1300
www.utoronto.ca/stmikes

University of Saskatchewan
105 Adminstration Place
Saskatoon, SK S7N 5A2
Canada
306-966-6718
www.usask.ca

University of Toronto
315 Bloor Street West
Toronto, ON M5S 1A3
Canada
416-978-2190
www.utoronto.ca

**University of Trinity College
at University of Toronto**
6 Hoskin Avenue
Toronto, ON M5S 1H8
Canada
416-978-2522
www.trinity.utoronto.ca

> **An education isn't how much you have committed to memory, or even how much you know. It's being able to differentiate between what you know and what you don't.**
>
> *—Anatole France*

Students who live on campus graduate at significantly higher rates than students who do not, and the effect is cumulative, i.e., the longer you live on campus the more likely you are to graduate on time. You may as well become a residence hall advisor and offset some room and board expenses while you're at it. Besides, graduate schools like to see such positions of responsibility.

University of Victoria
P.O. Box 1700 STN CSC
Victoria, BC V8W 3P2
Canada
250-721-8121
www.uvic.ca

University of Waterloo
200 University Avenue West
Waterloo, ON N2L 3G1
Canada
519-888-4567
www.uwaterloo.ca

University of Western Ontario
1151 Richmond Street
London, ON N6A 5B8
Canada
519-661-2111
www.uwo.ca

University of Windsor
401 Sunset Avenue
Windsor, ON N9B 3P4
Canada
519-253-4232
www.uwindsor.ca

University of Winnipeg
515 Portage Avenue
Winnipeg, MB R3B 2E9
Canada
204-786-9159
www.uwinnipeg.ca

V

**Victoria University at The
University of Toronto**
73 Queen's Park Crescent East
Toronto, ON M5S 1K7
Canada
416-585-4524
uvic.utoronto.ca

W

Wilfrid Laurier University
75 University Avenue West
Waterloo, ON N2L 3C5
Canada
519-884-0710
www.wlu.ca

Y

York University
4700 Keele Street
North York, ON M3J 1P3
Canada
416-736-5100
www.yorku.ca

The aforementioned list was gathered from the member list of the Association of Universities and Colleges of Canada (AUCC). This association serves the same functions as the American Association of Universities in the United States. It assists in helping its members develop public policy about education and serves as a forum for educational issues at the postsecondary level.

Association of Universities
and Colleges of Canada
350 Albert Street, Suite 600
Ottawa, ON K1R 1B1
Canada
613-563-1236
www.aucc.ca

The full list of recognized postsecondary institutions in Canada, set up by the Canadian Information Centre for International Credentials, is available at www.cmec.ca/cicic/index.stm

Also see:

The Complete Guide to Canadian Universities
by Kevin Paul
(Self-Counsel Press, 1998)

C

OTHER BOOKS
BY DONALD ASHER

Graduate Admissions Essays

This comprehensive guide removes
all the mystery and most of the
stress from the admissions process,
helping you choose the right school
or program, secure the best letters
of recommendation, write a winning
essay, and time your applications
effectively.

8 1/2 x 11 inches, 128 pages
$14.95 paper (Can $22.95)
ISBN 1-58008-042-1

The Overnight Résumé: The Fastest Way to Your Next Job!

While the promise of this book is
simple—a great, job-winning résumé
overnight—it offers much, much
more, including job-hunting techniques, insight from America's top
executives, and everything you need
to know about HTML, the Internet,
and scannable résumés.

8 1/2 x 11 inches, 164 pages
$14.95 paper (Can $29.95)
ISBN 1-58008-041-3

Asher's Bible of Executive Résumés and How to Write Them

This is the largest compendium of
advice and sample executive
résumés available to the general
public. Also includes hints on
upgrading your current job, getting
headhunted, and more.

8 1/2 x 11 inches, 600 pages
$29.95 paper (Can $48.00)
ISBN 0-89815-856-7

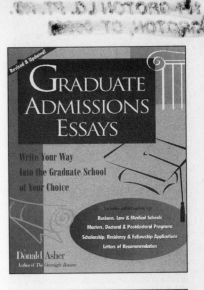

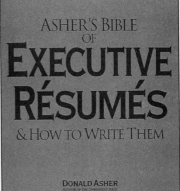

OTHER BOOKS FOR COLLEGE-BOUND STUDENTS

Write Your Way to a Higher GPA
by Randall S. Hansen and Katharine Hansen
Featuring hundreds of high-tech writing resources—Internet sites, CD-ROM's, and more—to help you dramatically boost your GPA simply by sharpening your writing skills.

7 3/8 x 9 1/4 inches, 240 pages
$11.95 paper (Can $18.95)
ISBN 0-89815-903-2

Major in Success:
Make College Easier, Fire Up Your Dreams, and Get a Very Cool Job
by Patrick Combs
With cool job and internship ideas, smart strategies for overcoming fears, hot tips on interviewing, and the best job-hunting Web sites, this savvy and inspiring guide will help you discover your passions and excel in life.

7 3/8 x 9 1/4 inches, 192 pages
$11.95 paper (Can $18.50)
ISBN 1-58008-209-2

Bears' Guide to Earning Degrees by Distance Learning
by John Bear and Mariah Bear
The classic resource for anyone who's looking to earn a college degree over the Internet, through evening and weekend classes, by passing exams, or through a number of other nontraditional methods.

8 1/2 x 11 inches, 480 pages
$29.95 paper (Can $46.95)
ISBN 1-58008-202-5

Available from your local bookstore, or by ordering direct from the publisher. Write for our catalogs of more than 1,000 books and posters.

TEN SPEED PRESS / CELESTIAL ARTS / TRICYCLE PRESS
P.O. Box 7123, Berkeley, California, 94707
Order phone (800) 841-2665 / Fax (510) 559-1629
Order@tenspeed.com / www.tenspeed.com